T0330536

Expansion of Trade and FDI in Asia

Foreign direct investment flows have increased dramatically in recent decades and continue to be a driving factor of economic globalisation. As a growth pole in the world economy, large parts of Asia in particular have become an attractive place for market-seeking FDI. In a high number of Asian countries FDI restrictions have been reduced, leading to accelerated technological exchange and globally integrated production and marketing networks. Overall, this has positively benefited the emerging countries that have opened their doors to FDI.

Expansion of Trade and FDI in Asia explores the trends of present FDI in Asia and their effects on multilateral regulation of FDI. It reviews the increasing attraction of FDI and the rise of Asian transnational corporations (TNCs) from an economic perspective. It also investigates the legal side of the development, in particular the changes in bilateral and regional FDI regulation, and the lessons that could be learned for international investment agreements (IIAs) and the constitution of trading blocs.

This book will be of interest to postgraduates and academics interested in Asian studies, Asian economics and international economics.

Julien Chaisse is Alternate Leader at the World Trade Institute, Bern, Switzerland. He coordinates the project research on investment international rules within the NCCR (National Centre of Competence in Research). He is Associate Professor at the University of Antwerp, Belgium. He is the co-editor of *Essays on the Future of the World Trade Organization* (2008).

Philippe Gugler holds the Chair of Economic and Social Policy at the Faculty of Economics and Social Sciences of the University of Fribourg. He is Director of the Centre for Competitiveness at the same university. Professor Gugler is Project-leader on investment policies within the NCCR (National Centre of Competence Research) International Trade located at the World Trade Institute.

Routledge Contemporary Asia Series

Expansion of Trade and FDI in Asia

Strategic and policy challenges

Edited by

Julien Chaisse and Philippe Gugler

Routledge
Taylor & Francis Group

LONDON AND NEW YORK

First published 2009
by Routledge
2 Park Square, Milton Park, Abingdon, Oxon OX14 4RN

Simultaneously published in the USA and Canada
by Routledge
270 Madison Ave, New York, NY 10016

Routledge is an imprint of the Taylor & Francis Group, an informa business

Typeset in Times New Roman by
Book Now Ltd, London

British Library Cataloguing in Publication Data
A catalogue record for this book is available from the British Library

Library of Congress Cataloging in Publication Data
Expansion of trade and FDI in Asia: strategic and policy challenges /
edited by Julien Chaisse and Philippe Gugler.
     p. cm.
1. Investments, Foreign—Asia. 2. International business enterprises—
Asia. I. Chaisse, Julien. II. Gugler, Philippe.
HG5702.E95 2009
332.67′3095—dc22   2008044832

ISBN10: 0–415–49084–7 (hbk)
ISBN10: 0–203–87899–X (ebk)

ISBN13: 978–0–415–49084–9 (hbk)
ISBN13: 978–0–203–87899–6 (ebk)

Contents

Illustrations

Figures

Tables

Appendices/annexes

Contributors

Bertram Boie is a research fellow at the NCCR/World Trade Institute Berne and at the University of Fribourg, Switzerland. His research focuses on the legal framework of Sino-European investment relations. Here, many matters relevant for enhancing coherence in international investment regulation come together, including in particular current fragmentation in regulatory issues, open substantive matters, and investment distortion. Before joining the WTI, Mr Boie worked at an investment advisory firm in Beijing and was a Carlo-Schmid fellow at UNCTAD's section for international investment agreements. He holds a LLM in European and international economic law from Maastricht University, and studied international relations at the TU Dresden's Centre for International Studies.

Tan Teck Boon has a Masters in Economics from the National University of Singapore and is currently a doctoral candidate at the Lee Kuan Yew School of Public Policy, National University of Singapore. His research interests include investment markets, institutional design, government sector reforms and intelligence systems.

Julien Chaisse holds a PhD in Law. He coordinates the multilateral rules on investment project of the National Centre of Competence in Research (NCCR) Trade Regulation and teaches WTO law at the University of Antwerp (Belgium). He has been Alternate Leader of NCCR-Trade Regulation's IP11, based at the World Trade Institute, since 2007. He was Visiting Professor at the International Law Institute of Wuhan University in China, where he taught WTO law and European Union law (2007–2008). Before joining the World Trade Institute, he taught Public International Law at the Institut d'Etudes Politiques of Aix-en-Provence (2004–2006). His previous experience includes two years in India, where he worked for the French Ministry of Foreign Affairs, as Scientific Secretary at the Centre de Sciences Humaines of New Delhi. His research interests include foreign trade and foreign direct investments, international business law, investment law, WTO law and the central question of its enforcement by its Members.

Debashis Chakraborty is currently working as Assistant Professor at the Indian Institute of Foreign Trade, New Delhi. He was educated at the University of

Calcutta and Centre for International Trade and Development, Jawaharlal Nehru University, New Delhi. His research interests include international trade policy, WTO negotiations and Indian economic development. He has presented and published his research at various academic and policy forums in India and abroad. He has also co-edited four books on WTO issues.

Andrew Delios is an Associate Professor and Head, Department of Business Policy, at the NUS Business School, National University of Singapore. He holds a PhD in General Management from the Ivey Business School, the University of Western Ontario. He has also held positions at the Hong Kong University of Science and Technology, the Chinese University of Hong Kong and the University of Toronto. His research interests include the study of the internationalization strategies of Japanese firms, and the ownership governance, growth and international expansion strategies of listed firms in China.

Ajai Singh Gaur is currently an Assistant Professor at the College of Business and Public Administration, Old Dominion University, USA. He holds a PhD in Strategy and International Business, a PhD in Management, a Master in International Business and a BTech in Mining Engineering. His research interests lie at the intersection of strategy and international business. His work has been published in leading management journals such as *Journal of Management*, *Journal of Management Studies*, *Management International Review* and *British Journal of Management*.

Philippe Gugler holds the Chair of Economic and Social Policy at the Faculty of Economics and Social Sciences of the University of Fribourg, Switzerland. He is Director of the Centre for Competitiveness at the same university. He is the co-author with John H. Dunning of the book *Foreign Direct Investments, Location and Competitiveness* (Oxford: Elsevier, 2008). Professor Gugler is an affiliate faculty member of the Harvard Business School, USA, a guest Professor at the University of Torino, Italy, and a Member of the Board of Directors of the World Trade Institute. In December 2005, Professor Gugler was elected President of the European International Business Association, which is the leading European association dealing with multinational enterprises.

Arup Guha is currently working as Assistant Manager at the Risk and Marketing Analytics division of the American Express Company, New Delhi. He was educated at the University of Calcutta, Centre for International Trade and Development, Jawaharlal Nehru University and the Indian Statistical Institute, New Delhi. His area of work is application of statistical and econometric methods to business problems. He has three years of experience in data analysis and interpretation. He is also the author of several research publications in the same field.

Darryl S.L. Jarvis is Associate Professor (International Relations) at the Lee Kuan Yew School of Public Policy, National University of Singapore. His research is concerned with risk and issues associated with regulatory and political risk for foreign investors in the Asia-Pacific region.

Shawkat Kamal is a PhD student at the National University of Singapore (NUS). He holds a BBA and an MBA from the Institute of Business Administration, University of Dhaka. Prior to Joining the PhD program at NUS, he worked as faculty at the Business School at BRAC University, Dhaka, Bangladesh for more than four years. His past education was in Finance. However, currently he is working on International Strategy.

Chang-fa Lo is Chair Professor/Distinguished Professor at National Taiwan University (NTU) and Director, Asian Center for WTO and International Health Law and Policy, NTU College of Law. He is a former Director, NTU Center for Ethics, Law, and Society in Biomedicine and Technology, and former Dean of NTU College of Law.

Jayant Menon is Principal Economist in the Office for Regional Economic Integration at the Asian Development Bank, Manilla. He holds Masters and PhD degrees in Economics from the University of Melbourne. He joined the Asian Development Bank Institute in 2005 from the Asian Development Bank, where he was Senior Regional Economist in the Southeast Asia Department. Before joining ADB, he was at the Centre of Policy Studies at Monash University in Melbourne. He has also worked at the University of Melbourne and Victoria University, and has held visiting appointments at the Australian National University, University of Malaya, Institute of Southeast Asian Studies in Singapore, and American University in Washington, DC.

Sébastien Miroudot is trade policy analyst at the OECD Trade and Agriculture Directorate. He holds a PhD in International Economics from Sciences Po Paris, where he teaches in the Master's degree program. Before joining the OECD, he worked for several years at Groupe d'Economie Mondiale as research assistant and lecturer. His research interests include trade in services, the relationship between trade and investment and the role of multinational enterprises in international trade.

Jianqiang Nie holds a PhD in Law from the University of Bern (World Trade Institute), Switzerland. He is presently Professor of Law at Wuhan University, China and vice-director of its prestigious Institute of International Law. Jianqiang Nie teaches international economic law with a strong emphasis in his research agenda on World Trade Organization law and in particular intellectual property law. He is the author of the book *Enforcement of Intellectual Property Rights in China*, published in 2006 by Cameron May.

Joël Ruet is a Researcher from Centre National de la Recherche Scientifique (CNRS) at LATTS-Université Paris Est and Director of the Observatory on Global Industry and Emerging Economies at Mines-ParisTech. Since 2000 he has been associate researcher at the Centre for Industrial Economics at the Ecole des Mines de Paris. He is the author or editor of five books, an alumnus of Ecole des Mines de Paris, a doctor in industrial economics and a researcher at the Centre National de la Recherche Scientifique (CNRS). He teaches at the Hautes Etudes Commerciales Paris, Ecole des Mines, and Barcelona

University. A former Fellow of the London School of Economics, he directed the French Research Centre in New Delhi and taught at Jawaharlal Nehru University, Delhi and was Consultant to the Governments of France and India and a member of the economic team of Dominique Strauss-Kahn' s Presidential campaign in 2006. His research expertise covers the globalization of firms in emerging countries, the impact on state–industry relations, and global recomposition of capitalism and its political economy. Joël Ruet is an expert on essential urban services, reforms of state administration and utilities, and urban governance. His research fields are India and comparative research with China and Egypt.

Chen Shaofeng is a researcher at the East Asian Institute, National University of Singapore. His research interests focus on the oil and gas market and policy analyses in East Asia, foreign direct investment, and comparative studies on government–business relationships.

Jun Xiao is Associate Professor at the Wuhan University Institute of International Law. He did his doctoral studies at the University of Saarland, Germany and has published in German *Das Prinzip der Nichtdiskriminierung in einem kuenftigen multilateralen Investitionsabkommen* (Nomos-Verlag, 2007). His research activities mainly relate to international investment law and international trade law.

Foreword

I am pleased to recommend the novel and interesting chapters in this book, examining the extent and institutional response to foreign direct investment in Asia and the recent expansion of emerging economy multinationals from Asia. In particular, the expansion of multinationals from China and India is changing the nature of international business research. This has implications for public policy towards multinationals, as is debated throughout. I have found that this book both complements and expands upon some of my current research interests.

Over my career I have examined the performance of the world's largest 500 firms. Most of these are from the core triad of the United States, the European Union, and Japan. In 1981, 445 of the 500 were from the core triad, and there were still 428 from the core triad in 2001, with 34 from emerging economies. However, in 2007 only 365 were from the core triad, whereas 77 were from emerging economies, most of these from Asia. Over the last seven years, the rise of emerging economy multinationals is the most important change in the composition of the world's top 500 firms. As discussed in this book, most of the emerging economy multinationals in Asia are from China (a total of 24 in 2006) and from India (6 in 2006). There were 69 emerging economy multinationals in total in 2006.

In my research examining the growth and performance of emerging economy multinationals from Asia, I have been frustrated by the lack of published data. For the 13 Chinese firms reporting data for 2006, I find that they have 18.5 percent foreign-to-total sales. They also have well over 90 percent of their total sales in Asia, mostly in China itself. The three firms from India with data average only 7 percent foreign-to-total sales, and again have well over 90 percent of their total sales in Asia. In contrast, nine Korean firms average 33.4 percent foreign-to-total sales and have 79 percent of their total sales in Asia. These rather spotty data on emerging economy multinationals from Asia basically confirm their focus on the home region. Thus, these provisional findings for Asian firms are broadly consistent with the more reliable data showing that North American and European firms operate solidly within their home region of the triad. Despite the unusual nature of the US/Chinese trading relationship, on average Chinese firms have not succeeded in operating across two (or three) regions but rather focus within Asia.

The implications of the regional nature of international business activity in Asia are vitally important and are further examined by careful case studies and more aggregate empirical work on foreign direct investment (FDI) in this book. There is broad support for the regional nature of Asian business. It is found here that FDI in Asia is regional; in particular, outward FDI by Chinese firms. This is why this book is much more useful than the dozens of books about Asia which simply assume that Asian business is global rather than regional.

Given the nature of the regional effect, scholars in international business must be as careful as those in this book to examine the complexities of international business and globalization. This has particular relevance when international institutions and trade agreements are being considered. Here it is found that policy measures affecting FDI in Asia are being handled at a regional level, even within the structures of bilateral investment agreements (BITs). These BITs are spread like a 'noodle bowl' across Asia and an integrated regional trade agreement is currently not available. Clearly, if international business is regional, rather than global, this implies that multilateral trade and investment agreements are less important than a regional trade and investment agreement for Asia. Eventually such a regional trade and investment agreement might be rolled into a future round of the World Trade Organization, but at this time regionalism is more relevant for Asian business than is multilateralism.

Another interesting finding in this book is that the conventional investor–state provisions for dispute settlement are likely to be redefined in Asia. This is because many emerging economy multinational enterprises from Asia (especially from China) are state-owned enterprises. Thus, investor–state investor provisions are really being replaced by state-to-state investor provisions. The implications of this for public policy towards FDI have not yet been resolved. It is interesting that these issues have already arisen in an Asian context and are now likely to arise between state-owned Chinese firms (as well as those from the Gulf states) and the policy-makers and lawyers in North American and European economies.

I hope that readers of this book will find it as interesting and challenging as I have and that future research in international business will continue to examine the challenges to globalization exhibited by studies of the regional nature of Asian international business.

Alan M. Rugman
Indiana University and
The Henley Business School of the University of Reading

1 Editors' introduction

Patterns and dynamics of Asia's growing share of FDI

Philippe Gugler and Julien Chaisse

Introduction

Capital throughout the world has become increasingly mobile in recent decades and international trade has been exploding. Advances in information communications technology and the accelerated pace of international distribution in recent years have promoted the growth of foreign investment which divides the various processes of research and development (R&D), procurement, production, manufacturing and sales, among others, between a number of countries. Until the recent past, foreign direct investment (FDI) and trade mainly flowed from the developed countries into the developed countries: in particular, the 'triad' (the European Union, the United States, and Japan). Until the mid-1980s, the role of developing and transitional Asian economies as sources of investment was negligible.

A regional pattern of FDI flows has emerged, with investors' attention shifting away from traditionally important locations in developed countries in favour of emerging markets (Sauvant, 2005), especially Asia and South-eastern Europe. A survey by the United Nations Conference on Trade and Development (UNCTAD) found prospects for Asia and the Pacific to be most positive, with over 85 per cent of experts, multinational corporations and investment promotion agencies expecting significantly increased FDI flows to the region (UNCTAD Investment Brief 2007).

As a result, more bilateral investment treaties (BITs) and double taxation treaties (DTTs) are now in force between developing countries than between developed and developing countries. Asia has, in fact, been the most active developing region in terms of concluding preferential trade and investment agreements (PTIAs). Asia concluded 38 per cent of a total of 14 PTIAs in 2005, followed by Latin America with a quarter of that percentage share.

FDI flows have increased dramatically in recent decades and continue to be a driving factor of economic globalization. As a centre for growth in the world economy, large parts of Asia have become a particularly attractive place for market-seeking FDI. It is in Asia that many of the recent and most innovative agreements have been signed and for which a detailed analysis of preferential commitments is available (Fink and Molinuevo 2008). In numerous Asian countries FDI restrictions have been reduced, leading to accelerated technological exchange and globally integrated production and marketing networks. Overall, this has benefited the emerging countries that have opened their doors to FDI.

According to the *World Investment Report* 2007, global FDI inflows rose in 2006 for the third consecutive year (UNCTAD 2007). This growth was shared by countries in various stages of development. FDI inflows to South, East and Southeast Asia maintained their upward trend last year, rising by 19 per cent to reach a new high of US$200 billion, according to UNCTAD's annual report on global investment trends. South and Southeast Asia saw a sustainable increase in FDI flows, while growth in East Asia was slower. However, FDI in East Asia is shifting towards more knowledge-intensive and high value-added activities.

China and Hong Kong currently top the list of recipients of the largest amounts of FDI, absorbing approximately half of the total FDI inflow into Asia in recent years. China and Hong Kong are followed by Singapore and India, according to the *World Investment Report 2007*. Inflows to China fell by 4 per cent to US$69 billion last year, dropping for the first time in seven years due mainly to declining investments in financial services. Hong Kong attracted FDI worth US$43 billion, Singapore US$24 billion and India US$17 billion, which was equivalent to India's inflows for the preceding three years added together. Meanwhile, FDI inflows to Thailand rose by 9 per cent in 2006, reaching a record of US$10 billion and consolidating the country's position as the second-largest FDI recipient in Southeast Asia.

FDI in the service sector in the region was considerably increased but FDI related to mergers and acquisitions in manufacturing dropped. The report predicts that rapid economic growth in this region should continue to attract FDI to its countries in the coming year. In the first half of 2008, the value of cross-border merger and acquisition deals in the region rose nearly 20 per cent compared to 2007. FDI outflows from the region are also expected to increase. The report also showed that rising demand for oil and gas and metals, particularly from Asia, has spurred a boom in FDI in mineral exploration and extraction industries. These industries largely account for the recent increases in FDI in many mineral-rich developing countries, notably in Africa.

A large share of the FDI inflows into Asia originated from other Asian countries. Of the US$138 billion of FDI inflows into South, East and Southeast Asia in 2004, approximately 40 per cent is estimated to have originated from other Asian countries. China, Hong Kong, Indonesia, the Philippines and Thailand stand out as having inward FDI that is dominated by Asian investors.

Numerous factors have driven the increasing levels of intra-Asian FDI. Examples include:

- *Competitiveness*: A large component of international competitiveness for Asian firms is achieved through intra-regional sales within the home region (Rugman and Hoon Oh, 2008). International competitiveness should not be confused with globalization. Asian firms do not compete globally; instead, they mainly operate regionally.
- *Need for global presence*: Multinational enterprises (MNEs) are undergoing an attitudinal change, realizing that they operate in a global economy in which Asia is a rising force. In addition, developing country MNEs are

investing in other countries to reduce the risk of overdependence on the home market. Offshore centres of excellence, such as India's data recovery centres in Singapore, are examples of this trend.

- *Costs of production*: Labour costs are of concern to most MNEs, especially those from more developed nations. Production has increasingly been relocated to developing economies where costs are lower. This practice is commonplace in industries such as electrical and electronics, and garments and textiles – FDI in the electrical and electronics industry is strongly regionally focused while FDI in the garments industry is more geographically dispersed.

- *Market access*: Production and distribution centres are in due course set up close to consumer markets. This reduces the problems of transportation of perishable goods such as agricultural food products and processed food. The Indonesian-owned Indofood Corporation, for instance, has located production in China where a large part of its market resides.

- *Favourable FDI regulatory trends in Asian host countries*: Changes in government policy have facilitated FDI through creating greater openness to foreign investors, reducing taxes, simplifying procedures and enhancing incentives. In host economies, liberalization policies have created many investment opportunities, such as the privatization of state-owned enterprises and assets. As competition for FDI intensifies, countries are becoming more proactive in their investment promotion efforts. Dedicated bodies such as the investment promotion agencies are being established to attract FDI. The investment promotion agencies now consider developing Asia as a key FDI source region.

This volume focuses on the theme of the Annual Conference of the National Centre of Competence in Research (NCCR) Trade Regulation, which took place at the National Institute of Development Administration (NIDA) in Bangkok in January 2008. The theme of the conference was *Expansion of FDI in Asia: Strategic and policy challenges*. All contributions to this book (with one exception) are based on the papers and keynote addresses presented during the conference. The multidisciplinary approach provides an opportunity to explore the trends of recent FDI in Asia and their effects on multilateral regulation of FDI. The aim is to offer a review of the increasing attraction of FDI and the rise of Asian multinational enterprises from an economic perspective. A second objective is to add a political and legal analysis of these developments, in particular the changes in regulation of bilateral and regional FDI and the lessons that can be learned for international investment agreements (IIAs) and the constitution of trading blocs.

The book comprises three parts to investigate the current scenario in Asia. The first part addresses the internationalization strategy of emerging Asian firms with examples from China and India. The second part relates to the national and regional initiatives affecting trade and investment in Asia. The third part focuses on the Asian interest in multilateral rules on trade and investment. It raises the question of a potential new paradigm. We outline below the background against which the different chapters are set.

Table 1.1 Outward FDI stocks as percentage of GDP

Region/economy	1990	2000	2006
China	1.2	2.6	2.8
East Asia	5.5	24.5	22.7
Hong Kong, China	15.5	230.1	363.5
India	–	0.4	1.5
Indonesia	0.1	4.2	4.8
Korea, Republic of	0.9	5.2	5.3
Malaysia	1.7	17.6	18.7
Philippines	0.3	2.1	1.8
Singapore	21.2	61.2	89.0
South, East and South-East Asia	3.6	18.4	18.0
Taiwan, Province of China	18.3	20.7	32.0
Thailand	0.5	1.8	2.7

Source: WIR 2007, pp. 266–268.

Internationalization strategy of emerging Asian firms: examples from China and India

The share in the total stock of FDI deriving from developing and transition economies stood at 23 per cent in 1980. It had increased to 46 per cent by 1990 and to 62 percent in 2005 (UNCTAD 2007). Focusing primarily on the outbound side of Asian FDI, the book analyses the geographical and sectoral trends involved. Further, it looks at the key players in these FDI activities that have become the Asian MNEs. In understanding why their number has multiplied during the past decade, a number of salient characteristics should be explored to answer the question: What are the location and types of investments from Asian MNEs (financial services, high-tech industries, geographical interests and so on)?

Traditionally, the main Asian source countries for FDI have been Japan, Korea, Taiwan, Hong Kong and Singapore. However, in recent years, the developing countries of Asia have begun to pull their weight (Tables 1.1 and 1.2).

China and India, for instance, are two giants on the move towards securing a greater share of energy assets overseas. Their strategy for controlling oil and natural gas reserves has led to rising FDI outflows. The China National Oil Company, for instance, has made major investments in the offshore oil and gas industry in Indonesia. The rapid development of China and India, the most populous countries in the world, has attracted the attention of international policymakers and industry leaders and should be given a particular place in this book.

China and India together account for about 37.5 per cent of the world population and 6.4 per cent of the value of world output and income at current prices and exchange rates.[1] As the two countries play an increasingly weighty role in the world economy, their expansion is having a noticeable impact on global growth,

Table 1.2 Outward FDI flows as percentage of GDP

Region/economy	1990	2000	2006
China	0.7	2.5	2.9
East Asia	5.9	4.3	6.0
Hong Kong, China	129.5	73.1	105.3
India	1.2	1.4	5.0
Indonesia	6.2	4.5	3.9
Korea, Republic of	2.3	1.9	2.8
Malaysia	8.5	11.4	20.1
Philippines	4.1	1.3	0.6
Singapore	31.5	19.3	28.3
South, East and South-East Asia	5.5	4.0	6.0
Taiwan, Province of China	10.5	8.5	10.3
Thailand	0.2	1.1	1.3

Source: WIR 2007, pp. 266–268.

through a number of channels, with trade, arguably, being the strongest and most direct (World Bank Development Indicators 2007).

China's and India's foreign trade patterns are largely dissimilar and have always been so (Winters and Yusuf 2007). In the case of China, using its vast resources of cheap labour and domestic savings to initiate building of infrastructure and inviting large amounts of FDI to spur the development of the manufacturing industry in the coastal areas has been seen as one of the initial and leading drivers for the country's economic success. India's strength, on the other hand, is based on its knowledge-based sectors such as IT and pharmaceuticals, its more developed financial markets and a more robust private sector.

FDI is an area in which India appears to lag behind China. In 2006, China attracted ten times more FDI than India. This is because China's policies for foreign investors are more liberalized than those of India. Moreover, the Chinese economy is growing faster and the infrastructure is better. FDI in China has been increasing and this is not surprising bearing in mind the sheer size of the market and the opportunities for resource exploitation. In addition, the open-market policies pursued by China over the last two decades and the concerted efforts made to attract FDI have spurred FDI growth and a consequent interest in scientific analysis. The further economic development of China depends to a large extent on continuous FDI and policy-making that will facilitate inward investment. Moreover, foreign investment and development of specific industrial sectors are essential for establishing the infrastructure and superstructure of a modern market economy. The manufacturing and technology sectors form a core for production and productivity. In addition, there must be facilitation of trade and transport of manufactured goods and information processing. China's entry into the World Trade Organization (WTO) suggests that trade will play an important role in the country's economic development.

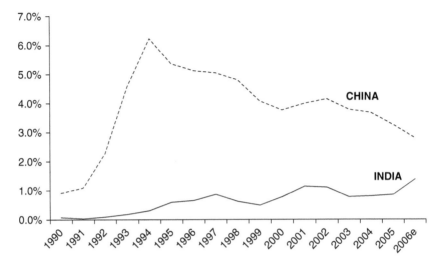

Figure 1.1 FDI in China and India, as a percentage of GDP
Source: UNCTAD FDI database.

Although strict protection policies remain in place in China in selected sectors such as the motor industry, India's restrictive labour laws and limits affecting foreign shares in ownership restrain foreign investment in general. In particular, India's inadequate infrastructure development makes it very difficult for multinational companies to ship products in and out of the country, and even within the country.

China is certainly a star performer in attracting FDI, but India did not perform as badly as expected in comparison to China. China accounts for 5 per cent of world GDP and India about 2 per cent, at current exchange rates (World Bank 2007). Development Indicators as bigger economies normally attract more investment, China currently tends to be the preferred destination of the foreign investors. But in terms of FDI's percentage in GDP, China's figure is less remarkable – little more than twice that of India (Figure 1.1).

Within South Asia, India is by far the leading host country for FDI. It received around US$19.4 billion in the fiscal year 2006, or about 80 per cent of total regional FDI (Table 1.3). India's dominance in FDI in South Asia is largely due to the size of its economy, the largest in the region. However, India's policy reforms geared towards liberalization also played an important part in India's dominance of FDI. After its independence in 1947, India adopted a socialist planned economy. Inefficiency was a problem in all sectors, making it a high-cost economy. Regulations on imports and FDI were strict, and the domestic market was virtually closed for the next 40 years.

In the late 1980s, however, the Indian Government gradually liberalized the economy and lifted restrictions on FDI. Consequently, India achieved high economic growth in 1988 and 1989. In July 1991, the New Industrial Policy was

Table 1.3 Net FDI inflows for South Asian countries (2005–2006)

	FDI ($ Million)		Annual growth	Share of regional FDI total (%)
	2005	2006		
Afghanistan	271	231	−14.8	1
Bangladesh	800	743	−7.1	3.1
Bhutan	9	6	−32.2	0
India	7661	19442	153.8	79.9
Maldives	10	14	46.3	0.1
Nepal	2	−6	−441.6	0
Pakistan	1459	3451	136.5	14.2
Sri Lanka	234	451	92.7	1.9

Source: Compiled by authors from Asian Development Bank, *South Asia Economic Report: Social sectors in transition*, Manilla 2007.

announced. Under this policy, foreign investment was approved without conditions, formalities for granting import licences were simplified, and private companies were permitted to enter fields that had previously been dominated by government-owned companies. India changed itself from a closed economy to an open economy. Movement towards liberalization in terms of FDI promotion is now common to all countries in South Asia.

In terms of business environment, the World Bank ranks China in the top 100 while India is not listed. But in some areas such as starting a business, obtaining credit, protecting investors and paying taxes, India still leads China.

The World Bank reported that South Asia is the second-least business-friendly region in the world, after Sub-Saharan Africa, based on its 'Doing Business' 2007 survey of the perceptions of foreign investors of 178 countries (World Bank Group 2007). India, the largest economy in South Asia, ranked relatively low, at 120, but this was an improvement over its 2007 ranking of 132. Only India and Bhutan could boast of slight improvements in their global rankings in 2008, suggesting an improving business climate in those countries. Conversely, the global rankings of the remaining South Asian countries deteriorated in 2008, indicating a worsening business environment in those countries. These deteriorating rankings are considered to result from foreign investor perceptions of poor infrastructure, restrictive labour policy and labour unrest, political uncertainties and civil conflicts, weak regulatory systems, and rampant corruption. Political instability and civil conflicts have been found to be a major factor in reducing the attractiveness of South Asia as a host for foreign capital. Afghanistan, Pakistan, and Sri Lanka continue to face political uncertainties and security challenges that are likely to hinder FDI. Empirical evidence demonstrates that FDI inflows into Sri Lanka are vulnerable to the ongoing civil conflict there. Likewise, in Afghanistan, the pace of foreign investment may be slow because of the sporadic suicide bombings, kidnappings and attacks. Political instability is also a major drawback for foreign investment in Nepal, while the worsening political situation in Pakistan (particularly in late 2007) may hamper FDI inflows into that country.

It may have been assumed that OECD countries took the lead in investing in China, but actually OECD countries only started to look at China from 2002 onwards. A large proportion of FDI into China comes from its diasporas abroad, from Hong Kong and Taiwan and from domestic companies, which go to Hong Kong and reinvest in China.

China has invested three times more in infrastructure than India, whose fiscal deficits, both at the national and state levels, impede its infrastructure development. This is partly the reason why China attracts more FDI than India. But there is at least one sector in which India has been doing well and that is telecommunications, one of the most competitive and lowest cost fields in the world (Thomsen 2007).

China is more open to trade liberalization than in the past and more open than other countries. However openness is a relative concept. China may be more open to foreign investment, but that does not mean that foreign investors find it easy to operate in the country, not only because of the difficulties in understanding Chinese values (Faure and Fang 2008), but also because technology transfer and intellectual property rights are still difficult issues for multinational companies in China.

In Chapter 2 Philippe Gugler and Bertam Boie deal with the rise of Chinese multinational enterprises. Chinese investors are increasingly exploring opportunities overseas in a wide range of industries. In this chapter the authors intend to contribute to the analysis of Chinese FDI. They first present a factual analysis of Chinese FDI and the emergence of Chinese MNEs, giving a statistical overview of the flows and stocks of Chinese FDI in different areas of the world, in various industries, and with regards to key characteristics of the Chinese MNEs expanding abroad. Against this background they analyse the strategies of Chinese MNEs going international and pose the question: What are the comparative advantages specific to Chinese firms, and how do they translate into motivations to expand abroad?

This question is crucial because the major impact of the growth of Chinese outward FDI, and the development of Chinese-based MNEs, will be to enhance the internal efficiency of the Chinese economy. The traditional theory on MNEs offers valuable tools with which to analyse their activities. However, Philippe Gugler and Bertram Boie underline that the Chinese characteristics in this process are particularly striking, and make the emergence of Chinese MNEs a special phenomenon. According to the analysis presented in this contribution, the most important differences between Chinese MNEs and Western MNEs going international are not to be found in their motivations, but in the special characteristics of their home country, namely the Chinese institutional and cultural context, and the home country resources. By far the largest outward investments by Chinese MNEs are made by state-owned enterprises (SOEs), and all investment projects follow a scheme that ensures that they are strictly in line with government policies (Buckley *et al.* 2007). Motivations of Chinese firms to a internationalize and the government interest in this are to a large extent aligned and institutionally intertwined.

Chapter 3 by Andrew Delios, Ajai Gaur and Shawkat Kamal explores the international acquisitions and the globalization of firms from India. The internationalization process in the subcontinent has undergone a considerable shift since the beginning of the 1990s. Whereas previously, India was a destination for the technologies and brands of foreign firms acquired primarily through licensing and technology transfer arrangements, since the mid-1990s, India's participation in the global economy has transformed into one in which it has become a more important recipient of FDI, and a more active participant in investing in overseas markets. As part of the trend towards outward FDI from India, firms domiciled in India have increasingly turned to international acquisitions as their modality of FDI.

Aside from the relatively high propensity of Indian firms to engage in FDI via an international acquisition, India's position as the second largest emerging economy after China makes it important to understand the international growth strategies of its firms. This trend is notable, particularly given its contrast to the relative lack of propensity for firms based in Asian economies such as Japan, South Korea and Taiwan to use acquisitions as a mode of FDI, as opposed to other modes such as wholly owned greenfield investments or joint venture entries.

This chapter on international acquisitions and the globalization of firms from India provides initial evidence of the notably positive performance outcomes of the international acquisitions of firms based in India. Indeed, these acquiring firms experienced a positive market reaction ranging from 2.2 per cent to 2.8 per cent, on average. This phenomenon of international acquisitions by these firms is only part of the wider phenomenon of the increasing globalization of the economy in India, in which outward FDI is playing an increasingly prominent role. It is also part of the larger phenomenon of the substantial growth in outward FDI by firms from emerging markets, in which acquisitions are also an important component as underlined by Andrew Delios, Ajai Gaur and Shawkat Kamal.

It is important to look at the broader picture. The *World Investment Report 2007* shows that while the 'triad' (the European Union, Japan, and the United States) is still home to most of the world's largest MNEs, the most significant change in recent years has been the increase in the number of firms from developing economies on the list of the world's 100 largest MNEs. Seven MNEs on the 2007 list were from developing countries, compared with five in 2006. The report ranks both the world's top 100 MNEs and the top 100 MNEs from developing economies. The transnational activities of the world's largest MNEs continued to increase in 2005 but, comparatively, the foreign activities of the 100 largest MNEs from developing economies have grown even more noticeably. Their foreign sales and employment rose by 48 per cent and 73 per cent, respectively, in 2005 (the most recent year for which data are available) compared to 2004. But the relative importance of their foreign operations compared with their domestic activities has remained more or less stable, the report notes. The most important focus for MNEs from developing economies remains the electrical/electronic equipment and computer industries, although the petroleum sector rose in value in 2005 (the most recent year for which data are available), confirming

the growing role of MNEs from developing economies in the extractive industries. The geographical spread of operations by transnational corporations
(TNCs) shows that companies from developing economies have, on average, foreign affiliates in fewer host countries than their counterparts from developed
countries. Developing-country MNEs have expanded mostly in their own
regions, although the top locations for their foreign affiliates are the United
Kingdom and the United States, with China now ranked third.

Asia dominates the list of the 100 largest developing-country MNEs, with 78
firms, followed by 11 each from Africa and Latin America. These MNEs operate
in a broader range of industries than the largest MNEs from developed countries.

In Chapter 4, Joël Ruet tackles this important issue. He explains how multinational companies from the 'South' are re-shaping global capitalism. He underlines
that since the 1980s and the upsurge of European and American multinational
companies, the strict coincidence between the economic interests of firms and of
countries ('what is good for General Motors is good for America, what is good
for America is good for general Motors') no longer applies. America and Europe
benefit equally from investments by Asian multinationals. But 'multinational'
continued to mean 'North' or 'West' until recently. The twenty-first century has
confirmed the rise of multinational firms from the South. FDIs and mergers and
acquisitions extend in all directions.

We would like to point out that a particularly sensitive question arose when
looking at the economic situation in Asia. From a political perspective, state ownership remains a common feature of the largest MNEs, bringing with it a very
specific situation in Asia. In response to the rising importance of state-owned
enterprises and sovereign wealth funds (collectively referred to here as 'state-
controlled entities') policy-makers are rethinking their own frameworks for the
regulation of investment. The role of state-driven outward FDI, mainly from
China, has generated considerable discussion in North America and Europe
(Marchick and Slaughter 2008). The world has thus witnessed a resurgence of the
role of the state vis-à-vis markets, with governments acting as both a source of,
and a potential impediment to, FDI.

Joël Ruet chapter focuses on two major consequential evolutionary paths. First,
some MNEs become 'simply global' and their origin will become increasingly
irrelevant because these actors act autonomously and separately from any particular territory. Second, these processes shape the production form of the firm as
they are both inter- and intra-firm. This in turn shapes the repositioning of industrial policies of countries of both the 'North' and the 'South'.

National and regional initiatives affecting
trade and investment in Asia

The global flows of inward and outward FDI worldwide have increased considerably over the past two decades and MNEs are increasingly considered as being
the most important agents worldwide. This is because they have the ability to
affect substantially the economic development of host and home countries and

are widely assumed to be the providers of knowledge, capital, capabilities and markets, the creators of jobs, the suppliers of foreign currency and the competition stimulator among other things (Dunning, 1992). A wide variety of national and international policy rules and principles govern many aspects of MNEs' operations – policy actions are important 'to the extent that they shift firm-level choices from one discrete governance structure toward another' according to Rugman and Verbeke (2004). The number of IIAs, instruments for the promotion and protection of foreign investment, has sharply increased over the past two decades, taking the form of a patchwork of bilateral, regional, interregional and plurilateral treaties.

What are the components of an attractive FDI policy framework? Corporate investment decisions depend to some extent on the legal framework governing international capital flows as well as on proactive policy measures to assist companies in their internationalization process. In addition, IIAs offer to help regulate investment and thus constitute an important tool for national policy-makers. Historically conceived as an instrument to be used by developed countries to protect their firms' investments against political risks, over the years the role of IIAs has undergone a change. With more and more emerging and developing countries finding themselves as both recipients and sources of FDI, these countries now have to consider not only the role of such agreements in facilitating inward FDI, but also in creating better opportunities for the internationalization of their firms. Many emerging economies today explicitly mention the promotion of outward FDI as one of the reasons for their participation in BITs and DTTs, both now proliferating (Adlung and Molinuevo 2008). Finally, with growing FDI flows, investment disputes involving investors from emerging economies are become increasingly important.

More and more regional economic agreements are currently being concluded in areas of the world with developing economic activity. As Asian developing countries, in particular, remove restrictions and implement policies to attract FDI inflows, trade and investment have become increasingly intertwined. This favours the negotiation and establishment of new Free trade agreements (FTAs). It seems that regional integration offers a larger potential market to investors, contributes to macroeconomic and political stability, often leads to domestic regulatory reforms favourable to foreign investors, and facilitates enforcement and harmonization of standards and regulations. What is the impact of regional integration schemes on FDI in Asia?

It seemed to us particularly relevant to see how investment policy in Asia contributes to an environment that is attractive to domestic and foreign investors and that enhances the benefits of investment to societies. This investment framework or 'investment climate', to use World Bank terminology, depends on the national and international regulations applicable to investment in a particular country. We know that the initiative of the OECD of the policy framework for investment (PFI) calls upon a detailed analysis of national and international investment issues, so as to create the policy environments needed to mobilize private investments (domestic and foreign) that support economic growth.

The objective of the PFI is to provide policy guidance for investment, mainly to support sustained efforts by developing countries to attract and generate more and better investment and thus continue to reap the demonstrated benefits of foreign and domestic investment flows. The PFI proposes guidance in ten policy fields identified as the most important elements influencing the investment environment. These include investment policy, trade policy, and competition policy – recognized as the prerequisites for the sound multilateral liberalization of investment – as well as other issues broadly influencing the investment environment, such as tax policy, human resource development and corporate governance among others.

The PFI is considered to be a non-prescriptive, flexible, operational and practical guide. It represents an overarching strategy for the cooperation of the OECD with developing countries on (national and international) investment issues.

Putting the PFI into action thus has significant effects on both the national and international policy framework for investment (Gugler and Ben Hamida 2007). The PFI encourages investment policy authorities from different economies to work together to expand international treaties on investment issues. It helps to ensure compliance of the policies in these treaties with international investment laws and hence facilitates the establishment of coherent international rules among economies. The policies of international treaties should also be in accordance with each country's own investment strategy.

Most countries offer incentives – tax concessions, tax holidays, tax credits, accelerated depreciation, export subsidies, import entitlements, and subsidized utility rates – to attract FDI. The People's Republic of China, for instance, offers income tax exemptions to foreign enterprises in the first and second years, and 50 per cent income tax reduction from the third to the fifth years. In addition, reduced income tax rates are levied on foreign investment enterprises in special economic zones and open coastal regions – 15 and 24 per cent, respectively, instead of the usual 30 per cent. Meanwhile, Thailand allows duty exemptions on imported raw materials and capital goods for FDI projects locating in export processing zones. Viet Nam also provides duty exemptions on imported capital goods and lower water and electricity rates for firms locating in export processing zones. Such incentives are aimed to encourage FDI and channel foreign firms towards the desired locations, sectors and activities.

It is important that this kind of national approach to investment regulation should be depicted in this book. Over the past few years, Chinese investment abroad has seen an upsurge since large companies such as Haier, Xoceco and Gree established production, research and development centres abroad. The governance of the Indian companies makes them completely independent of the state in their decisions regarding investments abroad, which is far from being the case of even the 'most private' Chinese companies. The Chinese financial services firms recently bought stakes in the investment banks Bear Stearns, Barclay's and Blackstone Group. Last year, the Anhui-based motor vehicle firm Chery, bought Britain's defunct MG brand. Three years ago, the China National Offshore Oil Corporation bid unsuccessfully for Unocal an appliance-maker and Hai'er lost out to Whirlpool in a bid for Maytag, but Lenovo bought IBM's old personal-computer unit. China's influence on the world's finances has generally received less attention than its influence on world trade, simply because Chinese overseas investment behaviour (unlike Chinese export growth) has generally not had any dramatic side-effects on the rest of the world. But in another decade that could well change. Since China affirms itself as one of the Asian growing investors going abroad, it was relevant to look in detail at the Chinese domestic policies from two different angles: how to promote and how to protect Chinese investment abroad; both elements being interdependent in practice.

As explained by Jianqiang Nie in Chapter 5, China's opening-up policy includes 'inviting in' and 'going global' as two interrelated strategies. While it is very important to attract further foreign investment, the Chinese Government is also encouraging Chinese enterprises to invest abroad. This chapter discusses Chinese overseas direct investments from the perspective of law. It presents two main results: an overview of increasing investments by China overseas and the promotion mechanisms of Chinese overseas direct investments. China's 'going global' strategy has strengthened interrelations between China and the world. China's economy is increasingly integrated into the world economy. China cannot develop in isolation from the rest of the world, nor can the world enjoy prosperity and stability without China.

As stated by Jianqiang Nie, since the Chinese Government adopted the 'going global' strategy, Chinese overseas investment has grown fast. The Chinese have made much progress in their overseas investments. A variety of promotion policies or regulations, especially those relating to the review and approval conditions, foreign exchange, financial support and investment insurance have been published. Although these policies or regulations are still in their initial stages and some of the provisions are tentative and short of precision, they have greatly contributed to the development of Chinese overseas investments. This indicates that China has evolved from being a country attracting large amounts of foreign investment to one that is fast becoming a major overseas investment power in its own right. However, China has not set up the institutions that manage its foreign investment in ways that insulate their decision making from the influence of China's top political leadership. Shenzhen's telecom giant Huawei has recently suffered a major setback in its bid to buy a stake in 3Com. Huawei hoped for a share of 3Com with the ambition of trying to prise an enterprise networking market share away from Cisco. The Chinese telecom-equipment company has been trying for months to become the junior partner in a deal led by Bain Capital to take over 3Com in a proposed US$2.2 billion deal. US lawmakers expressed concern about the security implications of a Chinese company allegedly tied to the People's Liberation Army gaining access to a second-tier American company.

The overall investment process seems incredibly politicized, with the key decisions being made by the top level of China's Government and this would explain why China's investments abroad are viewed with some suspicion. The extensive involvement of China's top leaders reflects the fact that in many ways China is just starting to invest in foreign equities, so each big investment effectively sets a new precedent and therefore makes policy. It may also be a consequence of the decision to spread the management of China's foreign exchange among different state institutions.

In Chapter 6, Xiao Jun analyses the transformation of Chinese BITs in recent investment policy and the particular strategic issue of investment protection. He observes that in the first decade of the twenty-first century, the rise of the Chinese economy and its outward investments has attracted worldwide attention. Interestingly, Chinese BITs concluded since 2000 contain some significant improvements that denote a high degree of investment protection.

Using the new China–Germany BIT of 2003 as an example, Xiao Jun's chapter compares the national treatment and investor–state dispute settlement provisions in the new agreements with those in the old Chinese BITs and analyses the differences. He argues that the difference is so important that these new agreements could be regarded as a new generation of Chinese BITs in the twenty-first century. Although attracting inward foreign investments is still important for China's economic development, the new Chinese attitude towards the protection of investment by means of BITs would be better explained by a desire to protect Chinese outward investments.

In general, FDI is not influenced solely by domestic policies, but also by international agreements. Foreign investors desiring to protect their investments and receive favourable tax treatment on their global profits and host countries wishing to attract greater inflows of FDI have entered into thousands of bilateral and, increasingly, regional agreements related to FDI. Most economies are now party to at least one international investment agreement. The situation in Asia is of great interest because of the proliferation of regional trade agreements (RTAs).

Before 1997 most economists considered economic cooperation in Asia (through trade and investment) as an example of a successful de facto regionalism, i.e. explained by the predominant interplay of market forces. To that extent, Asia appears as a latecomer in regionalism with very few agreements signed prior to 2000. However, in the past five years, many deals have been concluded and even more are under negotiation, giving rise to the 'noodle bowl syndrome'. This shift towards regionalism can be explained not only by the 1997 financial crisis and the necessity to promote regional economic cooperation, but also by the slow progress of WTO negotiations in the Doha Development Agenda. The financial crisis revealed the weaknesses of informal regional cooperation arrangements. The financial crisis and its knock-on effects on a number of economies in East and Southeast Asia painfully demonstrated that the East Asian economies were closely intertwined and that a resolution of the crisis called for heightened regional cooperation in the trade and financial fields (Sauvé 2007).

The regional and plurilateral agreements are also a popular means of formalizing international rules on investment. These treaties may involve a number of countries as for example the European Union model, the North American Free Trade Agreement (NAFTA), and more recently the Framework Agreement on the ASEAN Investment Area involving ten Southeast Asian countries. This agreement, signed in 1998, aimed at establishing the ASEAN Investment Area to enhance the attractiveness of the region for direct investment flows. The degree of integration and cooperation required by these agreements differs depending on the treaty and the member states (Gugler and Tomsik 2007a). The EU agreements are argued to be the most integrated and are characterized by their strong impact on FDI among member countries and investment in and from developing countries. The NAFTA agreements involve lesser degrees of integration but have a great impact on FDI regulations.

With the exception of ASEAN, most of these regional trade agreements are bilateral trade agreements. In Chapter 7, Darryl Jarvis, Chen Shaofeng and Tan Teck Boon seek to evaluate the situation in the ASEAN countries. Their chapter entitled 'Investment liberalization in the Association of Southeast Asian Nations' explores ASEAN's cooperative endeavours in investment liberalization. Investment liberalization is variously associated with net positive effects on inflows of investment capital, technology transfer, employment, export generation, economic growth and development.

As a net historical beneficiary of investment flows, the chapter hypothesizes that ASEAN's stated commitment to investment liberalization should by now be making progress in each of four areas: absolute reductions in national autonomy in relation to investment screening and conditionality provisions; increased transparency in respect of member states' national investment regimes; enhanced standardization and codification of regulatory standards governing investment-related provisions across member states; and enhanced centralized coordination and decision making in respect of investment governance. The results of this study show that the performance of ASEAN is disappointing in terms of intra-regional investment liberalization.

Can ASEAN remain in the driving seat of regional integration and be an effective hub? Despite proclamations of reduced barriers to entry and ease of access for ASEAN nationals, the evidence appears to be to the contrary with intra-ASEAN investment flows remaining largely unchanged. As a result of delays in the latest WTO negotiations, East Asia has now resorted to a multitude of bilateral trade and investment arrangements.

Sebastien Miroudot's chapter (Chapter 8) analyses the economic impact of investment provisions in Asian RTAs. The author presents an analytical framework within which to examine such an impact in particular by looking at the scope of commitments in services industries where most of the restrictions on foreign investment occur. There is no multilateral agreement on investment covering both goods and services and including the provisions formerly found in BITs. Only RTAs provide a wide coverage of investment issues and deal with the interaction between investment disciplines and services trade. Asian RTAs include deep commitments, in particular in the area of services trade and investment, and as such are good candidates for studying the economic impact of their investment provisions in the context of 'factory Asia' and the fragmentation of world production.

Chapter 8 presents new quantitative work on the economic impact of investment provisions found in RTAs with a focus on Asia where multinational enterprises have been particularly active in reorganizing their production across countries and where many agreements with deep commitments have recently been signed. The results confirm that investment provisions in RTAs are associated with higher inward and outward investment flows, as well as increased cross-border trade in services and higher trade flows in goods.

Asian interest in multilateral rules on trade and investment: a new paradigm?

From an international perspective, two major attempts to build a multilateral framework on investment (MFI) can be identified: the OECD Multilateral Agreement on Investment (MAI) exercise and the efforts of the Working Group on the Relationship between Trade and Investment at the WTO. Both of these attempts ultimately failed. The MAI negotiations ended in 1998, at a time when it had become clear that key differences between the parties could not be resolved (Sauvé 2006). The discussions at the WTO effectively ended with the Cancún Ministerial Conference in 2003 when investment, as a prospective candidate for a stand-alone agreement, was jettisoned from the WTO agenda. With a continuing need for coherent multilateral regulation, what are the consequences of the Asian developments in FDI for a potential, future MFI? Is the important role of FDI in Asia, in particular for regional integration, increasing outbound investment activities, and the rise of MNEs from Asia, leading to a new paradigm for the regulation of FDI on a global level?

In recent times trade and investment have been complementary, and achieving one is impossible in the absence of the other. However, the inclusion of the relationship between trade and investment in the WTO forum for negotiation with the establishment of a Working Group on Trade and Investment, one of the four Singapore Issues, has been the subject of fiery debates since the beginning. Investment had been the subject matter leading to the derailing of the WTO's Cancún meeting. The conflict of interest between two groups of countries has played a key role, resulting in the current scenario. In general the developed countries believe that inclusion of trade and investment under the negotiating agenda of the WTO would be a major step towards ensuring the WTO objective of a freer trade and investment regime, leading to increased FDI to Members (Kennedy 2003). Adopting this perspective, Japan and the EU pushed forcefully for the commencement of negotiations on investment while the USA did not strongly support this initiative. The 'flying geese model' describing the experience of the Asian tigers has always been a case in point. However, a number of developing countries remained averse to that idea, mostly owing to the potential risk involved with capital flight and the development consequences observed following the Southeast Asian currency crisis, which led even the International Monetary Fund (IMF) and the World Bank to acknowledge the importance of maintaining a strict investment regime in developing countries (Lee 2005).

Concerning inconsistencies with the Agreement on Trade-related Investment Measures (TRIMs Agreement), the domestic automobile development industry policies of Indonesia, India, Brazil, and the Philippines have been suited to WTO or made subject to consultation for dispute settlement. Also, developing countries were not easily able to obtain extensions of the period allowed for removing measures that do not comply with the agreement. As a result, developing countries remain concerned that adoption of a new agreement would impede their freedom to implement their own domestic development policies. Conflict over the interpretation of the TRIMs reflects the fact that it was a compromise agreement in the first place.

The TRIMs Agreement constrains the use of performance requirements by a host country government and the General Agreement on Trade in Services (GATS) provides investors with national and most-favoured-nation treatment, movement of personnel and transfer rights in service sectors selected by Members. WTO rules cover some forms of investment ('commercial presence' for service suppliers under the GATS) or address issues highly relevant to investment (e.g. TRIMs and subsidies) but do not address for instance, investment protection. It can be concluded that both agreements could represent a 'departure' from BITs because many BITs include some performance requirements and investment obligations as well as provisions on investment protection. Undoubtedly, addressing these issues in more detail would improve conditions for business and facilitate investment. The current state of affairs challenges all countries and their economic policies to commit themselves to ongoing efforts towards the improvement and further liberalization of investment regimes.

In any event, while the economic incentives favouring liberalization of national investment rules are likely to persist, much of that liberalization has originated either directly or indirectly in response to national commitments to international agreements such as the Agreement on Trade-Related Aspects of Intellectual Property (TRIPS) and the GATS.

Parallels have been drawn between the investment talks and how services negotiators are addressing the question of 'non-discrimination'. Non-discrimination in the WTO means treating all countries the same through most-favoured-nation and national treatment (treating foreign and domestic firms the same way). Under the GATS, countries can theoretically put limitations on national treatment awarded to sectors they choose to liberalize, while allowing exceptions to most-favoured-nation treatment. This idea of being able to pick and choose which sectors to liberalize is referred to as the 'positive list' approach. Trade negotiators have to make the choice between taking a positive or a negative list approach. The positive list approach is used where only those sectors and services listed in the agreement will be liberalized. In contrast, under a negative list approach, all sectors and services will be liberalized except for those explicitly named in the agreement. The negative list approach requires Members to stipulate exceptions and conditions regarding the pace and scope of liberalization, which can be more difficult and may reduce the control exerted on the scope of liberalization of investment. An investment agreement could follow a 'GATS-type' positive list approach in the 'pre-establishment' phase, meaning that countries could pick and choose which commitments they wanted to make.

The advantage of the positive list approach over the top-down or negative list approach is its greater flexibility. With the NAFTA-type negative list approach, some countries might feel deprived of an important policy tool. This is because in some sectors and industries it is very difficult to anticipate their future development and character at the moment of writing down the negative list. Here the combined national and most-favoured-nation treatment approach offers less flexibility to host countries in FDI flows into such sectors. In this sense, the GATS provides a realistic approach for dealing with the admission of foreign investment. The positive list approach would probably permit a more gradual liberalization (Egger *et al.* 2007), which some countries may prefer. Under GATS, no Member of the WTO is a priori forced to make any commitments in any given sector (Gugler and Tomsik 2007b).

But the GATS type approach has disadvantages as well – primarily that the level of investment liberalization is probably much lower than if the top-down approach were adopted. Generally it can be said that:

> experience with GATS showed that a positive list approach was preferable when a new area was for the first time the subject of liberalization at a multilateral level. However, the flexibility inherent in this approach has considerably weakened the scope of the national treatment principle. It was noted that the positive list approach needs constant updating if it is to assist to transparency and the aim of investment liberalization.[2]

Besides, understanding exactly which sectors to open up and which types of limitations and exceptions to put under each sector so that a country is not economically, socially or politically harmed requires extensive understanding of the various economic sectors. It also requires an understanding of how certain commitments will impact on constitutional and legislative mandates as well as on domestic regulation in each country. Currently, many countries in the WTO are struggling with these issues in the services negotiations and realizing that the negotiations involved in constructing a positive list can be quite overwhelming for effective and informed negotiations.

In Chapter 9, Jayant Menon focuses on the noodle bowl effect in Asia. The outcome of this proliferation of often overlapping bilateral free trade agreements (BTAs) and plurilateral free trade agreements (PTAs) is described as the spaghetti bowl effect or, in the Asian region, the noodle bowl effect. This development is costly and welfare reducing. How do we remedy the situation? In this chapter, Jayant Menon considers the various options proposed for dealing with the noodle bowl, and assesses their ability to do so. A general limitation of these proposals is their tendency to group all kinds of BTAs together, treating them as homogeneous. Thus, the proposals ignore underlying differences in motivation in forming BTAs. To overcome this, Jayant Menon develops a taxonomy for classifying BTAs by motivation before considering the effectiveness of the different remedies proposed. He finds that each proposal has its pros and cons, and can cater for different types of BTAs. Thus, a combination of the various proposals may be warranted, even in the event of an expeditious and *bona fide* conclusion to the Doha Round.

In Chapter 10, Julien Chaisse, Debashis Chakraborty and Arup Guha evaluate the approach of India towards FDI regulation and in particular towards a potential multilateral framework for investment. The inclusion of a multilateral framework for investment at the WTO is proposed with the aim of coordinating the global regulation of trade and investment. In addition to the difficulties arising during these negotiations, one major concern is that certain countries such as India have no interest in going for full-scale capital account convertibility. As a part of the G4, India is currently a major player in the trade-related international regulatory framework. It is argued here that the question of a multilateral framework for investment cannot be solved without taking into account the Indian reluctance for a freer investment regime. There is a historical reluctance of developing countries to establish freer investment regimes. The project on a new international economic order has already given pre-eminence to the sovereignty of States and their necessary control of the private sector, notably of foreign capital. But that political approach is reinforced by objective arguments analysed here. First the authors briefly discuss the debate on having a freer investment framework and the foreign investment regime in India. India's submissions to the WTO on this front are reviewed next. Then, in order to evaluate the legitimacy of India's concerns, an empirical model is applied to analyse the potential impact of a destabilizing shock on her capital account. Finally, based on the findings, the policy lessons are drawn.

In his contribution (Chapter 11), Chang-fa Lo examines the conditions and ways of restoring investment to the WTO negotiation agenda. He suggests establishing a linkage between BITs and the WTO. Investment and trade norms are generally developed in parallel. But there are also important points of intersection between the rules governing investment and those governing trade. This chapter divides the development of the linkage and relations between trade and investment into four stages: the rudimentary stage, the parallel development stage, the re-emerging stage, and the decoupling stage. After examining these stages, the author proposes an approach to encourage closer ties between these two fields by putting the investment issues back into the future WTO negotiation agenda. He argues that the way to achieve this does not rely on the possible wide range of substantive commitments but rather on allaying concerns and on the building of confidence of developing countries.

For this purpose, there are a number of elements to be included in the approach recommended by Chang-fa Lo: to recognize the existing BITs and their functions; to recognize the power and discretion of host countries to decide on the admission of foreign investment; to impose procedural requirements on notification and transparency; to introduce institutionalized technical assistance and capacity building; and to make available the multilateral dispute settlement mechanism for BIT disputes to unify the legal views on certain commonly occurring issues.

This approach raises the question of investor to state arbitrations. This is now the key feature of international investment agreements. We see from the pursuit of BITs by ASEAN states that these BITs might also be assessed in terms of the superior dispute resolution procedures they typically contain. Most BITs have recourse to independent arbitration in third-party countries in the case of investment disputes or breach of investment guarantees. This is not the case with the ASEAN Investment Area which has relied on political-cum-bureaucratic dispute resolution mechanisms. The relevant provisions are not geared to investment disputes per se and are more applicable to state–state than to firm–state dispute settlement procedures. ASEAN, in a sense, is thus being outclassed and is in danger of becoming outdated if renewed commitment to investment liberalization is not forthcoming.

The idea of promoting a harbour agreement to coordinate BITs at the global level is more modest than the suggestion of a GATS-type agreement on investment (Chaisse and Gugler 2008). Applying this hypothesis, an investment agreement could follow a 'GATS-type' positive list approach in the 'pre-establishment' phase, meaning that countries could pick and choose which commitments they wanted to make. The advantage of the positive list approach over the top-down or negative list approach is its greater flexibility. However, such an approach raises the question of the future of the BITs and FTAs already in existence all over the world and constantly expanding. For this fundamental reason, the harbour agreement is an option which should be supported and put on the negotiating table. It will not solve all the problems and will not be a perfect solution but it is surely the most politically feasible option.

When looking at the expansion of FDI in Asia we considered it important to address these three levels of analysis: the role of MNEs; the domestic and regional frameworks; and finally the impacts at the global level or, in other words, on the multilateral regulation of FDI. We believe that the contents of each chapter will justify such an approach.

Notes

1 Statistics from World Bank Development Indicators (2007) quoted in the book *Dancing with Giants: China, India and the global economy*, World Bank and Institute of Policy Studies, 2007.
2 WTO (2002): WT/WGTI/W120 *Modalities for pre-establishment commitments based on a GATS-type, positive list approach*, Geneva: World Trade Organization.

References

Adlung, R. and Molinuevo, M. (2008) 'Bilateralism in services trade: Is there fire behind the (bit-) smoke?', *Journal of International Economic Law*, 11: 365–409.

Buckley, P.J., Clegg, L.J., Cross, A.R. and Liu, X. (2007) 'The determinants of Chinese outward foreign direct investment', *Journal of International Business Studies*, 38: 499–518.

Chaisse, J. and Gugler, P. (2008) 'Investment issues and WTO law – dealing with fragmentation', in Chaisse, J. and Balmelli, T. (eds) *Essays on the Future of the World Trade Organization*, Geneva: EDIS.

Dunning, J.H. (1992) *Multinational Enterprises and the Global Economy*, Wokingham: Addison-Wesley.

Egger, P., Larch, M. and Pfaffermayr, M. (2007) 'Bilateral versus multilateral trade and investment liberalisation', *The World Economy*, 30: 582–583.

Faure, G.O. and Fang, T. (2008) 'Changing Chinese values: Keeping up with paradoxes', *International Business Review*, 17: 194–207.

Fink, C. and Molinuevo, M. (2008) 'East Asian free trade agreeements in services: Key architectural elements', *Journal of International Economic Law*, 11: 263–311.

Gugler, P. and Ben Hamida, L. (2007) *How the PFI May Contribute to a More Coherent International Policy Framework on Investment*, NCCR Trade Regulation Working Paper, No. 27.

Gugler, P. and Tomsik, V. (2007a) 'General agreement on investment: Departure from the investment agreement patchwork', in Dunning, J. and Gugler, P. (eds) *Foreign Direct Investments, Location and Competitiveness*, Oxford: Elsevier, 229–254.

Gugler, P. and Tomsik, V. (2007b) 'The North American and European approaches in the international investment agreements', *Transnational Dispute Management Review (online)*, 4 (5).

Kennedy, K. (2003) 'A WTO agreement on investment: A solution in search of a problem?', *University of Pennsylvania Journal of International Economic Law*, 24: 77–188.

Lee, Y.S. (2005) 'Foreign direct investment and regional trade liberalization: A viable answer for economic development?', *Journal of World Trade*, 39: 701–717.

Marchick, D.M. and Slaughter, M.J. (2008) *Global FDI Policy: Correcting a protectionist drift*, United States Council on Foreign Relations, Paper No. 34, Council on Foreign Relations Press.

Rugman, A. and Hoon Ho, C. (2008) 'The international competitiveness of Asian firms', *Journal of Strategy and Management,* 1 (1): 57–71.

Rugman, A. and Verbeke, A. (2005) 'Towards a theory of regional multinationals: A transaction cost economics approach', *Management International Review*, 45 (Special Issue 1): 3–15.

Sauvant, K. (2005) 'New sources of FDI: The BRICS – outward FDI from Brazil, Russia, India and China', *Journal of World Investment and Trade*, 6 (5): 639–710.

Sauvé, P. (2006) Multilateral rules on investment: Is forward movement possible? *Journal of International Economic Law*, 9: 325–355.

Sauvé, P. (2007) *Investment Regulation through Trade Agreements: Lessons from Asia*, Asia-Pacific Research and Training Network on Trade, Working Paper Series, No. 49.

Thomsen, S. (2007) 'India and China: Investment and development strategies' PowerPoint presentation for Chatham House workshop on The Expansion of China and India: Impact and Consequences for Japan, UK and the World Economy', London, 2 March, 2007. Online. Available HTTP: http://www.chathamhouse.org.uk/pdf/research/ie/020307thomsen.pdf (accessed 15/09/2008).

UNCTAD Investment Brief 2007, UNCTAD/PRESS/PR/2007/001. Online. Available HTTP: http://stats.unctad.org/fdi (accessed 15/09/2008).

UNCTAD (2007) *World Investment Report 2007, Transnational Corporations*, New York and Geneva: United Nations, 323.

Winters, L.A. and Yusuf, S. (2007) *Dancing with Giants: China, India and the global economy*, Washington, World Bank and Institute of Policy Studies.

World Bank and International Bank for Reconstruction and Development (2007), Development Indicators 2007, Washington: World Bank, 432.

World Bank Group (2007) *Doing Business 2007: How to reform*, Washington: World Bank, 185.

Part I

Internationalization strategy of emerging Asian firms

Examples from China and India

2 The rise of Chinese MNEs

Philippe Gugler and Bertram Boie

Introduction

Chinese outbound foreign direct investment (FDI[1]) is becoming an increasingly important phenomenon. In 2006, China's outbound FDI totalled about US$21 billion (MOFCOM 2007a), and it is expected to rise to a tremendous US$60 billion by 2010 (MOFCOM 2007b). Chinese investors are increasingly exploring opportunities overseas in a wide range of industries (Ming and Williamson 2007). A few high-profile acquisitions such as Lenovo's acquisition of IBM's personal computer business have become widely known, but the majority of such investments have received comparatively little attention and a systematic understanding of the phenomenon is lacking.

A scientific analysis of, and academic debate on, Chinese FDI and its characteristics has started, with a growing number of relevant articles published in recent years. Looking at the motivations of Chinese multinational enterprises (MNEs) to go international, most scholars (Buckley *et al.* 2007; Morck *et al.* 2007; Poncet 2007) agree that classical motivations play the key role: Chinese MNEs are to various extents market-seeking, resource-seeking, and strategic asset-seeking. However, most scholars, including Buckley (Buckley *et al.* 2007), Morck (Morck *et al.* 2008), and Child and Rodriguez (Child and Rodriguez 2005), feel that these characteristics, originally developed in a Western context and for Western companies, do not completely explain the phenomenon and cannot reveal all motivations of Chinese MNEs. They have thus proposed explanations for the phenomenon to complement the classical theory.

This chapter intends to contribute to the analysis of Chinese FDI. It is divided into two parts. The first part presents a factual analysis of Chinese FDI and the emergence of Chinese MNEs, giving a statistical overview of the flows and stocks of Chinese FDI in different areas of the world, in various industries, and with regard to key characteristics of the Chinese MNEs expanding abroad. The second part analyses the strategies adopted by Chinese MNEs going international: What are the comparative advantages specific to Chinese firms, and how do they translate into motivations to expand abroad?

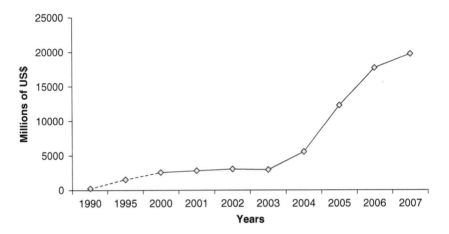

Figure 2.1 China's total outward FDI flows

Source: 1990–2002: Various editions of UNCTAD's World Investment Report (WIR); 2003–2007: MOFCOM

EMERGENCE OF CHINESE FDI

Main trends

Flows and stock of Chinese FDI

China's net outflows of FDI[2] have shown a strong positive trend over the past few years. As illustrated in Figure 2.1, at the beginning of the 1990s, outflows stood at about US$25.00 million. They rose to some US$2,500.00 million at the beginning of this century (MOFCOM 2006: 53). Since then, FDI outflows from China have increased more then sixfold from US$2,854.65 million in 2003 (MOFCOM 2006: 67) to a total of more than US$18,000.00 million in 2006 (MOFCOM 2007a). Of this, US$5.17 billion (24.4 per cent) was incremental equity investment, US$6.65 billion (31.4 per cent) profits reinvestment and US$ 9.34 billion (44.2 per cent) was related to other kinds of investment (MOFCOM 2006: 51). Stock value increased from US$33,222.22 million in 2003 to US$75,025.55 million in 2006 (MOFCOM 2006: 58). This stock breaks down to US$37.24 billion (41.1 per cent) equity investment, US$33.68 billion (37.2 per cent) profits reinvestment and US$19.71 billion (21.7 per cent) other kinds of investment (MOFCOM 2006: 51).

Compared to flows of outward investment from other countries, China's share is still comparatively small, but the country is catching up rapidly. According to the *World Investment Report 2006* of the United Nations Conference on Trade and Development (UNCTAD), the world's FDI outflows reached US$778.7 billion and the stock volume of FDI amounted to US$10,671.9 billion in 2005 (UNCTAD WIR 2006: 5). Taking this as the baseline period, China's FDI outflow and stock constituted 2.72 per cent and 0.85 per cent, respectively, of the world's total in 2006, ranking China thirteenth among all countries in the world's total FDI outflow (MOFCOM 2006: 52). Already in 2005, when China's FDI outflows stood at US$11 billion, which is only about half of today's value, this was the fourth largest outflow from a developing or transition economy (UNCTAD WIR 2006: 114). Furthermore, a recent survey by investment promotion agencies predicts that China will become a top four source of FDI over the period 2005–2008 (UNCTAD 2005a: 17).

Sectoral distribution of Chinese FDI

Looking at Chinese FDI in terms of stock until 2006, leasing and business services are the most relevant sectors, accounting for US$19,463.60 million (MOFCOM 2006: 65). They are followed by mining (US$17,901.62 million) and the financial sector (US$15,605.37 million) (MOFCOM 2006: 65). The importance of the financial sector may be illustrated by the information that, according to China's Ministry of Commerce (MOFCOM), by 2006, the Chinese state-owned commercial banks had established 47 branch offices, 31 affiliated institutions and 12 representative offices in 19 countries, including the United States, Japan and the United Kingdom (MOFCOM 2006: 51). The next most important sectors are wholesale and retail (US$12,955.20 million), and transport, warehousing and postal services (US$7,568.19 million) (MOFCOM 2006: 65). Manufacturing plays the least important role, valued at some US$7,529.62 million (MOFCOM 2006: 65). Also, Hobdari *et al.* underline the importance of outbound FDI in services (Hobdari *et al.* 2007: 7).

With regard to investment flows, in 2006, mining accounted for the highest share in Chinese outbound investments (US$8,539.51 million) (MOFCOM 2006: 64). Together manufacturing and mining have seen the highest growth rates over recent years, accounting for 60 per cent of total Chinese outbound FDI flows in 2005. The rise of the primary sector is an increasingly important factor in Chinese outbound investment and reflects the overall development of the industry. Mining includes the whole primary sector with exploration and mining activities associated with oil and gas and other commodities. Leasing and business services (US$4,521.66 million), rank above the financial sector (US$3,529.99 million), followed by transport, warehousing and postal services (US$1,376.39 million) (MOFCOM 2006: 64). Figure 2.2 shows flows and stocks of Chinese outward FDI in 2006.

The high importance of services among Chinese FDI is in line with the international trend. According to UNCTAD *World Investment Report 2006*, a breakdown of international outbound investment shows that services dominate in overall outbound investment. In 2004, this share worldwide was approximately 67 per cent for developed countries and 81 per cent for developing and transition economies (71 per cent excluding Hong Kong) (UNCTAD WIR 2006: 115).

Geographical distribution of Chinese FDI

Chinese outward investments to all continents have been rising over the past few years. As illustrated by Figure 2.3, although some regions have gained and others have lost importance as outbound investment locations, flows and stock of

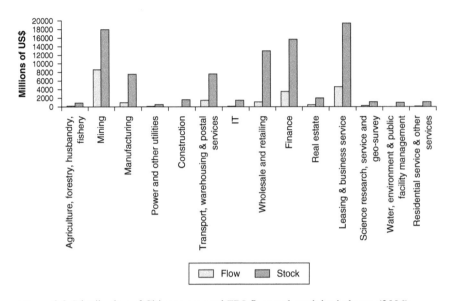

Figure 2.2 Distribution of Chinese outward FDI flow and stock by industry (2006)

Source: Authors' own illustration based on information from *MOFCOM Statistical Bulletin 2006*.

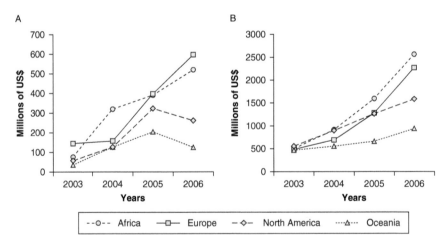

Figure 2.3 China's outward FDI flow (A) and stock (B) to Africa, Europe, North America and Oceania (non-financial)

Source: Authors' own illustration based on information from *MOFCOM Statistical Bulletin 2006*.

FDI from China to Africa, Europe, North America and Oceania, as well as to Latin America and Asian countries, all show an overall positive trend.

China's most intense outbound investment activities are in its Asian neighbouring countries, particularly the countries of the Association of Southeast Asian Nations (ASEAN). High levels of investment are noted for Mongolia,

Central Asian countries, Indonesia, South Korea, Singapore, Vietnam, and also Iran (MOFCOM 2006: 53). China's special administrative region (SAR), Hong Kong, plays a very important role with regard to outbound FDI. In fact, Hong Kong attracts by far the greatest amount of outbound investment from mainland China. Most of this FDI is in services, and a great deal must be assumed to constitute round-tripping investment or investment directed to offshore financial centres (see section on 'Unspecified and round-tripping investment'). While it is difficult to assess the specific characteristic investment transacted via Hong Kong in detail, it is obvious that Hong Kong is of crucial importance to mainland China as a financial marketplace.

Also noteworthy is that Chinese outbound investment directed towards Africa is comparatively high and continues to develop positively. With a flow of US$2,556.82 million, Africa is receiving more FDI from China than any other continent except Asia (MOFCOM 2006: 59). According to a survey by the Multilateral Investment Guarantee Agency (MIGA), investment projects planned by Chinese companies for the period after 2005 even exceed the number of investment projects per year before 2005 (FIAS/MIGA, Battat 2005: 19).

Chinese FDI also plays a role of growing importance for Europe and North America. Within the European Union, most Chinese FDI is directed to Germany (MOFCOM 2006: 61). In 2006, its stock of Chinese FDI amounted to US$472.03 million, compared to a total of US$2,269.8 million for all of Europe (MOFCOM 2006: 60). The United Kingdom, which ranks second, is receiving less than half of the amount invested in Germany (US$201.87 million). Spain, Poland, Italy, Romania, Hungary and France follow with stock values between US$136.72 million and US$44.88 million (MOFCOM 2006: 60).

Different viewpoints have been expressed with regard to the question of a preference of Chinese investors between North America and Europe. According to the statistics of MOFCOM, depicted in Figure 2.3, more Chinese FDI is reaching Europe than North America (MOFCOM 2006: 60, 63). This finding is supported by an analysis by MIGA, according to which Europe is attracting more investment projects and is likely to be more attractive for Chinese FDI in the years to come (FIAS/MIGA, Battat 2005: 21). Research undertaken by Roland Berger Consultants in 2003, however, indicates that the North American market remains the developed market of choice, with nearly 20 per cent of China's top 50 giving it high investment priority (von Keller and Zhou 2003: 18). This may point to a change in the perspective of Chinese decision-makers in recent years, towards valuing opportunities in Europe more positively.

Types of investors

State-owned enterprises versus private enterprises

Both Chinese state-owned enterprises (SOEs) and private enterprises are engaged in FDI, and no clear breakdown has been published on the shares of SOEs and private enterprises in the total number of investment projects. The high number (5,000) of Chinese companies investing abroad (MOFCOM 2006: 51) suggests considerable activity by companies from both SOEs and the private sector. However, a number of aspects characteristic of Chinese investors give a strong indication that the role the Chinese Government is playing in Chinese FDI is tremendous.

Most of the large-scale investment projects that weigh heavy in Chinese FDI statistics have so far been executed by Chinese SOEs. As Cheng reports, in recent years the shares of FDI flows of SOEs under the Central Government were 73.5 per cent (2003), 82.3 per cent (2004), and 83.2 per cent (2005) (Cheng and Ma 2007: 10). The remaining shares of FDI flows are split between investments of SOEs administered by regional governments, non-SOEs that are owned collectively, and, finally, privately owned companies. Examples of companies largely owned by regional governments, such as the governments of Beijing, Shanghai and Guangdong include TCL, and Beida Jade Bird (Cheng and Ma 2007: 10). Lenovo, today mostly in private hands, was still in majority state ownership at the time of its famous acquisition of IBM's personal computer business. This underlines the very strong role of the Chinese Government at various levels in large Chinese FDI projects.

Furthermore, until 2003, outward investment was, in principle, only allowed for Chinese SOEs (Buckley *et al.* 2007: 500). This considerably limited the amount private Chinese companies invested abroad compared to SOEs. Moreover, a number of FDI projects will naturally be executed by SOEs or majority SOEs, since the specific industry sector may be closed or nearly closed to private companies. In particular, nearly all Chinese companies in the natural resources industry are SOEs (Brett and Ericsson 2006: 27). Given the importance of the minerals sector in Chinese outbound investment, this constitutes an important factor.

Analysis by Morck confirms the very strong role the government is playing in Chinese FDI. According to him, Chinese private sector firms can, in principal, conduct outward FDI, but 'the scale is too small to register' (Morck *et al.* 2008: 22). Morck also notes that the largest FDI players overlap substantially with the most profitable SOEs in China. The bulk of FDI is thus executed by the Chinese SOEs, which are the large domestic players in major industries in China. They are often backed up with an officially sanctioned monopoly in their industry, such as natural resources, telecommunications or infrastructure (Morck *et al.* 2008: 340).

Finally, FDI by any Chinese firm requires the approval of the Chinese authorities. Approval processes include MOFCOM, the State Administration of Foreign Exchange (SAFE), and the National Development and Reform Commission (NDRC) (FIAS/MIGA, Battat 2005: 7, 8). Approvals are usually needed initially and for a yearly review. Investment projects are expected to follow the catalogue of encouraged FDI, and may be rejected or restricted, for example via foreign currency exchange limitations (Buckley 2007: 503). With these instruments, the government ensures that all investment activities, even if executed by privately owned companies, are strictly in line with government policies. Clearly, this needs to be taken into consideration when analysing the motivations and strategies of Chinese MNEs going international.

Table 2.1 The 30 largest Chinese companies as of 2006, ranked by outward FDI stock

No.	Name of enterprise
1	China Petrochemical Corporation
2	China National Petroleum Corporation
3	China National Offshore Oil Corporation
4	China Resources (Holdings) Co., Ltd
5	China Mobile Communications Corporation
6	China Ocean Shipping (Group) Company
7	CITIC Group
8	China National Cereals, Oils & Foodstuffs Corp.
9	China Merchants Group
10	Sinochem Corporation
11	China State Construction Engineering Corporation
12	China National Aviation Holding Corporation
13	China Telecommunications Group Corporation
14	China Shipping (Group) Company
15	China Network Communications Group Corporation
16	GDH Ltd
17	China Power Investment Corporation
18	Shanghai Automotive Industry Corporation
19	China National Chemical Corporation
20	China Minmetals Corporation
21	Legend Holdings Ltd
22	Shum Yip Holdings Company Ltd
23	China National Foreign Trade Transportation (Group) Corporation
24	Huawei Technologies
25	Shanghai Baosteel Group Corporation
26	China Huaneng Group
27	SinoSteel Corporation
28	China Poly Group Corporation
29	China Nonferrous Metal Mining & Construction (group) Co., Ltd
30	Haier Group

Source: *MOFCOM Statistical Bulletin 2006.*

Large enterprises versus small and medium enterprises (SMEs)

Two aspects are noteworthy with regard to the size of Chinese companies investing abroad. The first is the high number of companies engaged in FDI. As MOFCOM reports, by the end of 2006, more than 5,000 domestic Chinese investment entities had established nearly 10,000 overseas direct invested enterprises in 172 countries around the world (MOFCOM 2006: 51).

Second, as outlined in the previous section, it is the large Chinese companies that rank high with regard to FDI. These companies are active in the natural resources business, or in the businesses that closely follow minerals and metals in the value chain, such as chemical and steel making or construction. Companies involved in finance, logistics and infrastructure are also among the top 30. Most of them are SOEs or majority-SOEs. An overview of these companies is presented in Table 2.1.

This leads to the assumption that a comparatively small number of large Chinese SOEs are responsible for the current rise in Chinese FDI. In their shadow, numerous smaller companies, possibly privately owned, have started to emerge internationally, but do not yet do significant international business. This observation also seems to be in line with the work of Papanastassiou who reports that the average size of investment projects by Chinese companies is comparatively small (Hobdari *et al.* 2007: 9).

Types of investments

Greenfield investments versus mergers and acquisitions and joint ventures

Internationally, the recorded number of greenfield investments has seen a sharp increase since 2003. In 2005, 15 per cent of the recorded projects had originated as new investments from developing and transition economies, with the largest share being projects from Asia (UNCTAD WIR 2006: 110). Chinese companies are part of this trend, and greenfield investments are to date the preferred vehicle for expansion abroad. A survey by Roland Berger Consultants among Chinese business leaders reveals that greenfield investment ranks first among expansion strategies (48 per cent), followed by strategic alliances (39 per cent), and acquisition (13 per cent) (von Keller and Zhou 2003: 21).

Outright acquisitions are a complicated process that requires considerable experience for successful execution. Many Chinese companies still lack this experience. In addition, intercultural challenges as well as lengthy and challenging processes for gaining the approval of the Chinese authorities make acquisitions generally less attractive for Chinese firms (Buckley *et al.* 2007: 506).

However, joint ventures (JVs) and mergers and acquisition (M&A) have grown in importance in recent years (Wu 2005: 7), and are expected to increase in number, size and complexity in the years to come (von Keller and Zhou 2003: 22). In fact, M&As and JVs are often the only means of acquiring strategic assets, such as technology, intellectual property, business knowledge, and knowledge of the functioning of foreign markets. The importance of M&As for Chinese MNEs must thus not be underestimated, especially in securing their position in highly competitive, developed markets.

A number of scholars have put forward arguments that support this view. In an early analysis, Zhan notes that large investment projects are generally realized through acquisition or partial acquisition, while smaller projects are more likely to be executed as greenfield projects (Zhan 1995: 83). According to Poncet, a policy of selective support by the Chinese Government is applicable for appropriate cases. In October 2004, a circular issued by the the National Development Research Council and the Export–Import Bank of China explicitly promoted M&As that could enhance the international competitiveness of Chinese enterprises and accelerate their entry into foreign markets (Poncet 2007: 7). From a statistical analysis on Chinese outward FDI, Guohua Jiang finds that 'developing country acquirers are more likely to carry out a cross-border M&A in developed

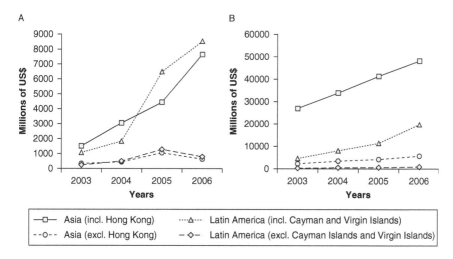

Figure 2.4 China's outward FDI flow (A) and stock (B) to Asia (incl./excl. Hong Kong), and Latin America (incl./excl. Cayman and Virgin Islands)

Source: Authors' own graphic based on information from *MOFCOM Statistical Bulletin 2006.*

countries for strategic asset-seeking purposes, but in developing countries for resource-seeking purposes' (Jiang *et al.* 2007: 16).

It is thus not surprising that the most well-known recent examples of Chinese companies going abroad have taken the form of acquisitions, for example Lenovo's acquisition of IBM's personal computer division, Shanghai Automotive Industry Corporation (SAIC)'s acquisition of the Korean SsangYong, or TCL's quasi acquisition of Thomson's television section and Alcatel's mobile phone division (Hagiwara, Bank of Tokyo 2006: 5).

Unspecified and round-tripping investment

By far the largest amount of Chinese outward investment in terms of transaction volume is executed via tax havens (Lunding 2006: 3). The preferred tax havens are Hong Kong (SAR), Macau (SAR), Singapore, the Cayman Islands, the Virgin Islands and the Bermuda Islands. Nearly 20 per cent of all Chinese outward FDI between 2003 and 2005 was invested in the Cayman and Virgin Islands, whereas almost 64 per cent of the investment went to Hong Kong. Figure 2.4 illustrates this situation, depicting the flows and stocks of Chinese FDI to Asia including Hong Kong (SAR) compared to flows and stocks of Chinese FDI to Asia excluding Hong Kong. Similarly, Chinese FDI to Latin America including the Cayman and Virgin Islands is compared to Chinese FDI to Latin America excluding the Cayman and Virgin Islands.

The motivations for investments in tax havens are difficult to investigate in detail, but are often made for financial reasons. In fact, it has been regularly noted that considerable parts of these investments do not stay in tax havens, but are rein-vested in China for the purpose of tax optimization (UNCTAD WIR 2006: 112). These investments are referred to as round-tripping investments. In addition, sources from the financial sector report that it must be assumed that a number of investments transacted via tax havens are flowing into the natural resources sector (Hagiwara, Bank of Tokyo 2006: 4). For various reasons, a hidden investment in anonymous bank accounts is occasionally also a preferred business strategy.

The significance of round-tripping and unspecified investment flows within Chinese FDI underlines the necessity to identify the phenomenon in a statistical analysis of Chinese outbound investment. Especially when comparing Chinese outbound investment to Asia or Latin America with investment flows to Africa, Europe, North America and Oceania, the amount of round-tripping investment must always be kept in mind. However, round-tripping investment being a mere financial flow of investment is less relevant for an analysis of the character and purpose of Chinese outbound investments. For such an analysis, financial invest-ment flows for tax optimization play no important role. Consequently, this chapter relies on the UNCTAD definition of investment, which characterizes FDI as an investment involving a long-term relationship and reflecting a lasting inter-est and control by a firm in an enterprise resident in a foreign country (UNCTAD WIR 2005b: 297). Thus, no further reference will be made to round-tripping investment in this chapter.

INTERNATIONALIZATION STRATEGIES OF CHINESE MNEs

Theoretical background

The theory of MNEs

The theory of MNEs indicates that the goal of firms in a global market econ-omy is to increase or protect their profitability and/or capital value (UNCTAD WIR 2006: 142). As noted by UNCTAD WIR (2006: 142), 'One of the ways in which TNCs [transnational corporations] are achieving this goal is by engaging in FDI, either to better exploit their existing competitive advantages or to safe-guard, increase or add to these advantages'.

Various theories and concepts of MNEs and international competitiveness are available to explain in detail these competitive advantages. Among the theories developed over recent decades, the eclectic or OLI paradigm, pointing out own-ership, location and internationalization advantages, is one of the most powerful tools for understanding the extent and pattern of FDI (Dunning 1981; Dunning *et al.* 2008). According to Dunning, firms may be in a position to international-ize by using their ownership advantages (Dunning 2000). The ownership advan-tages are defined as a unique capability proprietary to the firm, which may be built upon product or process technology, marketing or distributional skills (Rugman 2008: 93). These advantages could be assets possessed by a firm (e.g. brands, or patents) or they could involve more efficient organization of these assets across national boundaries. The type of MNE strategy based on this kind of advantage is referred to as 'asset exploiting' and the choice of host country is determined by one or more of four types of motivations (Dunning 1998; Dunning and Lundan 2008: 67ff.): market-seeking FDI, efficiency-seeking FDI, resource-seeking FDI and strategic asset-seeking FDI.

Market-seeking FDI may be undertaken to sustain or protect existing markets, or to exploit or promote new markets (Dunning and Lundan, 2008:70). Apart from market size and the prospects for market growth, there are several other reasons which might prompt firms to engage in market-seeking investment, such as the need to adapt products to local tastes or needs, to cultural mores and to indigenous resources and capabilities.

The motivation of efficiency-seeking FDI is to rationalize the structure of established resource-based or market-seeking investment in such a way that the investing firm can benefit from the common governance of geographically dispersed activities (Dunning and Lundan, 2008: 72). Such gains are essentially those of economies of scale and scope, and of risk diversification.

The aim of resource-seeking FDI is to acquire abroad particular and specific resources of a higher quality at a lower real cost than could be obtained in the home country (Dunning and Lundan 2008: 68). The theory distinguishes three main types of resource seekers: those seeking physical resources of one kind or another; those seeking plentiful supplies of cheap and well-motivated unskilled or semi-skilled labour; and those seeking to acquire technological capabilities, management or marketing expertise and organizational skills (Dunning and Lundan 2008: 68).

Finally, strategic asset-seeking investors play a key role in the theory of MNEs. As noted by Dunning and Lundan (2008: 72),

> [this] group of MNEs comprise those which engage in FDI, usually by acquiring the assets of foreign corporations, to promote their long-term strategic objectives – especially that of sustaining or advancing their global competitiveness. The investing firms involved include both established MNEs pursuing an integrated global or regional strategy, and first time foreign direct investors seeking to access or to buy some kind of competitive strength in an unfamiliar market.

In contrast to the strategies of asset-exploiting MNEs, firms engaged in asset augmenting strategies may not possess competitive advantages, in particular ownership advantages.

> In order to address this shortcoming, such firms may therefore be motivated to venture into international markets and exploit their limited competitive advantages in order to acquire 'strategic' created assets such as technology, brands, distribution networks, R&D facilities and managerial competences (quite commonly through M&As).

> (UNCTAD WIR 2006: 142)

A theory for Chinese MNEs?

In addition to the above theory, the literature has pointed out characteristics of the current political and economic situation in China, which have an effect on Chinese FDI and which might not be sufficiently covered by the usual theoretical approach. As Buckley notes, 'the question arises as to whether Chinese outbound investment is indeed to be explained by traditional theoretical approaches, or whether a special theory is needed to explain the phenomenon' (Buckley *et al.* 2007: 500).

John A. Mathews proposes a new theoretical approach to explain the phenomenon of MNEs from the Asia-Pacific region (Mathews 2006: 6). He identifies a generally new characteristic of these MNEs. He calls this new type of MNEs 'dragon multinationals', and defines them as being firms from the Asia-Pacific region that have successfully internationalized and, in some cases, have become leaders in their own fields. Starting from behind and without initial resources, skills and knowledge, they succeed due to a number of specific factors and special characteristics. Overall, their sudden appearance cannot be explained by conventional multinational strategies, and thus helps to 'expose the weaknesses and limits to traditional accounts of MNEs and to existing theories and frameworks of International Business' (Mathews 2006: 8). The main difference between the approach taken by new MNEs from the Asia-Pacific region and that of the established MNEs, according to Mathews, is that they are of such recent origin that they are perfectly adapted to a globalized world. While 'the incumbents see the world full of competitors who are trying to imitate their success [...] the newcomers and latecomers see the world as full of resources to be tapped' (Mathews 2006: 9).

Some scholars have found it useful to apply a concept of push and pull factors to categorize constraints and incentives relevant for investors (Dunning 2008). Such a categorization does not oppose or contradict the traditional approach, but arguably takes a wider perspective, since various motivations for investors deriving from conditions in the home as well as the host country may be addressed with such a scheme. Cheng, for example, categorized resource-acquiring FDI, market-expanding FDI, efficiency-improving FDI and asset-seeking to be pull factors. These pull factors are 'favorable natural and economic endowments abroad [that] lure Chinese corporations [to] invest and expand their businesses overseas' (Cheng and Stough 2007: 15). Push factors, on the other hand, are conditions inside China 'that facilitate, if not force, Chinese firms to actively participate in international and global investment and production' (Cheng and Stough 2007: 15). These push factors are mainly derived from market conditions such as domestic competition and excess production capacity, and macroeconomic considerations of the state, such as abundant foreign exchange reserves, high demand for natural resources, and political goals of the Chinese Government to support Chinese companies in their efforts to internationalize (Cheng and Stough 2007: 15). Many scholars agree with these points. Poncet adds that companies may see a need to bypass trade barriers (Poncet 2007: 11). Business intelligence, such as research by Roland Berger, underlines the importance of internal corporate motives to provide impetus for overseas expansion (von Keller and Zhou 2003: 9).

Finally, a large number of scholars insist on the application of the general theory, accepting, however, that FDI from China is unique in certain regards (Buckley *et al.* 2007; Hobdari *et al.* 2007; Poncet 2007). Buckley states that 'Chinese FDI is indeed distinctive in certain respects with implications for the theory. This, however, does not exclude the application of the general theory' (Buckley *et al.* 2007: 500). Analysing whether the emergence of significant outbound investment from China derives from China's institutional and idiosyncratic economic reforms, or whether Chinese outbound direct investment could still be explained in terms of China's stage of development and the established, but refined, investment development paths (IDP) hypothesis, he finds that the IDP hypothesis proves to be a valid tool to explain Chinese FDI:

'We find that the traditional theory is most appropriate to explain Chinese FDI' (ibid.). It is the most applicable to explain Chinese outbound FDI with the known, main motivations for companies to invest abroad, such as market- and resource-seeking motivations (see section on Motivations and strategies of Chinese MNEs'). The traditional theory is complemented by various explications to address Chinese specifications. Two aspects seem to be most relevant to understanding the specificities of the Chinese situation, which in many academic papers are hardly differentiated. On the one hand, the particular situation of Chinese MNEs is key to an understanding of Chinese particularities; this includes the companies' background, ownership and administrative structure, and the landscape of political support and constraints they are bound to. These are the competitive advantages and disadvantages Chinese MNEs possess or have to deal with. They are deeply rooted in Chinese tradition and largely follow from the historical and cultural development of the country. While they are thus obvious and self-explanatory for Chinese scholars and the management of the companies concerned, they create a considerably different starting point for analysis by Western scholars. These competitive advantages and disadvantages of Chinese MNEs will thus be reviewed below. This review is then followed by an analysis that will focus on the particular motivations for Chinese MNEs to invest abroad.

Competitive advantages and disadvantages of Chinese MNEs

As indicated by Cantwell and Barnard, 'in order to understand the advantages firms gain from FDI, it is important to understand their initial (ownership) advantages' (Cantwell and Barnard 2008: 60). A number of Chinese characteristics that make up the landscape for business of Chinese MNEs have been identified. Together, they are an expression of the political, economic and cultural features of today's People's Republic of China. Due to the supportive policy of the Chinese authorities, these characteristics will often have a positive effect on Chinese MNEs and thus constitute competitive advantages for these enterprises. However, in certain cases they may also condition and restrict managerial freedom, and may consequently constitute disadvantages for Chinese MNEs, compared to companies based in a less regulated political system. A number of such features possessed by developing-country MNEs have been identified and developed in the theory, namely 'expertise and technology', 'access to home resources and activities' and 'production and service capabilities' (UNCTAD WIR 2006: 148).

Expertise and technology-based features

Expertise and technology-based advantages are a key factor in the success of companies in global competition. These include, among others, appropriate and specialized expertise and technology; early adoption of new technologies; sustainable investment in R&D and other resources. These advantages are particularly relevant in industries that depend largely on innovation, such as consumer electrical and electronic products, machinery and transportation equipment (UNCTAD WIR 2006: 147–148).

At first sight, Chinese companies do not possess a particular competitive advantage in these areas. Chinese companies to date depend on the knowledge and expertise of their foreign partner rather than having a reputation for their own technological innovation. Typically, Chinese companies are being perceived as imitating successful products instead of taking the lead in technological innovation based on their expertise in technologies.

However, a number of up and coming Chinese MNEs have in the meanwhile taken a leading international position in innovative goods. Typical examples include the household electronics producer Haier and consumer electronics producer Hisense. In light of these success stories, it has been argued that the particular expertise of Chinese MNEs does not consist in knowledge as such, but rather in knowing how to deal with the challenges they face. According to Mathews, latecomers and newcomers engage in 'accelerated internationalization', 'organizational innovation' and 'strategic innovation' (Mathews 2006: 13ff.). This means that they develop expertise in meeting the challenge of catching up with the established MNEs in an innovative manner. Organizational innovation motivates companies to take an international approach to their business right from the beginning. In this way, they are able to engage in international business directly, instead of having to adapt their business to international activity at a later stage. Experience in strategic innovation approaches allows companies to engage in contract services, licensing models of technologies, or opt directly for joint ventures and strategic alliances. Latecomers such as Chinese MNEs have thus quickly gained experience in innovative resource generation and utilization, leverage and improved learning abilities (Mathews 2006: 14).

Further, a number of relevant features in expertise have been discussed by Morck, according to whom, Chinese companies have a particular expertise in managing large, complex markets. One possible example of this might be the recent attempt of Chinese telecommunication companies to expand in Southeast Asia. Using this interpretation, the FDI of these Chinese firms nicely fits the standard internalization model (Morck *et al.* 2008. p. 345).

Moreover, MNEs with a Western background tend to be experienced in operating in stable markets with transparent regulation and weak government influence on business decisions. Corrupt or otherwise dysfunctional institutions create difficulties for their operations. By contrast, Chinese firms are more experienced with such institutional features, and as a result are likely to be more capable of dealing with troublesome regulation and navigating around the opaque political constraints. Such experience is an intangible asset for Chinese companies and arguably puts them in a better position than many other foreign, especially Western, firms (Morck *et al.* 2008: 346). As has been pointed out, many target countries for Chinese FDI, especially in Asian and African countries are characterized by comparably weak institutions, a high level of direct state intervention, insecure property rights' protection, and opaque corporate governance, and thus fit comparably well with the expertise of Chinese companies.

Access to home country resources and activities

As underlined by Cantwell and Barnard, home country characteristics play an important role in shaping the nature of the initial firms' ownership advantages (Cantwell and Barnard 2008: 80). According to Dunning, home-country-specific advantages are the main feature that enables the firms of emerging countries, such as Chinese firms, to invest abroad. Such firms rarely have the firm-specific ownership advantages to ensure success in their FDI (Dunning and Lundan 2008: 120). Factors relating to home country resources and activities often relate to natural resources, clusters of knowledge and expertise, access to funds or alternative forms of financing, and development of utilities and infrastructure (UNCTAD WIR 2006: 149). Developing and transition economies are typically characterized by the active involvement of their governments in business, both through ownership and through regulation (Sun *et al.* 2008: 79; Yamakawa *et al.* 2008: 66).

This is certainly the case for China, and the consequences for the internationalization of Chinese firms are significant. Home market resources and activities are crucial for any Chinese company wishing to engage in global investment. From a broader perspective, all extensive government engagement and interference with the activities of firms may be seen as an element of home country activities. To some extent, these activities may offer companies strategic support, constituting a tremendous comparative advantage over other international MNEs. For example, companies that have been designated as 'national champions' will receive all the government support necessary to overcome their latecomers' disadvantage internationally. This will include financial aid and political back-up, as well as restriction of internal Chinese competition, to give these Chinese companies opportunities to grow large internally before facing the international competition (cf. also Child and Rodriguez 2005: 384 and 388). On the other hand, regulation, interference and surveillance by state authorities of the activities of companies in the process of internationalizing might considerably constrain companies in their business development, as is discussed at the end of this section.

Looking at these special characteristics of Chinese home country resources and activities, Buckley differentiates between capital market imperfections, special ownership advantages of Chinese MNEs and certain institutional factors that need to be taken into consideration (Buckley *et al.* 2007: 501ff.), of which the first and the last seem to be of greatest relevance.

Capital market imperfections generally make capital available at a cheaper rate than the market rate. Such capital may be available directly through (state-approved or guaranteed) loans or subsidies, or in soft forms, for example in the form of soft budget constraints. Further, the acceptance and support of companies running an inefficient business activity in the internal market will effectively subsidize FDI. Finally, family structures or the Chinese '*guanxi*' relationships, basically a form of cooperation by 'give-and-take' may include government officials and thus bring about strong strategic advantages, for example in the form of cheap capital (see also Buckley *et al.* 2007: 506).

There is strong evidence that these capital market imperfections are 'daily business' in China. Based on the government policy to support outward investment by Chinese companies, close interaction between government officials and business on individual cases of investment projects will find appropriate ways to realize the respective investment goals. In October 2004, a circular issued by the National Development Research Council and the Export–Import Bank of China explicitly promotes M&As that could enhance the international competitiveness of Chinese enterprises and accelerate their entry into foreign markets through preferential credit and an accelerated screening process (Poncet 2007: 7). The structure of the interaction is already characterized by the financial institutions supervising the internationalization by providing funds and foreign currency. The four biggest banks, which together are responsible for about three-quarters of all commercial loans and just over half of total banking assets, the Bank of China (BOC), Industrial and Commercial Bank of China (ICBC), China Construction Bank (CCB), and Agricultural Bank of China (ABC) are all state-owned. Further, the key role in financing outbound investment is played by the China International Trust and Investment Corporation (CITIC), which is a state-owned conglomerate active in a variety of financial services, and which was established by the Chinese Government as the first investor abroad. Other big companies have even been allowed by the Government to establish their own banks and financial sections to take care of their investment activities. Examples are the Sinochem Group and China's premier steel producer, the Beijing-based Shougang Group (Buckley *et al.* 2007: 502).

Institutional factors go a step further than capital market imperfections, and address the complete set of tools available to government bodies and authorities to shape the form and activities of Chinese MNEs. The emergence of the so-called 'national champions', first-ranking global players, in particular, has been viewed in the light of institutional factors. In particular, companies engaged in industries of strategic importance to the development of China, such as natural resources and infrastructure, have been supported so actively by government authorities that it has been argued that China 'built' some of its MNEs (Buckley *et al.* 2007: 503). Also, the acquisition of strategic assets and capabilities such as brands, distribution networks, and foreign capital markets, and so on, is often supported by the Chinese Government.

The potential risks of the domestic market and the institutional interference in business activities have also been noted. Approval processes include that of

NDRC to check the firms' capabilities, SAFE to survey and approve the sources of funds, and MOFCOM to check the conditions of the host country. Finally, state-owned banks have to be consulted to clear the transaction. Annual review procedures are obligatory for companies overseen by MOFCOM and SAFE. At the same time, the very firms that might be expected to internationalize with the advantage of support from national governments could be weakened because they 'remain beholden to administrative approval and bear a legacy of institutional dependence' (Child and Rodriguez 2005: 385).

Indeed, all major challenges faced by Chinese companies when going global are issues that may be addressed effectively by government intervention. Listing 'limitations on foreign exchange use', the 'application time', 'limited sources of finance', 'costs to comply with procedures and regulations', 'check of source of funds' and 'industrial policies' as their main areas of concern (FIAS/MIGA, Battat 2005: 9), it becomes clear that the crucial elements for Chinese companies wishing to go international are government policies and intervention. The institutional framework thus plays the key role in promoting or hindering Chinese FDI.

Production process capabilities

Features relating to production process capabilities concern primarily production of components and products as well as distribution and delivery capabilities. In this area, firms derive their advantages mainly from specialization in the production part of the value chain in sectors such as electronics, motor vehicle components, garments and footwear (UNCTAD WIR 2006: 149). Most of them are specialized in low-cost, high-quality manufacturing, mostly for sale to retailers or manufacturers (UNCTAD WIR 2006: 149).

According to a survey conducted in China by FIAS/MIGA, and illustrated in Figure 2.5, some of the most important advantages of Chinese MNEs rely on production process strengths (UNCTAD WIR 2006: 152). Chinese companies intend to exploit these advantages. According to UNCTAD 'this echoes China's role as a major global production base' (UNCTAD WIR 2006: 152). Market-seeking motivations are a direct consequence for Chinese MNEs.

However, Chinese MNEs have a clear understanding that they may not be able to rely in the long term on the competitive advantage of their production strengths. According to UNCTAD, 'the relatively low self-assessment by the firms surveyed across different aspects of the value chain implies that they will see themselves as having, at most, an average level of competitiveness'. In consequence, this creates a powerful reason for asset-seeking motives for internationalizing by Chinese MNEs, especially in industries in which they face intense competitive pressures (UNCTAD WIR 2006: 152).

Cultural proximity and ethnic Chinese businesses

Finally, academic research and the literature have suggested that international, 'ethnic Chinese' business cooperation plays a crucial role in the internationalization

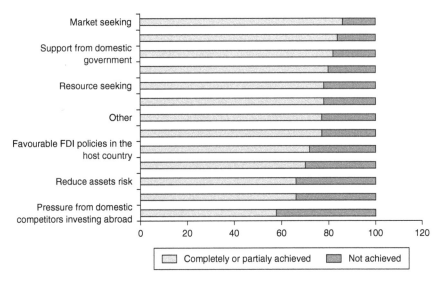

Figure 2.5 Extent of achievement of goals sought by FDI (percentage of firms)

Source: Survey on China's Outward Foreign Direct Investment, FIAS/MIGA Firm Survey. Joseph Battat, FIAS, the WBG, 2005.

process of mainland Chinese business. 'Ethnic Chinese' business means business that is undertaken by people with an ethnic Chinese background, although they have lived abroad for a long time and have possibly also adopted a foreign nationality. Due to their ethnic background they still feel strong ties with their former homeland, China. The existence and support of these ethnic Chinese business undertakings abroad for domestic firms going international is arguably a considerable competitive advantage. In fact, some of the biggest and most successful Southeast Asian MNEs outside China are 'ethnic Chinese' companies.

In his book *The Internationalization of Ethnic Chinese Business Firms from Southeast Asia'*, Yeung gives an impressive statistical analysis of the influence of ethnic Chinese business firms from Southeast Asia. According to him, at the end of the 1990s, the 'overseas Chinese' controlled some 80 per cent of corporate assets and 160 of the 200 largest enterprises in Indonesia, 40–50 per cent of corporate assets in Malaysia, 90 per cent of manufacturing and 50 per cent of services in Thailand. Furthermore, in 1995, every reported Indonesian billionaire had an ethnic Chinese background. In Thailand, the 'overseas Chinese' control the four largest private banks, of which Bangkok Bank is the largest and most profitable in the region. In the Philippines, the 'overseas Chinese' control over one-third of the 1000 largest corporations (Yeung 1999: 105). UNCTAD statistics on large ethnic Chinese MNEs prove the importance of the phenomenon (UNCTAD WIR 2006: 129f.).

What is most relevant for the analysis of the emergence of Chinese MNEs is that ethnic Chinese players are part of the overall globalization process and largely act as international players already. In this sense, they offer new Chinese players examples to learn from and to follow, and, given the close cooperation of ethnic Chinese in the international sphere, helpful partnerships (Yeung 1999: 166ff.).

In addition to the truly 'ethnic Chinese' business cooperation, cultural proximity in a wider sense has been put forward as an argument to explain investment decisions in regions where a culture with a proximity to the culture of the investors is to be found. For China, this would be its neighbouring countries such as North and South Korea, and possibly Vietnam or Myanmar. Real, physical distance might thus be complemented by psychologically perceived proximity, due to a similar culture, or a close relationship existing between countries and regions. These factors may act as door openers and catalysts for business development. Empirical research by Buckley underlines the importance of cultural factors (Buckley *et al.* 2007: 506 and 513).

While not disputing the phenomenon, it may sometimes have a less beneficial effect though. The strong particularities of Chinese business behaviour, including cultural, linguistic, institutional and organizational elements may prove to be a disadvantage for Chinese firms when internationalizing. These characteristics may give Chinese firms a comparative advantage when emerging in areas with similar cultural conditions, or where they can connect to ethnic Chinese businesses. Yet, these characteristics may hinder the success of Chinese businesses in areas with a different cultural heritage, mainly outside Asia. According to Child and Rodriguez, this implies

> that even if the lack of tangible assets such as technology and branded products can be met through their purchase abroad, a liability of foreignness may still jeopardize the effectiveness of how they are put to use. Distinctive Chinese styles of management … could thus prove a handicap …
>
> (Child and Rodriguez 2005: 386).

Motivations and strategies of Chinese MNEs

The process of China's reintegration with the global economy began with the 'open door' policies at the end of the 1970s. Soon afterwards, in the middle of the 1980s, clear and concrete political motivations for the opening were stated. As Zhan notes, the important aims were to secure a stable supply of resources that cannot be sourced within China, to contribute to foreign exchange earnings and generating export opportunities, and channelling advanced technology and equipment to China (Zhan 1995: 69). The early, selective approach for approval of investment projects has been applied less and less over the years, but the intention of the government to use Chinese FDI has remained. As a keystone, in 1999, the 'go-global' initiative (*zou chu qu*) was established, aiming at promoting the international competitiveness of Chinese firms. As part of this initiative, foreign-exchange-related, fiscal and administrative obstacles to international investment were gradually removed (Sauvant 2005: 676). An important step towards accelerated opening was finally achieved with the accession of China to the World Trade

Organization (WTO) in 2001 (Buckley *et al.* 2007: 499). The unchanged political intention was reiterated in 2003 by the Chinese Vice-Premier Wu Yi: 'We will actively foster our own multinational companies...We will create all kinds of [favourable] conditions to help our multinational companies further explore overseas markets and engage more strongly in global economic competition and cooperation' (*China Daily*, November 7 2003, cited in Cheng and Stough 2007: 16).

This section will analyse the motivations and strategies of Chinese MNEs. We will examine the main drivers of Chinese MNEs separately for the sake of clarity, but it is worth noting that in most cases motivations might be mixed, complementary or evolutionary. In fact, as stated above, the application of traditional approaches to explain motivations for FDI (as extensively covered by Dunning) seems to be the most appropriate way to address the phenomenon, since Chinese MNEs are engaging in an international, capitalist business environment. Their motivations will thus be mostly business driven, and consist of market-seeking, resource-seeking, efficiency-seeking and strategic asset-seeking motivations.

However, the political intention of the Chinese Government to promote FDI that had been developed in the late 1970s, and continually stated afterwards, points to political motivations for Chinese outbound FDI other than classical theory suggests. Given the great influence of institutional factors, cultural elements and home country resources and activities (see section on 'Competitive advantages and disadvantages of Chinese MNEs'), and, even more important, the extensive state ownership of Chinese MNEs heading abroad (see section on 'Emergence of Chinese FDI'), affect the motivations for Chinese FDI. Some of these motivations differ from those of Western MNEs, whereas others are quite close to the interests of Western MNEs. Where the latter is the case, Western MNEs are facing international competition from emerging MNEs with a different background. As state-owned or state-controlled enterprises, they are competing for markets and resources with Western MNEs, but being backed up by the Chinese Government. In this sense, the internationalization of (state-owned) Chinese MNEs is an expression of the going global of the People's Republic of China.

Market-seeking FDI

As noted by UNCTAD, 'market-seeking FDI is by far the most common type of strategy for developing-country TNCs in their process of internationalization' (UNCTAD WIR 2006: 158). Several recent studies point to the rise of market-seeking motives driving Chinese MNEs particularly towards large markets (Taylor 2002, Deng 2003, Zhang 2003). The FIAS/MIGA global survey confirms the prevalence of Chinese market-seeking FDI. In the survey, Chinese companies were asked to rate whether or not a motivation was important on a scale of 1 to 3. Of the 148 firms which responded to this question, 85 per cent regarded market-seeking as important or very important (FIAS/MIGA, Battat 2005: 11ff., UNCTAD WIR 2006: 167). In their study covering Chinese FDI from 1984 to 2001, Buckley *et al.* discovered that market-seeking was a key motive for

Chinese FDI in the period under study (Buckley *et al.* 2007: 509; 2008: 137). However, over this period, Chinese firms have moved away from using mainly market-seeking strategies in nearby foreign markets towards the securing of raw materials even in riskier markets (Buckley *et al.* 2007: 511).

As suggested by the theory, nearby regions are the most common location for market-seeking affiliates in the case of most developing countries' FDI. However, in examples such as Chinese FDI in many manufacturing industries, India in IT services, the Republic of Korea in advanced manufactures, and the Russian Federation in natural resources, proximity is less relevant for some important FDI attracted by developed-country markets (UNCTAD WIR 2006: 158). In the case of Chinese FDI, most investments do follow successful, established export streams, and destinations might be neighbouring countries as well as markets overseas. As Zhan points out, market-seeking motivations are the logical consequence of China's export-oriented policy of recent years. The firms follow their export channels to expand market shares and avoid trade barriers (Zhan 1995: 87). Buckley adds that trade-supporting reasons for FDI include distribution networks, the facilitation of exports of domestic products and enhancement of exports from the home country to other large and rapidly growing markets. Since market-seeking strategies are often positively correlated with large markets, the engagement of Chinese MNEs in large, foreign markets may largely be explained by market-seeking motivations (Buckley *et al.* 2007: 503).

Well-known examples of Chinese companies investing abroad for market-seeking purposes include Chinese home-appliance and consumer electronics manufacturers such as Haier, TCL, and Huawei Technologies, which have made repeated efforts to enter the more affluent developed economies such as the United States (Simmons 2008: 197). The TCL Group succeeded in purchasing the trembling Schneider AG in Germany, and the Haier Group purchased an Italian refrigerator facility. In addition, Shanghai Haixing Group's acquisition of Glenoit Textile, China Insurance's investment in Pacific Insurance, and the Wangxiang Group's acquisition of Universal Automotive Industries Inc. have been reported (von Keller and Zhou 2003: 12).

Apart from these motivations, which might also be described as 'pull factors', push factors provide incentives for Chinese companies to expand abroad. Increasingly strong competition and overcapacity are among the most important push factors, particularly in China's home-appliance sector (Cheng and Stough 2007: 15). According to a survey by the National Bureau of Asian Research (NBR), manufacturers of electronic appliances cite growing competitive pressure from MNEs in the domestic Chinese market, excess capacity and sliding profit margins to be the key reasons for searching for new markets abroad (Wu 2005: 7). According to Wu, overcapacity within China's home-appliance market is estimated by business consultancies to stand at over 30 per cent in washing machines, 40 per cent in refrigerators, 45 per cent in microwave ovens, and 87 per cent in televisions (Wu 2005: 7; cf. Cheng and Stough 2007: 15).

Efficiency-seeking FDI

> Efficiency-seeking FDI is an important motive, but its prevalence varies considerably among developing-country TNCs, especially in terms of their country or region of origin and industry. In the UNCTAD global survey, 22% of responses indicated this as a strategic motive. Most of the companies for which efficiency-seeking FDI is important are Asian and in three main industries, electrical and electronic products, garments and IT services.
>
> (UNCTAD WIR 2006: 159)

However, according to the survey, efficiency-seeking FDI is comparatively unimportant for Chinese MNEs because of the relatively low costs in their home economies (UNCTAD WIR 2006: 160). However, in some sectors where competitive pressure is very high, other cost-reducing factors, including national and international policies, seem to have induced efficiency-seeking investment by emerging country firms, including Chinese companies. For example, companies from China have invested in African countries such as Lesotho, Malawi, Senegal and Swaziland to benefit inter alia from the special treatment (duty-free) accorded by some developed countries to product exports from these African countries (UNCTAD WIR 2006: 160).

Most scholars agree that given the low production costs in China, efficiency-seeking motivations are not the most important factor for Chinese MNEs going global (Buckley *et al.* 2007: 501). However, a few examples may point to a growing role for efficiency-motivated Chinese FDI in the years to come. For labour-intensive production such as textiles, the situation has become more dynamic over the past months, since wages paid in the coastal areas of China have considerably increased. The Pearl River delta, in particular, is facing competition from even cheaper labour in neighbouring countries such as Vietnam or Thailand. Production in these regions will not necessarily be cheaper than that in remote provinces in China, but is more easily accessible for producers and entails lower transport costs.

Further, Shaoming Cheng notes that efficiency-improving and market-expanding outward FDIs are often intertwined and complementary. Market conditions (such as quota-free access for exporting to the United States and the European Union) in combination with good conditions for using mature low-tech and labour-intensive production will offer an economically efficient production environment. Such efficiency-enhancing and market-expanding outward FDI might grow significantly in ASEAN countries (Cheng and Stough 2007: 14).

Resource-seeking FDI

China's tremendous economic development requires a steady supply of natural resources, including ferrous and non-ferrous metals, precious metals, minerals and oil and gas. The country, is, however, comparatively poor in most natural resources except coal (Zhan 1995: 88). Chinese companies thus expend a great deal of effort in resource-seeking. FDI in natural resources is not driven by regional proximity, but simply by the availability of assets. The active acquisition of natural resources stands out among Chinese investments abroad, and destinations for Chinese outward FDI are resource-rich countries around the globe, such as African and Central Asian countries, along with Australia, Russia and Canada (Buckley *et al.* 2007: 511). The common rationale for setting up subsidiaries abroad is to ensure a stable supply of resources for operations of the Chinese companies at home in production and construction (Hobdari *et al.* 2007: 10).

Various studies have addressed this issue. According to UNCTAD, Chinese MNEs generally regard natural resources as an important motivation to invest abroad. Of all Chinese outward investors, 40 per cent indicate that natural resources are a very important motivation for their international engagement. This may seem a relatively low figure compared to market-seeking motivations (85 per cent of the firms) and created-asset-seeking (51 per cent of firms). However, the relatively low figure will essentially be explained by a higher concentration of firms in the natural resources sector (UNCTAD WIR 2006: 168).

FDI in natural resources can be undertaken by firms which are themselves based in the primary sector, or those from other sectors, mainly natural-resource-related such as metal manufacturing (UNCTAD WIR 2006: 161). Because of the strategic importance of securing supplies of resources for the home economy, a large proportion of Chinese MNEs engaged in these efforts are state-owned.

Generally, a division must be made between the oil and gas and the mining in mineral resources sectors. In the former, the big three national Chinese oil companies, China National Petroleum Corporation (CNPC), China National Offshore Oil Corporation (CNOOC), and China Petroleum and Chemical Corporation (Sinopec) are especially active. These companies invested in high-risk (and high return) projects in the 1990s, but have recently turned to the acquisition of existing, big oil fields which promise a stable and long-term production of oil and gas and considerable revenue. These acquisitions have largely been financed by the large-scale fund-raising by listing on overseas stock exchanges. Because these companies are acting as quasi monopoly players in China's enormous and fast-growing market, the companies' listings were tremendously successful. Today, these three companies are often referred to by business and the media as the 'Chinese oil majors'. According to industry knowledge, these companies have in recent years – backed up with the necessary political support – succeeded in acquiring over 100 projects, including several billion-dollar projects, in the Middle East, Africa, Latin America, Southeast Asia, Central Asia and Russia (Hagiwara, Bank of Tokyo 2006: 4).

With regard to the mineral resources industry, the number of Chinese players is bigger, and the projects invested in are less well-known. Companies such as Minmetals, China Aluminium Corporation (Chalco), and Zijin are important examples of the numerous Chinese companies investing in a wide variety of countries and regions to secure assets in minerals and metals. All resources are fundamental for China's further economic growth. The main industries driving the great need for resources are energy creation (coal and uranium) and construction.

The overview of the largest Chinese outward investors, as presented at the beginning of this chapter, further confirms the analysis. The top three Chinese outward investors are all companies in the natural resources field. As an example, in 2002 alone, CNPC acquired two oilfields in Azerbaijan and, together with Petrochina, the companies Devon Energy Corp. (Indonesia) and Salyan Oil (Azerbaijan); CNOOC acquired Repsol-YPF SA (Indonesia) (von Keller and Zhou 2003: 13).

Finally, less prominent but still relevant are the Chinese acquisitions in other natural resources, such as fishery, timber and agricultural products. As an example, Huaguang Forest Co. Ltd acquired the New Zealand timberland operation of Rayonier Inc.

Strategic asset-seeking FDI

While the UNCTAD global survey indicates that strategic asset-seeking FDI is a relatively modest motive for developing-country MNEs overall (14 per cent of responses compared to 51 per cent for market-seeking FDI), the picture is quite different for Chinese MNEs. The latter regard strategic asset-seeking as the second most important motivation after market-seeking. Among Chinese MNEs, 51 per cent regard created-asset-seeking as an important motive for their FDI, compared to 85 per cent for market-seeking, 39 per cent for efficiency-seeking and 40 per cent for resource-seeking FDI (UNCTAD WIR 2006: 168).

Strategic asset-seeking is often aimed at the acquisition of information and knowledge on how to operate internationally. However, with the growing experience of Chinese firms in this area, their goal has turned towards concrete intangible assets, such as advanced proprietary technology and immobile strategic assets, both through greenfield investments and through acquisitions. The acquisition of foreign technologies and brands is often regarded as a shortcut to establishing a company as an internationally known, quality producer with a portfolio of the latest technologies and services, and an efficient distribution channel. Acquisition will function as a fast track to such benefits, and at the same time, will also deny them to competitors (Child and Rodriguez 2005: 392).

Consequently, it is mostly countries with a highly developed industry and attractive technologies and brands which are of interest to Chinese strategic asset-seeking companies. Such countries are mostly industrialized countries in Europe or North America. Generally, developing country acquirers seem to carry out international M&As in developed countries for strategic asset-seeking purposes. Developing countries seem to be the preferred destination for their resource-seeking investment goals (von Keller and Zhou 2003: 22).

However, it seems that very few Chinese MNEs – or MNEs from other emerging countries – purely seek strategic assets, in marked contrast to market- or efficiency-seeking FDI. Most are established for mixed reasons (UNCTAD WIR 2006: 162). According to UNCTAD: 'One of the reasons why "pure" created-asset-seeking FDI might be rare is because developing-country firms seeking created assets must first master the capabilities to absorb them' (UNCTAD WIR 2006: 162). For that reason created-asset-seeking FDIs go hand in hand with asset-exploitation motivation, especially market-seeking and efficiency-seeking investments. For example, Lenovo, by acquiring IBM's computer division was simultaneously seeking to establish itself as a global brand and to gain expertise and technology to complement its existing specific advantages in China (Goldstein *et al.*, cited in UNCTAD WIR 2006: 251).

There are many other well-known examples of Chinese strategic asset-seeking FDI. In the automotive industry, Chinese companies have made tremendous efforts to overcome their greatest weakness compared to internationally established producers (Fetscherin and Sardy 2008: 184): the lack of a known, reputable brand. SAIC, the largest Chinese car producer has acquired the Korean Ssang Yong, and intended to acquire MG Rover. This British brand, however, was later acquired by Nanjing Automobile Group Corporation (Hagiwara, Bank of Tokyo 2006: 5). Other examples of technology and/or brand motivated investments for the years 2001–2003 have been reported by industry research sources: Dalian Machine Toll Group Co., Ltd invested in Ingersoll Production Systems (USA), the Holley Group acquired Philips CDMA chip design departments (USA/Canada), Shanghai Electric Group invested in Akiyama Publishing Machinery Co. (Japan), Shanghai Huayi Group acquired Moltech Power Systems, Inc. (USA), and the D'long Group invested in Fairchild Dornier (Germany) (von Keller and Zhou 2003: 14).

The ultimate success of these investments remains to be determined. Doubts have been expressed that the acquisition of often economically weak companies with a completely different business culture will not be easily dealt with by their new Chinese owners and partners. For Lenovo, for example, it has been stated that US$1.75 billion was a high price to pay for a manufacturing company in deficit (Hagiwara, Bank of Tokyo, 2006: 5). The confusion over the acquisition of MG Rover and the ownership of the brand name has not been a success story either. However, the ongoing boom of acquisitions for strategic asset-seeking purposes is an indication of a continued belief of Chinese companies in the benefits of this shortcut to technology and brands.

Other China-specific motivations for FDI

The above analysis of motivations for Chinese FDI gives clear evidence that Chinese MNEs have traditional motivations for their internationalization. A number of studies and surveys support this view and emphasize that these are the dominant motivations for Chinese MNEs. Evidence has been found that despite the country's enormous land area, large population and geographical position, refined IDP hypotheses are valid tools for explaining Chinese outbound investment (Buckley *et al.* 2005: 112). Research by Roland Berger Consultants underlines that internal corporate dynamics provide the greatest impetus for Chinese companies to expand overseas. But their evidence shows that at least 8 per cent of the motivations indicated by company leaders are not in line with traditional market motivations (von Keller and Zhou 2003: 10). This section looks at these additional motivations and points out various elements of China-specific FDI motivations.

Important work on this issue has been done by Buckley, Child and Rodriguez and, more recently, by Morck. Buckley applies known instruments to analyse Chinese FDI but admits that 'Chinese firms that invest abroad have to straddle environments, institutions and rules that differ probably more than for any other outward-investing country in the world' (Buckley *et al.* 2007: 511). Child and Rodriguez identify a number of prime areas of relevance to explain the characteristics of Chinese motivations for FDI: the latecomer perspective and catch-up strategies, institutional analysis with reference to the role of government, and the relation of entrepreneurs to the state's institutions (Child and Rodriguez 2005: 402ff.). Morck has contributed insights into the interconnections between government and business in China (Morck *et al.* 2008: 345ff.). Again, as noted above, motivations for Chinese FDI will usually be complementary and mixed. The following will distinguish particular Chinese motivations with regards to economic constraints, government interference, and individual interests of entrepreneurs.

From a macroeconomic perspective, the increasing Chinese foreign currency reserves have implications for outward investment activities. With more than one trillion dollars in foreign reserves (end of 2006, Cheng and Stough 2007), the question arises for China of how best to invest these savings. Purely financial options, for example, through the Chinese national investment fund, enable China to profit from worldwide economic growth. However, Chinese Government economists may consider that the reserves will best support the economic development of China if used to acquire international technologies, brands, and resources, and to smooth access to international markets. It is in this context of mixed motivations that fears about the intentions of Chinese FDI in developed countries have recently come up. Currency reserves may be used in strategic manner to support Chinese outward FDI. Morck, expresses a critical view of such state-policy-driven FDI activities, and questions their long-term efficiency:

> Grandiose and patriotism-inspiring initiatives, like takeovers of foreign companies, legitimize the continuation of the political status quo. Over the longer term, deflecting capital away from more efficient private sector ventures may compromise both continued economic growth and political stability.
>
> (Morck *et al.* 2008: 344)

Moreover, traditional theory has a tendency to explain motivations of companies in terms of incentives in the host countries. From the reverse perspective, the absence of certain factors in China may drive companies to go international to protect their business success. These factors may include lack of sufficiently developed intellectual property rights; lack of training and education and, consequently, limited access to skilled workers; poor local infrastructure; fragmentation of regional markets; and pressure from corrupt or otherwise illegitimately interfering officials. Chinese MNEs will in this sense be motivated by the desire to escape from poor business conditions in China, and the wish to profit from a more beneficial business landscape abroad.

Mathews identifies economic motivations for companies from the Asia-Pacific region, which might be seen as an overall global competitive strategy in light of the conditions of globalization. In fact, it is surprising how well Chinese MNEs seem to have adapted to the challenges of globalization, and are able to pursue their aims with ease. According to Mathews, the main difference in the approach of new MNEs from the Asian-Pacific region compared to that of the established MNEs is that they are of such recent origin that they are perfectly adapted to a globalized world (Mathews 2006: 13ff.). Their motivation to internationalize is consequently not based on established business operations and the wish to optimize these operations. Rather, for these companies, internationalization is an initial characteristic of their business and ex-ante an integral part of their organizational approach to globalization. In this sense, Mathews' framework provides a powerful tool for explaining the motivations of SMEs with limited capital resources and often weak institutional support.

Looking at government interference, a number of points need to be examined so that the interrelations between government officials and the private sector can be outlined. For many years, typical private sector businesses were non-existent in China. With economic opening and the introduction of private ownership in the 1980s, private sector activities began. They were built partly on individual, entrepreneurial initiative and partly driven by state policies such as privatization. In consequence, a range of different companies emerged, all of which comply with applicable government law and regulations, but which are to varying extents, through personal and institutional relationships, connected to and intertwined with government bodies. SOEs and companies that play a crucial role in China's development, or possibly those that have been selected by the authorities as future 'national champions', will have a very close relationship with the government. The leaders of such companies will usually be traditional state bureaucrats and members of the Communist Party. For these Party bureaucrats, the fact that companies may act as private players is a comparatively new phenomenon. The way they execute managerial tasks in these companies is thus characterized by their established and ongoing trust in and responsibility towards state interests. They experience their work in the 'private sector' largely as a continuation of their career as civil servants (Morck *et al.* 2008: 344).

Morck reports a striking recent example, illustrating the relationhip between these new Chinese MNEs and the government sector, and the career paths of the company leaders. In brief, within a short time, the leaders of the following (mostly internationally) listed Chinese MNEs had changed positions with high-ranking government officials and vice-versa:

'In April 2003, Mr. Li Yizhong, then Chairman of the Board of CNPC, was appointed to the [State-owned Assets Supervision and Administration Commission of the State Council] SASAC and replaced by Mr. Chen Tonghai, a former State Planning Commission official. In October 2003, Mr. Wei Liucheng, then CEO, Chairman of the Board, and Party Secretary of China National Offshore Oil Corp. (CNOOC) was appointed Governor of Hainan Province. In November 2004, the top managers of the three largest telecommunication companies in China – China Mobile, China Telecom and China Unicom – exchanged positions almost overnight without prior notice to public shareholders.

(Morck *et al.* 2008: 344)

Furthermore, the Chief Executive Officers (CEOs) of the 53 largest national SOEs are generally directly appointed by the Communist Party, and holders of senior management positions are largely appointed by SASAC, under direct control of the State Council (Morck *et al.* 2008: 344).

In light of the interrelationships between the government and companies described above, a number of motivations for Chinese FDI activities emerge. They relate not only to the decision to internationalize, but also explain how Chinese MNEs will effectively carry out investment projects. The focal point for motivations of Chinese MNEs is the challenge of efficiently exploiting government support while keeping the entrepreneurial freedom necessary to compete in a competition-driven international business context.

Government influence has a positive effect on companies' internationalization motives where it supports the companies' business goals, for example by opening up business opportunities that the Chinese firms would not have been able to take advantage of on their own. Companies will rely on their government's support in countries where arbitrary interference of the host Government in the host countries' private sector is possible, and where a positive trade-off may be achieved for the business of Chinese companies through the political influence of the Chinese Government. Such countries are usually non-democratic countries with a weak rule of law, for example in Africa or Central Asia.

For developed, Western markets, strategic asset-seeking motivations of companies might be supported by the action of the Chinese Government. Child and Rodriguez note that the distinctive role that the state can play in the FDI of Chinese MNEs is particularly strong when the companies are partly, but not wholly, state-owned (Child and Rodriguez 2005: 400). For a number of companies, strategic government support has given them considerable assistance in their internationalization, and has thus shaped their motivation strategies. Home appliances producer Haier, on its way to becoming a national champion, and Lenovo, in its move towards becoming the word's third-largest computer manufacturer, have profited from support in their internationalization strategies in the form of financial back-up or assistance in succeeding in the domestic market, which makes them more valued potential partners internationally.

Chinese companies expanding in both developing and in developed markets will seek to exploit the support provided by state authorities. It is difficult to assess whether government interference and back-up in FDI activities of Chinese firms is greater when the companies invest in developing or developed host countries. Yet, it seems evident that government interference will be more efficient in countries where the state leaders have strong discretionary powers and market forces are weak. Conversely, it will be less efficient where market forces are the main drivers of business development and potential business partners are private sector players with an exclusive interest in the economic feasibility of the proposed cooperation or investment project.

Both Morck and Buckley identify contradictions and surprises with regards to Chinese FDI, which might be partially explained in light of these findings. Morck notes that in accordance with internationalization theory, Chinese firms with large investments in enhanced productivity should lead China's FDI surge. Instead, 'large relatively inefficient SOEs lead the charge, and more efficient private enterprises remain largely domestic' (Morck *et al.* 2008: 345). Also, Chinese companies might be expected to aim at realizing economies of scale and consequently to focus on large, developed markets. However, Chinese FDI is to a large extent entering Southeast Asia and Africa, and to a lesser extent Europe, Japan and North America (Morck *et al.* 2008: 345). Looking at risk perception, Buckley's empirical results reveal that Chinese FDI seems to be attracted rather than deterred by political risk (Buckley *et al.* 2007: 513). Both observations can be seen as upholding the analysis that the supportive hands of the Chinese Government can play a bigger role in Chinese FDI in countries with a weak rule of law, and can provide weaker support in highly developed markets.

The two parts of this chapter have provided evidence that most current Chinese FDI, in terms of value, derives from the big new Chinese MNEs, which are companies that typically have the relationships to the government outlined above. The current focus of academic literature on these companies is thus justified. However, as a recent phenomenon, new Chinese investors with currently still comparably small FDI have been found to be on the rise in recent years. Their relations and interaction with the government authorities might be weaker than those of the large Chinese MNEs. Their business activities are more characterized by entrepreneurial engagement and ordinary domestic and international competition. They will thus also have a slightly different view on government engagement. For these companies especially, government interference may also have partially constraining effects.

Indeed, business needs the freedom to base strategic decisions on market requirements rather than on the need to fulfil institutional instructions and ideals. Foreign partners may take a critical view of strong government interference. In this context, Child and Rodriguez state that currently successful internationalizing Chinese firms are non-state-owned enterprises or companies that have made arrangements for protecting themselves from bureaucratic interference. Examples may include Galanx and Holly as typical town and villages enterprises (TVEs), Haier and Huawei as collective enterprises, and Lenovo and TCL with mixed international–domestic ownership structures. This has positive effects on managerial autonomy (Child and Rodriguez 2005: 392). Consequently, an important driver for Chinese FDI must also be the intention of Chinese firms to escape domestic institutional restrictions. In particular, 'legal uncertainties, obstruction of domestic acquisitions, and regional protectionism through license restrictions' are challenges for (privately owned) Chinese companies (Child and Rodriguez 2005: 401). The international sphere may offer the freedom for unrestricted business development without any limiting government influence.

To sum up, it seems that the key to success for Chinese companies in their internationalization strategies is their relationship to the Chinese Government, and their ability to use the embeddedness in formal and informal government structures strategically in combining the support of the government with the need to escape institutional restrictions.

Finally, the motivations of business leaders on a private level must not be neglected. International engagement of 'their' companies offers opportunities for a better reputation among colleagues and government officials. Arguably, corporate executives will gain respect and status by internationally 'restoring China's honor as a true economic power' (Morck *et al.* 2008: 347). In addition, business leaders may see chances to escape the control of the Chinese State and the uncertainties of the Chinese regulatory market, and the potential to store their wealth and that of their families in international tax havens.

Conclusion

Chinese FDI has gained in importance over recent years. A large number of Chinese companies have invested abroad and have become emerging Chinese MNEs. The growing importance of Chinese FDI is expected to continue. According to the survey by FIAS/MIGA, 58.9 per cent of Chinese MNEs that responded had concrete plans to continue to expand abroad, and 12.9 per cent had at least an intention to continue their international engagement (FIAS/MIGA, Battat 2005: 19). Further, as Shaoming Cheng notes, a future stronger Chinese currency will greatly enhance Chinese firms' purchasing strengths in international M&As and therefore lead to rising outflows of Chinese FDI (Cheng and Stough 2007: 15). In addition, the competitive pressure in the domestic Chinese market is expected to accelerate, and will continue to push Chinese enterprises to globalize. In particular, a further liberalization of the services sectors will intensify the pressure on services companies over the next years (Wu 2005: 19). Finally, the goal of the Chinese Government to help Chinese companies integrate into the world economy and China to participate in international economic growth will continue to lead it to support the globalization of Chinese MNEs.

The main motivations of Chinese MNEs are thus derived from their operation in an international capitalist market economy. Chinese MNEs have mostly market-seeking, resource-seeking, strategic asset-seeking and efficiency-seeking motivations. They are, to this extent, independent of their ownership structure, part of a global business undertaking. The traditional theory on MNEs offers valuable tools to analyse their activities.

However, there are characteristics of the Chinese approach to FDI that are particularly striking, and make the emergence of Chinese MNEs a special phenomenon. According to the analysis upon which this chapter is based, the most important differences between Chinese MNEs and Western MNEs going international are not in their motivations, but in the special characteristics of the home country in terms of the Chinese institutional and cultural context and with regards to home country resources. By far the largest outward investments by Chinese MNEs are made by SOEs, and all investment projects follow a scheme that ensures that they are strictly in line with government policies. The motivations of Chinese firms to internationalize and the government interest in this are to a large extent aligned and institutionally intertwined.

Chinese particularities are so strong and the motivations of government, state, and business so deeply integrated and interlinked, that it is doubtful that Chinese MNEs emerge with traditional motivations, but Chinese characteristics. Indeed, the emergence of Chinese MNEs is an expression of a broader development in the sphere of today's international business landscape: it is the People's Republic of China going global.

Notes

1 This paper uses the common abbreviation FDI as a short form for Chinese outward foreign direct investment, unless explicitly stated otherwise.
2 This paper relies on the UNCTAD definition of investment, which characterizes FDI as an investment involving a long-term relationship and reflecting a lasting interest and control by a firm in an enterprise resident in a foreign country (UNCTAD WIR 2005: 297). Thus, any reference in text or graphics to Chinese FDI does not include investment executed for purely financial aims such as portfolio investment.

References

Brett, D. and Ericsson, M. (2006) 'Chinese expansion to create new global mining companies', *Commodities Now*, October 2006. Online. Available HTTP: http://www. rmg.se/RMG2005/pages/attachments/COMMODITIES_NOW_2006_Oct,_Chinese_Expansion_to_Create_New_Global_Mining_Companies.pdf (accessed 13 May 2008).

Buckley, P.J., Clegg, L.J., Cross, A.R. and Liu, X. (2007) 'The determinants of Chinese outward foreign direct investment', *Journal of International Business Studies*, 38: 499–518.

Buckley, P.J., Clegg, L.J., Cross, A.R., Liu, X., Voss, H. and Zhen, P. (2008) 'Explaining China's outward FDI: An institutional perspective', in K.P. Sauvant (ed.) *The Rise of Transnational Corporations from Emerging Markets.* Northampton, MA: Edward Elgar, pp. 106–157.

Cantwell, J. and Barnard, H. (2008) 'Do firms from emerging markets have to invest abroad? Outward FDI and the competitiveness of firms', in K.P. Sauvant (ed.) *The Rise of Transnational Corporations from Emerging Markets.* Northampton, MA: Edward Elgar, pp. 55–85.

Cheng, L.K. and Ma, Z. (2007) *China's Outward FDI: Past and Future.* Working paper, National Bureau of Economic Research, Cambridge, MA. Online. Available HTTP: http://www.nber.org/books_in_progress/china07/cwt07/cheng.pdf (accessed 13 May 2008).

Cheng, S. and Stough, R.R. (2007) *The Pattern and Magnitude of China's Outward FDI in Asia.* Working paper, Indian Council for Research on International Economic Relations. Online. Available HTTP: http://www.icrier.org/pdf/25-26April07/Session2/Shaoming%20Cheng%20and%20Roger%20R%20Stough.doc (accessed 13 May 2008).

Child, J. and Rodriguez, S.B. (2005) 'The internationalization of Chinese firms: A case for theoretical extension?', *Management and Organization Review,* 1: 381–410.

Deng, P. (2003) 'Foreign direct investment by transnationals from emerging countries: The case of China', *Journal of Leadership and Organizational Studies*, 10: 113–124.

Dunning, J.H. (1981) *International Production and the Multinational Enterprise.* London: George Allen & Unwin.

Dunning, J.H. (1998) 'Location and the multinational enterprise: A neglected factor?', *Journal of International Business Studies*, 29: 45–66.

Dunning, J.H. (2000) 'The eclectic paradigm as an envelope for economic and business theories of MNE activity', *International Business Review*, 9: 163–190.

Dunning, J.H. (2008) 'Space, location and distance in IB activities: A changing scenario', in J.H. Dunning and P. Gugler (eds) *Foreign Direct Investment, Location and Competitiveness*. Oxford: Elsevier, pp. 83–109.

Dunning, J.H. and Gugler, P. (eds) (2008) *Foreign Direct Investment, Location and Competitiveness*. Oxford, Elsevier.

Dunning, J.H. and Lundan, S.M. (2008) *Multinational Enterprises and the Global Economy*. 2nd edn. Cheltenham: Edward Elgar.

Dunning, J.H., Changsu, K. and Donghyun, P. (2008) 'Old wine in new bottles: A comparison of emerging-market TNCs today and developed-country TNCs thirty years ago', in K.P. Sauvant (ed.) *The Rise of Transnational Corporations from Emerging Markets*. Northampton: Edward Elgar, pp. 158–80.

Fetscherin, M. and Sardy, M. (2008) 'China shifts into gear in the global auto market', in I. Alon and J.R. McIntyre (eds) *Globalization of Chinese Enterprises*. Basingstoke: Palgrave Macmillan, pp. 181–93.

FIAS/MIGA, Battat, J. (2005) *Firm Survey – Chinese Outward Foreign Direct Investment*. Online. Available HTTP: http://rru.worldbank.org/Documents/PSDForum/2006/joe_battat.pdf (accessed 13 May 2008).

Hagiwara, Y. (2006) 'Outward investment by China gathering stream under the go global strategy', *Economic Review*, 1, The Bank of Tokyo-Mitsubishi UFJ, Ltd, Economic Research Office. Online. Available HTTP: http://www.bk.mufg.jp/report/ecorev2006e/review_e200 61108.pdf (accessed 13 May 2008).

Hobdari, B., Sinani, E., Papanastassiou, M. and Pearce, R. (2007) *Chinese Multinationals in a New World: Micro-Evidence on Outward FDI*. Working Paper ,Copenhagen Business School. Online. Available HTTP: http://ir.lib.cbs.dk/download/ISBN/x656555377.pdf (accessed 13 May 2008).

Jiang, G., Zhang, F. and Thakur, P. (2007) 'The location choice of cross-border mergers and acquisitions: The case of Chinese firms'. Conference paper presented at EIBA 2007, available online at Rutgers University: http://eab.rutgers.edu/THE%20LOCA-TION%20CHOICE%20OF%20CROSS-BORDER%20MAs%20-%20THE%20CASE%20OF%20CHINESE%20FIRMS.doc.

Lunding, A. (2006) 'Global champions in waiting – Perspectives on China's overseas direct investment', *Deutsche Bank Research*. Online. Available HTTP: http://www.dbresearch.com/PROD/DBR_INTERNET_EN-PROD/PROD0000000000201318.pdf (accessed 13 May 2008).

Mathews, J.A. (2006) 'Dragon multinationals: New players in 21st century globalization', *Asia Pacific Journal of Management*, 23: 5–27.

Ming, Z. and Williamson, P.J. (2007) *Dragon at your Door*, Boston: Harvard Business School Press.

MOFCOM (2006) *Statistical Bulletin of China's Outward Foreign Direct Investment 2006*. Homepage, Chinese Ministry of Commerce. Online. Available HTTP: http://preview.hzs2.mofcom.gov.cn/accessory/200710/1192783779118.pdf. (accessed 13 May 2008).

MOFCOM (2007a) 'China revises direct outbound investment in 2006 to 21 bln USD', *News Release 16 September 2007*. Online. Available HTTP: http://il2.mofcom.gov.cn/aarticle/chinanews/200709/20070905099544.html (accessed 13 May 2008).

MOFCOM (2007b) 'Direct outbound investment to exceed US$60b by 2010', *News Release 5 June 2007*. Online. Available HTTP: http://eg2.mofcom.gov.cn/aarticle/chinanews/200706/20070604751016.html (accessed 13 May 2008).

Morck, R., Yeung, B. and Zhao, M. (2008) 'Perspectives on China's outward foreign direct investment', *Journal of International Business Studies*, 39: 337–350.

Poncet, S. (2007) *Inward and Outward FDI in China*. Working paper, Panthéon-Sorbonne-Economie, Université Paris I CNRS and CEPII. Online. Available HTTP: http://team. univ-paris1.fr/teamperso/sponcet/Perso/Book%20chapter%20Poncet% 20April%2028% 202007.pdf (accessed 13 May 2008).

Rugman, A. (2008) 'How global are TNCs from emerging markets?' in: K.P. Sauvant (ed.) *The Rise of Transnational Corporations from Emerging Markets*, Northampton, MA: Edward Elgar, pp. 86–106.

Sauvant, K.P. (2005) 'New sources of FDI: The BRICs. Outward FDI from Brazil, Russia, India and China', *Journal of World Investment and Trade,* 6: 639–709.

Simmons, M.S. (2008) 'Huawei Technologies: The internationalization of a Chinese Company', in I. Alon, and J.R. McIntyre (eds) *Globalization of Chinese Enterprises*. Basingstoke: Palgrave Macmillan, pp. 194–207.

Sun, L., Peng, M., and Tan, W. (2008) 'Competing on scale or scope lessons from Chinese firms' internationalization', in I. Alon, and J.R.McIntyre (eds) *Globalization of Chinese Enterprises*. Basingstoke: Palgrave Macmillan, pp. 77–97.

Taylor, R. (2002) 'Globalization strategies of Chinese companies: Current developments and future prospects', *Asian Business and Management*, 1: 209–225.

UNCTAD (2005a) *Prospects for Foreign Direct Investment and the Strategies of Transnational Corporations*. New York and Geneva: United Nations.

UNCTAD (2005b) *World Investment Report 2005*. New York and Geneva: United Nations.

UNCTAD (2006) *World Investment Report 2006*. New York and Geneva: United Nations.

UNCTAD (2007) *World Investment Report 2007*. New York and Geneva: United Nations Press.

von Keller, E. and Zhou, W. (2003) 'From Middle Kingdom to global market – Expansion strategies and success factors for China's emerging multinationals', *Roland Berger Study*. Online. Available HTTP: http://www.rolandberger.com/expertise/publications/2003-08-03-rbsc-pub-82-publications_sc_middle_kingdom_to_global_market.html (accessed 13 May 2008).

Wu, F. (2005) *The Globalization of Corporate China*. Report by The National Bureau of Asian Research. Online. Available HTTP: http://www.nbr.org/publications/analysis/pdf/ vol16no3.pdf (accessed 13 May 2008).

Yamakawa, Y., Peng, M. and Deeds, D. (2008) 'What drives new ventures to internationalize from emerging to developing economies', *Entrepreneurship Theory and Practice*, 1: 59–82.

Yeung, H.W. (1999) *The Internationalization of Ethnic Chinese Business Firms from Southeast Asia: Strategies, processes and competitive advantage*. Singapore: Blackwell Publishers, pp. 104–127.

Zhan, J.X. (1995) 'Transnationalization and outward investment: the case of Chinese firms', *Transnational Corporations*, 4: 67–100.

Zhang, A. (2003) *China's Emerging Global Business: Political economy and institutional investigations*. Basingstoke: Palgrave Macmillan.

3 International acquisitions and the globalization of firms from India

Andrew Delios, Ajai Singh Gaur and Shawkat Kamal

Introduction

The internationalization process in India has undergone a considerable shift since the onset of the 1990s. Whereas previously India was a destination for the technologies and brands of foreign firms acquired primarily through licensing and technology transfer arrangements, since the mid-1990s, India's participation in the global economy has transitioned to one in which it has become a more important recipient of foreign direct investment (FDI) as analyzed by Chaisse, Chakraborty and Guha (this book, Chapter 10). It has become simultaneously a more active participant in investing in overseas markets (Mavlonov 2007; Pradhan 2008).

As part of the latter trend – outward FDI from India – firms domiciled in India have increasingly turned to international acquisitions as their modality of foreign direct investment. This trend is notable, particularly given its contrasts to the relative lack of propensity for firms based in Asian economies, such as Japan, South Korea and Taiwan, to use acquisitions as a mode of FDI, as compared to other modes, such as wholly owned greenfield investments or joint venture entries.

Aside from the relatively high propensity of Indian firms to engage in FDI via an international acquisition, India's position as the second largest emerging economy, behind China, makes it important to understand the international growth strategies of its firms. India's place in the global economy is increasingly being strengthened by its rapid growth in the first decade of the 2000s, as coupled to its large population base. Further, the strategies of firms from India are not burdened by a legacy of strong government participation in the management of these companies, again unlike in other large transition economies such as China, Taiwan and Russia, for example. (Ruet, this book, Chapter 4) Accordingly, the strategies of firms from India, as they seek positions in international markets, are likely to be motivated by growth and profitability considerations, that are similar, although not necessarily identical, to those of companies operating in mature markets, such as the United States and the developed economies of Western Europe.

Given the importance of understanding the phenomenon of the international acquisition strategy of firms from India, our approach is to explore the performance implications of their international expansions by acquisition. The methodology and conclusions for the analysis of the performance outcomes of international and domestic acquisitions is well-established in the finance and strategy literatures. A series of studies on international acquisitions has established a positive relationship between internationalization by acquisitions, and firm performance, as related to the internalization and extension of core competitive assets into international markets (Markides and Ittner 1994; Morck and Yeung 1991). Yet, this evidence, obtained primarily from an event study methodology, has not been a consistently repeated finding in the literature. A performance decline, in the form of negative gains in the stock market performance of a firm, tends to also emerge in many studies (e.g. Dewenter 1995; Eun *et al.* 1996, Moeller and Schlingemann 2005; Seth *et al.* 2000), illustrating the considerable strategy formulation and implementation challenges associated with an international acquisition. Consequently, although there is the potential to make competitive gains through the internalization and extension of a firm's proprietary assets to international markets, through an acquisition, these gains are often ephemeral.

A notable point of this aforementioned literature is that the evidence has been primarily derived from samples of the internationalization of firms from developed-country markets. Consequently, there is an empirical need to understand if the same trends or patterns will exist for the internationalization strategies of firms from developing countries and transition economy markets. A variety of features of developing and transition economies might lead to a net of antecedents that can lead to a different performance outcome for the acquisition strategy of firms from a developing-country market. These antecedents primarily relate to the institutional context in which the firm is situated. Although we will not go into detail in examining such institutionally related influences on the effectiveness of a firm's strategy, because of our focus on understanding the performance-related aspects of this phenomenon, we do note it here as a potential underlay for the relationships we observe. Our primary question to be addressed in this study is 'What are the performance-related implications of the internationalization by acquisition strategy of firms indigenous to India?'

International acquisitions

'Acquisitions refer to the purchase of stock in an already existing company in an amount sufficient to confer control' (Kogut and Singh 1988: 412). Acquisitions allow a firm to acquire new technological resources (Prahalad and Hamel 1990). Acquisitions can also have a positive effect on organizational learning and can play a vital role in aiding a firm in escaping competency traps (Vermeulen and Barkema 2001). Acquisition of an existing firm can provide a parent firm with new managerial and financial resources (Caves and Mehra 1986). In their study of 75 major MNCs headquartered in the United States, Europe and Japan, Gupta and Govindarajan (2000) found that the subsidiaries that are acquired provide higher knowledge outflows to peer subsidiaries compared to those that are set up as greenfield operations. For a foreign entrant, an acquisition mode of entry creates the opportunity to acquire local brand names and to combine them with their firm-specific marketing skills (Hennart and Park 1993).

Table 3.1 The largest acquisition deals worldwide (2000–2006)

Rank	Year	Acquirer	Target	Deal value (US$ millions)
1	2000	*Merger*: America Online Inc. (AOL)	Time Warner	164,747
2	2000	Glaxo Wellcome Plc.	SmithKline Beecham Plc.	75,961
3	2004	Royal Dutch Petroleum Co.	Shell Transport & Trading Co.	74,559
4	2006	AT&T Inc.	BellSouth Corporation	72,671
5	2001	Comcast Corporation	AT&T Broadband & Internet Services	72,041

Table 3.2 The largest acquisition deals in the Asia-Pacific (2000–2006)

Rank	Year	Acquirer	Target	Deal value (US$ millions)
1	2005	*Merger*: Mitsubishi Tokyo Financial Group Inc.	UFJ Holdings Inc.	41,431
2	2000	Pacific Century CyberWorks Ltd	Cable & Wireless HKT	37,442
3	2000	Beijing Mobile, Shanghai Mobile, Tianjin Mobile Ltd, Hebei Mobile Ltd, Liaoning Mobile Ltd, Shandong Ltd, and Guangxi Mobile Ltd	China Mobile (Hong Kong) Ltd	34,008
4	2003	Deposit Insurance Corporation of Japan	Resona Bank Ltd	16,650
5	2000	Sanwa Bank Ltd	Tokai Bank Ltd	14,984

Acquisitions also allow a firm to quickly obtain market share and take advantage of the current opportunities (Andersson and Svensson 1994). This aspect of acquisitions can emerge as a consequence of the institutional environment of the market a firm is entering. Often legal barriers also require companies to consider acquisitions. For example, in many countries central governments can restrict the total number of mobile phone operators through the issuance of licenses. In such cases, a foreign company that is interested in entering the market only has the option to enter via acquisition.

These beneficial aspects of acquisitions have made an international acquisition strategy a common although not a necessarily dominant form of internationalization, particularly for firms from developed-country markets. As noted in Tables 3.1 and 3.2, acquisitions can also involve transactions that are very large in size.

Motivations acquisitions

Researchers have proposed several hypotheses to explain motivations behind acquisitions. These can generally be categorized under value-creating and non-value creating motivations. Value-creating motivations include the synergy hypothesis and the market power hypothesis. Non-value creating hypotheses include the managerial discretion hypothesis and the hubris hypothesis (Roll, 1986).

Value-creating motivations

Value-creating arguments claim that an acquisition takes place when the value of the combined firm is greater than the sum of the values of the individual firms (Bradley *et al.* 1988; Seth 1990a). Value creation, as defined by Seth (1990a), is realized by making the best use of a firm's assets and resources under environmental opportunities and constraints faced by the firm. In these instances, the combination of various resources of the acquirer and target firms in an acquisition provides the source of value creation.

Studies have shown that the additional values, or synergistic gain from acquisitions, are often derived from an increase in operational efficiency, or some form of financial gain (Seth 1990b; Singh and Montgomery 1987). Operating synergies refer to acquisitions that are undertaken with the goal of achieving economies of scale or scope by pooling various functions and resources of the merging firms. Such functions include production, R&D, marketing and management resources (Kitching 1967; Seth 1990a). Pooling of technological and marketing resources for example, could help the combined firm minimize redundant capacities, reduce costs, and in turn, enhance firm performance (Porter 1980; Seth 1990a).

The combined firm from an acquisition may also experience financial synergies in various forms. It may be able to attain scale economies when it raises money in capital markets due to its increased size (Wiggins 1981). When income streams of merging firms are imperfectly related, the variability and risk of cash flows are reduced. This may positively affect the firm's ability to borrow capital, again potentially improving firm performance.

According to the dominant-firm model, prices will rise as a consequence of an acquisition by a dominant firm (Seth 1990a). Firms can reduce the competition in a market through an acquisition and hence strengthen their ability to control prices, quantities, or the nature of products, generating abnormal profits as a result. In high-technology markets, acquisitions can provide small players with an opportunity to achieve a larger size so that they might be better able to share their operating and R&D costs and improve their competitive positions in the market. Empirical studies have provided evidence that market power serves as a source of value creation in mergers and acquisitions (Eckbo 1983; Stillman 1983).

Non-value increasing motivations

In addition to the idea that acquisitions can be a value-enhancing tool for a firm, researchers have also proposed another set of arguments stating that acquisitions might be driven by other factors that are unrelated to value enhancement. Among such arguments, the managerialism hypothesis and the hubris hypothesis are the most widely cited explanations.

The managerialism hypothesis suggests that managers will knowingly overpay in takeovers: managers embark on acquisitions to maximize their own utility at the expense of the shareholders of the acquiring firm (Jensen 1986; Morck *et al.* 1990). Individual managers might try to enhance their power, prestige, job-security and salaries by seeking corporate expansion or controlling a large empire (Baumol 1962). Since managerial compensation frequently is tied to the amount of assets under control, managers are more likely to seek higher rates of growth in assets than profits. Mueller (1969) suggested that acquiring firms' managers have discretionary control over decision making and attempt to maximize the growth of the firm subject to a profit constraint.

Mergers and acquisitions motivated by this managerial discretionary behavior have no synergistic gains to be allocated among the firms. Often termed empire building, managers tend to be willing to overpay for the target firms (Eun *et al.* 1996). This leads the managerialism hypothesis to predict that value is destroyed upon acquisition, since there is a transfer of value from the combined firm to the managers of the acquiring firm (Seth *et al.* 2002). Mathur *et al.* (1994) also pointed out three types of managers might probably demonstrate this managerial discretionary behavior: managers of firms with free or excess cash flows, manager of firms in declining industries, and managers of firms in slow-growth economies with limited investment opportunities.

The hubris hypothesis (Roll 1986) suggests that acquisitions occur because managers make mistakes in evaluating target firms, and the takeover premium merely reflects a random error. He further pointed out that each manager is likely to be over-confident in his or her ability to better manage the acquired assets than the average acquirer. Roll's (1986) extreme version of the hubris hypothesis predicts that there are no synergistic gains from takeover bids and the entire premium paid to the target firm is a transfer from the acquirer.

Seth *et al.* (2000) presented empirical evidence for a moderate version of the hubris hypothesis. If some corporate combinations do indeed result in synergistic gains, rational managers are motivated to undertake acquisitions seeking these gains. Although the expected synergistic gains are positive, because the valuation of the target may be erroneous, some such acquisitions may result in overpayment by the acquirer to the target, resulting in a loss to shareholders of the acquiring firm.

Motives and the empirical evidence

Studies have found evidence that suggest the presence of multiple motives such as synergy, managerialism and hubris in acquisition transactions both in domestic and international acquisitions (Berkovitch and Narayanan 1993; Seth *et al.* 2000). Seth *et al.* (2002) suggested that a possible reason to explain why previous studies have not found strong empirical evidence regarding the sources of value creation in international acquisitions is that they do not take into account that different motives may exist for undertaking these acquisitions. In effect, early studies tended to test the joint hypothesis that the acquisitions in their sample are characterized by synergy, and that some underlying source of this synergy is relevant for explaining value creation.

Empirical studies on the performance of acquisitions generally use one of two major approaches: event studies and outcome studies. The results from various event studies suggest that overall, acquisitions create value for shareholders of the target and acquirer as a whole; however, most of the gains accrue to the target firm's shareholders (Jarrell *et al.* 1988; Jensen and Ruback 1983). Most studies find evidence that within a time window of several weeks prior to and after the announcement of the acquisition, the target's stock price rises sharply, such that shareholders of the target firm earn substantial positive abnormal returns (Asquith 1983; Bradley 1980; Bradley *et al.* 1983; Dodd and Ruback 1977; Eckbo 1983). Less consistent however, are the results for acquiring firms.

Using a time period of 20 days before the announcement as the event window, Asquith *et al.* (1983) examined 214 merger bids initiated by Fortune 1000 firms during the period from 1963 to 1979. Their study shows that the acquiring firms experienced an average cumulative abnormal return (CAR) of 2.8 percent. Bradley *et al.* (1988) also finds evidence that acquiring firms in the United States earned positive returns during the unregulated period of 1963–1968. Contrary to the findings mentioned above, many other studies present opposite results. These studies provide considerable evidence that acquiring firms' shareholders experience zero or negative gains. Asquith (1983), and Asquith *et al.* (1983) find that acquiring firms' shareholders tend to experience either zero or small negative returns; Bradley *et al.* (1988) showed that bidders obtained negative but insignificant returns.

Several other studies have extended the time horizon examined beyond the usual announcement-period event windows (Loughran and Vijh 1997; Mitchell and Stafford, 2000; Rau and Vermaelen 1998). The long-horizon event studies suggest a negative drift in the stock prices of acquiring firms. Using a sample of 204 acquisitions undertaken during the period 1977–1996, Megginson *et al.* (2004) found that acquirers suffered abnormal returns of negative 13 percent within the three-year period that an acquisition transaction had taken place. Loughran and Vijh (1997) find the abnormal returns over the five-year period after the acquisition announcements are a negative 24 percent for acquirers where the acquisition is financed by a stock transaction.

Empirical research on international acquisitions

Empirical research on international acquisitions can be broadly categorized into three main streams. The first stream explores broad topics of international acquisitions, including the integration between the acquirer and target. The second stream examines post acquisition performance using relatively longer term measures in comparison with other modes of entry. Finally, researchers examine the issue of wealth creation to shareholders by international acquisitions. This stream is common to finance literature and is usually conducted by observing stock market reactions to acquisition announcements.

Firms are able to gain positive returns from an international acquisition based on the assumption that firms enter foreign markets to exploit their specific resources to take advantage of imperfections in the markets (Buckley and Casson 1976; Morck and Yeung 1992). Studies show that wealth is created for both acquirer and target firm shareholders and that this wealth creation accrues from the integrating benefits of internalization, synergy, and risk diversification (Kang 1993; Markides and Ittner 1994; Morck and Yeung 1991, 1992).

Unlike domestic acquisitions which are often reported to reduce the acquirer's shareholder value while only improving the target's shareholder value (Kaplan and Weisbach 1992), market reactions to international acquisitions show significant differences. Several studies on US acquirers purchasing non-US firms find evidence of wealth creation for the acquiring firms' shareholders (Markides and Ittner 1994; Morck and Yeung, 1992). Studies also find wealth creation effects for non-US acquirers purchasing US firms (Kang, 1993), providing further evidence that international acquisitions provide positive returns for acquirer firm shareholders.

Morck and Yeung (1992) found that the acquirers' R&D intensity, advertising intensity and management quality were positively associated with acquirer's abnormal returns. These firms had information-based resources that allowed them to more effectively internalize the assets of the target firm (Shimizu *et al.* 2004). Markides and Ittner (1994) used a similar sample of 276 international acquisitions by US firms between 1975 and 1988. They found several other factors that were positively related to acquiring firms' abnormal returns. These factors specifically are the acquirer's home currency strength, industry advertising intensity, industry concentration, prior international experience, business relatedness, and acquirer relative size compared with the target firm.

Harris and Ravenscraft (1991), examined non-US acquiring firms and US target firms and found that US targets of foreign buyers had significantly larger wealth gains than those purchased by US firms. Kang (1993) examined 119 Japanese firms that bid on 102 US firms from 1975 to 1988. His findings supported those of studies mentioned earlier, and that Japanese acquisitions of US firms created wealth for both target and acquirer firms. He also found that returns to Japanese acquirers were positively related to the acquirers' total debt and borrowings from financial institutions as well as the appreciation of the yen against the dollar. The debt level in this case was used as a proxy for agency costs, in that a high debt level often reduces potential agency costs (Jensen 1986).

There is, however, some research which finds conflicting evidence regarding wealth creation in international acquisitions, compared to the studies mentioned above. Examining 112 international acquisitions by US firms from 1978 to 1990, Datta and Puia (1995), reported opposite results from those mentioned above. They found that acquisitions, on average, do not create value for acquiring firm stakeholders. This could possibly be due to the inclusion of newer acquisitions compared to earlier studies, and to the fact that the impact of globalization has reduced the differences between domestic and international acquisitions (Shimizu *et al.* 2004). They also found that the cultural distance between target and acquirer firms was inversely related to wealth gains for acquiring firm shareholders.

Several studies find evidence that the tax system of the country in which the acquisition deal is consummated is highly influential. Cebenoyan *et al.* (1992) and Manzon *et al.* (1994) found that US acquirers benefit from wealth gains when their targets are located in high-tax countries, while they tend to earn lower returns when their targets are in low-tax countries. However, there is contradicting evidence regarding the influence of the tax systems as well. Cakici *et al.* (1996), in studying wealth creation in foreign acquirers, found that tax effects, exchange rate effects, as well as R&D intensity, were not relevant, and that wealth effects were most influenced by country factors.

International acquisitions in Asia

Cross-border acquisitions in Asia can be classified into three types: firms of developed countries (especially the United States and Western and Europe) acquiring Asian targets, intra-regional international acquisitions, and outbound acquisitions. Acquisitions into Asia account for the majority of cross-border acquisition activity that takes place, but the last decade has seen outbound and intra-Asian acquisition activity increase significantly. The value of international acquisitions by Asian acquirers was US$25 billion in 2001 compared to just US$2.5 billion a decade earlier. (UNCTAD 2003: 291)

Even though the number of acquisition transactions in Asia continues to grow, limited research has been conducted in this area. Kale (2004), studied acquisitions in India using a sample of 698 acquisitions during the period 1992–2002. He found that acquisitions in India created positive value for acquired and acquiring companies over the entire study period. The value creation was significantly greater for acquired companies (8.79 percent) compared to the acquiring companies (1.71 percent). In addition, he found that multinational acquirers, on average, created significantly greater value in their transactions than local acquirers did; but this difference in value creation reduced significantly over time. He concluded that the greater value creation of multinational acquirers might be seen as a reflection of their greater acquisition experience and superior acquisition skills.

Chari *et al.* (2004), studied a sample of 1629 observations of international acquisitions by firms from developed markets that purchased publicly traded emerging market target firms from Asia and Latin America between 1988 and 2002. They find evidence that both target and acquirer firms experience positive returns, with the value created accruing more to the target firms' shareholders. They further note that the benefits of the acquisitions seem to stem from the transfer of majority control from the emerging market targets to developed market acquirers.

Pangarkar and Lie (2004) using a sample of 115 acquisitions by Singapore acquirers find robust support for the idea that acquirers experience significantly positive returns. In contrast, Koh and Lee (1988) find zero returns to acquiring firms based on their study of a sample of 85 acquisitions by Singaporean acquirers of Singaporean targets during the period from 1973 to 1984. Using a smaller sample of 23 Singapore acquirers, Ding *et al.* (1996) concluded that acquirers experience insignificant returns. In the next section, we extend this line of research on the performance effects of acquiring firms based in Asia, using a sample of firms based in India.

Sample and methods

We develop our sample of firms using the acquisition experience of firms based in India.

The internationalization of firms from India is part of a larger trend of the internationalization of firms from other developing-country markets. Firms situated in emerging economies have been steadily increasing their contribution in the outward FDI flows. This flow increased from a mere US$65 billion in 1980 to US$849 billion, which was 12 percent of the world's FDI outflows in 2002 (Wright *et al.* 2005), to even more substantive levels of FDI by the late 2000s.

Even though the growth has been strongest most recently, incidents of investing abroad by firms from developing nations is not a recent event. Lecraw (1977) was among the earliest to examine this phenomenon and he found that market protection and development in the host country, avoidance of quotas in high-income countries, and risk reduction through diversification, were among the main motives for undertaking foreign direct investment. Investments tended to be in the direction of neighboring less-developed countries (Lecraw 1993).

In the 2000s, there has been a marked shift in the destination for FDIs of firms from developing nations. In addition to investing in less-developed countries and newly industrialized economies, firms from emerging economies are also investing in developed economies. In their study of 328 Taiwanese firms, Makino *et al.* (2002) found that firms from newly industrialized economies tended to invest in developed countries when they had a strategic asset-seeking and market-seeking motivation. Emerging market multinational enterprises often engage in aggressive acquisitions of strategic resources to overcome their latecomer disadvantage on the global stage (Luo and Tung 2007). Firms from India are part of this race to invest abroad.

Sample

We derived our sample from the population of all the acquisitions made by Indian firms during the 1986–2006 time period. We collected information on acquisitions made prior to 1998 from the reports put forth by the India Investment Centre. The India Investment Centre provided a comprehensive list of foreign acquisitions made by Indian firms until 1998, after which it stopped publishing these reports. For later years, we relied on the information provided in the Thomson Financial Database. We focused only on the acquisitions in which an Indian firm acquired a majority stake. Further, we removed the acquisitions which were made by firms that were not publicly traded on the Bombay Stock Exchange. These procedures gave us a list of 330 acquisitions. Since we could not obtain reliable share-market data for the years prior to 2002, we limited our calculations of the cumulative abnormal return (CAR) to the parent firm to the acquisition events that happened post-2002. This resulted in a sample of 224 acquisition events for the final analysis.

The 224 acquisition events included in our analysis involved 127 different acquiring companies. The targets in our sample were from 44 different countries with the maximum number coming from the USA (30.36 percent) and the United Kingdom (16.07 percent). The acquiring companies were from 33 different industries. The acquisition activities were dominated by firms operating in the business services (25.45 percent), pharmaceuticals (12.95 percent) and prepackaged soft-ware industry (10.27 percent). The targets were from 31 different industries with more than half of them operating in business services (22.32 percent), pharmaceu-ticals (15.18 percent) and prepackaged software (13.39 percent). A large majority (70.54 percent) of the acquisitions took place between firms operating in related industries, based on the two digit SIC code of the acquirer and target.

Methodology

We used the standard techniques of event study analysis and regression analysis to estimate the impact of an acquisition on shareholder wealth for the acquiring firms during the immediate period, before and after, of an acquisition announce-ment. This technique allowed us to determine whether there was an abnormal stock-price effect associated with the acquisition announcement. The abnormal return on the share price reflected the difference between the return associated with the acquisition announcement and the firm's expected return based on the past performance of its shares in the market. The announcement day of the acqui-sition was treated as the '0' day for the event. We used a short event window as we wanted to reduce any dilution in the effect on shareholder wealth due to events outside that of the acquisition itself. Hence, the maximum event window was kept to a period of 15 days.

As capital markets in emerging economies such as India might not be very effi-cient, there was a possibility of finding inconsistencies in the outcome of the analysis for different time windows. Accordingly, we needed to check the consis-tency of the outcomes. Thus, we calculated the CAR using four different time win-dows ranging from $t = -1$ (one day before the announcement), 0 to $t = -7$ (seven days before the announcement), $t = +7$ (seven days after the announcement). The share price of the acquiring companies and the market index used were collected initially for the $t = -7$ to $t = +7$ period to cover all four time windows. For analyt-ical purposes, $t = -1$ year to $t = + 30$ days was used as the period for collecting data for the share price of the acquiring companies and the market index. We decided to use a side benchmark index and we thus used the BSE-500 index. The BSE-500 index, inaugurated on 9 August 1999, represents nearly 93 percent of the total market capitalization on the Bombay Stock Exchange. It includes stocks from all 20 major industries of the Indian economy.

We used a market model to represent the return-generating process,

$$R_{it} = \alpha_i + \beta_i R_{mt}$$

where,
  R_{it} = daily return for firm i over day t
  R_{mt} = the return on the market portfolio over day t

We used a simple linear regression to estimate the model parameters. After obtain-ing the value of the parameters (α/β) from the regression, we calculated the daily abnormal returns for the four different time windows for each acquisition transaction. The formula used was as follows (this is an example of an event window of 15 days);

$$AR_{it} = R_{it} - \hat{\alpha}_i - \hat{\beta}_i \, R_{mt,} (t = -7 \,\, to \,\, t = +7)$$

Finally we obtained the cumulative abnormal returns for each firm by aggregating the daily abnormal returns over the different event periods (the following formula shows the example of a 15 day event window):

$$CAR_i = \sum_{t=-7}^{t=+7} AR_{it}$$

Results

We begin our depiction of the results by describing essential trends in acquisitions by Indian firms. As indicated in Figure 3.1, there has been a significant increase in the number of cross-border acquisitions by Indian firms since the year 2000. Of all the international acquisitions undertaken by the Indian firms after 1985, more than 80 percent were undertaken on or after the year 2000. This phenomenon might have its roots in the economic liberalization policy of the Indian Government during the early 1990s, although the effect was not immediate. Despite some negative speculation at the outset, this economic liberalization program ultimately benefited domestic companies as they became more competitive and started operating with a broader geographic horizon. Also, the economy as a whole has done very well since, with high GDP growth rates for India since the early 1990s.

There was a notable decrease in the number of international acquisitions by Indian firms immediately after 2001. One reason for this change in direction might be the effect of the 11 September 2001 events on the global economy. However, this downturn was soon reversed, with continued growth to 2008. It has to be noted though that this outward investment was concentrated in a few sectors only. The three leading sectors for international acquisition accounted for almost 50 percent of the total acquisitions by Indian firms after 2001. The Indian companies have made their mark in the world with their expertise in providing business services and software development. Thus it was no surprise that these two were amongst the leading sectors where acquisitions took place. The pharmaceuticals sector also saw a substantial number of international acquisitions taking place, thanks largely to the numerous acquisitions by companies such as Ranbaxy Laboratories.

Our analysis of the cumulative abnormal returns (CARs) suggested that the shareholders of acquiring companies from India gained from the international acquisitions that took place (Table 3.3). For all the different time windows we studied, we found positive average CARs for the shareholders of the acquiring

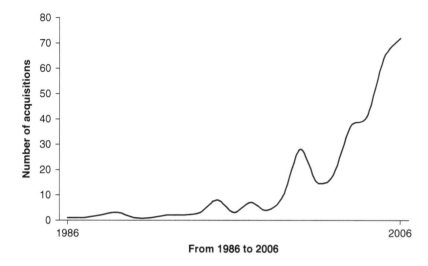

Figure 3.1 International acquisitions by Indian firms

Table 3.3 Effect of acquisitions on the market value of acquiring companies

Returns	Average change in value	Gainers	Losers
CAR (−1, 0)	2.24%	143	81
CAR (−1, +1)	2.80%	154	70
CAR (−3, +3)	2.64%	131	93
CAR (−7, +7)	2.53%	121	103

companies. The average CARs were more or less consistent for all time periods considered, hovering between 2 and 3 percent. In addition, it was found that more companies were gainers rather than losers as far as the CAR for their stocks were concerned. This was true in all the different time windows considered for the analysis. However, the gainer to loser ratio was not consistent and varied widely ranging from 1.17 to 2.20. All these pieces of evidence suggest that, in general, Indian firms are creating shareholder wealth through international acquisitions. The fact that we found the results to be consistent over different time windows enhances the level of confidence we place in this finding.

As one sensitivity test for these results, we also looked at the difference in the average change of value between acquisitions made in the developed and the developing nations (Table 3.4). We found that for all the time windows, acquisitions made in developed countries resulted in seemingly greater level of returns for the acquiring company's shareholders than acquisitions made in the developing countries. However, a two-tailed *t*-test indicated that the difference in the mean CAR between acquisitions made in developed and developing countries was only significant (at a 90 percent confidence interval) in the case of CAR

Table 3.4 Performance of acquiring firms grouped by region of target

Returns	Average change in value	
	Developed country	Developing country
CAR (−1,0)	2.56%	1.16%
CAR (−1,+1)	3.14%	1.64%
CAR (−3,+3)	3.07%	1.19%
CAR (−7,+7)	2.85%	1.45%
Number	173	51

Table 3.5 Performance of acquiring firms grouped by industry of target

Returns	Average change in value		
	Service	Manufacturing	Extracting
CAR (−1,0)	3.01%	1.66%	1.22%
CAR (−1,+1)	3.42%	2.37%	1.41%
CAR (−3,+3)	3.31%	2.06%	2.90%
CAR (−7,+7)	2.43%	2.67%	1.78%
Number	99	117	8

(−1, 0) and CAR (−1, +1) only. Hence, we are reluctant to draw firm conclusions about a country of destination effect in terms of generation of positive CARs for Indian acquirers.

Next, we looked at the differences in the change of the average CAR values between acquisitions made in three broad industry categories – manufacturing, services, and extractive industries. The results showed that acquisitions made in the services and manufacturing industries had higher positive CAR values compared to that of extractive industries. Between the two of them, acquisitions made in the service industry performed better than those made in the manufacturing industry. Our *t*-tests indicated that the difference in the mean CAR was significant (at a 95 percent confidence interval) only between service and manufacturing sectors and only in the case of CAR (−1, 0). The other cases were not significant, even at the 90 percent confidence interval level. The insignificance in the *t*-test result for the differences between the average CAR values of the extractive industry firms and firms in the other two industries is most likely caused by the fact that the sample had only eight observations from the extractive industry firms (which was less than 4 percent of the total number of acquisitions in the sample).

Finally, we performed tests to analyze differences in average CAR values between firms that entered the same industry by an acquisition, entered a related industry by acquisition and entered a new industry by acquisition. These tests yielded mixed results. Although the firms that entered related or new industries seemed to do better than firms that entered the same industry, the overall finding was

Table 3.6 Performance of acquiring firms grouped by industry relatedness of acquirer and target

Returns	Average change in value		
	Same industry	Related industry	New industry
CAR (−1,0)	1.96%	3.10%	2.09%
CAR (−1,+1)	2.45%	3.10%	3.51%
CAR (−3,+3)	2.34%	3.27%	2.82%
CAR (−7,+7)	2.64%	2.06%	2.77%
Number	131	50	43

not conclusive, as different time periods showed different outcomes. Our *t*-tests also indicated that differences in mean CAR values were not significant (at 90 percent confidence interval) for all possible mean comparisons between these categories.

Conclusion

International acquisitions by firms based in India have grown strongly through much of the first decade of the 2000s. The strong growth is a marker of the expansion of the Indian economy both in terms of GDP growth and in terms of growth into international markets. The growth of international acquisition activity coupled alongside the persistent question of whether and how gains are obtained for acquiring firms motivated our investigation in the performance outcomes of acquirers based in India.

Our study focused on the analysis of 224 acquisition transactions. We utilized a standard methodology to explore whether value was created in the acquisitions for the acquiring firm. Our event study analysis revealed that Indian acquirers obtained a positive return, with their average cumulative abnormal return ranging from 2.2 percent to 2.8 percent, depending on the length of window over which a firm's stock price movements were observed. Among the transacting firms, approximately two-thirds of firms achieved a positive return, while the other third had a negative market response on the news of the international acquisition.

This evidence tends to stand at odds with much of the event study performance analysis of international acquisitions. Although key studies have pointed to a potential positive performance impact of international acquisition announcements, through the effective internalization of a firm's proprietary assets when moving into overseas markets (Markides and Ittner 1994; Morck and Yeung 1991, 1992), empirical evidence rarely supports this point unambiguously. Indeed, much of the evidence points to a negative impact of an international acquisition announcement on the acquiring firm's market performance. This general trend aligns well with the similar empirical observation made for domestic acquisition announcements and the market performance of acquiring firms.

The positive performance impact of an acquisition announcement for acquiring firms based in India suggests that the market recognizes that the strategy of these firms is creating value through several possible mechanisms. Although it was not the focus of our study to investigate the antecedents to the performance outcomes of acquisitions announcements, there are several possible means by which a competition-enhancing outcome can be created in an international acquisition.

One prominent means of creating value is through the effective internalization and extension of the proprietary assets of the acquiring or target firms involved in the acquisition. A second means is a reconfiguration of the resources of the acquiring and target firms to reduce costs through the elimination of redundancies, or to create value through a more effective alignment of the potentially complementary competencies of the acquiring and target firm. A third means is again a reconfiguration of resources, but this time oriented towards a shift to structuring the acquired and target firms resources on a global level, instead of on a multi-local level. A fourth, but more long-term outcome, is an organizational learning influence that results in the development of new competencies for competition in new markets. Clearly there is much potential in the empirical trends we observed to extend this research to identify the determinants of value-creating in the international acquisitions of firms from India.

Although it was not our objective to make this form of analysis and inference in our study, we did investigate several key characteristics of these acquisitions to identify whether one feature or another was driving this result in part or in full. We grouped acquisitions into the country of origin of the target, as well as industry of origin and finally by whether the target operated in the same, related or unrelated industry as compared to the acquirer. Across these analyses, there was no clear category in which positive returns were more prominent, and accordingly, we could draw no firm conclusions from these analyses.

The study was conducted on data obtained from companies listed in one stock exchange only. In addition, we could only conduct the study over a rather short period of time as sufficient data were not available. Future researches may take necessary steps to avoid these limitations and conduct a more comprehensive study. Although the gainers were more than the losers in our sample, some firms did fail to create positive value for the shareholders. Future researches may also focus on this aspect and try to find out why some firms can create positive value for their shareholders while others fail to do so.

Our study hence provides initial evidence on the notably positive performance outcomes of the international acquisitions of acquiring firms based in India. We found that acquiring firms experienced a positive market reaction ranging from 2.2 percent to 2.8 percent, on average. This phenomenon of international acquisitions by these firms is but part of the larger phenomenon of the increasing globalization of the economy in India, in which outward foreign direct investment is playing an increasingly prominent role. It is also part of the larger phenomenon of the substantial growth in outward foreign direct investment by firms from emerging markets, in which acquisitions are also an important component. In a related fashion, the challenge remains for research to establish the basic trends in these prominent phenomena as a means by which we can deepen our understanding of the characteristics of these events, and provide good empirical grounding for future research into the causal nature of these events.

References

Andersson, T. and Svensson, R. (1994) Entry modes for direct investment determined by the composition of firm-specific skills, *Scandinavia Journal of Economics*, 96 (4): 551–560.

Asquith, P. (1983) Merger bids, uncertainty, and stockholder returns, *Journal of Financial Economics*, 11: 51–83.

Asquith, P., Brunner, R.F. and Mullings, D.W. (1983) The gains to bidding firms from mergers, *Journal of Financial Economics*, 11: 121–139.

Baumol, W.J. (1962) On the theory of the expansion of the firm, *American Economic Review*, 52 (5): 1078–1087.

Berkovitch, E. and Narayanan, M.P. (1993) Motives for takeovers: An empirical investigation, *Journal of Financial and Quantitative Analysis*, 28: 347–362.

Bradley, M. (1980) Interfirm tender offers and the market for corporate control, *Journal of Business*, 53: 345–376.

Bradley, M., Desai, A. and Kim, E.H. (1983) The rationale behind interfirm tender offers: Information or synergy?, *Journal of Financial Economics*, 11: 183–206.

Bradley, M., Desai, Anand and Kim, E. Han (1988) Synergistic gains from corporate acquisitions and their division between the stockholders of target and acquiring firms, *Journal of Financial Economics*, 21: 3–40.

Buckley, P. and Casson, M. (1976) *The Future of the Multinational Enterprise*. London: Macmillan.

Cakici, N., Hessel, C. and Tandon, K. (1996) Foreign acquisitions in the United States: Effect on shareholder wealth of foreign acquiring firms, *Journal of Banking and Finance*, 20 (2): 307–329.

Caves, R.E. and Mehra, S. (1986) Entry of foreign multinationals into US manufacturing industries, in M. Porter (ed.) *Competition in Global Industries*. Boston, MA: Harvard Business School Press, 459–481.

Cebenoyan, A.S., Papaioannou, G. and Travlos, N.G. (1992) Foreign takeover activity in the US and wealth effect for target firm shareholders, *Financial Management*, 21 (3): 58–68.

Chari, A., Ouimet, P., and Tesar, L. (2004) 'Cross border mergers and acquisitions in emerging markets: The stock market valuation of corporate control,' Working Paper, University of Michigan Business School, Ann Arbor, MI.

Datta, D.K. and Puia, G. (1995) Cross-border acquisitions: An examination of the influence of relatedness and cultural fit on shareholder value creation in US acquiring firms, *Management International Review*, 35 (4): 337–359.

Dewenter, K.L. (1995) Does the market react differently to domestic and foreign takeover announcements? Evidence from the us chemical and retail industries, *Journal of Financial Economics*, 37 (4): 421–441.

Ding, D.Y.K., Ang, J., Khoo, B.G. and Toh, S.F. (1996) Is shareholders' wealth affected by acquisition announcements?, *SES Journal*, October: 32–36, 74.

Dodd, P. and Ruback, R. (1977) Tender offers and stockholder return: An empirical analysis, *Journal of Financial Economics*, 5: 351–374.

Eckbo, B.E. (1983) Horizontal mergers, collusion and stockholder wealth, *Journal of Financial Economics*, 11 (April) 241–273.

Eun, C.S., Kolodny, R. and Scheraga, C. (1996) Cross-border acquisitions and shareholder wealth: Tests of the synergy and internalization hypotheses, *Journal of Banking and Finance*, 20 (9): 1559–1582.

Gupta, Anil K. and Govindarajan, Vijay (2000) Knowledge flows within multinational corporations, *Strategic Management Journal* 21 (4): 473–496.

Harris, R.S. and Ravenscraft, D. (1991) The role of acquisitions in foreign direct investment: evidence from the U.S. stock market, *Journal of Finance*, 46: 825–844.

Hennart, J. and Park, Y. (1993) Greenfield vs acquisitions: The strategy of the Japanese investors in the United States, *Management Science*, 39 (9): 1054–1070.

Jarrell, G.A., Brickley, J.A. and Netter, J.M. (1988) The market for corporate control: The empirical evidence since 1980, *Journal of Economic Perspectives*, 2: 49–68.

Jensen, M.C. (1986) Agency costs of free cash flow: Corporate finance and takeovers, *American Economic Review*, 76 (May): 323–329.

Jensen, M. and Ruback, R. (1983) The market for corporate control: The scientific evidence, *Journal of Financial Economics*, 1: 5–50.

Kale, P. (2004) 'Acquisition value creation in emerging markets: An empirical study of acquisitions in India', *Academy of Management Best Paper* Proceedings, New Orleans, LA.

Kang, J.K. (1993) The international market for corporate control: Mergers and acquisitions of US firms by Japanese firms, *Journal of Financial Economics*, 34: 345–371.

Kaplan, S.N. and Weisbach, M.S. (1992) The success of acquisitions: evidence from divestitures, *Journal of Finance*, 47: 107–138.

Kitching, J. (1967) Why do mergers miscarry? *Harvard Business Review*, 45 (6): 84–102.

Kogut, Bruce and Singh, Harbir (1988) The effect of national culture on the choice of entry mode, *Journal of International Business Studies*, 19 (3): 411–432.

Koh, F. and Lee, S.H. (1988) Risks and returns of acquiring and acquired firms in Singapore, *Asia Pacific Journal of Management*, 5 (3): 157–168.

Lecraw, Donald J. (1977) Direct investment by firms from less developed countries, *Oxford Economic Papers*, 29 (3): 442–457.

Lecraw, Donald J. (1993) Outward direct investment by Indonesian firms: Motivation and effects, *Journal of International Business Studies*, 589–600.

Loughran, T. and Vijh, A.M. (1997) Do long-term shareholders benefit from corporate acquisitions?, *Journal of Finance*, 52 (December): 1765–1790.

Luo, Y. and Tung, Rosalie L. (2007) International expansion of emerging market enterprises: A springboard perspective, *Journal of International Business Studies*, 38 (4): 481–498.

Makino, S., Lau, C. and Yeh, R. (2002) Asset-exploitation versus asset-seeking: Implication for location choice of foreign direct investment from newly industrialized economies, *Journal of International Business Studies*, 33 (3): 403–421.

Manzon, G.B., Sharp, D.J. and Travlos, N.G. (1994) An empirical study of the consequences of US tax rules for international acquisitions by US firms, *Journal of Finance*, 49: 1893–1904.

Markides, C.C. and Ittner, C.D. (1994) Shareholder benefits from corporate international diversification: Evidence from US international acquisitions, *Journal of International Business Studies*, 25 (2): 343–366.

Mathur, I., Rangan, N., Chhachhi, I. and Sundaram, S. (1994) International acquisitions in the United States: Evidence from returns to foreign bidders, *Managerial and Decision Economics*, 15 (2): 107.

Mavlonov, Ibrokhim R. (2007) Achievements of India's foreign investment policy, *Finance India*, 21 (4): 1337–1354.

Megginson, W., Morgan, A. and Nail, L. (2004) The determinants of positive long-term performance in strategic mergers: Corporate focus and cash, *Journal of Banking & Finance*, 28 (3): 523.

Mitchell, M.L. and Stafford, E. (2000) Managerial decisions and long term stock price performance, *Journal of Business*, 73: 287–329.

Moeller, S.B. and Schlingemann, F.P. (2005) Global diversification and bidder gains: A comparison between cross-border and domestic acquisitions, *Journal of Banking and Finance*, 29: 533–564.

Morck, R. and Yeung, B. (1991) Why investors value multinationality, *Journal of Business*, 64 (2): 165–187.

Morck, R. and Yeung, B. (1992) Internalization: An event study test, *Journal of International Economics*, 33: 41–56.

Morck, R., Shleifer, A. and Vishny, R.W. (1990) Do managerial objectives drive bad acquisitions? *Journal of Finance*, 45, (March): 31–48.

Mueller, D.C. (1969) A theory of conglomerate mergers, *Quarterly Journal of Economics*, 83 (4): 643–659.

Pangarkar, N. and Lie, Junius, R. (2004) The impact of market cycle on the performance of Singapore acquirers, *Strategic Management Journal*, 25, (12): 1209–1317.

Porter, M. (1980) *Corporate Strategy*. New York: Free Press.

Pradhan, Jaya Prakash (2008) The evolution of Indian foreign direct investment: Changing trends and patterns, *International Journal of Technology and Globalization*, 4 (1): 5–5.

Prahalad, C.K. and Hamel, G. (1990) The core competence of the corporation, *Harvard Business Review*, 68 (3): 79–91.

Rau, P.R. and Vermaelen, T. (1998) Glamor, value and the post-acquisition performance of acquiring firm, *Journal of Financial Economics*, 49 (2): 223–253.

Roll, R. (1986) The hubris hypothesis of corporate takeovers, *Journal of Business*, 59 (2): 197–216.

Seth, A. (1990a) Value creation in acquisitions: A re-examination of performance issues, *Strategic Management Journal*, 11: 99–115.

Seth, A. (1990b) Sources of value creation in acquisitions: An empirical investigation, *Strategic Management Journal*, 11: 431–446.

Seth, A., Song, K.P. and Pettit, R. (2000) Synergy, managerialism or hubris? An empirical examination of motives for foreign acquisitions of us firms, *Journal of International Business Studies*, 31 (3): 387–405.

Seth, A., Song, K.P. and Pettit, R.R. (2002) Value creation and destruction in cross-border acquisitions: An empirical analysis of foreign acquisitions of US firms, *Strategic Management Journal*, 23 (10): 921–940.

Shimizu, K., Hitt, M., Vaidyanath, D. and Pisano, V. (2004) Theoretical foundations of cross-border mergers and acquisitions: A review of current research and recommendations for the future, *Journal of International Management*, 10: 307–353.

Singh, H. and Montgomery, Cynthia A. (1987) Corporate acquisition strategy and economic performance, *Strategic Management Journal*, 8 (4): 377–386.

Stillman, R. (1983) Examining antitrust policy towards horizontal mergers, *Journal of Financial Economics*, 11 (April): 225–240.

UNCTAD (2003) world Investment Report 2003: FDI Policies for Development: National and international perspectives. New York and Geneva: United Nations, 294.

Vermeulen, F. and Barkema, Harry (2001) Learning through acquisitions, *Academy of Management Journal*, 44: 457–476.

Wiggins, S.N. (1981) A theoretical analysis of conglomerate mergers, in R.D. Blair and R. Lanzilotti (eds), *The Conglomerate Corporation*. Cambridge, MA: Oelgeschlager, Gunn & Hain, 53–70.

Wright, M., Filatotchev, Igor Hoskisson, Robert E. and Peng, Mike W. (2005) Strategy research in emerging economies: Challenging the conventional wisdom, *Journal of Management Studies*, 42 (1): 1–33.

4 The reshaping of global capitalism by MNEs from emerging countries

Joël Ruet

Introduction

For a long time, the term multinational company (MNC) was synonymous with American (northern) or European (western) companies. On the other hand, for numerous left-wing critics, this term has long been synonymous with 'the northern countries' where there was a correspondence between the interests of the economic territories and their companies in a world economy largely closed until the 1970s.[1] The early twentieth century was an era in which what was 'good for General Motors' was 'good for America' and vice versa. The situation changed, at first with the arrival of the 'global' firms, whose major production facilities are situated outside their country of 'origin' and given the helpful liberalization of financial markets, the ownership of these companies has become more widespread. Since the 1980s, what is good for a 'European' or an 'American' multinational has no reason to necessarily coincide with the interests of these territories. But 'multinational' continued to signify 'North'. It seems today that the current decade will be the one to mark the emergence of multinationals 'from the South'. The foreign direct investments (FDI) 'from the South' are multiplying as are the mergers and acquisitions by firms from the South. This chapter posits that this evolution underlines two major phenomena:

- Multinational firms that are 'simply global' come into existence and these economic players become completely independent from all the territories, whether from their 'territory of origin' or any other territory they operate from; this evolution is not necessarily a result of exchanges and inter-company international commerce, but instead is largely shaped by the globalization of the intra-company production process.
- Consequently this evolution determines the repositioning of the economic territories themselves in the worldwide setup of production; at the *industrial* level, the concepts of 'South' and 'North' are losing their meaning.

But to understand the current dynamics, it would be useful to review the origins of these groups. If they nowadays autonomize or try to autonomize their business model from the state and their country of origin, they have nonetheless all originated from very country-specific and state-created forms of political economy.

The existing literature has developed many analyses on the competitive advantages of emerging companies (for the last few years, mostly focusing on Chinese and Indian companies). It has in particular focused in the forms of joint ventures (JVs) and entry modes (Meyer *et al.* 2005), on the country assets and on the resilience of partnerships and funding of acquisitions (Deloitte *et al.* 2003), on learning strategies and vision (Bartlett and Goshal 2000), and sometimes on global institutional environment (Huang and Khanna 2003). However, unlike what was done by Hall and Soskice (2001) in the case of developed economies, seldom have the varieties of capitalism been studied for emerging economies. Indeed, very few studies have contemplated integrative explanations, sifting through all these explanatory lines, and, as a result, mainly case studies have been reported (Goldstein *et al.* 2006). Here we try to provide such an integrative framework of explanatory lines rooted in the trajectory of the political economy of a state to explain how different varieties of capitalism emerged.

After citing a few useful figures on the emergence of the MNCs 'of the South', the chapter goes on to show that even their present characteristics are the product of the industrial regulations and the 'national' trajectories of the last three decades. Thus, there is at once an 'emergent model' and a contribution 'to the varieties of capitalism'. The examples of India (Delios *et al.*, this book, Chapter 3) and China (Gugler and Boie, this book, Chapter 2) will be expanded to illustrate this point. However, the chapter then suggests that their multinationalization strategies and their business models increasingly converge (particularly those of the Indian, Chinese, Brazilian and Mexican companies) and reflect those of the 'historic' global companies. The fourth section reviews several examples, and considers the importance of entering the Asian economy as the privileged area of the world economy on the one hand and the entry into global chains of production on the other. Here we propose a stylization of evolutions informed by such 'model-making' examples as that of the Indian company, Tata. The chapter then explains in detail the *Mittal Steel* model. The case of Tata does not require a justification. *Mittal Steel* is a company governed by European laws. Nevertheless, we consider it to be one of the first purely global companies 'from the South' because it built itself from the emerging (and post-socialist) economies before multinationalizing itself completely. In a sense, it points towards the direction in which the 'converged' models, whose advent we predict, will go. We will conclude with a discussion of the contemporary upheavals prompted by the companies from the South, and the Asian companies in particular.

The emergence of multinational companies 'from the South': some facts

In 1990, 91.4 per cent of MNCs were from the developed countries (Japan and South Korea included). At the beginning of 2000, only 70.7 per cent of them were in this category. During the same period, the share of the MNCs from countries in transition grew, but only slightly, increasing from 2 to 3 per cent of the total number of companies. The major occurrence of the 1990s was thus the rapid development of the MNCs from the South. In ten years, the share of MNCs from emerging economies out of the total number of MNCs has increased fourfold, climbing from 6.6 to 26.3 per cent.[2] The progress in terms of total numbers is even more impressive, as, during this period, the total number of MNCs listed by the World Investment Report (WIR) had almost doubled. The number of MNCs from the South went up from nearly 2,800 to almost 18,000 companies.[3] This progress is largely explained by the emergence of Asian multinationals, which climbed from 5.8 to 21.2 per cent of the total MNCs. The 2000s have seen the deepening of internationalization at the company level and the acceleration of this phenomenon in numerical terms. The 2007 WIR mentions that:

> Large TNCs [transnational corporations] from emerging economies are internationalizing particularly fast. In 2005, the foreign sales and foreign employment of the top 100 TNCs from developing economies increased by 48% and 73% respectively. However, these TNCs are still significantly less transnational in their reach than the world's top 100, with a presence in fewer countries abroad.

> Asia dominates the list of the 100 largest developing-country TNCs, with 78 firms, followed by 11 each from Africa and Latin America. These TNCs operate in a broader range of industries than the largest TNCs from developed countries. As in previous years, the single most important industry in 2005 was electrical/electronic equipment, especially for a large number of companies from Asia.

We will see that this rise is in part linked to the emergence of the 'Asian System of Production' (assembly processes that spread across several Asian countries, notably China, led by Asian capital, but with a smaller amount of Chinese capital). This sees the Asian companies globalize their production process in many countries of the Asian continent, but this would not be able to overshadow the rise of Asian companies at the world level. The increase in the number of MNCs coming from Latin America, moving up from 1.6 to 4.2 per cent[4] of the total number of MNCs, confirms the emergence of companies from the large economies of the South. Chinese companies have seen almost a tripling of their share (from 1 to 2.8 per cent), and for Indian companies the progress has been fantastic, multiplying almost 70-fold: from 0.05 to 3.4 per cent. These latest figures themselves illustrate many points: on the one hand they underline that the potential of the Indian companies appears to be more than that of the Chinese companies and on the other hand they reveal the constraints that the Indian companies had to face until the reforms in 1991.

In short, these facts suggest that the dynamism of the companies can be distinct from that of the territories (Indian companies internationalize quickly unlike Chinese ones; in the meantime China has managed to secure a major part of the world market, but India has not[5]): micro and macro economies no longer follow the 'Rule of General Motors', which in reality was the Rule of Fordism.

But the phenomenon is widespread: according to the UNCTAD statistics, in 2005, the overseas turnover and workforce of the first 100 MNCs from developing countries increased from 48 to 73 per cent, respectively. Asia is the major player in this group, with 78 companies, followed by 11 companies from Africa and 11 from Latin America. Direct investments from the South and the mergers and acquisitions by the South correspond to these developments. Mergers and acquisitions (for developing countries and countries in transition) surged from US$10 billion per year in 1993 to US$90 billion in 2005, half of this coming from Asia. In terms of destination, from 2004 and 2005, half of the mergers and acquisitions (M&As) that were initiated by the South were 'South–South' M&As, the other half was dedicated to buying commercial and industrial assets in the OECD countries. Since then the share of the South–South investments has been increasing slowly but continuously. No continent has been left behind, and the FDIs in Africa have reached US$36 billion in 2006, twice that of the foreign investments (FIs) in 2004. This is obviously linked to the search for natural resources, but the 2007 WIR also mentions 'the improved profit prospects of the companies and (…) a more favourable economic climate'. In all, 'the foreign acquisitions in Africa were to the tune of US$18 billion, of which half were acquired by developing countries from Asia. The FIs coming from Africa also broke new growth records: US$8 billion in 2006, against US$2 billion in 2005…'.

But the South–South M&As are essentially intra-regional, and hence it is here that the multinationalization of emerging firms is taking place: during the period 2002–2004, intra-Asia deals accounted for US$ 47.8 billion (even though crossed FIs between India and China have not really taken off), intra- Latin America deals accounted for US$2.7 billion and intra-African deals for US$2.1 billion. Over the same period, the FIs for M&As from Latin America to Asia represented US$750 million, an inverse flow of 400 million, an Asia–Africa flow of 1.2 billion and an inverse flow of 700 million. So far, the flow between Latin America and Africa is negligible.[6] This primarily reflects the fact that the Asian economy is in the process of rapid integration: this integration was initiated in the 1970s by the Japanese investments directed towards the New Industrialized Economies (NIE, namely the Dragon countries: Hong Kong, Taiwan, Singapore and South Korea and then the Tiger countries: Malaysia, Thailand and Indonesia), followed by the FIs of the latter towards China in the 1990s and by the multinationalization of the Japanese companies.

The general data include both the small and large MNCs. It makes sense to deal with the large MNCs separately as they are precisely the ones that 'leave their geographical zones'. The most objective grading is based on turnover, but this is not always known. The UNCTAD monitors this for the 50 largest MNCs. The transnationality index[7] of the first 50 emerging MNCs joins with that of the first 100 MNCs with mixed backgrounds: from 20 as against 46 in 1993, to 47 against 55 in 2003 (UNCTAD). A recent Boston Consulting Group (BCG)[8] report focuses on companies from emerging economies (with rapid growth) and includes a few small companies whose business models show a particularly rapid growth. According to the criteria used by the BCG, amongst the first 100 MNCs 'from the fast growing economies' (this classification does not exclude the countries in transition), there are (public and private companies included) 44 Chinese, 21 Indian, 12 Brazilian, 7 Russian and 6 Mexican companies (plus 10 'others').

But the problem is that MNCs helped by their States and private companies or even companies exploring raw material and natural resources are not the same as industrial and commercial companies.

In reality, to better understand the current dynamics of this last category, one has to look at the business models of these firms at the microeconomic level. These models still carry imprints of the national trajectories of industrial regulation that are still inherent to the company structures.

Today's companies as products of the former national industrial regulations

Given the weight of China and India in the emergence of MNCs in the South, these countries are given more importance in the analysis. The higher collective dynamism of Indian companies was underlined earlier. Among the first 100 companies, the Chinese firms are in large numbers, but this largely concerns public companies and/or companies whose main activity is to search for raw materials. These are not representative of the dynamics of their counterparts in other sectors, and hide the fact that the private Chinese companies as of now lack the critical mass. Even if it is certainly not the only model, in numerous cases the development of Chinese MNEs is largely backed by the State. For these reasons, preference will be given here to discussion of the Indian trajectory, which is better able to explain the very capitalist dynamics associated with the emerging industrial firms.

India: numerous and powerful private conglomerate companies

India began to catch up economically from the 1980s with an average growth of 6 per cent and a current trend of 7 per cent as a base (with peaks at 9 per cent). This was firstly the result of a continuous public and private investment effort in terms of physical and human capital beginning at the time of independence in 1947. In the nineteenth century, the country had an industrial base and among others, the Tata group, the premier group in the country today, was born in this era. In 1947, 70 per cent of the nascent industry was the property of Indian entrepreneurs. As the leader of the country, Jawaharlal Nehru, supported by the 'Bombay Club', a network that brought together the important families of the business world, launched an economic plan with the double objective of modernizing the countryside and developing industry. The Indian way of planning essentially allocated resources to the sectors that were considered to be top priority, in short, it was a system of 'mixed socialism'. Certain sections of the industry were 'reserved' for the public sector, while an administrative authorization system for production[9] allowed private firms to operate in 'mixed' sectors within certain limits and with restrictions on product capacity. In each sector, the government first allocated a role to the private sector to promote its initial development. Then, past a threshold of production, the public sector would curb the development of the private sector so as to take over, but in general without privatizing the earlier existing capacities. This system worked until 1991. The strategy (typical of the 1950s and 1960s) was one of 'imports substitution', ensured by the combination of public industrial investment and private initial investment and tariff regulations.

This system gave birth to a capitalism of conglomerates: each time their expansion was blocked by the limits fixed for private investors in a given sector, the companies would get another one to invest, after having duly obtained the new 'licence'. A good number of today's industrial giants are still flagships of the 'Licence Raj'. Reliance Industries, the country's premier private group in terms of capitalization, is one of them: it amassed its fortune through import permits and permits to exclusively manufacture certain synthetic fibres; then it spread its activities based on the same principle to the fields of petrochemicals, energy, and more recently (in the liberalization era) oil exploration and high technology. The Indian socialist regulation had produced situations of private oligopoly that were to have a lasting effect. Indeed, 'Indian socialism' has never been very far from 'Indian capitalism', so much has the link between the State and the big private companies always been at the heart of the system. This situation remains the same today, dictating the pace of the adoption of liberal reforms.

In fact, during the phase in which the reforms took place, initially gradual in the 1980s and then becoming more widespread during the 1990s. From this economy managed by and within closely knit personal networks, the opening was virtually orchestrated, so as to leave time for the conglomerates to reorient themselves towards their main activities. Since 1984, the joint venture created in the automobile industry between Maruti India and Suzuki Japan, today the leading player in this rapidly growing market, has been symbolic of this new logic of import and transfer of selected technologies. For the State it meant identifying, along with the business world, the sectors in which fast modernization of an obsolete production apparatus would lead to the greatest results. Despite the withdrawal of the 'Monopolies and Restrictive Trade Practices Act' in 1991, 16 sectors, such as 'new' household goods, chemicals or the automobile industry, remained for some time under strict regulations and were only gradually 'de-licensed' (during this decade eight critical sectors remained under the exclusive control of the State; today two remain: the atomic sector and the railways). This historical perspective leads us not to overestimate the role of the service sector in Indian development: as important as they are, we should not focus so much on the software and biotechnology industries that we forget the diversity in the industrial infrastructure of the country, especially for exports.

It was within this relatively protected context, that Indian conglomerates, from the mid-1990s, accelerated the reorganization of their activities, in particular, by multiplying their strategic alliances with foreign companies. Their conglomerate form allowed them to extend to their other branches a technology or a know-how initially transferred to only one of them (as a form of spill-over effect), and this explains the very rapid restructuring of the Indian groups. But the explosion in the field of new technologies is without doubt the best example of the return to the world by Indian companies. In the 1990s, the Indian 'brains' who had migrated to the United States returned to India to create their own software companies (Infosys, Satyam), with contracts from their previous American employers in their pockets. At the same time, the big conglomerates developed software subsidiaries, such as Wipro and TCS (Tata group). As a result, since 1994, the growth of the information technology sector has been varying from 40 to 50 per cent per annum. Today it represents around 5 per cent of the GDP and more than a quarter of the exports. The Indian software companies began with less demanding subcontracting jobs, but the situation today is completely different: nowadays these companies offer world-class services and consulting. Some 'start-ups', right from their creation adopted a global strategy and 'global localization'. Already half of the world's companies that have been awarded the 'SEI-CMM5' certification – the highest quality norm for software – since 2001 are Indian (no French company received this certification in 2006). And some companies from the sub-continent are quasi-integrated with their American clients, whose software systems they develop, putting them at the very heart of the decision-making bodies of the whole organization.

India's numerous establishments abroad had multiplied by more than 40-fold over the span of 20 years, from 208 (in 1986) to 8620 (in 2006). From 1995 to 2006, the stock of the FIs had gone from US$212 million to US$8,181 million. The purchase of the British steel maker Corus by Tata in 2007 for a sum of US$11 billion, followed by the purchase of Jaguar and Rover by Tata Motors could mark the beginning of a new chapter for Indian FIs. Before 1990, Indian FIs (for the few private groups authorized to invest abroad) were mainly directed towards the manufacturing sector, energy and raw materials. Most of these FIs were made by big public companies. After 1991, a triple evolution took place: a massive increase in the sums invested, diversification of sectors, and the arrival of new players from the private sector who would quickly become the principal source of Indian FIs. But it is probably more appropriate to subdivide this period with a break around the years 2001–2002. Before this turning point, the major industrial groups in India spent a decade refocusing on their core businesses and rationalizing their most 'exotic' 'Licence Raj' activities.

With all the FI operations, the mergers and acquisitions have also increased. But, until 2006, they largely remained beneficial to the foreign companies: the exceptional deal by Tata Steel over Corus, followed by a much more modest but significant deal by Suzlon over Repower, however, definitely indicated a new phase in the making. In 2006, the value of overseas acquisitions reached a peak of US$30 billion which is much higher than the inflow of the FDI in India (US$5.5 billion, not counting the 'financial' inflows) for the same fiscal year (the net outflow would then represent around 3 per cent of the GDP).

Furthermore, Indian industrial groups are today devising new car models at a third of the cost of their development in Europe. In short, India has already become a platform for manufacturing and re-exportation on a global scale. The country is at the heart of the industrial strategy of the 'global production chain' of multinationals such Hyundai, Toyota, ABB, and Nokia. The importance of partnerships in the context of internationalization of conception and production has been perfectly understood by the Indian Government, which is multiplying its means of support, relying notably on research and higher education, by financing the creation of 'technological parks' and by maintaining a special link with the Confederation of Indian Industry, the federation of employers. Today the big Indian firms aim for a 'global' strategy and approach the international market directly, without necessarily trying to fit in with subcontracting or with a 'supply chain'. Since 2006, the motor and the motor parts and accessories industries are multiplying plants, subsidiaries, and greenfield investment abroad with Bajaj, Bharat Forge, Mahindra & Mahindra, Tata Motors, and TVS Motor Company. The engineering sector is not to be outdone thanks to Crompton Greaves and Larsen & Toubro. Many deals in the iron and steel industry have also been struck, in the sectors of energy and raw materials, for example, with Hindalco (non-ferrous metals), Tata Steel, the Reliance conglomerate (energy), and last but not least, the state sector with ONGC (oil and gas). The investments abroad in the oil and gas sectors accounted for 19 per cent of Indian FDIs in 2006.

China: the feeble power of the large private companies

As stated by Gugler and Boie in their chapter, the largest outward investments by Chinese MNEs are made by state-owned enterprises (SOEs), and all investment projects follow a scheme that ensures that they are strictly in line with government policies. The Chinese companies, by contrast, are the products of a much more troubled history. China's entry into 'European' modernity was much slower, even though the Chinese elite had spoken about it from the end of the nineteenth century. The civil war and the Japanese invasion did not make the creation of a modern State easy. It was only in 1949 with the arrival of the communists in Beijing that the creation of a State began on a firmer footing, but we cannot say the same about the industrialization of the country. The communists were suspicious of the industries in the north (Manchuria) developed by the occupying Japanese in the 1930s, as they challenged the entrepreneurs from Shanghai and the coastal province of Zhenjiang. The 'gentlemen's agreement' between the State and capital was broken in 1953 and these entrepreneurs disappeared. The Maoist regime first industrialized the centre of China (the city of Wuhan, capital of the province of Hubei) basing itself on the Soviet model, only to discard it again after the 'giant leap forward' of 1958 when it launched itself into the micro-industrialization of the countryside, which negated all the principles of layered output. The industrial production finally collapsed with the Cultural Revolution of 1966 to 1976. Even today China has to manage this double legacy (obsolescence and socialism in the north and in the centre of the country, and the ineffectiveness typical of the Maoist model of industry in the entire country). The key reforms consisted of developing an industry that later was gradually privatized by using the resources of the state sector. This 'growing out of Plan' of the 1980s decade, later giving birth to private industries; but these are rarely of a size to rival their Indian counterparts, in terms of either turnover or capitalization. The biggest Chinese companies are still public companies. In both Indian and Chinese cases, the modernization of company governance has not yet been achieved. Only a few Chinese private companies which have made a mark are well known: Lenovo which successively bought IBM's PC division, and Haier which bought

Thomson's electronics division dealing in products for mass consumption, only to face a setback in integrating Thomson's activities.

The figures for outgoing Chinese outward FIs indicate a new level in the internationalization of Chinese firms from 2001 onwards and a rapid acceleration since 2005 with US$12.3 billion, then US$21 billion in 2006.[10] The stock of Chinese FIs is admittedly modest, being worth US$78 billion, that is, only 0.6 per cent of the world total. But the Chinese authorities foresee a strong increase in the annual flow of FIs which could rapidly exceed US$30 billion. This explains the strong activity of Chinese trade diplomacy and the numerous Free Trade Agreements (FTAs) or bilateral investment treaties recently concluded. The 2005 Agreement on the Encouragement and Reciprocal Protection of Investments between China and Germany is a key example (Xiao, this book, Chapter). At the end of 2006, the Chinese Ministry of Commerce listed just over 5,000 Chinese companies which had made investments abroad with nearly 10,000 establishments in 172 countries.[11] Since 2005, telecommunications, software, mass consumption electronic goods and the motor vehicle sectors have been progressing very rapidly: they currently represent nearly 35 per cent of the total Chinese FIs. Three companies – Huaiwei, Haier and ZTE – are especially active in these sectors. Haier for example, created 13 production units, 8 design centres, 22 business offices and more than 46,000 stores in less than a decade.

To say a quick final word on the differences between Chinese and Indian firms, the legacy of the industrial regulations of the previous decades explains the very different role of the private sector as well as the organizational forms: small single-product Chinese firms (and a less advanced sectorial rationalization) versus conglomerates that are admittedly restructured on certain core businesses, but are capable of transferring technologies and know-how from one branch to another. These differences between China and India particularly influence the flexibility in the development of technological skills. For instance, in India, out of its focused, technology-driven JVs, Mahindra was able to integrate organizational learning into its other branches and later develop its proprietary car models. Whereas in China, car companies multiplied the JVs for public agenda reasons (mostly, employment). Our field interviews show that, in this context of multi-partners and mandatory JVs, foreign partners trusted their local partner less; they equally show that many state car makers ultimately have become 'holdings' more than holders of technological skills. Finally, the governance of the Indian companies makes them completely independent of the State in their decisions regarding investments abroad, which is far from being the case of even the 'most private' Chinese companies.

Integration of companies in the Asian or the global economy? Converging trajectories towards a new model of capitalism and the case of Tata

On this basis, and from the 1990s onwards, the industrial evolution of emerging companies integrated itself more and more with the evolutions of the Asian industry first and then with the industry of the world as a whole.

The development of the Chinese economic territory in international commerce after 1993 was judged to be very high. A finer analysis, however, shows that on the whole Asia's place stabilized during the same period, 1993–2003. The place won by China (+3.9 per cent) and the Tiger countries (+0.7 per cent) in international exports was the one lost by Japan (which fell from 12.5 per cent to 7.5 per cent of international exports of manufactured goods between 1993 and 2003). In reality a large part of this commerce is intra-Asian commerce: Asia-Oceania is responsible for 32 per cent of world exports, of which 16 per cent is for its own consumption, 8 per cent is bound for Europe and another 8 per cent for America. The evolution noted from 1993 to 2003 thus represents in a large part a relocalization of Japanese companies and the companies from the Dragon countries towards China and the Tiger countries (the Asian commercial surplus follows exactly the same movement). This becomes clear when we note that 41 per cent of manufactured Chinese imports and 55 per cent of its manufactured exports are industrial assembling goods. China did not specialize in sectors so to speak, but in the function of industrial assembling. This function is largely carried out by the non-Chinese companies, mostly Asian companies, which have become multinational as a result: for example, if we observe the share of the technological components in the import of goods that are intended for assembly, 71 per cent come from Asia. If we break up these 71 per cent by studying the capital of the companies involved in the assembly procedure, only 17 per cent are controlled by Chinese companies, 15 by joint ventures and the remaining 39 are controlled by foreign companies.[12] The same is true for investments driven by R&D in China, for which the foreign multinational companies adjust their choices of sectors. In fact R&D investments in China by the first 1,000 MNCs tend firstly towards software (23 per cent), followed by telecommunications (18 per cent), semi-conductors (13 per cent), and cars (7 per cent),[13] all sectors in which no particular Chinese company is the leader. The Chinese are penetrating the world economy via an assembly activity which by its very structure favours multinationalization of the Asian companies. But on the whole Chinese companies do not control either the choice of sectors, or the capital or the orientation of the R&D in these procedures.

The trajectory of the Indian firms is completely different. India as a territory is less concerned with exchanges; the share of technological exports in manufactured Indian exports is only 5 per cent (as against 23 per cent for China); nevertheless the procedures of technological insertions are not only controlled by Indian companies (control of capital for assembly of technological contents), but the big private Indian companies have shown themselves to be quick in technological upgrading and multinationalization. In fact, from the middle of the 1990s, Indian conglomerates accelerated the reorganization of their activities, notably by multiplying their strategic alliances with foreign companies. The story of the automobile maker Mahindra will illustrate this: the firm first concluded a technological partnership with Ford, but did not hesitate to pull out some years later to launch its own model, and then finally concluded a new deal with Renault-Nissan. Having reinforced its position in the meantime, Mahindra was able to obtain better conditions in the technological partnership. Like Mahindra, the other Indian industrial groups thus fit into the world economy with a give and take strategy: to their partners they offer a point of entry into emerging but complex markets, in exchange for which they acquire the skills of the new industrial processes, are associated with R&D and gain increasingly in terms of technological range. Groups like Tata and Reliance carry out both these strategies, and are not indifferent to the explosion of software technologies in the Indian sector. Tata, the largest Indian group in terms of market capitalization, signed an international commercial alliance with Fiat in 2005 and is already exporting its models to the United Kingdom, and the software subsidiary of Tata already represents 50 per cent of the group's capitalization. At a time when General Motors, Ford and others are having to engage in some serious restructuring, Tata is developing car models for a third of the cost of their development in the West, and its software at a tenth of its cost.

In this context, the Indian groups are turning global by the minute: they are creating subsidiaries in Shanghai, London and New York just as they are doing in Africa (US$325 million worth of investments by Tata over the next five years); they are investing in the emerging countries such as Mexico, Brazil and South Africa; they are delocalizing part of the software industry to Southeast Asia or China. In the field of technology, they are moving up through acquisitions: 80 per cent of Indian investments for mergers and acquisitions in the USA are oriented towards information technology, and Indian purchases in Europe are targeted at information technology, pharmaceuticals, electronics and computers, and high-end chemicals: in 2004, Reliance bought a subsidiary of Dupont in Nemours, Germany. Clearly with its 24 per cent annual growth for the past 30 years, Reliance has the means to support its ambitions.

In reality, an accelerated dynamism of capitalism is taking place: the big groups from the emerging countries are going beyond a simple costs strategy. They are concentrating and structuring the increasing technological capacity present in the emerging economies (whose extent was predicted by Pierre-Noël Giraud[14]); very early technological upgrading is linked to industrial strategies which are today acquiring precise forms.

The recent developments certainly correspond to a search for strategic assets: technology, market shares in the developed economies, brands and new domains in the field of R&D. Indian firms are seeking to exceed their advantage in terms of initial costs in the domestic market by going up the value-added chain. It is thus interesting to note that in 2004 for example, the sectors in which Indian companies concentrated their FIs in the USA were the sectors of information technology (80 per cent), chemicals (7 per cent) and pharmaceuticals (7 per cent). Only 19 per cent of the FIs in the European Union targeted the IT sector, whereas 17 per cent were invested in pharmaceuticals, 10 per cent in electronics, 9 per cent in transport, 7 per cent in chemicals, 6 per cent in metal products, and the remaining 32 per cent in very diverse sectors.[15] These figures demonstrate quite well the industrial specializations of the economies concerned as well as a knowledge of and sectoral interactions between Indian industry and the European Union.

One major reason why FDI is sought by Indian trade diplomats, is that FDI generally brings with it the much needed state-of-the-art technology that developing countries lack (Chaisse *et al.*, this book, Chapter 10). The redefining of destinations for Indian FIs thus corresponds in large measure to the search for new technological competences and brands, leading to a natural increase in the power of the developed economies from within. But there is also a natural geographical evolution arising out of the necessity to come closer to the clients, in the sector of software outsourcing for example. It is for this reason that Indian companies are investing in Eastern Europe or in the Maghreb, to capture the Western European markets, or even in Mexico, so that they can penetrate the American market. By doing so, Indian firms are anticipating a major industrial revolution with the digitization of a part of the industrial design and conception. In May 2007, Tata Consultancy Services announced the opening of an office in Guadalajara. Tata already has 5,000 employees on its pay roll in Brazil, Chile and in Uruguay. Similarly, Wipro has established a presence in Saudi Arabia, Canada, China, Portugal and Romania, to name but a few. Cognizant Technology Solutions is present in Shanghai and in Phoenix, AZ (USA). At the same time, Indian companies in the information sector are looking to profit from their advantage in terms of costs by becoming dominant in the nascent outsourcing industry in the developing countries: that, for example, is the case of Infosys which recently purchased back-offices in Thailand and Poland.

Towards a 'model'?

Let us now study a 'cycle' that an increasing number of emerging companies are following. They operate in the markets where not only is the growth rate very high but also very consistent, leading to a tight flow of investments, without any delays between profits and reinvestments. This ensures a strong cash flow and very weak debt rates (this is the case of all those countries which were socialist until recently; India is a case in point, not all of China is yet in this position, but the argument remains true for its most dynamic companies), and thus an increase in reinvestment capacities. Over a period of time, it allows diversification of its investment model.

Our recent studies[16] show that numerous large groups from the emerging countries have been targeting the following objective 'type' for some years: 50 per cent of investments in the country of origin to continue 'to prime the pump'; 25 per cent in other emerging countries (the so-called 'BRIC' countries, Brazil, Russia, India and China, but also Mexico, Arab countries, African countries with oil, or mines for China,[17] or, for Indian companies, stable African countries in general; markets where the comparative advantage is not just the cost but the capacity to make 'adapted industrial design' and sizes adapted to small countries (cost advantage on conception and on incremental innovation, hence an economy that is already perfectly modern).

Finally, the last 25 per cent broadly serve to upgrade technology: either by traditional joint ventures with further transfer of procedure to other activities outside the initial purview of the joint venture, or through the purchase of patents or R&D. This can be, as one has seen, hostile or it can also be 'amicable', such as the case of the subsidiary of Dupont that was bought by Reliance in 2004 or Ranbaxy that took over the 'generic' subsidiary of Aventis. In fact, the strategic partnerships between emerging and global firms are multiplying. In effect, the latter use China, but also India and other emerging countries, as 'platforms for re-exports', which their 'local' partners make money thanks to the access they gain to the world market. In short, the players of the emerging countries are already partners in global firms, friendly one day, hostile the next. There is thus no room for 'Western' companies to become worried about the situation, rather they need to analyse it. Certain 'western' companies are in fact rushing their best managers to these countries to keep a watch on the strategic purchases of promising emerging companies … now is the right time.

In short, the size of the market, the inherent speed of the processes of 'economic upgrading' (we must remember South Korea, Japan, Germany at the end of the nineteenth century and France under the second empire 'catching up' with England), the short cycles of financing, establishment of communication between all the economic territories that would allow for a quick recombination of the procedures of intra-company production, are among the reasons why the accumulation of capital in emerging countries is today very speedy in certain sectors, including those with a strong 'technological' content. But there is an 'obligation to invest' which is today possible in an open world economy.

There is a difference between the initial growth of the first Asian country to upgrade, Japan, which established itself largely due to its solid internal market and technological upgrading before entering the export markets, and the Chinese and Indian strategies, which combine traditional upgrading and globalization of companies. It is this specific series of elements that justify the claim that the Indian and Chinese multinational companies should, with no difficulty, become profitable in the world market in the years to come. These countries will accumulate commercial excesses which they can over a period of time only invest in 'western' assets, and their companies will be 'condemned' to invest in the 'western' world, starting with repurchasing. These models are applicable to big emerging companies such as Cemex (Mexican cements), Petrobas (Brazilian petrol) and companies such as Arcor, Sabo and Acer or Haier or Lenovo. But as far as number of companies are concerned the Indians already seem to dominate. In certain sectors for equipment, such as steel, where the increase in growth is concentrated in Asia, the companies occupying the third to the sixth positions in the world are Asian: Japanese, Korean and Chinese; all have already internationalized themselves.[18] If this model has some foundation, then the truly global companies having a business model centred on the emerging countries will be successful. We think that *Mittal Steel*, whose 'nationality' has been a contentious issue, is one of these, and possibly the first among them.

Mittal Steel: the development of a purely global company with its origin in the south towards a 'model of convergence'?

If Mittal chose a model a little different from the stylized model presented above, the fundamentals are the same: presence in the emerging market with adapted products, a large cash flow that finances the expansion, R&D, the integration of information systems developed in India itself, and over a given period, industrial positioning over the OECD markets. Mittal represents a typical case study. It was already number one in the world steel market. Its takeover bid for Arcelor – the European giant and then number two in the world, heir to two centuries of industrial entrepreneurship – was only a last act in this model, a model of which this company has already become an exemplary symbol. Launched in February and won in June 2006, it was a standard takeover bid in which the industrial model judged as the most efficient by the markets won within a few months. It was an oligopolistic consolidation – an age-old capitalist market – with the only difference being that it operates at the international level today (and, furthermore, the new group constitutes only 12 per cent of the international market). But the new group's portfolio combines the effects of the 'old economy' with the production–research synergy of the 'new economy' within the elite of the world's economic and financial networks – after all *Mittal Steel* is listed on the stock exchange in the Netherlands, the country which invented modern finance in the eighteenth century and in New York, the city which internationalized finance and the old European 'world-economy'. Truly a case study for internationalization.

But the novelty is linked to the national origin of this group. Not to the fact that Mr Mittal is himself an Indian: after western employees had to adapt themselves for decade to allow them to become competitive, the times of the industrial hierarchy have arrived. *Mittal Steel* groups together its skills and key strengths with international financing and contemporary industrialization. The company has financial networks, especially with the Indian bank ICICI, who sits on *Mittal Steel's* non-executive board. Mr Mittal is also a member of ICICI's Board of Directors. Mittal's board also includes people who command networks into key emerging countries or into those who have already begun economic upgrading (India, Mexico, Brazil, Korea and Japan), but also the United States, Mauritius and its financial sector, and finally all the oldest of the large banks, Rothschild for example. The Board and the Management are perfectly internationalized, while at the same time being discreetly centred on India and its diaspora, as the compositions of the 'corporate directors' and the 'regional CEOs' would prove. Much more structured, the Mittal group created itself on the return investments between emerging and post-socialist countries. The industrial history of *Mittal Steel* marks its accession to the top place in the world within 30 years, or rather 14 if we consider that the purchase of a post-soviet-era complex in Kazakhstan in 1992 to sustain the Chinese market was the act that 'triggered' all that followed. Initially the adventure had begun in Indonesia, a country that was just emerging in 1976, accelerated by the recapitalization of the complexes of the old communist bloc (in short, partners with 'intermediate' level firms). Including Eastern Europe, the group conducted, before the merger, 43 per cent of its activities in Europe, as against 29 per cent in America and 28 per cent in the rest of the 'emerging' world. In 1992, Mr Mittal agreed to take the factory plus the mine, plus all the 'social' obligations of the previous complex in Kazakhstan, and to recapitalize the whole to modernize it. He reduced the cost through investment, did not lower the salaries, nor did he lay off the staff. He did what very few post-soviet groups could do, and achieved the task that many of the Chinese complexes had faced: that of repairing and utilizing the production capacities which the previous 'socialist' clients had avoided but for which new openings had to be found in an innovative manner, that is the Chinese market which was all ready to take-off. The assets were not expensive but the goods did not have any value either, with the exception of knowing how to enhance their value: the western steelmakers were not interested in them. The expansion over the past 30 years in Indonesia, then in Mexico, was followed by the more 'technological' purchases in North America. *Mittal Steel* is thus very representative of the large groups from the emerging countries and hence a harbinger of their development. At the same time *Mittal Steel* is also the representative of some 'oligarch' groups from the East. Here is definitely a 'model'.

Although it had a comparable production capacity, Mittal was making very high profits, double those of its rival Arcelor, by relying on the cost structures of its core activity and its principal markets: in Asia in particular and the emerging countries in general, we find the regularity and the rise in demand, and also the short cycles ('on-time' production and optimized capacity) for this central commodity led to economic upgrading. Thus a country where financial capacities for industrial expansion are to be found. And Mittal did not lose the opportunity of using its benefits for its development in the USA for example, or trying the operation in Canada yesterday, or in continental Europe today. Mittal's case, although exemplary, is not isolated. Cemex, the Mexican cement company has followed the same path. Even in the steel sector, 2006 also saw the friendly takeover bid by Tata Steel for the Anglo-Dutch group Corus. The industrial concentrations are far from being over in this sector where China represents 25 per cent of the production and where the rise of Indian demand is yet to be seen.

Towards a mixed 'developed–emerging' model of capitalism?

The phenomenon of international acquisitions by Indian firms is part of the larger phenomenon of the increasing globalization of the economy in India, in which outward foreign direct investment is playing an increasingly prominent role (Delios *et al.*, this book, Chapter). The motivations of Chinese firms to internationalize and the government interest in FDI are to large extent aligned and institutionally intertwined (Gugler and Boie, this book, Chapter). This is what characterizes the Chinese strategy and makes it distinctive. For global companies, many lessons have already been learnt, and we are, in all likelihood moving towards a mixed business model. This is a 'developed–emerging' capitalist model that has yet to stabilize but from which we should learn, right from this stage, three lessons.

The first lesson is that for industry accumulation of capital is far faster today in the emerging markets. Given that investments that were themselves pushed up by growing demand (and its anticipation) were going to result in an increase in capital, it was to be expected that strong (and regular) growth would finally pay off. There is evidence to support this assertion, but European industry very often remains torn between its necessary expansion to 'emerging' economies (especially in Asia) and the financial constraints linked to a race for technological modernization. It is not only necessary to do both, and the main lesson learnt from the '*affaire* Mittal' or from the observations of groups such as Tata and Reliance is that over a certain period of time it will be the growth in the emerging countries that will finance the R&D and hence the capitalization 'from above' for companies from developed countries. From this perspective, these markets will no longer be seen as marginal, and the epithet 'strategic' will no longer be synonymous with mimetic as has been the case for quite some time. As far as the standard directions are concerned, market expansion should not be consigned to the future in the context of the financial constraints, but should be a priority as it is a source of cash flow. The model is simple: the volume effect is present in Indonesia, China, Brazil, Mexico, South Africa and India and will very soon be seen in Central Asia. The old Soviet bloc countries that are taking off once again should also be mentioned here. On the technological front, the most advanced companies of these countries (or the global firms operating in these countries, such as Mittal) are not to be outdone: the economy of development tells us that when a critical mass is exceeded (roughly, when the human capital is united), the last to arrive has an advantage of quick access and low-price technologies that permit industrialization and accumulation of physical capital.[19] Taking into account the increase in technological competition in the developed economies, the techniques absorbed in the developed countries (which are in general the first to be transferred) are no longer techniques that are 'approching their end' as was the case of the old 'transfer of technology' towards the 'developing' countries with very limited human resources. The current techniques in the emerging countries conserve an industrial topicality and were certainly leading-edge technologies only yesterday. In some typical industrial sectors, barely a few years separate the technological levels of the companies of developed countries and those from the emerging countries. This image is most in contrast for sectors that have 'complex' industrial products (automobile, aeronautical propulsion, nuclear), but the industrialists in these markets know that outsourcing and co-conception have to be increasingly included in the industrial process in the emerging countries, without even having to mention the aggressive presence on these markets and the integration into the production chain or even the production for re-exports. All of them appear on the horizon. The first lesson can be summarized thus: in the world economy where the production process of the big firms is globalized, the emerging economies are stakeholders on many levels of production and its financing; the emerging companies are already positioned on these activities.

The second lesson is that western firms must accelerate their synergies with the emerging markets, as opposed to the scenario in which the companies from the emerging economies find themselves in the midst of cost competition between large volumes and technological advances. The meeting point of the developed and emerging firms will admittedly include competition, but also collaboration. In effect, the large emerging companies are already anticipating – in a very strategic manner – the limits of a cost competition whose generalization is already expected all over the South. These companies have surpassed the template, they are transforming their cost advantage by investing in technological upgrading, primarily through royalties (to develop the processes), and also through purchase or even development of patents. They are also making strategic acquisitions of technological firms, implementing indigenous R&D programmes and establishing themselves in the developed countries (to name a few examples, such companies include Lenovo, Bharat Forge, Tata, and Reliance). In this race, Indian firms undoubtedly have the advantage of their large size compared to that of their private Chinese counterparts, and an uninterrupted history of capitalism. Finally even in high-end technology, we have seen that competitive pressure between the USA and Europe is pushing transfers in the fields of nuclear technology and avionics, among others. A true upgrading will thus be the one that is financed by abundant capital and R&D which is inexpensive. The logic that demands that all truly global firms should have one 'developed' and one 'emerging' foot and should utilize these two types of territories not only as markets but also in an equal manner as a base for complete capitalist growth (a portfolio of clients but also adaptive technology and procedures) is a symmetrical logic: emerging companies will invest in the developed countries and vice versa. Of course, this reasoning becomes more refined in terms of the specificities of each sector, but in this general form it is relevant to most sectors: steel and capital goods manufacture, but also the motor industry, banks and to some extent the high-tech sector.

The third lesson is the emergence of a new question: will there be a convergence towards a North–South capitalism? This question is normally dealt with in terms of norms and governance – let us briefly consider the industrial determinants. To this day, companies from the 'advanced' economies retain a technological advantage and brand assets, but models are expected to converge because of the dissemination of R&D and future attempts to compel these markets to acquire brand assets: China will move in this direction, to be followed one day by India in the field of IT. Two certitudes are vital: access to emerging markets and to their weak unitary margins demands specific competences, especially when the competition with the other companies from developed countries is very strong. In effect, after decades of high-level competition, western markets have lost their know-how in markets with low-margin units. They will have to relearn the necessary skills. On the other hand 'in emerging situations' they need to innovate in terms of production procedure: adapt the assembly lines to a more intensive context in terms of labour and the transition demand (splitting up the demand, and a need for a wide range with price control). From this point of view, the experience gained in an emerging country improves competence or the knowledge portfolio, but necessitates an investment. This process takes time and during this period there is the risk of the competition contacting the local partners. The dynamics of upgrading thus prompts associations, joint ventures and other partnerships. It is the margin that will make the difference: capacity to create priviledged relationships with industrial districts and poles of competences, and keeping a watch on strategic purchases by emerging companies which are growing. Here too, some companies from the 'South' are learning fast.

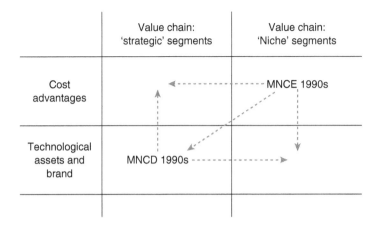

Figure 4.1 Dynamics of convergence: trajectories of firms and generalized competition

Note: MNCD and MNCE respectively signify 'multinational companies from developed countries' and 'multinational companies from emerging countries'.

This environment of competition/partnership can be summarized as in Figure 4.1, which attempts to give a broad outline of the 'trajectories' (shown as arrows, which represent temporal migrations, migrations in terms of business models, and 'movement of acquisition of complementary assets') of companies since the 1990s.

In the 1990s, the representation in terms of insertion in the world economy was that the MNCDs (MNCs originating from developed economies) mastered the value chain through their position in the strategic segment and the MNCEs (MNCs originating from emerging economies) entered (at best) in the 'niche' segments and often in the non-strategic segments where their advantage was that of a low-cost production structure. Since then migrations have been taking place. The MNCDs have worked on devocalizations, a productive redeployment, initially operated in the so-called non-strategic sectors. Today this is happening more and more in areas with a strong technological content or even with high-end technology, in the fields of innovation and design among others. To accelerate this movement, it has become necessary to look beyond joint ventures designed to facilitate administrative reach and to consider them from a strategic angle, even looking towards acquisitions and alliances. Moreover, today the MNCDs can afford even less to neglect the dynamic importance of certain 'niche' companies, destined to become the new business models.

In contrast, the MNCEs have developed three types of strategies to climb the value chain (sometimes called the 'change of value chain'). The first was to climb the value chain within a strategy of extension of capacities at low cost, quickly completed by a second one: technological development (and brands) of the niche companies. The third one is the combination of both, in a conducive financial context, and today allows the MNCEs to envisage a quick strategy of 'direct' technological acquisition (or even an indigenous development). It is this strategy that groups such as Geely and Chery have had difficulty in mastering but that groups like Huawei and Tata and even Mahindra and Mahindra have successfully adopted.

It is too early to talk about the nature or the scale of the 'convergence' to come. But what is certain is that in terms of multinational industrial companies, the concept of 'North' and 'South' will continue to lose its meaning.

Conclusion

The examples, stylizations and models we have surveyed suggest that in many ways emerging markets and their companies are changing global business models. One can summarize the dynamics at work through the fact that whatever their origin, and whether they operate by means of investments, acquisitions or partnerships, companies must combine assets and resources from emerging economies and from developed economies:

- Companies within developed economies must have a presence in emerging economies. This means more than learning about the countries, it is a matter of learning their own lines of business again from scratch.
- Companies in emerging countries need to capitalize on their assets quickly in order to climb the value chain, continue their technological development, and internationalize.

What this chapter tends to suggest is that, more than a convergence, this shift is already creating new opportunities for numerous companies. Original business models are being devised everywhere. These include accelerated technological development, rapid capitalization by means of diversifying client portfolios, through inter-sector technological synergies, the reorganization of production, design and distribution, the re-integration of specific human resources, mineral or energy resources, new financing models and so on.

Some business models are already changing several sectors and lines of business drastically: examples include the technological rise of suppliers from emerging economies in the automotive and aeronautical industries which in turn contribute to the rise of assembly companies from these economies; another example is the strategic rise of suppliers into innovation chains (facilitated by the computerization of innovation) or the industrial diversification into classical and renewable energy businesses (especially from Indian and Brazilian companies), not to mention vertical integration strategies (in the fields of raw materials and energy resources) or portfolio diversification (most notably among Chinese and Indian companies).

The research question as well as the strategic business issue in the coming years will be to see whether (or rather, how fast) some of them will migrate from one sector to the next, spread from one economy to the next and alter power ratios. Identification of innovative models constitutes a strategic pre-competitive advantage. In the face of this generalized re-invention, simply monitoring the traditional sector of each company is no longer enough and these innovations need to be identified wherever they emerge.

A forward-thinking look at the new emerging business models, sustained by a practical analysis of the convergence of emerging and developed assets, is a growing need.

Notes

1 UNCTAD, *World Investment Report 2004*, table I.1 and WIR 2005, table I.1. The statistics for capitalization are not available, given that many emerging MNCs were either public or private and family controlled or private but not listed on the stock market.

2 From 37,530 in 1990 to 69,727 in 2000, and 78,000 in 2007 for 780,000 subsidiaries (*World Investment Report 2007*).

3 Calculations by the author based on the World Investment Report data.

4 And hence multiplied by 4.9 in terms of the number of companies.

5 During the same ten-year period from 1993 to 2003, China's world exports of manufactured goods grew from 3.8 to 7.7 per cent and it imports from 3 to 5.2 per cent. Over the same period, India increased its exports marginally, moving from 0.7 to 0.8 per cent of manufactured products. We know that India as an economic territory has specialized in services, but the rise in power of its multinational firms has also extended to manufactured products. As for China, its international specialization is huge in terms of macro-economy but it has seen a limited international growth of companies. Meanwhile for India, a real dynamism of its companies abroad has transformed into a training effect in terms of international specialization.

6 Even though Brazilian firms have begun to export heavily to certain western African countries, especially in the agro-food industry (Source: personal discussions, Seventeenth International Fair, Dakar, December 2006).

7 Number of countries in which the MNCs have a permanent presence: at least one permanent sales office or a production or development site.

8 'The new global challenges: How 100 top companies from rapidly developing economies are changing the world', Boston Consulting Group, 32pp, May 2006.

9 The 'Licence Raj' or the 'Rule of Licences' in a reference to the 'British Raj', the colonial power.

10 Ministry of Commerce of The People's Democratic Republic of China.

11 *China Daily*, 17 September 2007.

12 Lemoine, F. (2006), China and India – Trade Specialisation and Technological Catch-up, in: Huchet, J.F. and Ruet, J. (Eds), *Globalisation and Opening Markets in Developing Countries and Impact on National Firms and Public Governance: The Case of India*, CSH-LSE-NCAER-ORF-CERNA report.

13 Source: *Business Week*, 22 August 2005.

14 Giraud, P.N. (1996), *L'inégalité du Monde* [*The Inequality of the World*], Paris: Gallimard, Folio Actuel.

15 Milleli, C. (2007), International expansion by Indian firms: What of European market entry?, in *The Indian Economy in the Era Of Globalisation*, Geneva, Center for Asian Studies, CAS Occasional Papers no. 26.

16 Huchet, J.F. and Ruet, J. (eds) (2006) Globalisation and Opening Markets in Developing Countries and Impact on National Firms and Public Governance: The Case of India, CSH-LSE-NCAER-ORF-CERNA report.

17 For reasons mentioned above, here we prefer to talk about China for operations concerning diversification of resource supplies, but refer to Indian companies for market-oriented commercial and industrial strategies.

18 To characterize the business models of the 100 largest emerging MNCs, the BCG, proposes the typology defining the six following models: 1. Internationalization of the emerging brands. 2. Global innovation with engineering component. 3. Establishing world leadership in a sector. 4. Monetarization of natural resources. 5. Expansion of new business models in multiple markets. 6. Acquisition of natural resources. While

the fourth and the sixth models might be beyond the scope of our analysis, we think that the other four do not describe in a systemic manner the actual dynamics. For BCG, 'expansion of business models' means the FIs coming from the South but without clearly mentioning their industrial articulation in terms of the markets (models 1 and/or 3), nor the technological upgrading (model 2). Generally, and even though they know that these models are interpenetrative, there is an absence of any link between the basic elements which help the emergence and the elements of the models which take them to the highest added value or towards more strategic elements. If our stylization is more heuristic and stylized, it has its balancing merits. On the other hand, given that for the MNCs with industrial characteristics adopted according to it models 1 to 3, the BCG classifies almost 75 per cent of the MNCS studied as having 'dominant' strategies of organic development – the BCG does not distinguish the organic development according to the origin of the market, the other emerging or developed markets – and for about 20 per cent as having 'dominant' rise by mergers and acquisitions or partnerships.

19 Thesis of advantage 'to those who became industrialised late' by Alice Amsden in the case of South Korea. See Amsden, A. (1989), *Asia's Next Giant: South Korea and late industrialization*, New York: Oxford University Press.

References

Amsden, A. (1989), *Asia's Next Giant: South Korea and late industrialization*, New York: Oxford University Press.

Bartlett, C.A and Goshal, S. (2000), Going global: Lessons from late movers, *Harvard Business Review*, Mar–Apr, pp. 132–142.

Deloitte, ISB, NSF, NYU Stern, Krannert School of Management (2007), Globalizing Indian Manufacturing: Competing in Global Manufacturing and Service Networks, Report on the Summit on Indian Manufacturing Competitiveness.

Giraud, P.N., (1996), *L'inégalité du Monde (The Inequality of the World)*, Paris: Gallimard, Folio Actuel.

Goldstein, A., Bonaglia, F. and Mathews, J. (2007), Accelerated internationalization by emerging multinationals: The case of the white goods sector, *Journal of World Business*, 42 (4), pp. 369–386.

Hall, P.A. and Soskice, D. (Eds) (2001), *Varieties of Capitalism: The institutional foundations of comparative advantage*, New York: Oxford University Press.

Huang, Y. and Khanna, T. (2003), Can India overtake China? *Foreign Policy*, Jul./Aug., pp. 76–81.

Huchet, J.F. and Ruet, J. (Eds), *Globalisation and Opening Markets in Developing Countries and Impact on National Firms and Public Governance: The case of India*, CSH-LSE-NCAER-ORF-CERNA report, New Delhi 407.

Lemoine, F., (2006), China and India – trade specialisation and technological catch-up, in: Huchet, J.F. and Ruet, J. (Eds), *Globalisation and Opening Markets in Developing Countries and Impact on National Firms and Public Governance: The case of India*, CSH-LSE-NCAER-ORF-CERNA report.

Meyer, K., Estrin, S. and Bhaumik, S. (2005), Institutions and Business Strategies in Emerging Economies: A Study of Entry Mode Choice, working paper.

Milleli, C. (2007) International expansion by Indian firms: What of European market entry?, in: *The Indian Economy in the Era Of Globalisation*, Geneva, Center for Asian Studies. CAS Occasional Papers no. 26.

UNCTAD (2005) *World Investment Report 2004*, New York and Geneva: United Nations.

Part II

Regional and national initiatives affecting trade and investment in Asia

5 Towards China's greater influence on the world's finances

A legal analysis of Chinese overseas direct investment

Jianqiang Nie

Introduction

Since 1978, the Chinese Government has been implementing its opening-up policies. The Chinese economy has been developing rapidly and is becoming an integral part of the global economy. Between 1978 and 2006, China has attracted a total of US$700 billion of foreign direct investment (FDI), ranking first for 16 consecutive years among developing countries as a destination for FDI. The wise and active utilization of foreign investment has contributed to China's economic development and has played an important role in shaping and improving the Chinese socialist market economy.[1]

China's opening-up policy includes 'inviting in' and 'going global', two interrelated strategies: the Chinese Communist Party (CCP) officially put forward the strategy at its Sixteenth National Congress of the CCP on 8 November 2002. While it is very important to attract further foreign investment, the Chinese Government is also encouraging competent Chinese enterprises to invest abroad. By the end of 2006, nearly 8,000 enterprises had been established by Chinese investors in some 160 countries and regions with direct investment amounting to more than US$73 billion (non-finance part). The sectors covered by Chinese overseas investment have been expanded from the business of import and export, shipping and catering to include manufacturing, agricultural cooperation, resource development, project contracting, research and development (R&D) and others. The forms of investment have also diversified from the simple business establishment to cross-border mergers and acquisitions, equity swaps, overseas listing, R&D centres and industrial parks.

China's 'going global' strategy has strengthened interrelations between China and the rest of the world. Foreign investment by Chinese businesses is increasing rapidly for two reasons. First, China's high rates of economic growth are promoting investment abroad. Second, the Chinese Government is encouraging and supporting foreign investment by businesses for the purposes of avoiding economic friction, acquiring resources, and cultivating global enterprises. Furthermore, at the individual business level, factors such as global management as part of survival and development strategies, as well as plans for acquiring overseas markets and technology, are also actively spurring on investment abroad. China's economy is increasingly integrated into the global economy. This indicates that China has evolved from a country attracting large amounts of foreign investment to one that is fast becoming a major overseas investment power (see Gugler and Boie, this book Chapter 2).

As explained by Joel Ruet (in Chapter 4 of this book), the governance of Indian companies makes them completely independent of the State in their decisions regarding investments abroad. This is far from being the case for even the 'most private' Chinese companies whose decisions to invest abroad are always backed by public authority. According to Chinese Government statistics, state-owned enterprises (SOEs) are the key drivers of China's industrial economy, accounting for almost half of industrial production and more than two-thirds of fixed assets. This is true of all provinces, even in the entrepreneurial south, where, for example, SOEs account for 35 per cent of Guangdong's industrial output. In addition, SOEs provide essential raw materials and dominate such capital-intensive sectors as power, steel, chemicals, and machinery (Gugler and Boie, this book, Chapter 2). Of the Chinese companies engaged in investment abroad, major SOEs are being watched particularly closely.

This chapter will discuss Chinese overseas direct investments (ODI) from the perspective of law. China's influence on the world's finances has generally received less attention than its influence on world trade, simply because Chinese overseas investment behaviour has generally not had any dramatic side-effects on the rest of the world. In future, Chinese economic development and the augmentation of corporate capability will lead to further expansion of foreign investment by Chinese enterprises abroad. This chapter is intended to help readers to better understand the present state of Chinese investment abroad and to anticipate the future trends of these investments. We will explore first the tools used by the Chinese Government to promote investment abroad. Then we will look at the review process used by the national authorities, as well as the rules applied to foreign exchange. To complete the analysis, the financial support of the Government will be discussed as well as the investment insurance syatem, which is of great importance when investors decide to orient strategies in foreign countries.

The promotion of Chinese overseas investment

Since the Chinese Government adopted the policy of implementing a combined 'inviting in' and 'going global' strategy in 2002, Chinese overseas investments have increased significantly, the value of the investments (in flow) in 2006 was more than US$20 billion and the annual growth rate of Chinese ODI (non-finance part) reached 60 per cent during the five years from 2002 to 2006.

As explained by Gugler and Boie (Chapter 2), Chinese overseas investment grew fast, from US$2.7 billion in 2002 to US$21.16 billion in 2006 (in terms of capital flow) and from US$29.9 billion in 2002 to US$90.63 billion in 2006 (in terms of investment in stock). A variety of Chinese investors invested abroad. Although Chinese SOEs (companies) still dominate, other types of Chinese investors, including private enterprises are becoming increasingly active in ODI. Furthermore, in addition to Chinese national (or central) SOEs, many local enterprises have also joined this investment movement. The sectors covered by

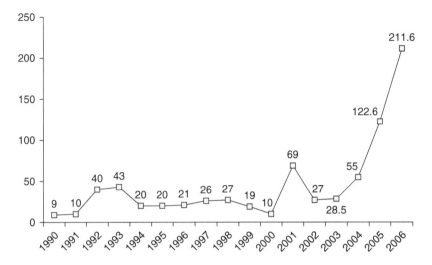

Figure 5.1 Chinese overseas investments (inflow) (including finance part) (1990–2006)

Chinese ODI expanded broadly, from agriculture, forestry, husbandry and fishery to public management and social communities. However, most of the investment goes to the sectors of commercial and leasing services, mining, finance, whole-sale and retailing, manufacturing and transportation, warehousing and postal services. By the end of 2006, the Chinese had invested in more than 200 countries or regions in the world, but investments were mainly concentrated in Asia and Latin American, especially in Hong Kong, China, the Cayman Islands and British Virgin Islands among others.

Although Chinese overseas investment has been growing fast, China has yet no uniform law on Chinese overseas investment promulgated by the Chinese National People's Congress – the top Chinese legislative body.[2] The regulations on Chinese overseas investment are mainly issued by the State Council (Chinese Central Government).[3] Chinese local governments also play active roles in regulating Chinese overseas investment.[4] Since the CCP, which exerts the strongest political leadership in China, first proposed in 2002 that China's basic policy of opening up should include both 'bring in' and 'go global' strategies, the Chinese State Council has issued several administrative policies on encouraging and regulating Chinese overseas investment.[5] For example, 'The Decision of the State Council on Reforming the Investment System' has been promulgated.[6] In addition, 'The Opinions on Encouraging and Regulating Overseas Investment and International Cooperation by Chinese Enterprises' was published by the State Council on 14 April 2007 (referred to as the '2007 State Council Opinions'). The Chinese National Development and Reform Commission (SDRC) has also published its 'Eleventh Five-Year National Program on Chinese Overseas Investment' (2007). The Program states that the guiding principle of Chinese overseas investment is to

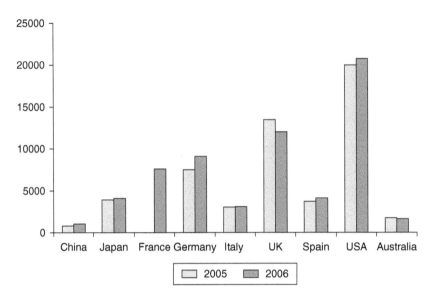

Figure 5.2 Comparisons of Chinese ODI (in stock) with those of the developed countries
(2005–2006)

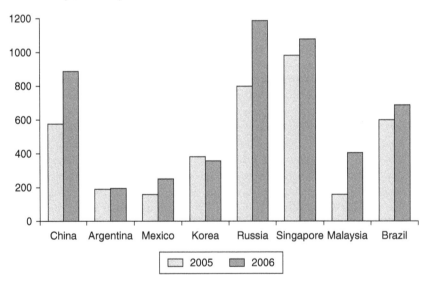

Figure 5.3 Comparisons of Chinese ODI (in stock) with those of the developing countries
(2005–2006)

encourage and regulate such investment and international cooperation, to realize
mutual support, and mutually beneficial common development. The main goals
expected to be achieved are to increase the scale of investment, expand investment
coverage, and improve investment efficiency; to establish and develop a long-term,

stable, economical and safe overseas natural resources supply system; to enlarge the investment sectors in the fields of high technology and new technologies and modern manufacturing industries; to transfer abroad the production capabilities over-supplied domestically; and to establish and develop several Chinese transnational corporations (groups); and to increase progressively the proportion of overseas investment by non-state-owned enterprises.

Under the political leadership of the CCP and the administrative guidance of the State Council, Chinese administrative authorities at both the national and local levels, according to their areas of responsibility, have issued a variety of regulations or rules on the promotion of Chinese overseas investments covering many subject matters. This chapter will mainly discuss the review and approval of an investment, the foreign exchange, the financial support and the investment insurance.

The review and approval of Chinese overseas investment

China's original investment system was established under the planning economy system and was strictly controlled by the government. All investments, no matter who made the investment, in what sector(s) the investment(s) were made, and where the capital resources originated, were subject to the review and approval of the governmental authorities at various levels. With respect to Chinese overseas investment, various Chinese administrative authorities, depending on their competences and functions, enjoyed the power of review and approval of the investments. Chinese investors had first to submit their applications to the specified responsible administrative authorities ('responsible authorities') and then go on to the competent Chinese regulating authorities ('regulating authorities') who were in charge of the review and approval of Chinese ODI. The responsible authorities and the regulating authorities were empowered to review all investment applications, project proposals, feasibility study reports, approval documents from other relevant administrative authorities, investment contracts or other business decisions, and any other documents required by them. The investors were not independent and could not make decisions by themselves. The formalities and procedures concerning overseas investments were complicated and time-consuming. Chinese overseas investments grew slowly.

Since the Chinese Government adopted the socialist market economy system, especially the 'going global' strategy, it has made a series of reforms of the investment system, including the system for the review and approval of Chinese overseas investments. In accordance with the reform(s), the government will only review and approve the major overseas investments as required under law. Other overseas investments will follow the registration or recording system. These are prescribed under 'The Temporary Regulatory Measures on Review and Approval of Overseas Investment Projects' issued by the State Development and Reform Commission (referred to as the '2004 Measures of SDRC').[7]

The 2004 Measures of SDRC are applicable to the approval of all Chinese overseas investment projects (including new establishment, merger by purchase, share participation, capital increase and reinvestment) of all types of legal person within China and the enterprises or organizations controlled by them (Article 2

SDRC). The designation 'overseas investment project' includes those activities which the investors pursue to obtain ownership, power of operation and management and other related rights and interests by investing in money, securities, material objects, intellectual property or technology, stock ownership, creditor's rights and/or by offering the security (Article 3 SDRC). According to the 2004 Measures of SDRC, the projects that need to be approved by the SDRC are the overseas investment projects relating to natural resource exploitation in which Chinese investment is more than US$30 million and those investment projects in non-natural resources which involve more than US$10 million foreign exchange by the Chinese investor; the projects that require authorization by the State Council include projects investing in natural resources with Chinese investment of more than US$200 million and projects in non-natural resources which involve investments of more than US$50 million by the Chinese investor (Article 4 SDRC). However, Chinese overseas investment projects relating to the exploitation of natural resources in which a Chinese investor(s) has an investment of less than US$30 million, and investment projects in non-natural resources overseas which involve less than US$10 million in foreign exchange by a Chinese investor can be authorized (Article 5 SDRC) by the Development and Reform Commissions at the level of provinces, autonomous regions, municipal cities directly under the control of the central government, and other cities separately listed by central government, and the Xinjiang Production and Construction Army Group (referred to as the 'SDRC at the provincial level').

Where the SDRC gives approval, only the following conditions shall be taken into account:

1   whether the projects abide by laws and regulations and state industrial policies, without prejudice to state sovereignty, safety and public interests, and without violations of international law;
2   whether the projects comply with the demands of sustainable economic and social development, are helpful to the exploration of the strategic resources required for national economic development; and comply with the requirements of the State on the adjustment of the industrial structure, strengthen the export of the technology, products, machines and labour services in which the Chinese have comparative advantages, and absorb foreign advanced technologies;
3   whether the projects comply with the regulations concerning national administration on capital projects and foreign debts; and
4   whether the investors have relevant capabilities for the investment projects (Article 18 SDRC).

This implies that the SDRC will not intervene in the investors' investment decisions. The enterprises shall make investment decisions by themselves.

In the case of the national enterprises under the administration of the central government (referred to as the 'national enterprises'), only the recording of the project is required for overseas investment projects relating to the exploitation of natural resources in which the Chinese party's investment is less than US$30 million and other overseas investment projects in which the Chinese party's foreign exchange is less than US$10 million. The national enterprises may make their investment decisions independently. The investment decision shall be reported to the SDRC for the purposes of record-keeping. The procedures concerning the recording have been simplified.[8]

The procedures and formalities concerning the approval are also clarified. Where the power to approve the projects remains with the SDRC, the investors shall first make an application for the projects to the 'SDRC at the provincial level', and after their review and approval, shall submit it to the SDRC at the national level. The enterprise groups in cities under separate state planning and national enterprises may directly submit the application for projects to the SDRC (Article 8 SDRC). The SDRC shall within 5 working days entrust qualified consulting organizations to make an assessment of the relevant key issues. The entrusted consulting organizations shall render their assessment report to the SDRC within the prescribed time (Article 10 SDRC). Moreover, the SDRC shall within 20 working days finish the review and approval of the application or render its suggestion of approval to the State Council. Where it is difficult to make the decision within 20 working days, the period may be extended for 10 working days with the approval of the SDRC (Article 11 SDRC). The last and most important point is that where the application is not approved, the SDRC shall notify the applicant in writing of the reasons and the rights to apply for an administrative review or to initiate an administrative lawsuit (Article 12 SDRC).

In addition to the SDRC, the Ministry of Commerce is another important regulating organ for approval of Chinese overseas investments. Although both the SDRC and the Ministry of Commerce are empowered to approve Chinese overseas investments, the SDRC does this mainly from the perspective of the overall national investment program or plan, whereas the Ministry of Commerce does so from the perspectives of the operation and supervision of the investment and establishment of overseas enterprises. Furthermore, the SDRC will only approve the natural resources exploitation projects and projects involving large amount of foreign exchange. The Chinese Ministry of Commerce, however, may approve all Chinese enterprises investing abroad and establishing overseas enterprises (with the exception of financial enterprises). The Ministry of Commerce has promulgated its 'Rules on the Review and Approval of the Investment and Establishment of an Enterprise Relating to Direct Overseas Investment' (2004) (hereafter referred to as the '2004 Rules of MC').[9]

The '2004 Rules of MC' stipulate that the objective 'to invest and establish an enterprise abroad' refers to Chinese efforts to establish an overseas enterprise through new investment (wholly-owned, joint-venture or cooperative), purchases, mergers and acquisitions, stock participations, capital investment and stock exchange, or to acquire the right of ownership or management of an existent overseas enterprise, etc. (Article 3 Rules of MC). The Ministry of Commerce or the commercial administrative authorities at the level of provinces, autonomous regions or municipal governments directly under the control of the central government and separately listed municipal governments (collectively known as 'provincial level commercial administrative authorities') may approve Chinese enterprises to invest abroad and establish enterprises in specified countries or regions.[10] When deciding whether to approve the investments, the Ministry of Commerce and the 'provincial level commercial administrative authorities' will take into account many factors. These factors include the investment environment and the security of the host country (region); the political and economic relationship between the host country (region) and China; the guidelines and policies for overseas investment; the locations of investment in the country (region); requirements relating to implementation of international obligations; and protection of legal rights and legitimate interests of foreign investors which may affect the operation of Chinese overseas investment (Article 5 Rules of MC). These factors have been further clarified in 'The Detailed Operational Provisions Relating to Approval of Investment and Establishment of an Enterprise Abroad' issued by the Ministry of Commerce on 17 October 2005. These operational provisions stipulate the following characteristics for the host country or region:

1   Country (region) investment environment, including: (i) political and social stabilities, no war and other social turbulences; (ii) sound economic situations, no economic crisis, stable foreign exchange rate and tax system; (iii) sound legal system, explicit laws, regulations and policies to encourage and protect foreign investment; (iv) water, power, gas, transport and telecommunication, etc., basic infrastructure and facilities and energy supply; and (v) labour resources.
2   Country (region) security situation including: (i) no large scale nationalizations and expropriations of foreign investments, no terrorism activities, personal safety and property security of foreign investments; (ii) stability of financial and foreign currency policies, legal protection of profit remittance of the foreign investment; (iii) no interferences into business operation from political parties, aggressive organizations or groups, good social order; and (iv) no sovereign disputes in the host country (region).
3   The political and economic relationships between the host country (region) and China include: (i) whether there is diplomatic relationship with China; (ii) whether it is a Chinese trade partner, or has adopted trade discriminations against China; and (iii) whether it has special restrictions on Chinese persons entry into or departure from the country (region).
4   The guidelines and policies for overseas investment include: (i) consistent with the guidelines and policies for overseas investment relating to countries (regions) and sectors; (ii) capable of contribution to export of goods, machines, technologies, services and labours where China owns comparative advantages; (iii) capable of utilization of advanced foreign technologies and management skills, improving the capabilities relating to technological research and development and international competitiveness; and (iv) contribution to realization of brand strategy and creation of world brands.

5   Locations of investment in the country (region) include: (i) whether the investments by Chinese enterprises are over-concentrated in the same sector in the host country (region); (ii) whether the production capabilities of the investment enterprises match with market needs of the host country (region); and (iii) whether the production is in the over competitive sector of the host country (region).

6   Implementation of international obligations include: (i) international agreements relating to non-diffusion of nuclear materials; (ii) international agreements relating to prohibition of research, production and sale of drugs; (iii) international agreements relating to environment protection and protection of endangered species of animals and plants; (iv) international agreements relating to food safety; and (v) international agreements relating to intellectual property rights protection.

7   Protection of foreign investors' rights and their legitimate areas interest covers: (i) whether there is a bilateral agreement on investment protection; (ii) whether there is a bilateral agreement on exemption of double taxation; and (iii) whether there were investigations and confiscations of Chinese enterprises without sound reason.

8   As regards overseas investment through mergers and acquisitions, emphasis should be paid to the following factors: (i) whether the investing sector is sensitive or restrictive in the host country (region); (ii) whether the relevant laws and regulations have been taken into account; (iii) whether the risks relating to the political system, security and financial affairs of the investment have been taken into account; and (iv) whether the issues relating to labour union, social responsibilities of the enterprise and culture integration have been taken into account.

After the investments have been approved, the Ministry of Commerce issues a Certificate of Approval of the People's Republic of China to Invest Abroad (hereafter referred to as the Approval Certificate) to the national enterprise applicants, and the 'provincial level commercial administrative authorities' issue an Approval Certificate to other enterprise applicants on behalf of the Ministry of Commerce (Article 9 Rules of MC). Only once they have obtained the Approval Certificate, can the applicants go on to deal with the matters relating to foreign exchange, banking, customs, foreign affairs, and so on (Article 9 Rules of MC).

The '2004 Rules of MC' have clarified the procedures concerning the approval of investment abroad by Chinese enterprises. The national enterprises may make an application directly to the Ministry of Commerce; other enterprises need to file an application to the 'provincial level commercial administrative authorities' (Article 7.1 Rules of MC). Where the application is incomplete or inconsistent with the statutory requirements, the Ministry of Commerce or the 'provincial level commercial administrative authorities' shall within 5 working days notify the applicant of the materials once and for all (Article 7.2 Rules of MC); where the opinions of China's economic and commercial counselor's office of the embassy (consulate) are solicited, the counselor shall make a reply within 5 working days (Article 7.3

Rules of MC). The 'provincial level commercial administrative authorities' shall decide within 15 working days whether to approve the application in accordance with the authorized power; if reporting to the Ministry of Commerce for approval is necessary, the 'provincial level commercial administrative authorities' shall conduct a preliminary review within 5 working days (Article 7.4 Rules of MC) and submit it to the Ministry of Commerce. The Ministry of Commerce shall decide whether to approve the application within 15 working days (Article 7.5 Rules of MC). The Ministry of Commerce will accept online applications and online issuance of approval certificates (Article 13 Rules of MC).

In a word, following the strategy of 'going global' and the 'Decision of the State Council on Reforming the Investment System', the Chinese Government is making the approval of overseas investment increasingly easier. The administrative items that need to be approved have been reduced.[11] The procedures for the approval have been simplified. The formalities concerning the approval have been clarified. Many overseas investments are now only required to be put on record rather than to be approved by government authorities. The formalities relating to the recording have been modified. The idea behind these changes is that under the market economy investors shall take all the responsibilities for their own economic and technical activities and for the risks of their overseas investments (Article 5 Rules of MC). Government authorities should not interfere with enterprises' business decisions except in those ways prescribed by law. The general principle of the Chinese administration regarding approval of overseas investments has transformed from the control of the investment to the promotion of the investment.

Foreign exchange

Foreign exchange has always been tightly controlled in China, especially under capital accounts. The transfer of foreign exchange abroad, opening a foreign exchange account abroad and use of foreign exchange to make an overseas investment usually has to be approved by the administrative authorities responsible for foreign exchange affairs. As regards Chinese overseas investment, the investors should use their own foreign exchange;[12] the State Administration for Foreign Exchanges Affairs (SAFEA) will review the sources of the foreign exchange and assess the risk of foreign exchange relating to overseas investment.[13] The transfer abroad of foreign exchange shall be approved by SAFEA (Article 4 Rules on Regulating Foreign Exchanges Relating to Investment Abroad); the Chinese investor shall submit the deposit into a special account as the security for remittance of the profit earned by the overseas investment (Article 5 Rules on Regulating Foreign Exchange Relating to Investment Abroad); Chinese investors shall bring home all the profits or other incomes earned in foreign exchange rather than deposit them abroad without authorization (Article 6 Rules on Regulating Foreign Exchanges Relating to Invest Abroad).[14] These foreign exchange controls are not consistent with the 'going global' strategy. The Chinese Government has progressively reformed its foreign exchange system to accelerate its overseas investments.

Chinese investors can now use self-owned foreign exchange, foreign exchange bought by Chinese currency, e.g. the "Renminbi" (RMB), or the domestic and overseas foreign exchange loans to make overseas investments.[15] The approval requirement concerning the amount of foreign exchange to invest abroad is no longer in force (Article 3 SAFEA 2006). In addition, the stipulations regarding the following have been lifted: the quota for purchase of foreign exchange to invest abroad;[16] the 'deposit for remittance security';[17] and the review requirement concerning foreign exchange risk relating to investment abroad.[18] The formalities and procedures relating to review of the sources (the 'sources review') of the foreign exchange have been simplified,[19] and the local SAFEA enjoy more powers to make the 'sources review'.[20] The new Chinese Regulations on Foreign Exchanges (2008) further prescribe that domestic investors, who invest abroad, shall make a registration according to the rules issued by SAFEA under the State Council. Where an approval or filing is required under law, the investors shall, prior to registration first handle the approval or filing matters.[21] In other words, for Chinese overseas investment, the foreign exchange approval or filing is required only for investors provided under laws. This may contribute further to increasing Chinese overseas investment.

Financial support

Various policies or regulations have been issued individually or jointly by the Ministry of Finance, the SDRC, the Ministry of Commerce, the State Development Bank of China (SDBC), China Import and Export Bank (CIEB) and other Chinese authorities to provide Chinese overseas investments with financial support. The financial support offered mainly takes the form of the special funds and special loan schemes.

One special fund scheme has been established by the Ministry of Finance and the Ministry of Commerce under the 'Measures Governing Special Funds for Foreign Economic and Technological Cooperation' (hereafter referred to as the '2005 Special Funds for FETC').[22] The special fund may be used to support Chinese overseas investment by means of direct subsidy or interest subsidy (Article 4 FETC). The 'overseas investment' refers to the establishment by a Chinese enterprise of an overseas enterprise through new investment (wholly-owned, joint-venture or cooperative), purchases, mergers and acquisitions, stock participations, capital investment and stock exchange, or to acquire the right of ownership or management of an existent overseas enterprise among others. The special fund will be appropriated by the Ministry of Finance under the fiscal budgetary grade (Article 16 FETC).

The direct subsidy refers to the relevant fees incurred prior to the registration of the overseas enterprise in the country where the project is located (hereafter referred to as the 'host country') (Article 5 FETC). It includes the legal, technical and commercial consultation fees for employing the third party, fees for producing the feasibility report on the project, fees for translation of the regulatory documents and bidding documents and fees for the purchase of the regulatory documents, bidding documents and other materials, and the operation fees for the foreign labour, establishment of overseas research and development platforms for high technology and new technologies, and overseas designing consultation projects (Article 5 FETC). The interest subsidy of the special fund pertains to the medium- or long-term loans provided by domestic banks for the overseas investment, cooperation and engineering projects (Article 5 FETC). The Ministry of Finance and the Ministry of Commerce will decide annually the priority sectors and scope of projects to be supported by the special fund (Article 6 FETC).

The '2005 Special Funds for FETC' provide that all enterprises which meet the following specified conditions can apply for financial support from the fund: (1) having registered within China and enjoying an independent legal personality; (2) having obtained the approval documents in written form (including approval or put on record) issued by relevant administrative authorities; (3) having committed no major illegal or irregular acts or malicious default acts of government funds for the past five years; and (4) having submitted statistical materials as required (Article 7 FETC). In addition, the projects should fulfill the following requirements: (1) having been approved, registered or put on record by the relevant state organs; (2) having been registered or put on record under the laws of the host country and the project has come into effect legally; (3) the amount of the investment by the Chinese party for the overseas investment project in principle shall not be lower than US$1 million (or the equivalent currencies) (Article 8 FETC). Where the interest subsidy for the medium- or long-term loans is applied, the project shall also satisfy the following conditions: (1) the term of the loan provided by the domestic bank(s) shall be more than one year; (2) the loan shall be used for construction and operation of a foreign economic and technological cooperation project; (3) the amount of a single loan shall not be lower than 3 million RMB (or equivalent foreign currencies); (4) the cumulative amount of loans to be applied for interest subsidy shall not be more than the total amount of Chinese investment or the contractual sum; and (5) one project cannot have interest subsidy cumulatively for more than 5 years (Article 8 FETC).

The proportion of direct subsidies in general shall not be more than 50 per cent of the fees paid by the applicant and each project can only receive the financial support once (Article 9 FETC). The ratio of the interest subsidy for the medium- or long-term loan shall be decided as follows: (1) the rate of interest subsidy for loans in RMB shall not exceed the base interest rate as promulgated or implemented by the People's Bank of China or the actual interest rate where the actual interest rate is lower than the base interest rate; (2) the annual rate of interest subsidy for loans in foreign currencies shall not exceed 3 per cent or the actual rate where the actual interest rate is lower than 3 per cent (Article 10 FETC).

Another special fund scheme for firms engaged in exploring overseas mineral resources has been set up by the Ministry of Finance (hereafter referred to as the '2005 Special Fund for Resources').[23] Under the '2005 Special Fund for Resources', the Chinese central government will make available certain financial subsidies and financial interest discounts specially for geological exploration units and mining enterprises to enable them to explore mineral resources and develop projects abroad, which are in short supply domestically and badly in need of national economic development (Article 2 Special Fund for Resources). The financial subsidies will mainly be provided for projects looking for mines, at the early stage of making pre-surveys and general surveys; a financial interest discount will support projects already at the stage of investigating, exploring and mining the resources (Article 8 Special Fund for Resources). Specified conditions must be satisfied in order to apply for the special fund.

Article 6 of the '2005 Special Fund for Resources' lists these conditions:

1   the implementation of the project shall accord with national laws and industrial policies, laws of the country where the project is located, and standards of international law, and shall not harm state sovereignty, safety and public interests;
2   the overseas investment and establishment of an enterprise has been reviewed and approved by the Ministry of Commerce or the 'provincial level commercial administrative authorities'; the overseas mineral resource project has been approved by or filed with the SDRC or the SDRC at provincial level, and put on record with the Ministry of Commerce and the Ministry of Land and Resources;
3   the project has obtained the licence (or permission) issued by the competent responsible authority for mineral resources of the host country for exploring and developing the mineral resources. The plan for executing the project has been approved by the host country; the contract or agreement (initialed text) should be signed for the joint venture and cooperative project with foreign partner(s);
4   the project should meet the requirements for raw materials, fuel, power, main equipment, communication and transport etc.;
5   the mineral area where the project is located has both excellent internal and external conditions. The mineral resources will have good market prospects and striking economic benefits;
6   domestic unit enjoys the mining right of the project exclusively or jointly with foreign joint venture or cooperative partner(s);
7   the main mineral resources (or rough products) will be brought back to China;
8   other conditions required by the Ministry of Finance.

As regards the special loan schemes, the CIEB, the SDBC and the SDRC have jointly circulated the notices relating to providing financial support to the key Chinese overseas investment projects. On 27 October 2004, the CIEB and the SDRC issued 'The Joint Notice of the State Development and Reform Commission and China Import and Export Bank on the Policies of Providing Loan Support to the Key Overseas Investment Projects Encouraged by the Chinese Government' (hereafter referred to as the '2004 Joint Notice'). According to the '2004 Joint Notice', the CIEB and the SDRC will jointly establish the credit and loan scheme to support overseas investments (Article 1 Joint Notice 2004). The CIEB will, in accordance with the national program on overseas investments, in its annual plan of loans for export, specially arrange a certain scale of capital to be used as the loans (referred to as the 'special loans for overseas investments') to support the key overseas investment projects encouraged by the State. The special loans enjoy the preferential interest rate of the loans for export (Article 1 Joint Notice 2004).

The 'special loans for overseas investments' will support the following main key overseas investment projects: (1) overseas resources exploitation projects which can supplement the shortages of domestic resources; (2) overseas production or infrastructure projects which can contribute to the export of the domestic technologies, products, equipment and labour services; (3) overseas research and development centres which can make use of international advanced technologies, management skills and professional talents; and (4) overseas merger and acquisition projects which can improve enterprises' international competitiveness and expand the international market (Article 2 Joint Notice 2004). The projects that can apply for the special loans shall be the ones approved in accordance with 'The Decision of the State Council on Reforming the Investment System' (2004) and 'The Temporary Regulatory Measures on Review and Approval of Investment Projects Abroad' (2004), and the CIEB will review the applications independently (Article 3 Joint Notice 2004). The CIEB will speed up the review of the applications for the special loans and provide for the facilities such as: (1) to confer a certain quota of loans in accordance with the credit class of the applicant and the economic returns of the overseas investment project; (2) to make direct loans to the overseas project company where the risks relating to the project are small and the investment returns are stable, on condition that the domestic investment entities of the project provide for the warranty and/or the mortgage on the assets of the project or other rights and interests; (3) to extend the loan term where the project is strategic and a long-term investment (Article 6 Joint Notice 2004).

The CIEB will also provide for other financial services relating to the projects utilizing the special loans. The financial services include the letter of guarantee (L/G) for bidding, the L/G for performance, the L/G for payment in advance, and the L/G for quality and international settlements. On certain conditions, some preferences will be provided for on the counter-warranty and security matters (Article 7 Joint Notice 2004).

The CIEB acts as the state's major financial institution to promote export credit to provide for the special loans for the key overseas investment projects. The SDBC, however, provides for special loans for the key overseas investment projects with the aim of promoting development. The SDBC and the SDRC have published their 'Joint Notice of the State Development and Reform Commission and the State Development Bank of China on the Relevant Issues Relating to Providing More Financing Support to the Key Overseas Investment Projects' (hereafter referred to as the '2005 Joint Notice') to deal with the loans issues.[24] Similar to the provisions of the '2004 Joint Notice', the '2005 Joint Notice' prescribes that the SDRC and the SDBC will, in accordance with the national development program on overseas investments, set forth annual plans on the financial support for the key overseas investment projects, and the SDBC shall, in its scale of annual loans for equities, specifically arrange a certain amount of capital for loans (hereafter referred to as the 'equities loans for overseas investments') so as to support the capital expansion of the key overseas investment projects encouraged by the State and improve their financing capacity (Article 1 Joint Notice 2005). The 'equities loans for overseas investments' will support the same key overseas investment projects as those under the '2004 Joint Notice' (Article 2 Joint Notice 2005). All the enterprises possessing legal personality registered within China can make applications for the 'equities loans for overseas investments' (Article 3 Joint Notice 2005). The SDBC will, pursuant to the relevant provisions, speed up the applications for the key overseas investment projects and provide certain preferential interest rates (Article 5 Joint Notice 2005). The SDBC will also provide for other supports and services to the key overseas investment projects (Article 6 Joint Notice 2005).

Investment insurance

China's overseas investment insurance is at an early stage of development. No uniform law on overseas investment insurance exists. However, the China Export Credit Insurance Company (CECIC), jointly with the SDRC, or the Ministry of Commerce, has issued several policies or rules concerning overseas investment insurance. As for the overseas investment projects, the CECIC and the SDRC published 'The Notice of the State Development and Reform Commission and the China Export Credit Insurance Corporation on Establishing an Insurance Scheme against Risks Deriving from the Key Overseas Investment Projects' on 25 January 2005 (hereafter referred to as the '2005 overseas investment projects insurance scheme'). With regard to promoting overseas investment by Chinese individual, private and other non-state owned enterprises (referred to as 'non-state owned enterprises'), the CECIC and the Ministry of Commerce have jointly drawn up 'The Notice of the Ministry of Commerce and the China Export Credit Insurance Corporation on Implementation of Export Credit Insurance' (hereafter referred to as the '2005 export credit insurance for non-state owned enterprises');[25] and for the purpose of developing Chinese brands abroad, the CECIC and the Ministry of Commerce on 24 June 2005 jointly issued 'The Notice of the Ministry of Commerce and the China Export Credit Insurance Corporation on Utilizing the Export Credit Insurance to Promote Development of Chinese Brands Abroad' (referred to as the '2005 Notice on Brands').[26]

Under the '2005 overseas investment projects insurance scheme', the SDRC and the CECIC have jointly established an insurance scheme against the risks deriving from key overseas investment projects (Article 1 insurance scheme). The CECIC will, in accordance with the national program on Chinese overseas investments and the arrangements of the national funds on export credit insurance, provide for the services of the investment consultation, risk assessment, risk control and investment insurance for key overseas investment projects encouraged by the State (Article 1 insurance scheme). Overseas investment projects include: (1) overseas resources exploitation projects which can supplement the relative shortages of domestic

resources; (2) overseas production or infrastructure projects which can contribute to
the export of domestic technologies, products, equipment and labour services; (3)
overseas research and development centers which can make use of international
advanced technologies, management skills and professional talents; and (4) overseas
merger and acquisition projects which can improve the international competitiveness
of enterprises and expand international markets (Article 2 insurance scheme). All
enterprises possessing legal personality registered within China (hereafter referred to
as 'domestic investment entities') can make applications for the services under the
investment insurance scheme (Article 3 insurance scheme). The CECIC will, under
the overall guidance of the SDRC, provide for the services as follows: (1) information consultations; (2) country risk assessments; (3) project risk control schemes; and
(4) insurance services relating to overseas investment, insuring against the political
risks such as appropriation and confiscation, war, restriction on foreign exchange
and governmental illegal acts (Article 3 insurance scheme).

   According to the article 4 insurance scheme, the projects that may apply for
overseas investment insurance are those that have been approved or put on record
in accordance with 'The Decision of the State Council on the Reforming the
Investment System' (2004) and 'The Temporary Regulatory Measures on Review
and Approval of Investment Projects Abroad' (2004). The CECIC will conduct
an independent review of the applications (Article 4 insurance scheme). As for
the projects where the country risk is large, the SDRC and the CECIC will
encourage the domestic investment entities to utilize fully the overseas investment insurance schemes to effectively prevent the risks of overseas investment
(Article 5 insurance scheme). For key overseas investment projects encouraged
by the State, the CECIC will provide for preferential insurance fees, simplify the
insurance formalities and speed up the insurance applications (Article 7 insurance
scheme). The CECIC may also provide for insurance services to the domestic (or
foreign) financial institutions that have financed the key overseas investment
projects (Article 8 insurance scheme). Furthermore, related export credit insur-
ances and warranties may also be provided by the CECIC to key overseas investment projects (Article 9 insurance scheme).

   In addition to the '2005 overseas investment projects insurance scheme' which
is mainly applicable to key overseas investment projects encouraged by the State,
the CECIC, jointly with the Ministry of Commerce, also offers some export credit
insurance policies to non-state owned enterprises. The '2005 export credit insurance for non-state owned enterprises' has granted special preferential support measures to non-state-owned enterprises. The measures include assistance to establish
an effective work coordination mechanism; help for non-state-owned enterprises to
actively use export credit insurance; providing non-state owned enterprises with
training in export trade risk management; assistance to such enterprises in establishing and improving their export trade risk management mechanism; publicizing
of policy-related functions of export credit insurance offered to non-state owned
export enterprises; formulation of special service plans; offering target-oriented
support; and customization of service program of export credit insurance for non-
state owned enterprises.[27] Furthermore, the small and medium-sized non-state

owned export enterprises shall be provided with a simplified procedure for applying for insurance and services, and the small and medium enterprises' comprehensive insurance covered by the short-term export credit insurance shall be fully available to small and medium non-state owned enterprises (Article 5 '2005 export credit insurance for non-state owned enterprises'). Non-state owned enterprises shall be also given active assistance in solving their financing problems and provided with trade financing facilities and guarantee services under export credit insurance (Article 6 '2005 export credit insurance for non-state owned enterprises'). The CECIC shall provide non-state owned enterprises with preferential services for export credit management, including such services as short-term export credit insurance, medium- and long-term export credit insurance, overseas investment insurance, domestic trade credit insurance and overseas collection of business debts (Article 8 '2005 export credit insurance for non-state owned enterprises').

The '2005 Notice on Brands' emphasizes the utilization of export credit insurance to support Chinese brands abroad. Where the export enterprises with famous brands are covered by export credit insurance, the CECIC shall render the qualifications of 'preferred client' or 'key client' to enjoy the relevant supporting policies (Article 4 Notice on Brands). In other words, exporters of famous brands will be given special status and offered policies appropriate to that status. Furthermore the CECIC shall provide the enterprises with the preferential services such as overseas investment insurance and overseas labour service insurance for the establishment of their research and development centre, production base and marketing network (Article 5 Notice on Brands). The CECIC shall also provide the export enterprises with such value-added services as a national risk report, an industrial analysis report and a risk management recommendation. In addition it will provide a free or preferential credit information report and give priority to the setting up of an online business operation and service system (Article 6 Notice on Brands). Finally, the CECIC shall actively develop new products and explore new modes to provide insurance credit support in such areas as production originality and research and development, brand marketing and extension, patent acquisition and protection (Article 7 Notice on Brands).

Conclusion

China cannot develop in isolation from the rest of the world, nor can the world enjoy prosperity and stability without China. In recent years, foreign investment by Chinese businesses has been rapidly increasing. While the investment so far is mostly in Asian countries, it also extends across the globe to Europe, Africa, and Central and South America. History tells us that without laws and institutions (both national and international), China's opening-up policy and its 'going global' strategy cannot work smoothly and effectively, nor can Chinese economic and social development be stable and sustained. Besides, this globalization of investment will probably create ties that reduce political friction between the countries involved in the investment. If governments in China, Russia and the

Middle East have large investments in the United States and the European Union, then they also have a direct stake in the continuing prosperity of the United States and the European Union.

Since the Chinese Government adopted the 'going global' strategy, Chinese overseas investment has grown rapidly. The Chinese have made much progress in their overseas investments. It is no coincidence that the Chinese bilateral investment treaties (BITs) concluded since 2000 contain some significant improvements which denote a high degree of investment protection. Chinese bilateral investment policy is mutating as explained by Xiao Jun in Chapter 6 of this book. A variety of promotion policies or regulations, especially those relating to the review and approval conditions, foreign exchange, financial support and investment insurance have been published. Although these policies or regulations are still in their initial stages and some provisions are tentative and lacking in precision, they have greatly contributed to the development of Chinese overseas investments.

Nevertheless several institutional issues remain to be clarified in practice. These issues include the division of approval power between the SDRC and the Ministry of Commerce; the division of supervisory power between the Ministry of Commerce and the State Commission on Administration of State-Owned Assets; and the approval and supervision of overseas investments made by non-state owned enterprises. Recently, the State Council has ordered the SDRC and the Ministry of Commerce to consolidate the administrative institutions concerning the 'going global' strategy and the corresponding policy measures and to improve the relevant coordination system. The Ministry of Commerce and the State Commission for Administration of the State-Owned Assets have been told to strengthen the supervision of Chinese overseas enterprises and institutions.[28] Although these institutional issues may be settled in the near future, this indicates that China is still at the primary stage of overseas investment.

In 2007, the Chinese Communist Party (CCP) further proposed that China should better integrate the 'bring in' and 'go global' strategies, make innovations in Chinese overseas investment and international cooperation, support Chinese domestic enterprises in carrying out international operations of R&D, production and marketing, and accelerate the growth of Chinese multinational corporations and Chinese brand names in the world market, and vigorously carry out mutually beneficial international cooperation in energy and resources.[29] For these reasons, it can be expected that Chinese policies and regulations on promoting Chinese overseas investment will develop to a new stage and contribute to a substantial increase in overseas investment.

Notes

1 The 'Expanding Opening-Up and Strengthening Mutually Beneficial and Win-Win International Investment Cooperation', speech at the 2007 WAIPA World Investment Conference by Ma Xiuhong, Vice Minister of the Ministry of Commerce of China, Geneva, 8 March 2007.

2 Under the Chinese Constitution, the National People's Congress (NPC) is the highest organ of state power, and its permanent body is its Standing Committee. The NPC and its Standing Committee exercise the legislative power of the State. The NPC enacts and amends, inter alia, criminal, civil, and other 'basic' laws. The Standing Committee enacts and amends laws, except for example the Foreign Trade Law and the Customs Law, which are enacted by the NPC. Executive power is vested in the State Council, which is the central government.

3 The State Council's functions include: formulation, adoption, and enactment of 'administrative regulations' in accordance with the Constitution and laws; submission of proposals to the NPC or its Standing Committee; the exercise of leadership over the work of local organs of state administration, and determination of the functional divisions between central and local authorities; drafting and implementing the national economic and social development plan and the State budget, and the direction and administration of urban and rural development work; and the conclusion of treaties and agreements with other States. The State Council reports to the NPC or, when the NPC is not in session, to its Standing Committee.

4 For example, the Shanghai Municipal Government issued 'The Several Opinions on Strengthening Implementation of the "Going Global" Strategy' on March 22, 2004.

5 Legislation in China includes the Constitution, laws, administrative regulations, departmental rules, local regulations, and rules. The Constitution is the highest law, followed by laws and administrative regulations; national administrative regulations take precedence over local regulations and rules. It should be emphasized that policies made by the CCP have a great influence on Chinese law. The CCP as the party in power enjoys the highest political leadership in China. The important policies made by the Central Commission of the CCP guide all Chinese law and other policy-making and implementation.

6 State Council, 'The Decision of the State Council on Reforming the Investment System', the State Council, 16 June 2004.

7 'The Temporary Regulatory Measures on Review and Approval of Overseas Investment Projects' (2004), adopted at the Meeting of the Board of Directors of the State Development and Reform Commission (SDRC) on 9 October 2004.

8 'The Notice on Certification of Recording Regarding Overseas Investment Projects', issued by General Office of the SDRC on 30 May 2007.

9 'The Rules on Review and Approval of Overseas Investment and Establishment of Overseas Enterprise' (2004), adopted at the Eleventh Session of the Ministry of Commerce Meeting on 23 September 2004.

10 Article 4 of the '2004 Rules of MC', 'The Notice on Adjustment of Relevant Items Relating to and Approval of Overseas investment', issued by the Ministry of Commerce on 19 December 2007.

11 See the several 'Decisions of the State Council on the Withdrawal and Adjustment of Administrative Approval Items'. Article 3 of 'The Rules on Regulating Foreign Exchanges Relating to Investment Abroad' (approved by the State Council on 5 February 1989 and published by the State Administration for Foreign Exchanges Affairs on 6 March 1989). Article 21 of 'The Regulations of the People's Republic of China on Foreign Exchanges' (1997) stipulated similarly that 'where a domestic investor makes an overseas investment, prior to being reviewed and approved by relevant administrative authorities, it has to be submitted to the State Administration for Foreign Exchanges Affairs (SAFEA) for review of the sources where the foreign exchanges come from; only with the approval of the SAFEA, can the foreign exchanges

be transferred abroad according to regulations issued by the State Council on foreign exchanges relating to overseas investment.

12 Where Chinese investors purchase foreign exchange for their overseas investments, there are limits on the amount of the foreign exchange that can be purchased.

13 Article 3 of 'The Rules on Regulating Foreign Exchanges Relating to Investment Abroad' (approved by the State Council on 5 February 1989 and published by SAFEA on 6 March 1989). Article 21 of 'The Regulations of the People's Republic of China on Foreign Exchanges' (1997) stipulated similarly that 'where a domestic investor makes an overseas investment, prior to being reviewed and approved by relevant administrative authorities, it has to be submitted to the State Administration for Foreign Exchanges Affairs (SAFEA) for review of the sources where the foreign exchanges come from; only with the approval of the SAFEA, the foreign exchanges can be transferred abroad according to regulations issued by the State Council on foreign exchanges relating to overseas investment'.

14 See also Article 19 of 'The Regulations of the People's Republic of China on Foreign Exchanges' (amended by the State Council on 14 January 1997).

15 Article 3 of 'The Notice of the State Administration for Foreign Exchange Affairs on Adjusting Some Foreign Exchange Management Policies Relating to Overseas investment', (adopted by the State Administration for Foreign Exchanges Affairs on 6 June 2006) (referred to as the 'Notice of the SAFEA 2006').

16 Item 1 of the 'Fourth Decision of the State Council on the Withdrawal and Adjustment of Administrative Approval Items' on 9 October 2007.

17 Item 746 of the 'First Decision of the State Council on the Withdrawal and Adjustment of Administrative Approval Items' on 1 November 2002. See also Article 1 of 'The Notice of the State Administration for Foreign Exchanges Affairs on Several Issues Relating to the Security Money for Remittance Back the Profit Earned by the Overseas investment', (issued by SAFEA on 12 November 2002).

18 Item 745 of the 'First Decision of the State Council on the Withdrawal and Adjustment of Administrative Approval Items' on 1 November 2002.

19 'The Notice of the State Administration for Foreign Exchanges Affairs on Simplifying the Review of the Sources of Foreign Exchange', (issued by SAFEA on 19 March 2003).

20 See 'The Notice of the State Administration for Foreign Exchanges Affairs on Expanding Reform of Foreign Exchanges Administration Pilot Work Relating to Invest Abroad', (issued by SAFEA on 19 May 2005), and 'The Notice of the State Administration for Foreign Exchanges Affairs on Transferring More Powers Relating to Review and Approval of Foreign Exchanges Business Under Capital Accounts to Local Authorities' (issued by SAFEA on 25 August 2005).

21 Article 17 of 'The Regulations of the People's Republic of China on Foreign Exchanges' (amended by the State Council on 5 August 2008).

22 'The Administrative Measures Governing Special Funds for Foreign Economic and Technological Cooperation', issued by the Ministry of Finance and Ministry of commerce on 9 December 2005, hereafter referred to as the '2005 Special Funds for FETC'.

23 'The Provisional Measures for Administration of Special Fund for the Exploration of Overseas Mineral Resources', issued by the Ministry of Finance on 31 October 2005 (hereafter referred to as the '2005 Special Fund for Resources').

24 'The Joint Notice of the State Development and Reform Commission and the State Development Bank of China on Issues Relating to Providing More Financing Support

to the Key Overseas Investment Projects', issued by the SDRC and the SDBC on 25 September 2005.
25 'The Notice of the Ministry of Commerce and the China Export Credit Insurance Corporation on Implementation of Export Credit Insurance', the Ministry of Commerce and the CECIC on 10 August 2005.
26 'The Notice of the Ministry of Commerce and the China Export Credit Insurance Corporation on Utilizing the Export Credit Insurance to Promote Development of Chinese Brand Names Abroad', the Ministry of Commerce and the CECIC on 24 June 2005.
27 Articles 1, 2, 3 and 4 of the '2005 export credit insurance for non-state owned enterprises'.
28 See 'The Notice of the General Affairs Office of the State Council to Transmit the Opinions of the State Development and Reform Commission Relating to Strengthening the Reform of Economic Institutions', issued by the General Affairs Office of the State Council on 20 June 2007.
29 See Hu Jintao, Report to the Seventeenth National Congress of the Communist Party of China on 15 October 2007.

References

Political documents

The State Council, 'The Decision of the State Council on Reforming the Investment System', adopted by the State Council on 16 June 2004.
The State Council, 'The First Decision of the State Council on Withdrawal and Adjustment of Administrative Approval Items', issued by the State Council on 1 November 2002.
The 'Expanding Opening-Up and Strengthening Mutually Beneficial and Win-Win International Investment Cooperation', speech at the 2007 WAIPA World Investment Conference by Ma Xiuhong, Vice Minister of the Ministry of Commerce of China, Geneva, 8 March 2007.
The General Office of the State Council, 'The Notice of the General Office of the State Council to Transmit "the Opinions of the State Development and Reform Commission Relating to Strengthening the Reform of Economic Institutions"', issued by the General Office of the State Council on 20 June 2007.
The State Council, 'The Fourth Decision of the State Council on Withdrawal and Adjustment of Administrative Approval Items', issued by the State Council on 9 October 2007.
Hu Jintao, *Report to the Seventeenth National Congress of the Chinese Communist Party*, 15 October 2007.

Legal documents

Administrative regulations

The State Council, 'The Regulations of the People's Republic of China on Administration of Foreign Exchange' (revised version), issued by the State Council on 14 January 1997.
The State Council, 'The Regulations of the People's Republic of China on Administration of Foreign Exchange' (Revised Version), issued by the State Council on 5 August 2008.

Departmental rules

The Ministry of Commerce, 'The Rules on Review and Approval of Overseas Investment and Establishment of Overseas Enterprise', adopted at the Eleventh Session of the Ministry of Commerce Meeting on 23 September 2004.

The State Development and Reform Commission, 'The Temporary Regulatory Measures on Review and Approval of Overseas Investment Projects', adopted at the Meeting of the Board of Directors of the State Development and Reform Commission on 9 October 2004.

The Ministry of Finance, 'The Provisional Measures for Administration of Special Fund for the Exploration of Overseas Mineral Resources', issued by the Ministry of Finance on 31 October 2005.

The Ministry of Finance and The Ministry of Commerce, 'The Administrative Measures Governing Special Funds for Foreign Economic and Technological Cooperation', issued by the Ministry of Finance and the Ministry of Commerce on 9 December 2005.

Other departmental documents

The State Administration for Foreign Exchange Affairs, 'The Notice of the State Administration for Foreign Exchange Affairs on Several Issues Relating to the Security Money for Remittance Back of the Profit Earned by Overseas Investment', issued by the State Administration for Foreign Exchange Affairs on 12 November 2002.

The State Administration for Foreign Exchange Affairs, 'The Notice of the State Administration for Foreign Exchange Affairs on Simplifying the Review of the Sources of Foreign Exchange', issued by the State Administration for Foreign Exchange Affairs on 19 March 2003.

The State Administration for Foreign Exchange Affairs, 'The Notice of the State Administration for Foreign Exchange Affairs on Expanding Reform of Foreign Exchange Administration Pilot Work Relating to Overseas Investment', issued by the State Administration for Foreign Exchange Affairs on 19 May 2005.

The Ministry of Commerce, 'The Notice of the Ministry of Commerce and the China Export Credit Insurance Corporation on Utilizing Export Credit Insurance to Promote Development of Chinese Brand Names Abroad', issued by the Ministry of Commerce and the China Export Credit Insurance Corporation on 24 June 2005.

The Ministry of Commerce, 'The Notice of the Ministry of Commerce and the China Export Credit Insurance Corporation on Implementation of Export Credit Insurance', issued by the Ministry of Commerce and the China Export Credit Insurance Corporation on 10 August 2005.

The State Administration for Foreign Exchange Affairs, 'The Notice of the State Administration for Foreign Exchange Affairs on Transferring More Powers Relating to Review and Approval of Foreign Exchange Business Under Capital Accounts to Local Authorities', issued by the State Administration for Foreign Exchange Affairs on 25 August 2005.

The State Development and Reform Commission and the State Development Bank of China, 'The Joint Notice of the State Development and Reform Commission and the State Development Bank of China on Issues Relating to Providing More Financing Support to the Key Overseas Investment Project', issued by the State Development and Reform Commission and the State Development Bank of China on 25 September 2005.

The State Administration for Foreign Exchange Affairs, 'The Notice of the State Administration for Foreign Exchange Affairs on Adjusting Some Foreign Exchange Management Policies Relating to Overseas Investment', issued by the State Administration for Foreign Exchange Affairs on 6 June 2006.

The State Development and Reform Commission, 'The Notice on Certification of Recording Concerning Overseas Investment Projects', issued by the General Office of the State Development and Reform Commission on 30 May 2007.

Local regulations or rules

The Shanghai Municipal Government, 'The Several Opinions on Strengthening Implementation of the "Going Global" Strategy' issued on 22 March 2004.

6 Chinese BITs in the twenty-first century

Protecting Chinese investment

Jun Xiao

Introduction

In recent years, along with China's economic growth, the outward investments from China have soared. While the stock of Chinese outward investments amounted to only US$4.5 billion in 1990, the figure had reached US$28 billion by 2000 and US$46 billion by 2005 (UNCTAD, 2006: 113). In 2006, China's outflows increased by 32 per cent to US$16 billion, and its outward investment stock to US$73 billion. This expansion involves considerable investment in other developing countries. The importance of Chinese FDI is expected to continue to grow in the future. According to the survey by the Foreign Investment Advisory Service/Multilateral Investment Guarantee Agency (FIAS/MIGA), 58.9 per cent of Chinese multinational enterprises (MNEs) taking part in the survey had concrete plans to continue to expand abroad, and 12.9 per cent had at least an intention to expand abroad (FIAS/MIGA, 2006: 19). Furthermore, as Shaoming Cheng notes, a future stronger Chinese currency will greatly enhance the purchasing strength of Chinese firms in international mergers and acquisitions and therefore lead to a rise in outflows of Chinese FDI (Gugler and Boie, this volume, Chapter 2). In addition, the competitive pressure in the domestic Chinese market is expected to accelerate, and will continue to push Chinese enterprises to globalize. For these reasons two free trade agreements (FTAs) recently entered into force (the China–Chile FTA on 1 October 2006, and the China–Pakistan FTA on 1 July 2007). The Agreement on Trade in Services of the China–ASEAN Free Trade Area also entered into force on 1 July 2007. Three further agreements (with Australia, the Gulf Cooperation Council and Iceland) are being negotiated while the China–New Zealand FTA entered into force on 1 October 2008.

Today, China is regarded as an important source of foreign investment (UNCTAD, 2007: 44). Has this development had an impact on China's international law practice? The new Agreement on the Encouragement and Reciprocal Protection of Investments between China and Germany entered into force on 11 November 2005.[1] It replaces the old China–Germany bilateral investment treaty (BIT) of 1983.[2] A comparison between these two BITs shows that the new agreement contains some significant improvements which denote a much higher degree of investment protection. As Germany is advocating and practising such a high level of protection of foreign investment, *inter alia*, through its model BIT, it would be worthwhile and interesting to know whether these improvements and high standards are specific to the Chinese BITs, or, if they indicate a new Chinese attitude towards the protection of investment by means of such agreements. On the basis of research on Chinese BITs, this chapter will argue that the high level of investment protection as provided for in the new China–Germany agreement has been a common feature of the Chinese BITs concluded since 2000, so that a new generation of Chinese BITs has arisen. The reason for this phenomenon is that China has stronger interests in protecting its outward investment in accordance with its economic development.

The role of BITs

The global flows of inward and outward FDI worldwide have increased considerably over the past two decades and multinational corporations (MNCs) are increasingly considered as being the most important agents worldwide. This is because they have the ability to affect substantially the economic development of host and home countries and are widely assumed to be the providers of knowledge, capital, capabilities and markets, the creators of jobs, the suppliers of foreign currency and the stimulators of competition among other things (Dunning 1992).

A wide variety of national and international policy rules and principles govern many aspects of the operations of MNCs – policy actions are important 'to the extent that they shift firm-level choices from one discrete governance structure toward another' according to Rugman and Verbeke (2004). The number of international investment agreements, instruments for the promotion and protection of foreign investment, has increased sharply over the past two decades, taking the form of a patchwork of bilateral, regional, interregional, and plurilateral treaties.

The World Trade Organization (WTO) and its predecessor, the General Agreement on Tariffs and Trade (GATT), have not directly tackled the broad issue of foreign investment rules. Instead, GATT and the WTO have dealt with a narrow set of very specific issues, which has left nations to formulate their own policies, either through BITs or FTAs (Gugler and Chaisse 2008). The WTO handles two major agreements that address investment directly: the General Agreement on Trade in Services (GATS) and the Agreement on Trade-Related Investment Measures (TRIMs). GATT and the WTO have dealt with specific aspects of the relationship between trade and investment through the GATS, which concerns the supply of services by foreign companies, and through TRIMs. To the extent that trade in services may require a commercial presence by a foreign service-provider in the territory of another state, the provider may enjoy certain investment rights under the GATS. Additionally, under WTO rules, investment measures, such as local content rules or trade balancing requirements, would be prohibited, to the extent that they impact upon trade and violate the GATT rules on national treatment and quantitative restrictions. Three further agreements (the Agreement on Trade-Related Aspects of Intellectual Property Rights (TRIPS), the Government Procurement Agreement (GPA), and the Agreement on Subsidies and Countervailing Measures (ASCM)) have only indirect effects on investment.[3] Of these the TRIPS Agreement is the most interesting. It provides protection for intangible assets that form the basis of the activities of multinational corporations. It further requires that Members provide effective legal procedures and remedies for the enforcement of such rights.

The first ever modern BIT has been identified as the agreement between Germany and Pakistan way back in 1959. Ever since then, capital exporting countries, mostly developed nations, have negotiated and concluded such agreements with capital importing countries, mostly least developed countries (LDCs). The origin of these treaties is attributed to the strong disagreement as to the customary international law standards of treatment owed to foreign investors before 1959, as well as the failure of diplomatic efforts to conclude a broader multilateral agreement. It has been widely accepted that customary law provides only very weak legal standards for foreign investment. BITs emerged as a solution to the complexities of multilateral agreements, as no multilateral treaty showed potential for overcoming the uncertainties of customary international law. Western investors had great concern and fears at the time (and many still do) about the likelihood of expropriation or nationalization and arbitrary treatment at the hands of the authorities in the LDCs. The number of these agreements soared from 385 to 1,857 between 1980 and 1990, according to the UNCTAD index. The UNCTAD index of 2000 showed that there were 2100 known BITs between 173 countries. At the end of 2006, there were 2,573 BITs between nearly 180 countries, showing that the number of countries that have entered into these treaties far exceed the membership of the WTO. The BITs concluded between two countries represent the core of the current international agreements (Gugler and Tomsik, 2007a). In 2005 alone, 162 international investment agreements (IIAs) were concluded, bringing the total number of agreements concluded since the early 1960s to almost 5,500 (i.e. IIAs including BITs, double taxation treaties and FTAs). In 2006 73 BITs, 174 IIAs totally, were concluded. Most BITs have been concluded between developed and developing countries. Whereas earlier agreements fell almost exclusively into this category, the number of BITs involving two developing countries is now increasing. Over the past five years, the share of such agreements has almost doubled, from 14 per cent to 27 per cent. This broad picture of the situation can be extended to China.

The preambles of the thousands of existing BITs state that their purpose is to promote the flow of FDI and, undoubtedly, BITs are so popular because policymakers in developing countries believe that signing them will increase FDI. Are BITs therefore playing a significant role in the inflow of foreign investments? Opinion on the subject remains divided. Investment agreements have been regarded by developing countries as an instrument to attract foreign investors. It has been said that despite expectations about the impact of BITs on FDI, there is no evidence indicating that the adoption of BITs has actually encouraged FDI flows to the developing countries that have signed such agreements. While half of the Organisation for Economic Co-operation and Development (OECD) FDI into developing countries was covered by a BIT by 2000, the increase in FDI flows to those countries over the previous two decades was accounted for by additional country pairs entering into agreements rather than by signatory hosts gaining significant additional FDI. Other authors are confident that although

BITs may not attract much FDI in the short run, a good reputation for honouring foreign investments will nevertheless have the desired effect in the long run.

Improvements in the new China–Germany BIT

China had signed 112 bilateral investment protection agreements by the end of May 2007 and 93 agreements or arrangements on avoidance of double taxation by the end of July 2007. The agreements on avoidance of double taxation incorporate 'tax sparing' provisions, which stipulate that in respect of certain 'taxable income', tax is to be levied by only one party to the agreement; they have no most-favoured-nation (MFN) provisions. In addition, China's Closer Economic Partnership Arrangements (CEPAs) with the special administrative regions (SARs) of Hong Kong and Macao provide certain privileges to investors from these SARs.

In the two decades between 1983 and 2005, the economic reform in China made significant progress. The Chinese economic system has now been liberalized to a large extent. Accordingly, the new China–Germany BIT includes some improvements reflecting the modified, i.e. liberalized, economic system, for example:

- The definition of investor with respect to China has been adapted to the liberalized administration of foreign trade. The old China–Germany BIT provided that only companies, enterprises and other economic organizations of China authorized, registered and entitled by the Chinese Government to make an investment could be an 'investor'.[4] This restriction is not included in the new BIT, because the new Foreign Trade Law of China, dating from 2004, principally permits any natural and legal person as having fulfilled the registration criteria to engage in foreign trade.[5]
- Corresponding to the relaxed foreign exchange controls,[6] a basically unlimited free transfer of investments and returns is provided for in the new China–Germany BIT. There are no general approval requirements for capital transfer in the BIT, except two special cases provided for in the Protocol to the agreement. Moreover, China promises free capital transfer without any restriction if the existing restrictions were to be abandoned.

These improvements are undoubtedly important for investors and investments. Nevertheless, with respect to international law, there are two amendments which are more decisive in the agreement being marked as a modernized framework with high-level investment protection: the national treatment provision and the investor–state dispute settlement mechanism.

The 1983 China–Germany BIT did not contain an explicit national treatment provision. Instead, Article 3(4) provided that, in accordance with domestic laws and regulations, neither contracting party shall take discriminatory measures against investments of investors of the other contracting party and enterprises involving such investments. To establish discrimination, the treatment of 'investments of investors of the other contracting party' has to be compared with the treatment of another group of investments. Accordingly, the latter had to be investments of investors of states other than the other contracting party. Because Article 3(1) explicitly granted MFN treatment, Article 3(4) forbids discrimination between investments of the other contracting party on the one hand and domestic investments on the other hand. Therefore, Article 3(4) did implicitly grant national treatment without mentioning a comparison to domestic investments.

By contrast, Article 3(2) of the new China–Germany BIT explicitly provides for national treatment in the post-establishment phase without the qualification of 'in accordance with laws and regulations' found in the former agreement between the two countries:

> Each contracting party shall accord to investments and activities associated with such investments by investors of the other contracting party treatment not less favorable than that accorded to the investments and associated activities by its own investors.

The Protocol to the agreement allows China to maintain its existing non-conforming measures, and to amend them as long as the amendment does not increase their non-conformity. On the other hand, China promises that it will 'take all appropriate steps in order to progressively remove the non-conforming measures' (Ad Articles Additions to 2 and 3 of the Protocol to the Agreement). Therefore, although the existing non-conforming measures are 'grandfathered', the treaty imposes a standstill obligation on China. Furthermore, the 'best efforts' rollback promise by China has to some extent been reinforced by the Note Verbal to the agreement where two countries agree to review 'in due course but not later than three years after the entry into force' of the agreement, the progressive elimination of the non-conforming measures. Hence, notwithstanding some limitations, the explicit national treatment provisions constitute an essential improvement over the old China–Germany BIT.

Another essential improvement is the new investor–state dispute settlement mechanism. In the 1983 China–Germany BIT, investors could only submit disputes concerning an amount of compensation to international arbitration. An *ad hoc* arbitral tribunal could be constituted. The tribunal could determine its own procedure with reference to the ICSID Convention.[7]

This limited access to international arbitration is superseded in the new China–Germany BIT by a far-reaching consent of the contracting parties to international arbitration for 'any dispute concerning investments'. After a waiting period of six months, investors can submit such disputes to ICSID arbitration or to an *ad hoc* arbitral tribunal established under the United Nations Commission on International Trade Law (UNCITRAL) or other arbitration rules. As the dispute will be submitted 'at the request of the investor', China does give a priori consent to such proceedings.[8]

This consent is conditioned by two rules provided in the Protocol to the Agreement.

- A German investor has to refer the dispute to an administrative review procedure according to Chinese law in the first place, and if the dispute still exists three months after the investor has brought the issue to the review procedure, he can submit the dispute to international arbitration.

- If the issue has been brought to a Chinese court, investors must be able to withdraw the case according to Chinese law. Otherwise, they cannot submit the dispute to international arbitration. This rule of so-called 'fork in the road' requires the investor to make a choice between submission to a domestic court or to international arbitration, and where the choice once made becomes final and irreversible. The *rationale* of this rule is that the international arbitral tribunal should not review domestic court decisions as an appeal court.

Despite these two conditions which are common in BITs,[9] the investor–state dispute resolution provisions in the new China–Germany agreement provide for almost unlimited access of foreign investors to international arbitration. This is in accordance with the usual BIT practice nowadays.[10]

The national treatment and investor–state dispute settlement mechanism are among the most important elements in BITs. By means of national treatment a competitive equality between foreign and national investments should be ensured, distortions in competition should be eliminated and efficiency should be enhanced. Consequently, the national treatment has been considered as 'the single most important standard of treatment' in international investment agreements.[11] The root of investor–state dispute resolution by international arbitration is the concerns of investors that national courts might be subject to the influence of the executive in host countries, and the belief that international arbitration is independent and fair (UNCTAD 1999: 13). Therefore, the improvements in the new China–Germany BIT with respect to these two elements will benefit investors from both contracting parties and are already significant *per se*.

In the following sections, the scope of the discussion is widened to look at whether the new China–Germany BIT is a special case or if it represents the current attitude of China towards the protection of foreign investment through BITs.

National treatment in Chinese BITs

Essentially, national treatment requires countries not to discriminate against foreign investors in favour of domestic ones. The standard of treatment can be defined in two ways: 'same' or 'as favourable as' treatment or 'no less favourable' treatment. The difference is subtle, but the 'no less favourable' formulation leaves open the possibility that investors may be entitled to treatment that is more favourable than that accorded to domestic investors, in accordance with international standards. Often the definition of national treatment is qualified by the inclusion of the provision that it only applies in 'like circumstances' or 'similar circumstances'. As the situations of foreign and domestic investors are often not identical, this language obviously leaves room for interpretation.

When 'national treatment' is applied to investment during the pre-establishment phase, it curtails or prohibits developing countries from having control over the entry of foreign investors and types of investments. And if national treatment is applied during the post-establishment phase, it would also impede the ability of a government to give preferential treatment to local firms, or to channel foreign investment in certain desired directions.

China has been one of the most important host countries for foreign investment for many years. According to the annual World Investment Reports by UNCTAD, China was among the five largest host economies in 2004, 2005 and 2006, and the largest of the developing countries.

China is also among the countries that have signed the most BITs. It has signed more than 120 BITs, second only to Germany (UNCTAD 2007: 18).[12] With respect to the treatment of foreign investment, most of the Chinese BITs signed in the 1980s and 1990s provide for fair and equitable treatment and most-favoured-nation treatment, but not national treatment.[13] The absence of national treatment provisions is a specialty of Chinese BITs in comparison to BITs signed by other countries (WTO 2002a: 18). Only a few of the Chinese BITs signed in this period contains a post-establishment national treatment clause, and if they do, its application is often limited. The 1983 China–Germany BIT was the first such agreement, but the only one in which the comparison regarding the treatment granted to domestic investments was not explicitly mentioned. The first Chinese BIT containing an explicit national treatment provision is that with the United Kingdom of 1986, Article 3(3) of this agreement provides:

> either contracting party shall to the extent possible, accord treatment in accordance with the stipulations of its laws and regulations to the investments of nationals or companies of the other contracting party the same as that accorded to its nationals or companies.

In view of the best-efforts feature and the restriction of 'in accordance with [...]', this national treatment clause is hard for investors to enforce (Zhou 2000: 120).

Two years later, Article 3(2) of the BIT between China and Japan of 1988 provided for national treatment without such vague language:

> The treatment accorded by either contracting party within its territory to nationals and companies of the other contracting party with respect to investments, returns and business activities in connection with the investment shall not be less favorable than that accorded to nationals and companies of the former contracting party.

Although the application of this clause is limited to a certain degree by the clarification of the terms of 'business activities' and 'treatment less favorable',[14] the clause *per se* does indicate the adoption of the usual formulation of the national treatment provision as in BITs of other states.[15]

The two national treatment clauses mentioned above, in BITs with two important home countries of foreign investment, are representative of such provisions in only a fraction of Chinese BITs concluded before 2000.[16]

In this respect, the situation changed significantly after 2000. The post-establishment national treatment obligation has since been provided for in most of the new Chinese BITs:[17]

- The new China–Netherlands BIT (2001) contains an almost identical national treatment clause, Article 3(3), to the one in the new China–Germany BIT.[18] The grandfathering of the existing non-conforming measures of China is also provided for in the Protocol to the China–Netherlands BIT.
- A national treatment obligation similar to the one in the BITs with Germany and the Netherlands is provided for in the Chinese BITs with Bosnia-Herzegovina (2002), Finland (2004), the Czech Republic (2005), Portugal (2005, MOFCOM 2008), Spain (2005, MOFCOM 2008), India (2006, MOFCOM 2008) and the Seychelles (2007, MOFCOM 2008).
- The China–Guyana BIT (2003) contains a national treatment clause conditioned by 'without prejudice to its laws and regulations'. Therefore, the contracting parties are still able to take certain measures, including new, non-conforming ones.[19]
- A similar national treatment clause to that in the China–Guyana BIT can be seen in BITs with Botswana (2000), Jordan (2001), the Cote d'Ivoire (2002), Trinidad and Tobago (2002), Djibouti (2003), Benin (2004, MOFCOM 2008), Latvia (2004, MOFCOM 2008), the Democratic People's Republic of Korea (2005, MOFCOM 2008), Russia (2006, MOFCOM 2008), as well as with Vanuatu (2006, MOFCOM 2008).

The developing countries acting as host countries for foreign investment are generally concerned that providing national treatment could prevent them from pursuing development objectives.[20] With the restriction of 'without prejudice to its laws and regulations', the contracting parties may to a certain degree reserve the right to grant preferential treatment to national investment. The practical significance of the related national treatment clauses would then be reduced by such a restriction, because the host country could enact 'laws and regulations' and thus refuse to grant the national treatment thereby.

Although some of the Chinese BITs concluded before 2000 do provide national treatment, they are only a fraction of Chinese BITs concluded at that time. Therefore, it is a remarkable change in China's BIT practice that most of the Chinese BITs concluded in the twenty-first century grant national treatment.

This change is consistent with the gradual acceptance of national treatment in China.[21] The initial reluctance to accept national treatment had historical and political roots.[22] Moreover, granting national treatment is difficult in an economic system where state-owned enterprises dominate and subsidies have been granted exclusively to such enterprises (UNCTAD 1999: 16). The economic reform in China, which is aimed at establishing a market economy including privatization, and the related legal reform form the present political background for the progressive acceptance of national treatment.[23] Last but not least, China's entry into the WTO is also a contributory factor (Zhou 2000: 146–47).

Notwithstanding the limitations in favour of the existing non-conforming measures of China, the national treatment obligation in the new China–Germany BIT is stricter than that in the Chinese BITs with other developing countries which are conditioned by 'without prejudice to its laws and regulations'. This restriction makes the related national treatment clauses little different from the few provisions of this kind in the old Chinese BITs conducted before 2000. Nevertheless, the investor–state dispute settlement provisions in the new agreements differentiate them from their old counterparts and have an impact on the practical significance of similar national treatment clauses.

Investor–state dispute settlement in Chinese BITs

Among the most crucial elements of a sound investment regime is the investor–state arbitration mechanism. Procedures for the settlement of investor–state disputes govern the settlement of disputes that arise when a state is alleged to be non-compliant with an investment-enabling institution. Unlike in the area of international trade, where the WTO has its own dispute settlement mechanism, investment-enabling institutions rely on external arbitral rules already in place. Investment-enabling institutions may however contain modifications or qualifications of the external rules that it refers to in the arbitration clause. Thus the rules, procedures and mechanisms for the settlement of investment disputes are not entirely independent of the investment-enabling institutions; however, for the purposes of this chapter they can be classified as a separate set of institutions.

Dispute settlement is about the interpretation of a set of rules and the application of these rules to a particular set of facts. Usually authors distinguish between inter-state and transnational dispute resolution: interstate dispute resolution is consistent with the view that public international law comprises a set of rules and practices governing interstate relationships. Legal resolution of disputes, in this model, takes place between states conceived of as unitary actors. In transnational dispute resolution, by contrast, access to courts and tribunals and the subsequent enforcement of their decisions are legally insulated from the will of individual national governments.

Investor–state arbitration can be supervised by an administrative body or can be unsupervised (*ad hoc*). The supervising body may assist in appointing arbitrators, determining the place of arbitration, determining costs and arbitrator fees, and so forth, and will itself charge a fee for the performance of these functions. The supervisory bodies most commonly referred to in investment-enabling institutions are the International Centre for the Settlement of Investment Disputes (ICSID) and the International Chamber of Commerce's (ICC) International Court of Arbitration; each body has its own set of arbitration rules. *Ad hoc* arbitrations most often follow the arbitration rules of the United Nations Commission on International Trade Law (UNCITRAL).

The awards of tribunals in investor–state disputes are not self-executing; they require enforcement within the host-state of the investment. International treaties have thus been signed in which states consent to the jurisdiction of international tribunals, and commit to enforcing the subsequent decisions of those tribunals.

The investor–state dispute settlement provisions in the old China–Germany BIT were typical of most of the Chinese BITs conducted before 2000.[24] A few of those agreements provide formally for a more liberal access of investors to international arbitration. In addition to the binding consent of the contracting parties with regard to disputes concerning an amount of compensation, any dispute concerning other matters may also be submitted to international arbitration by a special mutual agreement by the disputing parties, i.e. the host country and investors.[25] Because there is no obligation to enter into such an agreement, the scope of the consent to international arbitration in those BITs could not be wider than that in the old China–Germany BIT.

The far-reaching consent to international arbitration for 'any dispute concerning investments' in the new China–Germany BIT had never been seen in the Chinese BITs concluded before 2000, but is present in most of the BITs concluded in the twenty-first century. These include the BITs with Benin, Bosnia-Herzegovina, Botswana, the Cote d'Ivoire, the Czech Republic, Djibouti, Finland, Guyana, India, Jordan, the Democratic People's Republic of Korea, Latvia, the Netherlands, Portugal, Russia, Spain, Trinidad and Tobago, the Seychelles and Vanuatu.

The significance of this difference in regard to investor–state dispute settlement provisions should not be underestimated.

Investor–state arbitration is a key component of the negotiating objectives on investment as determined by many countries. Investor–state arbitration offers a neutral setting in which foreign investors can challenge government measures which they believe to be in violation of an investment agreement. Without investor–state arbitration, investors cannot be assured that wrongs committed against them will be redressed independently of the political interests of governments, as in the state-to-state dispute settlement process. Investor–state arbitration ensures that the interests of the investor will be protected.

As long as China's political attitude towards foreign investments remains friendly, it is almost impossible for foreign investments to be expropriated, or for a dispute to arise concerning the amount of compensation. According to the Chinese BITs concluded before 2000, no dispute concerning other matters can be submitted, without, for example, a special mutual agreement, which in reality is a special consent by the Chinese Government to international arbitration. For this reason, it is unlikely that China would be confronted with such proceedings.

By contrast, the possibility of such proceedings would be much greater under the new BITs. First, dirigisme still plays an important role in the economic politics of China. Second, the interpretation of some norms in the BITs, e.g. fair and equitable treatment, most-favoured-nation treatment and national treatment, is complicated and even contentious. As investors can invoke such norms and submit disputes about them to an international arbitral tribunal, the scope of China's challengeable measures is much wider. This can lead to greater potential for international arbitration against China.

As the Argentina case demonstrates,[26] on entering a BIT, one consents to surrender the decision power to an outside tribunal (such as ICSID). A good lesson from the case in question is that domestic courts and national legal systems are completely marginalized by recourse of investors to these international arbitration panels. ICSID and UNCITRAL only allow for the investor and government parties to the dispute to have legal standing. These bodies are thus given the responsibility to adjudicate virtually all investment disputes without democratic structures or transparency, despite the fact that they are not serving private goals but an international judicial function governed by treaty and international law.

Therefore, the investor–state dispute settlement mechanism in the new China–Germany BIT and other Chinese BITs concluded in the twenty-first century differ from their predecessors to an even greater degree than the national treatment does. While investors could now invoke national treatment according to the new mechanism, granting national treatment does have greater practical significance in the new BITs.

Foreign companies have won a string of rulings against Argentina at ICSID. Exxon Mobil is claiming billions of dollars compensation from Venezuela at ICSID after walking away from an oil project following government attempts to take control. With companies from emerging markets such as India and China investing abroad, the rich countries could find themselves increasingly the targets of litigation. These findings support the suggestion of Professor Chang-fa Lo in Chapter 11 of this book to develop a 'harbour agreement' to coordinate BITs at the international level. There is indeed a need to recognize the existing BITs and their functions; to recognize the power and discretion of host countries to decide on the admission of foreign investment; to impose procedural requirements on notification and transparency; to introduce institutionalized technical assistance and capacity building; and to make available the multilateral dispute settlement mechanism for BIT disputes to unify the legal views on certain commonly occurring issues (Chang-fa Lo, this volume, Chapter 11).

Conclusions

China has recently been moving towards a level playing field for foreign and domestic investors in China. Until the end of 2007, China had provided better than national treatment in its taxation policies for foreign-investment enterprises (FIEs); since 1 January 2008, a uniform enterprise income tax rate of 25 per cent has been applied to all enterprises (including FIEs) in accordance with the Enterprise Income Tax Law, with some exceptions, such as certain 'grandfathering' and lower rates granted for investment in certain industries. It would appear that all tax incentives now apply equally to domestic firms and FIEs. Several regulations and rules have been introduced or amended with a view to further liberalizing FDI and establishing a more rules-based and predictable business environment for foreign investors.

At the international level, it has been said that the multilateral trading system is at a crossroads. Some have argued that one road leads to the death of multilateralism and the emergence instead of a network of bilateral and regional trade deals, while the other road leads to a resurgence of the multilateral trade system and to fulfilment of the original ambitions of the 1947 General Agreement on Tariffs and Trade. In reality, the debate about multilateralism versus bilateralism or regionalism is a matter of balancing objectives rather than choosing between them. The WTO remains at the centre of the international trading system–it might be said that reports of the death of multilateralism are exaggerated. Nonetheless, the last five years have seen a dramatic growth in the number of bilateral and regional free trade agreements. As can be seen from this chapter, China has been an active participant in this field. By contrast, China's attitude towards a multilateral framework on investment is skeptical, like most of the developing countries. In discussions of a possible multilateral investment agreement in the WTO, China, India, Brazil and ASEAN countries built a group which was opposed to investment rules in the WTO (Sauvé, 2006). However, the relationship and interaction between obligations in existing WTO treaties, especially in the GATS, and those in BITs should not be ignored and underestimated (Adlung and Molinuevo, 2008).

The national treatment and investor–state dispute settlement provisions differentiate the Chinese BITs conducted since 2000 from their predecessors. This difference is so important that these new agreements could be regarded as a new generation of Chinese BITs in the twenty-first century.

There are many reasons for the development of this new generation of BITs. As mentioned above, the acceptance of national treatment could and should be understood in a wider context. In contrast, the investor–state dispute settlement mechanism is a particular phenomenon in international investment law. It clearly aims at the protection of foreign investments, which national investors cannot resort to. Therefore, the liberal consent to international arbitration in the new Chinese BITs indicates the new attitude of China towards international investment protection. There is surely also a desire to strengthen the confidence of investors in the pro-foreign investment politics of China and to attract more foreign investments. Because the wish to attract more foreign investments has existed since the 1980s, the new Chinese attitude would be better explained from the angle of the changing role of China in international investment protection: in parallel with the economic development of China, Chinese outward investment arises. This trend has become obvious since 2000 and is supported by the Chinese Government.[27] It has resulted in a growing interest in the protection of Chinese investors in foreign countries by means of BITs, e.g. the investor–state dispute settlement mechanism and national treatment. As long as such interest exists, China will not turn away from the BIT model represented by the new China–Germany BIT. On the other hand, it is quite possible that China will continue to play its (old) role of a developing country and a host country for investments from developed countries for many years. As long as investors perceive that the legal protection offered by China's domestic law is insufficient, other (home) countries such as Germany would deem the conclusion of BITs with China necessary. Therefore, it could be predicted that China's international law practice with respect to investment protection will be moulded by this new generation of Chinese BITs for a long time.

Notes

1 This agreement and other Chinese BITs available in an English version are at http://www.unctadxi.org/templates/DocSearch.aspx?id=779 (accessed 15 May 2008).
2 This agreement and other Chinese BITs only available in a Chinese version are at http://tfs.mofcom.gov.cn/h/h.html (accessed 15 May 2008). These BITs will be marked by 'MOFCOM 2008'.
3 See the analysis done by Gugler and Chaisse 2008.
4 It was also provided for by Article 1.2 of the China–Sweden BIT.
5 The Foreign Trade Law is available at http://www.fdi.gov.cn/pub/FDI_EN/Laws/law_en_info.jsp?docid=50900 (accessed 15 May 2008). For a general discussion of this new act, see Wang (2006).
6 For a discussion of the foreign exchange system of China, see Hall (2004).
7 No. 4 of the Protocol to the 1983 China–Germany BIT. The Convention on the Settlement of Investment Disputes between States and Nationals of other States, known generally as the ICSID Convention, established the International Centre for Settlement of Investment Disputes (ICSID) which provides facilities for the conciliation and arbitration of disputes between member states and investors who qualify as nationals of other member states; 155 States have signed the convention (China in 1990) and 143 of them have completed the process of ratification (China in 1993).
8 Article 9 of the 2003 China–Germany BIT. For a discussion of such *a priori* consent based on the dispute settlement provisions in BITs, see Sornarajah (2004), p. 251.
9 See for example *Emilio Agustin Maffezini v. The Kingdom of Spain*, ICSID Case No. ARB/97/7, Decision on Objections to Jurisdiction, 25 January 2001, 40 ILM 1129 (2001), para. 63.
10 For investor–state dispute settlement provisions in BITs in general, see UNCTAD (2003a).
11 'At the same time, it is perhaps the most difficult standard to achieve, as it touches upon economically (and politically) sensitive issues', see UNCTAD (1999), p. 1.
12 There are disputes in theory as well as among states whether and how BITs can promote foreign investments. On the one hand, there is a consensus that the macroeconomic conditions in host countries are the main reasons for multinational enterprises to invest, e.g. the size and potential of the domestic market, the availability of natural resources, the quality of local infrastructure and work force, the political and macroeconomic stability, etc. On the other hand, the BITs can internationalize the favourable domestic politics towards foreign investments, and thereby the host country does signal its pro-foreign investment position. For related discussions of WTO members in the Working Group on the Relationship between Trade and Investment (WGTI), see WTO (1998). For analysis of the role of BITs for investment promotion, see for example Salacuse and Sullivan (2005), Vandevelde (1998).
13 For example, the Chinese BITs with Kuwait (1985), Switzerland (1986), Australia (1988), Argentina (1992), Greece (1992), Egypt (1994), Ethiopia (1998) and Qatar (1999). For an analysis why there is no national treatment in such Chinese BITs, see UNCTAD (1999), p. 16.
14 Article 3(3) of the China–Japan BIT exhaustively enumerates the types of 'business activities'. In the Protocol to that agreement it is declared that 'the discriminatory treatment' 'in accordance with its applicable laws and regulations', and 'in case it is really necessary due to public order, national security or sound development of the national economy', shall not be deemed 'treatment less favorable'.

15 For examples of national treatment clauses in BITs, see UNCTAD (1999), pp. 19–25.

16 The Chinese BITs with Slovenia (1993) and Iceland (1994) contain an almost identical national treatment clause as in Article 3(3) of the China–United Kingdom BIT. The national treatment in the style of Article 3(2) of the China–Japan BIT is provided for, for example in the BITs with the former Czechoslovakia (1991), Republic of Korea (1992) and Saudi Arabia (1996), (MOFCOM: 2008). There is no official explanation why China has committed itself to national treatment obligation to these countries, and not the others. For another, not exhaustive, list of Chinese BITs containing national treatment, see Wang (2005), p. 776.

17 Not all of the Chinese BITs concluded since 2000 have been published. Some have not yet entered into force. Nevertheless, in view of the fact that 20 of the 22 BITs for which either an English or a Chinese version is available, except the agreements from 2000 with Iran and Brunei, respectively, provide for national treatment, a conclusion that most of the new Chinese BITs in the twenty-first century do that should be appropriate. Besides, it is worth noting that only six of the contracting parties, i.e. the Czech Republic, Finland, Germany, the Netherlands, Portugal and Spain, are OECD countries, and the related new BITs are the outcome of re-negotiations of the old agreements from the 1980s. Wang observes that all eight Chinese BITs concluded since 2002 provide for national treatment, see Wang (2005), p. 777.

18 Article 3(3) provides: 'Each contracting party shall accord to investments and activities associated with such investments by the investors of the other contracting party treatment no less favorable than that accorded to investments and activities by its own investors or investors of any third State.'

19 Article 3(2) of the China–Guyana BIT provides: 'Without prejudice to its laws and regulations, each contracting party shall accord to investments and activities associated with such investments by the investors of the other contracting party treatment not less favorable than that accorded to the investment and associated activities by its own investors.'

20 For example, some developing countries have stressed these concerns in discussions about standards of non-discrimination in international investment agreements that have taken place in the WGTI, see WTO (2002a), pp. 18–21. The cause of the concerns is that measures providing preferential support and protection to national investment could violate national treatment obligation, see WTO (2002b), p. 17.

21 For discussions of this gradual acceptance in a wider context, i.e. not only for BITs, but also for all of the economic policies, see Wang (2005), Zhou (2000).

22 The first international treaties providing national treatment signed by China at the beginning of the twentieth century were forced by Western powers. Moreover, the national treatment obligations in these treaties were unilateral and binding only on China. Therefore, these treaties and the national treatment therein were considered as closely connected with the oppression of imperialism and traitorous activities, see Wang (2005) p. 762–63, 779.

23 It is worth noting that Chinese private enterprises have also asked for national treatment, because foreign investors have been granted advantages in many respects and treated better than *private* national investors in China. Although this appeal for national treatment is based on a misunderstanding of this standard in international law, it did contribute to the acceptance of national treatment in China.

24 For example, the BITs with the United Kingdom (1986), Ghana (1989), Slovenia (1993), Egypt (1994), Saudi Arabia (1996), Ethiopia (1998) and Qatar (1999).

25 Article XII of the China–Australia BIT. Other examples are the BITs with Kuwait (1985), Japan (1988), Greece (1992) and the Republic of Korea (1992).

26 The consent to international arbitration, as well as the conclusion of BITs *per se*, signals the pro-foreign investment politics of host countries, see UNCTAD (2003a), p. 13.
28 There are extensive reports and commentaries in this respect. For just two documents from international organisations, see UNCTAD (2003b); WTO (2006), p. 51.

References

Adlung, R. and Molinuevo, M. (2006) 'Bilateralism in services trade: Is there fire behind the (BIT-)smoke?', *Journal of International Economic Law*, 11: 365–409.

Dunning, J.H. (1992) *Multinational Enterprises and the Global Economy*, Wokingham: Addison-Wesley.

FIAS/MIGA (2006) *Firm Survey – Chinese Outward Foreign Direct Investment.* Presented by Battat, J. Online. Available HTTP: http://rru.worldbank.org/Documents/PSDForum/2006/joe_battat.pdf (accessed 13 May 2008).

Gugler, P. and Chaisse, J. (2008) 'Foreign investment issues and WTO Law – Dealing with fragmentation while waiting for a multilateral framework', in Chaisse, J. and Balmelli, T. (eds), *Essays on the Future of the World Trade Organization*, Geneva: Editions Interuniversitaires Suisses, 135–71.

Gugler, P. and Tomsik, V. (2007) 'General agreement on investment: Departure from the investment agreement patchwork', in Dunning, J. and Gugler, P. (eds), *Foreign Direct Investments, Location and Competitiveness*, Oxford: Elsevier, 229–54.

Hall, T. (2004) Controlling for risk: An analysis of China's system of foreign exchange and exchange rate management, *Columbia Journal of Asian Law*, 17: 433–81.

MOFCOM (2008) *Statistical Bulletin of China's Outward Foreign Direct Investment 2008*. Online. Homepage, Chinese Ministry of Commerce.

Rugman, A.M. and Verbeke, A. (2004) 'Towards a theory of regional multinationals: A transaction cost economics approach', *Management International Review*, 44 (Special issue): 3–15.

Salacuse, J. and Sullivan, N. (2005) Do BITs really work? An evaluation of bilateral investment treaties and their grand bargain, *Harvard International Law Journal*, 46: 67–114.

Sauvé, P. (2006) Multilateral rules on investment: Is forward movement possible?, *Journal of International Economic Law*, 9: 325–55.

Sornarajah, M. (2004) *The International Law on Foreign Investment*. Cambridge: Cambridge University Press.

UNCTAD (1999) *National Treatment*. New York and Geneva: United Nation's. Online. Available HTTP: http://www.unctad.org/en/docs/psiteiitd11v4.en.pdf (accessed 15 May 2008).

UNCTAD (2003a) *Dispute Settlement: Investor-state*. New York and Geneva: United Nation's. Online. Available HTTP: http://www.unctad.org/en/docs/iteiit30_en.pdf (accessed 15 May 2008).

UNCTAD (2003b) *China: An Emerging FDI Outward Investor*. New York and Geneva: United Nation's. Online. Available HTTP: http://www.unctad.org/sections/dite_fdistat/docs/china_ebrief_en.pdf (accessed 15 May 2008).

UNCTAD (2006) *World Investment Report 2006*. New York and Geneva: United Nation's. Online. Available HTTP: http://www.unctad.org/en/docs/wir2006_en.pdf (accessed 15 May 2008).

UNCTAD (2007) *World Investment Report 2007*. New York and Geneva: United Nation's. Online. Available HTTP: http://www.unctad.org/en/docs/wir2007_en.pdf (accessed 15 May 2008).

Vandevelde, K. (1998) Investment liberalization and economic development: The role of bilateral investment treaties, *Columbia Journal of Transnational Law*, 36: 501–24.

Wang, H. (2006) Chinese views on modern Marco Polos: New foreign trade amendments after WTO Accession, *Cornell International Law Journal*, 39: 329–69.

Wang, W. (2005) Historical evolution of national treatment in China, *International Lawyer*, 39: 759–79.

WTO (1998) *WT/WGTI/M/6 Report on The meeting of 1 and 2 October 1998*. Geneva. Online. Available HTTP: http://docsonline.wto.org (accessed 15 May 2008).

WTO (2002a) *WT/WGTI/W/119 The Development Provisions*. Geneva. Online. Available HTTP: http://docsonline.wto.org (accessed 15 May 2008).

WTO (2002b) *WT/WGTI/W/118 Non-discrimination: Most-favoured nation treatment and national treatment*. Geneva. Online. Available HTTP: http://docsonline.wto.org (accessed 15 May 2008).

WTO (2006) *WT/TPR/S/161 Trade Policy Review, People's Republic of China*. Geneva. Online. Available HTTP: http://docsonline.wto.org (accessed 15 May 2008).

Zhou, J. (2000) National treatment in foreign investment law: A comparative study from a Chinese Perspective, *Touro International Law Review*, 10: 39–153.

7 Investment liberalization in ASEAN

Progress, regress or stumbling bloc?

Darryl S.L. Jarvis, Chen Shaofeng and Tan Teck Boon

Introduction

In 2007 the Association of South East Asian Nations (ASEAN) celebrated its fortieth birthday. The original founding members, Indonesia, Malaysia, the Philippines, Singapore, and Thailand, have subsequently been joined by Brunei Darussalam (1984), Vietnam (1995), Lao People's Democratic Republic, Myanmar (Burma) (1997) and Cambodia (1999). Originally a small five-state security community, ASEAN now comprises an association with a combined population of 600 million, a GDP of US$1 trillion and generates annual trade flows in excess of US$900 million.[1] Despite reaching its 'middle age' milestone, however, ASEAN's achievements remain the subject of intense debate, as does its role and relevance to a region experiencing rapid change in its economic, social and political composition. Indeed, despite its commitment to realizing economic integration via the 'free flow of goods, services, investment and a freer flow of capital', evidence of deeper economic engagement remains problematic.[2]

This chapter explores ASEAN's cooperative endeavours in investment liberalization. Investment liberalization is variously associated with net positive effects on inflows of investment capital, technology transfer, employment, export generation, economic growth and development (UNCTAD 2003; Quazi 2007). As a net historical beneficiary of investment flows, the chapter hypothesizes that ASEAN's stated commitment to investment liberalization should by now be realizing progress in each of four areas:

- absolute reductions in national autonomy in relation to investment screening and conditionality provisions;
- increased transparency in respect of member states' national investment regimes;
- enhanced standardization and codification of regulatory standards governing investment related provisions across member states; and
- enhanced centralized coordination and decision-making in respect of investment governance.

Each of these areas is investigated in relation to ASEAN's three primary investment agreements and the ensuing regimes that govern investment provisions and policy practices among member states.

ASEAN's investment regime: the architecture

Foreign investment has been the lifeblood of ASEAN's economies. Where goes foreign direct investment (FDI), so goes growth. As Figure 7.1 indicates, foreign investment is correlated strongly to economic performance and export activity and is responsible for an increasing share of gross fixed capital formation (Sakakibara and Yamakawa 2003). Investment promotion has thus been a key policy instrument used by all member states to steer investment into strategic sectors that complement national comparative advantage, promote export activity and generate employment. Recognizing the strategic importance of investment to development, ASEAN was one of the first regional groups in the South to adopt formal instruments that promote and protect cross-border investment among nationals of member states. These have comprised two sequentially related agreements that together define the policy architecture of ASEAN's investment regime:

1 The ASEAN Agreement for the Promotion and Protection of Investments (AAPPI) (1987, 1996).
2 The ASEAN Investment Area (AIA) Agreement (1998) (Amended 2001).

While each is a formal instrument that speaks to the legal strictures and obligations of member states, equally they embody the political aspirations of ASEAN heads of government and their stated commitment to increase intra-ASEAN investment as a proportion of total investment flows to the region, facilitate greater ease of movement of capital, technology and knowledge skills, and thus promote equitable development among member states as a means of achieving longer term economic integration through enhancing economic complementarities.[3] ASEAN's success and/or failure thus rests on the efficacy of these agreements and their outcomes.

The ASEAN Agreement for the Promotion and Protection of Investments

Adopted in 1987 at the ASEAN Heads of Government Meeting in Manila, the ASEAN Agreement for the Promotion and Protection of Investments (AAPPI) represents the culmination of a decade-long series of negotiations and ASEAN's first multilateral endeavour at enhancing investment cooperation. Its importance lies not only in the architecture it set in place and from which would evolve ASEAN's contemporary investment regime, but also in the procedural, cooperative, consultative and dispute processes and procedures that were to arise and largely embed themselves in ASEAN's subsequent investment agreements.[4] The AAPPI thus casts a long shadow over ASEAN's investment regime and the ensuing character of the association's liberalization efforts.

Despite the foundational importance of the AAPPI, the agreement itself is remarkably parsimonious. The protocols of the agreement are confined to three substantive areas:

- stipulation of investor treatment;
- investor protection and compensation; and
- disputation mechanisms.

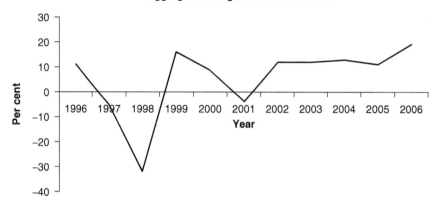

Aggregate GDP growth rate in ASEAN[1]

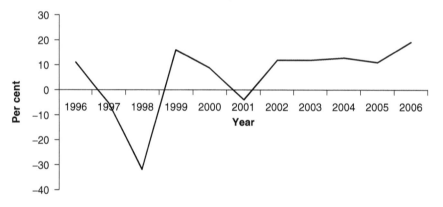

Aggregate GDP growth rate in ASEAN[2]

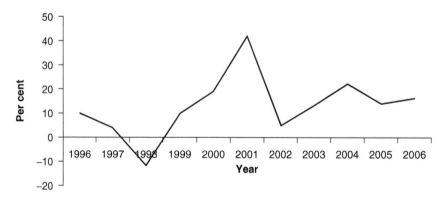

Aggregate export growth in ASEAN[3]

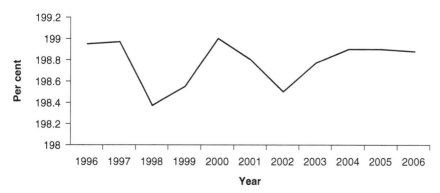

Figure 7.1 FDI inflows, growth, fixed capital formation and exports

Notes: All figures are based on the author's calculation using the World Development Indicators, World Bank, in current US dollars.
1 Data for Brunei Darussalam not available. Rounded off to the nearest billion.
2 Data for Myanmar not available. Rounded off to the nearest percentage point.
3 Data for Myanmar not available. Data for Singapore from 1995 to 2000 not available. Rounded off to the nearest percentage point.
4 Data for Myanmar not available/included. Data for Lao PDR from 1995 to 1999 not available. Rounded off to the nearest 1/100th of a percentage point.

The first of these provisions aspires to a broad set of minimum standards that define the treatment of ASEAN nationals by specifying a 'fair and equitable' treatment clause (Article IV) and stipulating that this cannot be less advantageous than that granted to investors accorded most-favoured-nation (MFN) status. Ostensibly, the intent is to discourage discrimination between ASEAN nationals while ensuring them treatment equivalent to MFN status. Further, Article IV stipulates that ASEAN nationals will receive protection in accord with that afforded to a host country's own nationals: 'each contracting party shall, within its territory ensure full protection of the investments made in accordance with its legislation' and that this 'shall not impair by unjustified or discriminatory measures the management, maintenance, use, enjoyment, extension, disposition or liquidation of such investments.'[5] Judicial, political and/or legislative measures that unfairly discriminate against investment from ASEAN nationals are therefore prohibited. This equivalency clause is also extended to the treatment of ASEAN nationals in the event of damages due to hostilities or a state of national emergency. Under the agreement, for example, both domestic and ASEAN investors are afforded equivalent treatment in the case of restitution, compensation or 'valuable consideration' with inbuilt measures designed to safeguard the remittance of compensation monies to home country domiciles.[6] The clause, however, does not guarantee compensation and/or restitution and is not intended as an instrument for providing investor indemnity against civil unrest or political risk.

The second of the provisions in the agreement address investor protection. Two sets of protection measures are identified: the repatriation of capital and earnings, and compensation in the case of expropriation. The former affirms the right of repatriation for all business activities associated with the remittance of net profits, dividends, royalties, interest, dispossession of assets and capital transfers by ASEAN nationals. Article VII also includes the repatriation of proceeds upon the liquidation of assets, earnings accruing to employees and remittance of all forms of debt settlement by ASEAN nationals. The second clause provides investor indemnity in the case of expropriation by providing ASEAN investors recourse to compensation at fair market values prevailing 'immediately before the measure of dispossession became public knowledge', and access to compensation monies 'without unreasonable delay' as well as committing signatories to assure the transferability of compensation monies in freely usable currencies.[7]

Third and finally, the AAPPI specifies disputation mechanisms in the case of disagreement between contracting parties covered by the agreement. Two sets of disputation mechanisms are incorporated into the agreement. The first is a defined arbitration mechanism that allows disputing parties to seek arbitration in specified international arbitration centres.[8] While the agreement makes the disputation mechanisms binding on the extant party and vests in the arbitration court a 'binding authority' clause, no enforcement mechanism is specified. Partly, this is accommodated in a second default mechanism that refers intransigent disputes to the ASEAN Economic Ministers (AEM) meeting, vesting in the AEM ultimate decision-making authority.

Assessing the impact and outcomes of the AAPPI

In the Joint Communiqué issued at the conclusion of the ASEAN Heads of Government meeting held in Manila, in 1987, the adoption of the AAPPI was lauded as one of the foundation stones that would propel expansion of intra-ASEAN investment 'to at least ten per cent of total foreign investments by the turn of the century.'[9] Plainly, the AAPPI was viewed as a facilitation mechanism that, over time, would see annual growth in intra-ASEAN investment and in the process would help lay the groundwork for deeper regional integration. As Tables 7.1 and 7.2 indicate, however, the AAPPI has fallen short of achieving its original aim, with the level of intra-regional investment remaining stubbornly static – not only in dollar terms, but also as a percentage of total capital flows to the region. As recently as 2005, for example, intra-ASEAN investment accounted for less than 10 per cent of total FDI inflows.

While there are countless factors that impact investment flows, making it hard to apportion causality and/or correlate variables with any degree of accuracy, the evidence suggesting a positive impact of the AAPPI is hard to discern. Partly, this reflects the limited and circumscribed nature of the agreement itself and partly the structural flaws in the agreement which fails to address underlying issues associated with the transparency of the investment regime or the removal of national barriers to investment entry. More obviously, the agreement also reveals fundamental tensions between the intent to create standards of equivalency in the treatment of

Table 7.1 FDI inflows into ASEAN by source country/region (US$ millions)

Source country/region	1995	1996	1997	1998	1999	2000	2001	2002	2003	2004	2005
ASEAN[a,b]	3,516.90	3,121.70	3,962.90	2,073.10	934.60	714.30	933.00	3,634.00	2,302.00	2,433.00	3,765.10
EU-15[c,d]	5,067.10	6,231.20	5,542.90	5,344.30	7,051.10	2,609.30	4,141.70	4,236.00	52,320.00	5,421.00	11,139.60
USA	2,119.00	4,586.50	6,669.40	3,427.30	4,992.30	2,404.60	3,150.00	358.00	1,395.00	5,052.00	3,010.60
Total inflows	23,389.40	25,544.40	29,612.30	21,778.60	22,169.70	8,513.60	10,293.30	13,705.00	18,447.00	21,804.00	41,067.80
ASEAN intra FDI inflows as a % of total FDI inflows to the region	15	12.2	11.4	9.5	4.2	8.3	9	26.5	12.4	11.1	9.1

Sources: *ASEAN Statistical Yearbook* (2003) Jakarta: ASEAN Secretariat; *ASEAN Statistical Yearbook* (2006) Jakarta: ASEAN Secretariat; *Foreign Direct Investment Statistics* (2007), ASEAN Secretariat, http://www.aseansec.org/18144.htm.

Notes
a Excludes Cambodia 1995–2004.
b Includes Cambodia 2005.
c Includes EU 15 1995–2004.
d Includes EU 25 2005.

Table 7.2 ASEAN foreign direct investment: net inflow from selected partner countries/regions

Partner country/region	Value (US$ million)				Share to total net inflow (%)			
	2004	2005	2006	2002–2006	2004	2005	2006	2002–2006
ASEAN	2,803.7	3,765.1	6,242.1	19,377.7	8.0	9.2	11.9	11.3
USA	5,232.4	3,010.6	3,864.9	13,736.1	14.9	7.3	7.4	8.0
Japan	5,732.1	7,234.8	10,803.3	30,813.7	16.3	17.6	20.6	18.0
EU-25[a]	10,046.1	11,139.6	13,361.9	44,955.6	28.6	27.1	25.5	26.3
China	731.5	502.1	936.9	2,302.9	2.1	1.2	1.8	1.3
Republic of Korea	806.4	577.7	1,099.1	3,347.3	2.3	1.4	2.1	2.0
Australia	566.7	195.9	399.2	1,444.3	1.6	0.5	0.8	0.8
India	118.7	351.7	(380.4)	295.1	0.3	0.9	(0.7)	0.2
Canada	301.2	161.3	274.0	1,184.9	0.9	0.4	0.5	0.7
Russia[b]	–	–	5.6	n.a.	n.a.	n.a.	n.a.	n.a.
New Zealand	3.5	480.7	(282.8)	392.1	0.0	1.2	(0.5)	0.2
Pakistan	4.8	3.5	7.8	16.8	0.0	0.0	0.0	0.0
Total selected partner	26,347.1	27,422.9	36,331.7	117,866.4	75.0	66.8	69.4	69.0
Others[c]	8,770.1	13,644.9	16,047.9	52,955.4	25.0	33.2	30.6	31.0
Total	35,117.2	41,067.8	52,379.5	170,821.9	100.0	100.0	100.0	100.0

Source: *ASEAN Foreign Direct Investments Database* (compiled from data submission of central banks, national statistical offices and other relevant government agencies), ASEAN Secretariat, Jakarta.

Notes
–, not available as of publication time.
n.a., not applicable.
0.0, less than 0.1%.
a Includes Austria, Belgium, Cyprus, Czech Republic, Denmark, Estonia, Finland, France, Germany, Greece, Hungary, Ireland, Italy, Latvia, Lithuania, Luxembourg, Malta, the Netherlands, Poland, Portugal, Slovakia, Slovenia, Spain, Sweden, and the United Kingdom.
b No separate data available; included in 'Others'.
c Includes inflow from all other countries, including Russia, as well as total reinvested earnings in the Philippines (local banks only), for 2002–2006.

ASEAN nationals while preserving national autonomy over investment policy. These conflicting agendas doubtlessly contributed both to the protracted decade-long negotiations leading to the adoption of the agreement and its problematic impact on intra-ASEAN investment flows.[10]

Tensions and contradictions: nationalism versus regionalism

The obvious shortcoming of the agreement lies in its inability to effectively negotiate a mechanism to decouple competitive national investment agendas from broader objectives aimed at creating region-wide standards in the entry and treatment privileges afforded ASEAN nationals. Specifically, the failure to identify a regional mechanism to protect developing domestic industries from parallel competitive ASEAN investments condemned the agreement to its current form; one that essentially enshrines national autonomy in respect of investment policy and investor treatment. The agreement, for example, affirms the centrality of autonomous national screening processes, allowing member states to leave untouched national requirements for investors to obtain written approval from the host government and/or to impose registration and annual renewal requirements on foreign investment. So too, the AAPPI does not delimit the conditionality rights of member states, allowing them to impose point of entry and operating conditions on investments and/or to discriminate through various tax, concessional or incentive systems as a means of directing or selecting investments deemed to be beneficial to the host country. Importantly, this preserves the ability of member states to screen foreign investment and to shelter domestic investment from competition from intra-regional investment. In short, the agreement does not grant investors a right of entry to member states but speaks more generally to post-entry standards of treatment once approval for the investment has been given by the host country.

Even in the case of post-entry standards of treatment, however, the AAPPI tends to preserve national discretionary autonomy, allowing states to withhold or confer national treatment to foreign investors on an *ad hoc* basis. Indeed, there is an obvious tension in the agreement between clauses stipulating equivalency standards in the treatment of ASEAN nationals, and broad exclusion clauses that seek to limit the scope of equivalency treatment. Article IV: 4, for example, notes that 'any two or more of the contracting parties *may negotiate* [my emphasis] to accord national treatment' but further adds that 'nothing herein shall entitle any other party to claim national treatment under the most-favored-national principle'.[11] Clearly, signatories to the agreement were not willing to grant national treatment even to ASEAN investors except on a case-by-case basis and subject to approval by the host country (Thanadsillapakul 2001). This provides signatory states with the latitude to specify modes of treatment and/or impose limitations on foreign investors as deemed appropriate. More obviously, making this clause beyond the scope of MFN consideration preserves the ability of member states to maintain a dual investment regime able to discriminate between domestic and foreign investors.

If examined closely, the AAPPI even preserves the discretion of member states in respect of rights to expropriate foreign invested assets. Article VI:1, for example, allows states to invoke a 'public use, or public purpose, or … public interest' clause in the case of state expropriation only stipulating a 'fair market value' compensation clause. Missing from the agreement, however, is any definitional clarity as to what constitutes 'public use' or 'public purpose', presupposing that member states may invoke this clause unchallenged or at least absent a mechanism to effectively investigate the rectitude of the action itself. It also precludes any legal challenge to an act of 'public use' expropriation by an ASEAN investor, privileging the actions of the member state and guaranteeing the state autonomy in respect of investment provisions. And while compensation is guaranteed ASEAN nationals in the case of expropriation, the technical means via which 'fair market' value is to be determined or the appeal mechanisms available to the investor to challenge this remain opaque – as do the compliance and enforcement mechanisms available to the investor.

This, perhaps, is the most telling omission in the agreement; the absence of rule-based dispute settlement procedures for foreign investors and the failure to vest ultimate decision-making authority in a non-political, non-partisan body. By default, the AEM has ultimate juridical authority over intransigent disputes. This makes dispute settlement a process of protracted political and bureaucratic negotiation and obfuscates the use of rule-based processes informed by technical, objective assessment criteria. The effectiveness of the investment guarantees and their availability to ASEAN investors is thus rendered problematic (Greenwalk 2006).

Finally, the AAPPI leaves untouched issues associated with the transparency of the investment regime or the standardization and formal codification of the regulatory regime responsible for oversight and governance of investment. Again, deference to national proclivities tended to arrest the development of transparent protocols across the membership base and limit the emergence of more effective intra-ASEAN investment coordination. Under the auspices of the AAPPI, for example, even the development of a centralized ASEAN repository providing information about the regulatory standards and compliance protocols for investors proved unfruitful. As before, navigating the rules concerning the entry and operational compliance obligations of investors continued to rest with national authorities and be defined by non-uniform national standards.

AAPPI: the 1996 emendations

Despite the shortcomings of the agreement and its problematic impact on intra-ASEAN investment flows, the AAPPI operated for nearly a decade before emendations were ratified in 1996. These were triggered in part by the accession of Vietnam to full membership of the association (July 1995) and, in part, by perceptions about the veracity of the agreement and the need to quicken the pace of investment cooperation. Two substantive emendations were incorporated into the amended agreement. Article 3 related to issues of transparency and 'predictability' of investment laws and Article 4 to dispute settlement mechanisms.[12] Article 3, in particular, dealt with the lack of investment transparency that by 1996 warranted deliberative corrective measures. More generally, the haphazard and superficial level of investment coordination under the AAPPI became increasingly evident and of growing concern at ASEAN ministerial meetings. The

Twenty-sixth ASEAN Foreign Ministers meeting in July 1993, for example, highlighted concerns about the apparent international trend towards deeper regionalism and coordination in blocs such as the European Union and the North American Free Trade Agreement (NAFTA), while intimating that similar developments would need to be realized in ASEAN if growth trajectories were to be sustained. Similarly, by the time of the AEM meeting in Brunei in September 1995, there was a general sense of urgency with regard to speeding up trade and investment liberalization and that ASEAN would need 'to move faster'.[13] Article 2 of the amended AAPPI thus urged members to 'endeavour to simplify and streamline its investment procedures and approval processes [in order] to facilitate investment flows', and further stipulated in Article 3 that:

> Each contracting party shall ensure the provision of up-to-date information on all laws and regulations pertaining to foreign investment in its territory and shall take appropriate measures to ensure that such information be made as transparent, timely and publicly assessable as possible.[14]

Both emendations essentially gave the game away, revealing within the agreement itself its tacit reification of national standards and proclivities in setting investment policy, yet appealing to member states to enhance the level of transparency of their investment regimes. In a sense, the pretext of cooperative, regionally based investment protocols that the AAPPI was meant to entertain, was set aside. By and large, the agreement now became a more explicit aspirational statement of goals concerning investment cooperation and appeals to members to codify, simplify and publish their investment laws in a manner that would make them more transparent and accessible to ASEAN nationals.

The one area where progress did appear to be being made was in the development of the 'ASEAN Protocol on Dispute Settlement Mechanism' (APDSM), which Article 4 of the amended AAPPI noted would henceforth apply to the settlement of disputes. While notionally a move towards initiating a rules-based dispute settlement system and attempting to decouple dispute procedures from political-cum-bureaucratic negotiation, the APDSM remained in limbo for several years and was never ratified. The then ASEAN Secretary-General, Ong Keng Yong, blamed the failure to immediately ratify the protocol on perceptions that it was 'ineffective because of its excessive bureaucratic nature'.[15]

AAPPI: triumph of nationalism over regionalism?

In terms of the four criteria outlined at the beginning of this chapter, the AAPPI (1987, 1996) obviously fails on all. The AAPPI preserves the ability of member states to engage in competitive investment promotional measures and investment screening, as well as impose conditionality clauses on the operational parameters of foreign investment in the context of a dual investment regime. Its impact should thus be assessed in terms of a circumscribed set of minimum standards defining compensation, restitution and repatriation principles that provide government guarantees to ASEAN nations regarding the transfer of capital, profits, earnings, and

Table 7.3 Major features of the AAPPI (1987, 1996)

	Present	*Absent*	*Implementation/administrative authority*
Non-discrimination clause	√		National
Fair and equitable treatment clause	√		National
Most-favoured nation clause	√		National
National treatment clause		√	–
Rules-based disputation mechanism		√[a]	Regional/ASEAN Secretariat
Rules-based dispute resolution process via independent body		√	
Treaty review mechanism		√	–
Independent administering entity/central statutory authority		√	–
Codified treaty reporting processes		√	National, regional/ASEAN Secretariat
Termination mechanism	√		National
National host country approval/registration required for FDI	Yes		
Allows national autonomous imposition of conditionality clauses on FDI	Yes		
Allows for autonomous national screening of FDI	Yes		

Note
a Attempted as part of the ASEAN Protocol on Dispute Settlement Mechanism (1996).

debt settlement. It is, in this sense, ASEAN's introductory foray aimed at mitigating the most obvious forms of political risk for ASEAN nationals while preserving the juridical sanctity of domestic-based investment regimes and state autonomy with respect to foreign investment policy.

The ASEAN Investment Area (AIA) Agreement

The ASEAN Investment Area (AIA) Agreement is the most comprehensive statement made by ASEAN on investment liberalization to date.[16] Ratified in October 1998 and amended in 2001, the AIA embodies a series of 'schemes, action plans and specific programs' that define the contemporary contours of ASEAN's investment regime.[17] Its coverage extends to various forms of FDI, excluding portfolio investment or investment pertaining to matters falling under the ASEAN Agreement on Services.[18]

The key instruments in the agreement are contained in Article 7 and cover four main areas. The first speaks to an immediate liberalization of all 'industries for investments by ASEAN investors' except for sectors listed on a temporary exclusion list (TEL) or sensitive list (SL). The second sets in place a 'national treatment' clause in respect of 'all industries and measures affecting investment … the admission, establishment, acquisition, expansion, management, operation and disposition of investments'. The third pillar specifies the procedural mechanisms in respect of sector/industry nomination for the inclusion of sectors on the TEL and SL lists. Specifically, Article 7 sets in place a time-line for the phasing out of the TEL (2010), except for Lao People's Democratic Republic, Vietnam (2013) and Myanmar (2015). Article 7 also stipulates procedures for the recurrent review of the TEL and SL lists by a newly formed ministerial-level AIA Council responsible for oversight, coordination and implementation of the AIA among member states (Wee and Mirza 2004). Finally, and most notably, the AIA Agreement provides the first tangible set of provisions for improving investment transparency among member states, stipulating procedural mechanisms and reporting requirements for signatories concerning the rules, regulations and ordinances governing investment provisions and which impact the AIA Agreement. These also extend to bilateral investment agreements entered into by member states with a requirement to disclose 'promptly and at least annually' changes to the regulatory provisions governing investment.[19]

Subsequent emendations to the agreement, in September 2001, did not alter the tenor of the agreement but did stipulate its specific coverage. Whereas the original AIA Agreement specified *all* industries, the amended protocol stipulated sector coverage exclusive to direct investments and services incidental to (a) manufacturing, (b) agriculture, (c) fishery, (d) forestry, and (e) mining and quarrying.[20] In addition, the 2001 protocol accelerated the phasing out of the TEL for the manufacturing sector to 2003 (except for Cambodia, Laos, and Vietnam, which have a deadline of 2010).

The AIA and investment liberalization: fact or fiction?

Despite being the most comprehensive agreement on investment liberalization produced by ASEAN, the AIA is exposed to a series of tensions concerning nationalist economic protectionism, growth objectives and, more broadly, philosophical debates about the role of state sponsorship in the promotion of domestic multinational enterprises (MNEs). Set against a backdrop of regional economic turmoil and financial crises, the ratification of the agreement in 1998 betrayed concerns over the ability of ASEAN member states to continue to attract large inflows of FDI, maintain growth and employment and quell increasing political discontent. While the negotiations leading to the adoption of the AIA preceded the regional financial crisis, the speed of its adoption and the unilateral implementation of various measures contained in the agreement prior to its formal ratification, reveal an environment fraught with anxiety. Malaysia, for example, strongly supported the AIA but saw it principally as a means of nurturing domestic Malaysian capital, whereby ASEAN's regional market would provide the economies of scale and testing ground for Malaysian enterprise to launch onto the world stage. Indonesia too saw the AIA as a means of forging 'ASEAN conglomerates' by privileging ASEAN investors over other foreign direct investors. One senior official in the ASEAN Secretariat, for example, noted that ASEAN 'saw the need to develop regional MNCs using the grace period [clause] before foreign investors would be accorded the same privileges' (Nesadurai 2003) Rather than being conceived strictly as a means of investment liberalization, the AIA was instead embraced as a means of protecting and advantaging regional enterprise in readiness to compete with Western multinational conglomerates. At one and the same time, the AIA thus represents a medium for investment liberalization and regional protectionism.

These competing policy concerns explain the contradictions evident in the various articles of the AIA. The instigation of a coordinating authority in the form of an AIA Council, for example, marked a significant step forward in institutionalizing investment coordination as a central pillar of ASEAN's 2020 vision to develop an economic community (ASEAN 2003). More obviously, it reflected the previous haphazard approaches to investment facilitation, policy coordination and implementation, much of which had been left to national discretion and fell prey to the pitfalls of dissimilar national institutional capacity. In adopting the AIA and the institutional architecture of the AIA Council, ASEAN members signalled their intention to get serious about policy coordination and investment policy harmonization, and to make their national investment regimes more transparent. Indeed, the ministerial level AIA Council moved quickly to institutionalize its processes, forming a Coordinating Committee on Investment (CCI), which meets regularly four to five times a year to oversee policy coordination and implementation, discuss regional investment matters and coordinate investment promotion. Likewise, the instigation under the auspices of the AIA Council of a Working Group on Foreign Direct Investment Statistics (WGFDIS), marked for the first time the adoption of formal procedural mechanisms to harmonize FDI data collection and measurement and thus make available annualized comparative regional FDI data to the AIA Council and policy planners (Wee and Mirza 2004).

While the AIA marks a significant advance in terms of the institutional environment governing intra-regional investment, the articles of agreement and their impact on investment liberalization are more problematic. For example, while the AIA accelerated the phase-out schedule for the TEL (ASEAN 6, 2003; Vietnam, Laos, Cambodia, Myanmar, 2010) it left the phase-out period for the SL unspecified, allowing national discretion in the nomination of sectors to the list and only suggesting that this would be periodically reviewed by the AIA council. Likewise, the commitment of member states to intra-ASEAN investment liberalization seemed to wane as the regional financial crisis subsided. Article 1 of the 2001 'Protocol to Amend the Framework Agreement on the ASEAN Investment Area (AIA),' for example, seemed to step back from a default blanket clause covering 'all' industries towards more exclusionist language covering only named sectors (manufacturing, agriculture, fishery, forestry, mining and quarrying). That the intent was to circumscribe coverage is revealed in paragraph 3, Article 1, which states that the 'agreement shall further cover direct investments in such other sectors and services incidental to such sectors as may be agreed upon by all

Member States.' In this regard, the agreement is probably more revealing for what it failed to include. Strategic sectors like telecommunications, financial services, infrastructure, transportation, and print, electronic and broadcast media, for example, remained unnamed in the agreement, indicative of an enduring depth of protectionist sentiment and strong national sensitivities.[21]

The impact of the AIA is also problematic in terms of its stated achievements to roll back closed and/or restricted sectors to foreign investment and the apparent progress in removing or de-listing sectors from the TEL and SL. Indeed, there is ample evidence to suggest that investment protectionism or sectoral sheltering persist in many ASEAN states. As Appendices 7.1 and 7.2 highlight, for example, the TEL and SL for various countries continue to be populated by numerous industry sectors where investment is either prohibited and/or subject to stringent conditionality clauses limiting investment access. Likewise, the TEL and SL for services incidental to the manufacturing, agricultural, fishery, forestry mining and quarrying sectors (Appendix 7.2), also continue to be heavily populated with and/or subject to stringent conditionality requirements, including ceilings on foreign equity participation, joint venture (JV) requirements, forced government business cooperation contracts (BCC), directed sourcing requirements, domestic market access restrictions and/or export-only clauses, stipulated land use provisions, or various approvals and/or screening requirements that place discretionary authority for investment approval in the hands of regional and local agencies – many of which have stipulated non-dislocation clauses pertaining to local populations as part of their approval requirement processes. In the case of the Philippines, Indonesia, Vietnam, and Lao People's Democratic Republic, for example, the sectoral inclusion and conditionality clauses speak openly to restricted investment access that affects small and medium sized enterprise in the manufacturing, forestry, fishery, agriculture and mining sectors. Equally, the retailing, food and beverage processing/manufacturing sector, construction and allied services, electronic component manufacturing, hospitality, hotel and tourism sectors are all typically restricted or prohibited on the basis of being 'reserved for domestic SMEs'. Far from being an open investment regime, many of ASEAN's member states continue to use protectionist measures despite the stated ambitions of the AIA.

The TEL and SL, however, do not betray the full extent to which investment screening and tacit investment protectionism persists among ASEAN states. Two factors would seem to be at work in this respect. First, regional political pressures and the need to 'keep up appearances' in terms of moving the AIA forward and achieving the targets aspired to, is doubtlessly leading to under-reporting of investment conditionality clauses and restrictions. While the ASEAN Secretariat thus dutifully carries the TEL and SL lists provided by member states, when cross-checked against the investment stipulations applied at point of entry by the relevant national authorities, a wide discrepancy appears to exist between the stated restrictions and the conditionality requirements listed with the ASEAN Secretariat. Second, the compliance requirements stipulated by the AIA in terms of the phasing out of the TEL by 2003 (except for Cambodia, Laos and Vietnam, which have until 2010) and ratified as part of the amended AIA Agreement of

2001, appears to have produced a flurry of reclassifications and redesignations. Vietnam, for example, publishes a 'temporary exclusion list' in which it designates 'nil' sectors under the categories of 'Industries closed to both national and foreign investors'. However, in the same 'nil' excluded sectors it proceeds to list 24 sectors where industries are open but with restrictions on foreign investors including ASEAN nationals. A further 24 sectors are listed on Vietnam's SL list and either subject to prohibition or BCC, equity and export-only requirements.[22] Likewise, while Indonesia does not publish a 'temporary exclusion list' in line with the 2003 phase-out agreement under the Amended 2001 AIA protocol, it does publish Presidential Regulations that essentially circumvent the TEL list. Presidential Regulation Number 77, for example, proscribes prohibitions, conditionality clauses and 'reserved' sectors in a document that runs to some 57 pages and lists more than 25 sectors 'closed' to foreign investment, 121 sectors 'open to investment with conditions' and/or reserved for domestic small and medium sized enterprise, 36 sectors where investment requires a domestic JV partnership, 129 sectors where capital ownership restrictions and/or foreign equity ceilings are imposed, 20 sectors where location restrictions are imposed, 26 sectors where 'special permits' are required, 48 sectors with 100 per cent domestic capital requirements and 17 sectors where combined foreign capital ownership ceilings and locality requirements are imposed.[23]

Similar trends are also apparent in the case of Malaysia and Thailand who no longer publish a TEL and/or claim 'nil' inclusion in terms of prohibited sectors, but have ramped up the SL list and/or moved to a series of increasing conditionality clauses that range from restricted locality clauses, equity restrictions, directed sourcing requirements to restricted market access and export quota requirements. Perhaps more obvious, however, has been the trend towards default blanket investment screening where obligations under the AIA are ostensibly adhered to in terms of non-published investment restrictions and/or closed sectors, but where all foreign investment is subject to a national approvals and/or permit approvals processes. Thailand, Malaysia and Singapore have each adopted this model, driven mostly by a desire to attract finite pools of extra-regional FDI and to appear 'open for business'. This 'knock on the door and ask' type policy approach has undoubtedly been highly successful and proven an attractive investment promotion device (OECD 2004). But to what degree it represents investment liberalization is questionable. Investment screening, approvals processes, compliance requirements and conditionality clauses keep the state front-and-centre in overseeing foreign investment and enable it to shelter sectors or industries from investment competition. What it does do, however, is give the appearance of investment liberalization if only by usurping the need to proscribe prohibitions or restrictions on investment. Much of the claimed progress of the AIA might thus be ascribed to mechanisms such as this.

Two trends thus appear evident in the case of the impact of the AIA. First, a combination of reclassification and redesignation has seen the migration of nominated sectors from the TEL to the SL lists and sectors previously 'closed' now being listed as 'open' but with stringent conditionality clauses that effectively render them protected. Second, policy changes in some ASEAN states towards a non-proscribed investment regime reliant on permits and approvals processes and thus a default investment screening system, has removed the need for blanket investment prohibitions or 'closed' sectors while leaving intact national discretion in investment screening. These two trends are significant since they betray a series of policy failures associated with the AIA. Specifically, they highlight the failure of the AIA to nurture the emergence of a more centralized investment governance regime mediated through regional authorities or to effectively coordinate national investment regimes in a way that produces more systematic standardization of national investment provisions. Rather than restrain national discretionary screening of investment or the imposition of conditionality clauses, the AIA continues to display weaknesses that allow it to be outmanoeuvred by protectionist domestic political constituencies. Despite the decade-long operation of the AIA, its impact on investment liberalization must thus be judged as problematic.

Intra-ASEAN investment patterns and the AIA

Perhaps most disappointing and illustrative of the failure of the AIA to fundamentally transform ASEAN's investment regime, is the near stasis in the composition and distribution of intra-regional investment flows. Despite proclamations of reduced barriers to entry and increased ease of access for ASEAN nationals, the evidence appears to be to the contrary, with intra-ASEAN investment flows remaining largely unchanged, disturbed only by gyrations associated with the Asian financial crisis in the late 1990s, the technology sector meltdown of 2001 and the impact of severe acute respiratory syndrome (SARS) in 2003–2004. Tables 7.5 and 7.6, for example, reveal little evidence that the AIA is leading to enhanced investment penetration among ASEAN states. Rather, two obvious and troubling trends appear evident. The first is the predominance of inflows to Malaysia, Singapore and Thailand. Over the ten-year period from 1995 to 2004, for example, Malaysia averaged 22.86 per cent of all intra-ASEAN FDI inflows, Singapore 24 per cent and Thailand 22.9 per cent. In other words, just three of ASEAN's ten member states absorb the vast bulk (some two-thirds) of intra-regional investment. Country-of-origin data indicate an analogous pattern with Singapore accounting for upwards of 63.3 per cent of intra-ASEAN investment outflows between 1995 and 2003, while Malaysia averaged 16.3 per cent. Just two of ASEAN's ten member states thus accounted for nearly 80 per cent intra-ASEAN investment outflows.

These trends reveal a number of challenges confronting ASEAN and which, potentially, diminish the prospects for deeper investment liberalization. First, the highly concentrated and unequal distribution of intra-regional investment flows highlights the dissimilar nature of ASEAN's economies and the problem of market capture. Singapore, for example, with its well-developed financial markets, efficient prudential capability and adept institutional and infrastructural capacity, is readily able to capture and intermediate the lion's share of the region's investment transactions, particularly in terms of capital raising, merger and acquisitions, and

Table 7.4   Major features of the AIA (1998, 2001)

	Present	*Absent*	*Implementation/administrative authority*
Non-discrimination clause	√		National
National treatment clause	√[a]		–
Rules-based dispute resolution process via independent body		√[b]	
Treaty review mechanism		√	Non-formalized but can be instigated through the AIA council
Independent administering entity/central statutory authority	√		Regional/ASEAN Secretariat (AIA Council endowed with coordinating function but subject to approval of the ASEAN Economics Ministers)
Codified treaty reporting processes	√		National, regional/ASEAN Secretariat (stipulated annualized reporting of national investment regulations to AIA Council)
Termination mechanism	√		National
National host country approval/registration required for FDI	Yes (various requirements as stipulated by national governments)		
Allows national autonomous imposition of conditionality clauses on FDI	Yes under the TEL and SL		
Allows for autonomous national screening of FDI	Yes		

Notes

a It is unclear to what extent the 'national treatment clause' is applied since the coverage of the AIA agreement is limited to stipulated industry sectors (manufacturing, agriculture, fishery, forestry, mining and quarrying).

b The AIA agreement does not contain a dedicated dispute settlement mechanism but the agreement comes under the auspices of the Protocol on Dispute Settlement Mechanism (1996) and as of 2004 the ASEAN Enhanced Dispute Settlement Mechanism. Neither of these mechanisms contain firm–state dispute settlement mechanisms.

allied financial, legal, and consulting support services. Similarly, Malaysia and Thailand offer infrastructural and skills capacities that have made them highly attractive production, assembly and component manufacturing platforms in the region. For the vast majority of ASEAN states, however, lower levels of economic development and poor institutional and infrastructural capacity limit their ability to

Table 7.5 Inward intra-ASEAN FDI by country of destination, 1995–2004 (US$ millions, percentage of total ASEAN FDI)

Host country	1995	1996	1997	1998	1999	2000	2001	2002	2003	2004
Brunei	311.32 (6.7)[a]	353.12 (8.26)	384.94 (7.35)	247.18 (8.84)	4.27 (0.19)	10.59 (0.74)	10.6 (0.40)	21.23 (0.58)	36.79 (1.59)	25 (1.05)
Cambodia	–	–	–	–	–	–	–	9	20	32
Indonesia[b]	608.88 (13.1)	193.33 (4.52)	272.48 (5.2)	(0) -38.36	(0) -427.83	(0) -232.55	(0) -239.98	1336.62 (36.76)	383.96 (16.68)	32 (1.34)
Laos	6.53 (0.14)	102.57 (2.40)	64.36 (1.22)	28.34 (1.01)	31.36 (1.41)	13.72 (0.96)	3.06 (0.11)	7.89 (0.21)	2.98 (0.12)	8 (0.33)
Malaysia	1676.54 (36.2)	1475.8 (34.5)	2261.49 (43.19)	469.94 (16.88)	535.99 (24.17)	258.12 (18.08)	79.99 (3.0)	0.02	251.12 (10.91)	980 (41.24)
Myanmar	96.7 (2.0)	228.6 (5.35)	323.3 (6.17)	153.9 (5.50)	41.2 (1.85)	74.02 (5.18)	67.36 (1.41)	25.11 (0.69)	24 (1.04)	12 (0.5)
Philippines	241.59 (5.2)	74.88 (1.84)	142.87 (2.72)	106.89 (3.82)	110.92 (5.0)	126.53 (8.86)	222.3 (8.44)	37.94 (1.04)	175.1 (7.60)	116 (4.88)
Singapore	1165.07 (25.1)	1206.71 (28.2)	941.57 (15.19)	794.57 (28.41)	632.1 (28.5)	353 (24.7)	356.9 (13.56)	774 (21.29)	637 (27.68)	649 (27.3)
Thailand	160.56 (3.46)	308.1 (7.2)	297.5 (5.68)	569.6 (20.37)	572.04 (25.8)	389.03 (27.2)	1650 (62.69)	1223 (33.6)	670 (29.1)	336 (14.14)
Vietnam	387.25 (8.36)	328.7 (7.6)	547.2 (10.45)	398.7 (14.25)	289.26 (13.0)	202.39 (14.1)	241.49 (9.17)	200.43 (5.51)	100.4 (4.36)	243 (10.2)
Total*	4627.41	4271.81	5235.71	2796.12 -38.36	2217.14 -427.83	1427.4 -232.55	2631.7 -239.98	3635.24	2301.08	2376

Source: ASEAN Foreign Investment Statistics, ASEAN Secretariat, Jakarta.

Notes
a Percentage of total ASEAN FDI in parentheses.
b Negative values in terms of net outflows of FDI have not been factored into the calculations.

Table 7.6 Outward intra-ASEAN FDI by country of origin, 1995–2003 (US$ millions, percentage of total ASEAN FDI)

Source country	1995	1996	1997	1998	1999	2000	2001	2002	2003
Brunei	85.67	146.73	36.21	67.23	18.74	24.54	41.33	17.96	9.13
	(1.87)[a]	(3.43)	(0.69)	(2.46)	(1.03)	(1.79)	(1.68)	(0.50)	(0.54)
Cambodia	1.83	2.19	3.83	0.05	1.35	2.31	0.37	−0.19	5
	(0.04)	(0.05)	(0.07)		(0.07)	(0.16)	(0.01)		(0.29)
Indonesia	538.29	618.53	501.09	333.15	436.26	310.57	340.79	384.4	228.33
	(11.79)	(14.47)	(9.57)	(12.21)	(24.07)	(22.56)	(13.86)	(10.80)	(13.68)
Laos	0.01	0.01	0.01	—	0.57	10.92	0.16	—	0.2
				(0)	(0.03)	(0.79)			(0.01)
Malaysia	769.48	713.82	623.78	578.65	327.25	313.71	119.47	389.41	398.82
	(16.85)	(16.70)	(11.91)	(21.2)	(18.0)	(22.79)	(4.85)	(10.94)	(23.91)
Myanmar	3.95	2.2	6.96	0.5	2.35	8.14	3.42	12.98	7.1
	(0.08)	(0.05)	(0.13)	(0.01)	(0.12)	(0.59)	(0.13)	(0.36)	(0.42)
Philippines[b]	89.6	71.09	17.44	−26.36	−22.43	58.94	33.12	15.18	−2.79
	(1.96)	(1.66)	(0.33)			(4.28)	(1.34)	(0.42)	
Singapore	2983.39	2394.87	3572.97	1620.05	897.05	641.87	1917.55	2421.95	1309.95
	(65.3)	(56.06)	(67.85)	(59.4)	(49.51)	(46.63)	(77.99)	(68.47)	(78.5)
Thailand[b]	181.44	321.95	472.13	155.69	123.75	−181.38	−66.69	278.06	108.25
	(3.97)	(7.53)	(9.0)	(5.74)	(6.83)			(7.81)	(6.48)
Vietnam	0.77	0.44	1.29	1.78	4.41	5.24	2.21	37.2	4.91
	(0.01)	(0.01)	(0.024)	(0.06)	(0.24)	(0.38)	(0.08)	(1.04)	(0.29)
Total	4564.83	4271.83	5235.73	2727.1	1811.73	1376.24	2458.42	3557.14	1667.87

Source: ASEAN Foreign Investment Statistics, ASEAN Secretariat, Jakarta.

Notes
a Percentage of total ASEAN FDI.
b Negative values in terms of net outflows of FDI have not been factored into the calculations.

absorb investment flows on a scale that would significantly change current investment patterns. Investment liberalization in ASEAN thus remains as much an issue of the ability to absorb investment as one of engineering agreements to facilitate intra-regional investment flows. While the AIA might thus be faulted for its shortcomings and individual ASEAN states for failing to honour the letter and spirit of the agreement, clearly ASEAN faces substantial obstacles to equalizing investment absorption if only because its membership continues to be composed of vastly dissimilar states whose economic composition is far from complementary.

Second, Indonesia, Thailand, the Philippines and, increasingly, Vietnam, occupy similar developmental niches in terms of low-value added manufacturing, particularly in the electronic component sector, but also in the areas of bio-fuels (palm oil in Malaysia and Indonesia; automobile parts manufacture and assembly in Thailand and Malaysia; and textiles and footwear in Indonesia, Vietnam and Thailand). Not only does this create competitive rather than cooperative regional dynamics, it also tends to bolster fiercely protectionist domestic political constituencies and competitive bidding wars through the provision of costly incentive systems for attracting and maintaining FDI. Competition for extra-regional FDI in ASEAN, for example, has witnessed what the OECD recently described as a 'proliferation of incentives' which national governments use as a means of driving their development and offering competitive advantages to encourage investors to locate in their jurisdictions (OECD 2004). Rather than seeing these abate or migrate to regional incentive schemes as one might expect if ASEAN was maturing toward a regional investment bloc, they appear to be deepening. Indonesia, for example, reinstated its incentive structures for FDI in the mid- 1990s and has continually intensified them, particularly after the Asian financial crisis. So extensive have these competitive incentive structures become that the OECD now estimates that the cost to ASEAN governments constitutes a significant proportion of their GDP. The estimated cost of Vietnam's incentives, for example, now runs to 0.7 per cent of GDP or some 5 per cent of non-oil revenues; for the Philippines some 1 per cent of GDP or US$2.5 billion of forgone taxation revenues year-on-year; and as much as 1.7 per cent of GDP for Malaysia (OECD 2004: 99–100). Perhaps more obviously, these incentives are likely to persist as the competition not only between ASEAN states but between ASEAN states and China for extra-regional FDI continues to intensify. Since the mid-1990s, for example, the investment patterns on which ASEAN's growth has been predicated have deteriorated. The result has been a systematic decline in ASEAN's share of region-wide FDI: down from 50 per cent in 1990 to between 17 and 19 per cent in 2003, with China now absorbing upwards of 50 per cent of all FDI into Asia (Jarvis 2004).

Third, highly unequal intra-regional investment flows have also tended to arouse nationalistic suspicions and intra-regional rivalry. As a financially dominant player in intra-ASEAN investment, Singapore, for example, is frequently perceived as predatory. Recent investments by the investment arm of the Singapore Government, Temasek Holdings, into Shin Corporation, Thailand's largest and dominant telecommunications company, and majority owned by then Thai Prime Minister, Thaksin Shinawatra, for example, triggered a military coup and the removal of Thaksin based on fears in part reflecting the sale of telecommunications assets to foreign regional interests (Kazmin 2008). Similarly, Temasek's investment via ST Telemedia and Singapore Technologies and their purchase of a 41.9 per cent stake in Indosat, Indonesia's satellite telecommunications company, met with Indonesian resentment and various legal manoeuvrings by the Indonesian anti-monopoly watchdog who, in November 2007, announced that they would move to impose sanctions and fine Temasek (Guerin 2007).

Recent examples such as this indicate enduring problems that lessen, or at least render problematic, the prospects for engineering further agreements that deepen investment liberalization in ASEAN. The prolonged delay in the emergence of the ASEAN Comprehensive Investment Agreement (ACIA) which remains 'under negotiation' despite the successful negotiation and partial ratification of the ASEAN Charter, for example, is illustrative of the depth of investment nationalism that persists in the grouping.[24] Finding meaningful ways to surmount such political stumbling blocks will be no easy feat.

Where next? The future of investment liberalization in ASEAN

Despite ASEAN's lacklustre achievements in facilitating intra-regional investment liberalization, individual member states have nonetheless displayed a zeal for investment liberalization principally through a spate of bilateral investment treaties (BITs). As Table 7.7 highlights, all ASEAN states with the exception of Myanmar and Brunei have aggressively pursued bilateral investment agreements, with ASEAN's membership collectively signing 326 BITs as of 2007. As Table 7.7 also demonstrates, however, the pattern of BIT agreements appears to lie beyond the region. Excluding Myanmar which remains blacklisted by most Western states, and Cambodia and Laos where limited investment opportunities have constrained the engagement of extra-regional parties, the vast majority of BITs entered into by ASEAN's members (some 85 per cent or 278 of BITs) have been with non-ASEAN states.

This trend is likely prescient of the future direction of investment liberalization in Southeast Asia; one potentially dominated by a 'spaghetti bowl' effect of overlapping BITs and bilateral trade agreements (BTAs) that will collectively define the region's investment architecture. The implications of this are varied but all are potentially significant for ASEAN. For example, with the failure of WTO talks in 2006 and 2008 to realize further liberalization in the global trade and investment system, states have been forced to place greater emphasis on bilateral initiatives as their principal tool for enhancing trade and investment. By their very nature, bilaterally negotiated agreements have proven relatively efficient, simple and effective instruments for achieving stated economic goals and, judging by their number, are now the preferred means for trade and investment enhancement. The problem for ASEAN, of course, is that they effectively usurp or bypass regionally orchestrated agreements such as the AIA and pose the risk of marginalizing ASEAN as the region's most proactive and central vehicle for securing inter-state economic cooperation and mutual welfare gains. To put it another way, BITs, because they are targeted and nested in mutually defined interests, appear to produce deeper

Table 7.7 ASEAN member state BITs

Country	Total number of BITs signed by ASEAN states	Number of BITs signed with an ASEAN member	Percentage of total number of BITs signed with an ASEAN member state
Brunei	5	0	0
Cambodia	16	6	38
Indonesia	60	7	12
Laos	21	6	29
Malaysia	66	4	6
Myanmar	4	3	75
Philippines	35	5	14
Singapore	31	4	13
Thailand	39	5	13
Vietnam	49	8	16

Source: UNCTAD *World Investment Report: Transnational corporations, extractive industries and development,* New York & Geneva: United Nations Conference on Trade and Development (UNCTAD), 2007b. See also WorldTradeLaw.net: http://www.worldtradelaw.net/fta/ftadatabase/ftas.asp

liberalization measures and superior welfare effects than has been the case with the AIA; this, after all would explain why some ASEAN states have pursued BITs with other ASEAN states even in the presence of the AIA Agreement.

Further, the pursuit of BITs by ASEAN states might also be assessed in terms of the superior dispute resolution procedures they typically contain. Most BITs have recourse to independent arbitration in third-party countries in the case of investment disputes or breach of investment guarantees. This is not the case with the AIA which, under both the 1998 and 2001 agreements, relied on political-cum-bureaucratic dispute resolution mechanisms contained first in the Protocol on Dispute Settlement Mechanism (1996) and second in the ASEAN Protocol on Enhanced Dispute Settlement Mechanism (APEDSM) (2004).[25] As Walter Woon, the Attorney General of Singapore notes:

> The heart of the Vientiane Protocol … provides for the establishment of a panel to look into the dispute and make findings to assist the Senior Economic Officials Meeting (SEOM) to come to a discussion. SOEM, on its part, shall adopt the panel's report, unless it decides by consensus not to, or if one of the parties signals its intention to appeal …
>
> Woon 2008

The APEDSM, in other words, is not strictly a legal-based instrument but can defer matters of disputation to economic officials and political organs that can disregard the recommendations of the appointed adjudication panel. More obviously, neither of these agreements is geared to investment disputes *per se* and apply more to state–state than to firm–state dispute settlement procedures. All this points to shortcomings in the AIA which likely explain the prevalence and deepening web of BITs entered into by ASEAN's member states. It also points to a further irony in the liberalization process in ASEAN; that much if not most of it is being driven by instruments and mechanisms external to the association rather than the various agreements constructed by the association. BITs and BTAs, for example, signal much deeper levels of penetration into protectionist practices than those achieved by the AIA or the AAPPI. In the case of tariff liberalization, for example, one commentator went so far as to note that:

> In practice AFTA [the ASEAN Free Trade Agreement] and its core agreements (on tariff, investment and services) have so far merely given the appearance of political cooperation on economic liberalization policy changes that were happening anyway. Also, because of the depth of unilateral liberalization in ASEAN countries, there do not appear to have been any significant tariff or investor benefits for being an ASEAN member as opposed to a non-ASEAN member.
>
> (As quoted in Pagaduan-Araullo 2007)

Paradoxically, then, many of the standards associated with liberalization highlighted at the beginning of this chapter, particularly national autonomy in relation to investment screening and conditionality provisions, transparency in respect of national investment regimes and codification of regulatory standards governing investment related provisions, are being moderated more by the outcomes of bilateral initiatives than by ASEAN-based ones. The danger, of course, is that since the majority of these bilateral agreements reside with countries outside the region, the investment provisions and patterns they create will skew relationships in ways that do not necessarily complement regional ideals or the longer term goals of ASEAN economic integration.

ASEAN, in a sense, is thus being outclassed, outmanoeuvred and is in danger of becoming outdated if renewed commitment to investment liberalization is not forthcoming. Making ASEAN relevant to investment liberalization and to enhancing investment volumes across its membership base will require considerably more effort than has thus far been displayed. Much, of course, will depend on the outcomes of the long awaited ASEAN Comprehensive Investment Agreement (ACIA) which is set to supersede the AIA when formalized sometime in 2008–2009. It might, however, be premature and over optimistic to assume that the ACIA will prove to be the answer to reinvigorating investment liberalization in ASEAN. As Walter Lohman and Anthony B. Kim note:

> ASEAN's ambition is clear, its record in implementing agreements to facilitate economic integration is spotty, and its commitment to economic freedom is subpar. ASEAN requires a resolution of vision to get to ASEAN Economic Community by 2015. It also needs tools and resources to manage the undertaking effectively.
>
> (Lohman and Kim 2008)

Historically, ASEAN has been long on talk and short on concrete deliverables. Singapore's former Foreign Minister, Professor S. Jayakumar, for example, noted that ASEAN has at times been widely perceived to be 'ineffective' and in danger of being marginalized by its dialogue partners and international investors alike.[26] Transforming ASEAN from what Hadi Soesastro described as a 'diplomatic community' into a true economic community is, of course, the intent behind recent political initiatives and the newly minted ASEAN Charter (Soesastro 2001). The ambitions are again clear and concisely articulated. Whether these ambitions will be realized, however, remains the preserve of individual member states and of their commitment to enhancing the supranational capabilities of ASEAN. With a secretariat that is only 210 people strong, resource capabilities well below those required to service a community of some 600 million people, and an ambitious agenda for economic integration, it is obvious that considerably more effort, resources and political commitment will be required in the coming years.

Notes

1 ASEAN Secretariat web page http://www.aseansec.org/64.htm.
2 ASEAN Secretariat, 'Overview of ASEAN' http://www.aseansec.org/64.htm.
3 See the Joint Communiqué, Third ASEAN Heads of Government Meeting. Manila, 14–15 December 1987, Point 29. ASEAN Secretariat, http://www.aseansec.org/1225.htm.
4 The AAPPI was signed in 1987 between the original six ASEAN states (Indonesia, Malaysia, the Philippines, Singapore, Thailand and Brunei). It was subsequently amended in 1996 with the accession of Vietnam to the association.
5 AAPPI Agreement, 1987, Article IV:1. ASEAN Secretariat.
6 AAPPI Agreement, 1987, Article IV:3. ASEAN Secretariat.
7 AAPPI Agreement, 1987, Article VI:1. ASEAN Secretariat.
8 Article X clause 2 of the AAPPA agreement (1987) nominates the International Centre for the Settlement of Investment Disputes (ICSID), the United Nations Commission for International Trade Law, the Regional Centre for Arbitration at Kuala Lumpur, 'or any other centre for regional arbitration in ASEAN, whichever the parties to the dispute mutually agree to appoint for the purposes of Conducting the arbitration'. See AAPPI Agreement, 1987, Article X:2. ASEAN Secretariat.
9 Joint Communiqué, Third ASEAN Heads of Government Meeting, Manila, 14–15 December 1987, Article 29. ASEAN Secretariat, http://www.aseansec.org/1225.htm.
10 Negotiations to explore the possibility of formalizing an ASEAN investment agreement were commenced soon after the Second ASEAN Heads of Government meeting in Kuala Lumpur, August 1977, when the joint communiqué urged the commencement of bilateral agreements on investment guarantees between ASEAN members and 'directed that measures be taken to stimulate the flow of technology, know-how and private investments among the member countries'. Joint Communiqué, Second ASEAN Heads of Government Meeting, Kuala Lumpur, 4–5 August 1977, communiqué points 16 and 25. Jakarta: ASEAN Secretariat, http://www.aseansec.org/1224.htm.
11 AAPPI Agreement, 1987, Article IV:4 ASEAN Secretariat, http://www.aseansec.org/6464.htm.

12 Protocol to Amend the Agreement among the Governments of Brunei Darussalam, the Republic of Indonesia, Malaysia, the Republic of the Philippines, the Republic of Singapore and the Kingdom of Thailand for the Promotion and Protection of Investments, Jakarta, 12 September 1996. ASEAN Secretariat, http://www.aseansec. org/6465.htm. The other Articles in the amended protocol of the AAPPI refer to procedural issues related to the accession of new members and the deposit of articles with the ASEAN Secretariat.

13 See the Joint Communiqué of the Twenty-sixth ASEAN Ministerial Meeting, Singapore, 23–24 July, 1993. ASEAN Secretariat, Jakarta. Joint Press Statement of the Twenty-seventh ASEAN Economic Ministers Meeting (AEM) Bandar Seri Begawan, Brunei Darussalam, 7–8 September, 1995. ASEAN Secretariat, Jakarta, http://www. aseansec.org/2116.htm.

14 Protocol to Amend the Agreement among the Governments of Brunei Darussalam, the Republic of Indonesia, Malaysia, the Republic of the Philippines, the Republic of Singapore and the Kingdom of Thailand for the Promotion and Protection of Investments, Jakarta, 12 September 1996. ASEAN Secretariat, http://www.aseansec.org/6465.htm.

15 ASEAN Secretary-General Ong Keng Yong as quoted in Greenwald, A. (2006) 'The ASEAN–China Free Trade Area (ACFTA): A legal response to China's Economic Rise', *Duke Journal of Comparative & International Law*, 16:207. Only in November, 2004, did ASEAN adopt a formal dispute resolution mechanism entitled the 'ASEAN Protocol on Enhanced Dispute Settlement Mechanism'. ASEAN Secretariat, Jakarta, http://www.aseansec.org/16754.htm. In 2004, the ASEAN Protocol on Enhanced Dispute Settlement Mechanism (APEDSM) was eventually ratified.

16 See the 'Framework Agreement on the ASEAN Investment Area (AIA)' 7 October 1998, Makati, Philippines. ASEAN Secretariat, http://www.aseansec.org/7994.pdf. See also 'Protocol to Amend the Framework Agreement on the ASEAN Investment Area', Ha Noi, 14 September 2001. ASEAN Secretariat, http://www.aseansec.org/6467.htm.

17 ASEAN Secretariat (ND) *Handbook of investment agreements in ASEAN. ASEAN Secretariat*, Jakarta, p.3, http://www.aseansec.org/12814.htm.

18 See the ASEAN Framework on Services Agreement, Bangkok, 15 December 1995. ASEAN Secretariat, Jakarta, http://www.aseansec.org/19087.htm. Protocol to Amend the ASEAN Framework Agreement on Services, Phnom Penh, Cambodia, 2 September 2003. ASEAN Secretariat, Jakarta, http://www.aseansec.org/AFAS_Amendment_Protocol.pdf.

19 Article 11, Framework Agreement on the ASEAN Investment Area, 8 October 1998. ASEAN Secretariat, http://www.aseansec.org/2280.htm.

20 Protocol to amend the Framework Agreement on the ASEAN Investment Area, Ha Noi, 14 September 2001. ASEAN Secretariat, http://www.aseansec.org/6467.htm.

21 Protocol to amend the Framework Agreement on the ASEAN Investment Area, Ha Noi, 14 September 2001. ASEAN Secretariat, http://www.aseansec.org/6467.htm.

22 'Temporary Exclusion List for the Opening up of Industries for the Manufacturing, Agriculture, Fishery, Forestry, Mining and Quarrying Sectors: Vietnam', ASEAN Secretariat, Jakarta, http://www.aseansec.org/18657.htm.

23 Presidential Regulation of the Republic of Indonesia, Number 77 of 2007, 'Concerning the list of lines of Business Closed and Open with Conditions of Investment',. Republic of Indonesia, http://www.bkpm.go.id/en/downloads/31.

24 At the time of writing, the ASEAN Charter has been ratified by six of the ten member states. The ACIA has been under negotiation for several years but, as yet, has not been formalized. At the Tenth ASEAN Investment Area (AIA) Council Meeting on 23 August 2007, the AIA Council agreed to 'complete the ACIA by the Eleventh AIA Council

meeting in Singapore in August, 2008'. Tenth ASEAN Investment Area (AIA) Council Meeting Joint Media Statement, 23 August 2007, Makati City, Philippines. ASEAN Secretariat. Jakarta http://www.aseansec.org/20834.htm.

25 Protocol on Dispute Settlement Mechanism, Manila, 20 November 1996. ASEAN Secretariat, Jakarta <http://www.aseansec.org/16654.htm>. ASEAN Protocol on Enhanced Dispute Settlement Mechanism, Vientiane, Lao, People's Democratic Republic, 29 November 2004. ASEAN Secretariat, Jakarta http://www.aseansec.org/16754.htm.

26 Professor S. Jayakumar as quoted in Simon S.C. Tay, Jesus P Estanislao and Hadi Soesastro (2001) *Reinventing ASEAN*, Singapore: Institute of Southeast Asian Studies, p. ix.

Bibliography

Adlung, R. and Molinuevo, M. (2008) 'Bilateralism in services trade: is there fire behind the (bit-)smoke'? *Journal of International Economic Law*, 11: 365–409.

Greenwalk, A. (2006) 'The ASEAN–China Free Trade Area (ACFTA): A legal response to China's economic rise', *Duke Journal of Comparative and International Law*, 16: 193–217.

Guerin, Bill (2007) 'Telecom tangle for Singapore's Temasek', *Asia Times Online*. 22 November. Online. Available HTTP: http://www.atimes.com/atimes/Southeast_Asia/IK22Ae01.html (accessed 8 May 2008).

Hew, D. (2007) (ed.) *Brick by Brick: The building of an economic community*, Singapore: Institute of Southeast Asian Studies.

Jarvis, D.S.L. (2004) 'The changing economic environment in Southeast Asia: ASEAN, China and the prospects for enhanced cooperation', in *Building Institutional Capacity in Asia,* Ministry of Finance, Japan and the Research Institute for Asia and the Pacific, University of Sydney, Australia. p.1.

Kazmin, A. (2008) 'Temasek to reduce stake in Shin Corp,' *The Financial Times*, 17 June.

Lohman, W. and Kim, A.B. (2008) 'Enabling ASEAN's Economic Vision', *Backgrounder*, *No. 2101*. Washington, DC: The Heritage Foundation.

McDougall, D. (1997) *The International Politics of the New Asia Pacific*, Boulder, CO: Lynne Rienner.

Narine, S. (2002) *Explaining ASEAN: Regionalism in Southeast Asia*, Boulder, CO: Lynne Rienner.

Nesadurai, H.E.S. (2003) *Globalization, Domestic Politics and Regionalism: The ASEAN Free Trade Area*, London: Routledge.

OECD (2004) *International Investment Perspectives*, Paris: Centre for Cooperation with Non-Members, Organisation for Economic Co-operation and Development.

Pagaduan-Araullo, C. (2007) 'ASEAN Hype' *Bulatat (Manila)* 7, 5–11August, as posted on the website of Bilaterals.org. Online. Available HTTP: http://www.bilaterals.org/article.php3?id_article=9251&var_recherche=ASEAN+investment+liberalization (accessed 5 March 2008).

Presidential Regulation of the Republic of Indonesia, Number 77 of 2007, Concerning the list of lines of Business Closed and Open with Conditions of Investment. Republic of Indonesia. Online. Available HTTP: http://www.bkpm.go.id/en/downloads/31 (accessed 20 April 2008).

Quazi, R. (2007) 'Economic freedom and foreign direct investment in East Asia', *Journal of The Asia Pacific Economy*, 12: 329–44.

Sakakibara, E. and Yamakawa, S. (2003) 'Regional integration in East Asia: Challenges and opportunities: Part II'. *Trade, Finance and Integration. Policy Research Working paper 3079*. World Bank, East Asia and Pacific Region. Poverty Reduction and Economic Management Sector Unit, pp.18–19.

Soesastro, H. (2001) 'ASEAN in 2030: The long view', in S.C. Tay, J.P. Estanislao and H. Soesastro (eds) *Reinventing ASEAN*, Singapore: Institute of Southeast Asian Studies, pp. 226–42.

Thanadsillapakul, L. (2001) 'International investment law: The investment regime of ASEAN countries', *Thailand Law Source*. Online. Available HTTP: http://members.tri-pod.com/asialaw/articles/lawaninvestment.html (accessed 14 February 2008).

UNCTAD (2003) *World Investment Report 2003: FDI Policies for Development: National and international perspectives*, New York: United Nations Conference on Trade and Development.

UNCTAD (2007a) 'Development implications of international investment agreements', *International Investment Agreements Monitor, Number 2*: New York and Geneva: United Nations.

UNCTAD (2007b) *World Investment Report 2007: Transnational Corporations, Extractive Industries and Development*. New York and Geneva: United Nations.

Wee, K.H. and Mirza, H. (2004) 'ASEAN investment cooperation: Retrospect, developments and prospects', in N.J. Freeman and F.L. Bartels (eds) *The Future of Foreign Direct Investment in Southeast Asia*, London: Routledge, pp. 201–54.

Woon, W. (2008) '*The ASEAN Charter Dispute Settlement Mechanism*'. Online. Available HTTP: http://www.agc.gov.my/agc/agc/rev/agcjc/3rd/pdf/SingaporeThe_ASEAN_Charter_Dispute_Settlement_Mechanisms.pdf (accessed 21 April 2008).

ASEAN official documents

ASEAN (2003) *An Overview Declaration Vision 2020*, Jakarta: ASEAN Secretariat.

ASEAN Foreign Investment Statistics, Jakarta: Asian Secretariat.

ASEAN Framework on Services Agreement, Bangkok, 15 December 1995, Jakarta: ASEAN Secretariat. Online. Available HTTP: http://www.aseansec.org/19087.htm (accessed 12 March 2008).

ASEAN Investment Report 2007, Jakarta: ASEAN Secretariat.

ASEAN Protocol on Enhanced Dispute Settlement Mechanism, Vientiane, Lao, PDR, 29 November 2004, Jakarta: ASEAN Secretariat. Online. Available HTTP: http://www.aseansec.org/16754.htm 14/4/2008

ASEAN Secretariat (No date given) *Handbook of Investment Agreements in ASEAN,* Jakarta: ASEAN Secretariat, Online. Available HTTP: http://www.aseansec.org/12799.htm

Framework Agreement on the ASEAN Investment Area, 8 October 1998, Jakarta: ASEAN Secretariat. Online. Available HTTP: http://www.aseansec.org/2280.htm (accessed 4 February 2008).

Joint Communique, The Third ASEAN Heads of Government Meeting. Manila, 14–15 December 1987, Point 29, Jakarta: ASEAN Secretariat. Online. Available HTTP: http://www.aseansec.org/1225.htm (accessed 15 April 2008).

Joint Press Statement of the Twenty-seventh ASEAN Economic Ministers Meeting (AEM) Bandar Seri Begawan, Brunei Darussalam, 7–8 September 1995, Jakarta: ASEAN Secretariat. Online. Available HTTP: http://www.aseansec.org/2116.htm (accessed 2 May 2008).

Protocol to Amend the Agreement among the Governments of Brunei Darussalam, the Republic of Indonesia, Malaysia, the Republic of the Philippines, the Republic of Singapore, and the Kingdom of Thailand for the Promotion and Protection of Investments, 12 September 1996, Jakarta: ASEAN Secretariat. Online. Available HTTP: <http://www.aseansec.org/6465.htm (accessed 12 April 2008).

Protocol to Amend the Framework Agreement on the ASEAN Investment Area, Ha Noi, 14 September 2001, Jakarta: ASEAN Secretariat Online. Available HTTP: http://www.aseansec.org/6467.htm (accessed 28 April 2008).

Protocol on Dispute Settlement Mechanism, Manila, 20 November 1996, Jakarta: ASEAN Secretariat Online. Available HTTP: http://www.aseansec.org/16654.htm (accessed 12 March 2008).

Temporary Exclusion List for the Opening up of Industries for the Manufacturing, Agriculture, Fishery, Forestry, Mining and Quarrying Sectors: Vietnam, Jakarta: ASEAN Secretariat. Online. Available HTTP: http://www.aseansec.org/18657.htm (accessed 12 April 2008).

Tenth ASEAN Investment Area (AIA) Council Meeting Joint Media Statement, 23 August 2007, Makati City, Philippines, Jakarta: ASEAN Secretariat. Online. Available HTTP: http://www.aseansec.org/20834.htm (accessed 14 April 2008).

Appendix 7.1 ASEAN foreign direct investment temporary exclusion list and sensitive list, 2008: manufacturing, agriculture, fishery, forestry, mining and quarrying sectors

Country	Temporary exclusion list/restricted investment: sector/industry	Restriction/conditionality requirements	Sensitive list: sector/industry	Restriction/conditionality requirements
Brunei Darussalam[a]	Growing of cereals and other crops	30% local participation requirement for eligibility to access government facilities and sales to domestic market	Arms and ammunition	Prohibited
			Spirits and other alcoholic beverages	Prohibited
			Fireworks	Prohibited
	Growing of vegetables, horticultural specialties, nursery products, fruits, nuts, beverage and spice crops	30% local participation requirement for eligibility to access government facilities and sales to domestic market	Tobacco and tobacco substitute products	Prohibited
			Polluting industries affecting the environment	Prohibited
			Retail	Prohibited
			Other manufacturing industries according to previously published list	Prohibited
Indonesia[b]	Sawn timber	Special permissions required and/or approvals and subject to discretionary conditionality clauses	Food and beverage (F and B) industries involving preparation of shredded, boiled, fried or jerked meat; salted/pickled fish and other marine biota	Prohibited investment (reserved for small-scale enterprise)
	Veneer woods industry Plywood industry	Special permissions required and/or approvals and subject to discretionary	F and B industries involving food preparation of chips produced from	Prohibited investment (reserved for small-scale enterprise)

(Continued)

Appendix 7.1 (Continued)

Country	Temporary exclusion list/restricted investment: sector/industry	Restriction/conditionality requirements	Sensitive list: sector/industry	Restriction/conditionality requirements
	Laminated veneer lumber	conditionality clauses	flour flavoured with shrimp/fish; fish/shrimp condiment	
	Wood chip industry	Materials sourcing stipulations/requirements	F and B industries preparing/processing grains, cereals, legumes and tubers, including rice flours of various kinds; flour made of legumes; flour made of dried cassava	On condition of partnership with small scale enterprises
	Security printing/security paper printing/security ink; Pulp industry	Permit approvals/ministerial authority and approvals		
	Clove, cigarette and other cigarette industries	Clearance/recommendation from relevant ministries/cooperation/sourcing requirements with small enterprise	F and B industries making bread, cookies and the like	Prohibited investment (reserved for small scale enterprise)
	Port facilities (connecting port)	Joint venture (JV) or business cooperation contracts (BCC) with domestic partner as stipulated by government	Postal services	Prohibited
			Non-ferrous metal industry (lead)	Prohibited
			Cyclamate and saccharin industry	Prohibited
	Agricultural business greater than 25 hectares	Maximum equity ownership of 95%	Chlor alkali industry with mercury containing materials	Prohibited

(Continued)

Appendix 7.1 (Continued)

Country	Temporary exclusion list/restricted investment: sector/industry	Restriction/conditionality requirements	Sensitive list: sector/industry	Restriction/conditionality requirements
	Domestic/international sea transportation/port loading facilities/port infrastructure services – jetty, container terminal, liquid bulk terminal, dry bulk terminal/port waste reception facilities	Maximum equity restrictions of 49%	Alcoholic beverage industry (liquor, wine, and malt beverage)	Prohibited
			Chemical industry and potentially environmentally harmful chemical production, such as: penta chlorophenol, dichloro diphenyl trichloro ethane (DDT), dieldrin, chlordane, carbon tetrachloride, chloro fluoro carbon (CFC), methyl bromide, methyl chloroform, halon, and the like	Prohibited
			Air traffic service (ATS) providers	Prohibited
			Telecommunication/marine aids to navigation	Prohibited
			Provider and operator of terminal	Prohibited
			Public broadcasting service (LPP) of radio and television	Prohibited

(Continued)

Appendix 7.1 (Continued)

Country	Temporaryexclusion list/restricted investment: sector/industry	Restriction/conditionality requirements	Sensitive list: sector/ industry	Restriction/conditionality requirements
			Management and operation of station monitoring spectrum radio frequency and satellite orbit equipment/infrastructure	Prohibited
			Sawmill and plywood operation and manufacture	Prohibited
Malaysia			Pineapple canning	Prohibited except for projects with source of supply drawn from own plantations
			Palm oil milling	Prohibited except for projects with source of supply drawn from own plantations
			Palm oil refining	Prohibited in Peninsular Malaysia; permitted in Sabah and Sarawak with source supply from own plantations
			Sugar refining	Prohibited

(Continued)

Appendix 7.1 (Continued)

Country	Temporary exclusion list/restricted investment: sector/industry	Restriction/conditionality requirements	Sensitive list: sector/industry	Restriction/conditionality requirements
			Liquors and alcoholic beverages	Prohibited
			Tobacco processing and cigarettes	Prohibited
			Sawn timber, veneer and plywood	Prohibited for Peninsular Malaysia and Sabah; permitted in Sarawak
			Wood based products utilizing local logs as raw materials	Prohibited for Peninsular Malaysia; permitted in Sabah and Sarawak
Philippines			Manufacturing cooperatives	No (nil) foreign equity permitted
			Agriculture, fishery, mining and quarrying cooperatives	No (nil) foreign equity permitted
			People's small scale mining programme (mining activities which rely extensively on manual labour using simple implements/ methods, not exceeding 20 hectares with investment not exceeding	Only Philippine citizens or corporations with minimum of 60% capital owned by Philippine citizens who voluntarily form a cooperative licensed by Department of Environment and Natural

(Continued)

Appendix 7.1 (Continued)

Country	Temporary exclusion list/restricted investment: sector/industry	Restriction/conditionality requirements	Sensitive list: sector/industry	Restriction/conditionality requirements
			P10.00 million (US$1,000)	Resources may engage in the exraction/removal of minerals or ore bearing materials
Thailand[a]	Artificially propagated or plant breeding	Foreign equity participation restricted to less than 50% of registered capital		
	Fishery and marine animal culture	Foreign capital participation of 50% or more of registered capital permitted subject to: i) permission of Director General of Business Development and approval of Foreign Business Committee; ii) permission under law governing Industrial Estate Authority of Thailand or other related laws		
	Logging from plantation			
Singapore			Chewing gum/bubble gum/dental chewing gum or any like substance	Prohibited on the basis of safety and social reasons
			Firecrackers/matchsticks	Prohibited on the basis of safety and social reasons
			Pig farming	No more licences issued
			Quarrying	No more licences issued

(Continued)

Appendix 7.1 (Continued)

Country	Temporary exclusion list/restricted investment: sector/industry	Restriction/conditionality requirements	Sensitive list: sector/industry	Restriction/conditionality requirements
			Publishing and printing of newspapers	Foreign equity subject to approval of relevant ministry
Cambodia			Poisonous chemicals	Disallowed
			Agricultural pesticides/insecticides	Disallowed
			Any other goods/manufactured items using chemical substances that affect public health and the environment	Disallowed
			Psychotropic and narcotic substances	Disallowed
			Electricity production using imported waste products	Disallowed
			Forestry exploitation/harvesting	Disallowed
Lao People's Democratic Republic	Manufacture of beverages including soft drinks, ethyl alcohol and spirits, drinking and mineral water, fruit juices	Various conditionality clauses imposed at the discretion of national authorities. Conditionality clauses are 'negotiated with the Lao	Manufacture of Lao dolls	Prohibited (reserved for Loa nationals)
			Manufacture of products	Prohibited (reserved for Loa national)

Country	Temporary exclusion list/restricted investment: sector/industry	Restriction/conditionality requirements	Sensitive list: sector/industry	Restriction/conditionality requirements
	Manufacture of cigarettes Leather tannery and leather dressing	Authorities concerned' and are discretionary	of copper, silver, and gold (jewellery)	
	Manufacture of wood products, including plywood, laminboard, particle board and other wood panels and boards Sawmilling and planing of wood		Manufacture of Lao musical instruments Manufacture of blankets/mattresses with cotton and kapok	Prohibited (reserved for Loa national) Prohibited (reserved for Loa national)
	Manufacture of pulp paper, paper and paper-board Manufacture of soap, detergents, cleaning and polishing preparations, perfumes and toilet preparations		Manufacture of beer	Subject to joint venture with domestic investors and/or export of 100%
	Manufacture of PVC pipes, plastic products, electrical accessories, rubber tong shoes, electrical wires		Manufacture of rice noodles	Subject to high ratio of local content (use of local raw material) and/or export
	Manufacture of steel rods, casting of iron and steel Manufacture of agricultural tools, machinery and equipment Manufacture of furniture			

(Continued)

Appendix 7.1 (Continued)

Country	Temporary exclusion list/restricted investment: sector/industry	Restriction/conditionality requirements	Sensitive list: sector/industry	Restriction/conditionality requirements
Myanmar[a]	Manufacture of refined petroleum products	Prohibited (reserved for state sector)	Electricity generating services other than those permitted by law to private and cooperative electricity generating services	Prohibited
	Extraction of hardwood and sale of hardwood	Prohibited and subject to national policy on forestry	Saw milling	Reserved for government
	Exploration, extraction and sale of petroleum	Prohibited except as where prescribed by notification of the government	Aquaculture (fish and prawn) breeding	Reserved for government and village cooperatives
	Fishing of marine fish, prawns and other aquatic organisms	Prohibited except as where prescribed by notification of the government	Forestry and forest plantations	Prohibited
	Manufacture of veneer sheets, plywood, laminboard, particle board and other panels and boards.	Prohibited and subject to national policy on forestry	Manufacture of pulp of all kinds	Prohibited
			Exploration/extraction/export/sale of jade, precious stones	Prohibited
	Air transport service and rail transport service	Prohibited	Distilling, blending, rectifying, bottling and marketing of all kinds of spirits, beverages and non-beverages	Prohibited
	Production and marketing of basic construction materials, furniture, parquet, using teak extracted and sold by state-owned economic organization	Prohibited	Manufacture of malt, liquors, beer and other	Prohibited

(Continued)

Appendix 7.1 (Continued)

Country	Temporary/exclusion list/restricted investment: sector/industry	Restriction/conditionality requirements	Sensitive list: sector/industry	Restriction/conditionality requirements
			brewery products, soft beverages, aerated and non-aerated products, drinking water	
			Manufacture of cigarettes	Prohibited
	Ownership of land	Prohibited	Manufacture and sale of corrugated galvanized iron sheets	Prohibited
			Prohibited investment in telecommunications services, broadcasting or television services of any kind	Prohibited
			Banking and insurance services	Prohibited
Vietnam	Processing of aqua-products and canned sea foods	Subject to JV, stipulated materials and technology requirements; output must be 80% for export market	Exploration/processing of oil, gas, precious and rare minerals	Restricted to JV or BCC or as stipulated by government
	Vegetable oil production and processing	Subject to association and development of local raw materials, resources, and	Air, railway, sea transportation, public passenger, airport and port infrastructure	

(Continued)

Appendix 7.1 (Continued)

Country	Temporary exclusion list/restricted investment: sector/industry	Restriction/conditionality requirements	Sensitive list: sector/industry	Restriction/conditionality requirements
		subject to export requirement	Press. radio and television activities	
	Dairy processing	Subject to association and development of local raw materials, resources, and subject to export requirement	Provision of public telecommunication networks, telecommunication services, domestic or international courier services	
			Construction and operation of international telecommunication networks	
			Production of cement, steel, iron	
			Industrial explosives	
			Aforestation and planting of perennial industrial crops	
			Construction and operation of industrial facilities of industrial zones, export processing zones and high-tech zones	
			Manufacture of: • 2-wheeled motorized bicycles;	Minimum of 80% must be for export market

(Continued)

Country	Temporaryexclusion list/restricted investment: sector/industry	Restriction/conditionality requirements	Sensitive list: sector/ industry	Restriction/conditionality requirements
			• tourism cars and trucks of less than 10 tonnes; • irrigation water pumps; • medium and low voltage electric cables; • common use telecommunication cables; • sea transportation vessels of less than 30,000 tonnes; • audiovisual products; • pre-shaped aluminum products; • common steel for building; • facing tiles and sanitary ceramics; • nitrogen–phosphorus–potassium (NPK) fertilizer; • detergents; • common use paints and building paints; • lead and acid batteries; • PVC plastics; • tyres for bicycles and motorcycles;	

(Continued)

Appendix 7.1 (Continued)

Country	Temporary exclusion list/restricted investment sector/industry	Restriction/conditionality requirements	Sensitive list: sector/ industry	Restriction/conditionality requirements
			• Soda and acid; • electric fans of all kinds; • bicycles and spare parts; • electrical transformers of less than 35kV; • diesel engines of less than 15cc; • garments; • foot wear; • common use plastic products	

Source: ASEAN Secretariat, Jakarta, Indonesia.

Notes

a Brunei Darussalam, Thailand and Myanmar do not publish a 'sensitive list' as such but include on their temporary exclusion list restrictions and/or conditionality clauses. These are not indicated for phasing out but only for 'periodic review'.

b Presidential Regulation of the Republic of Indonesia, Number 77 of 2007, Concerning the List of Lines of Business Closed and Open with Conditions of Investment.

Appendix 7.2 ASEAN foreign direct investment temporary exclusion list and sensitive list, 2008: industries for services incidental to the manufacturing, agriculture, fishery, forestry, mining and quarrying sectors

Country	Temporary exclusion list/restricted investment: sector/industry	Restriction/ conditionality requirements	Sensitive list: sector/industry	Restriction/ conditionality requirements
Brunei Darussalam[a]	Agricultural and animal husbandry service activities on a fee or contract basis Services rendered on a fee or contract basis for the following areas: • renting of agricultural machinery/equipment • veterinary services • agricultural research/experimental development • agricultural market research Forest plantations and nurseries Forest based industry processing	Foreign equity participation restricted to a maximum of 70% to be eligible to access government facilities and sales to domestic market		
Indonesia[b]	Livestock market on a fee or contract basis Manufacture of food and beverages on a fee or contract basis, including: i) fruit and vegetable canning; ii) fruit and vegetable pulverizing, juicing and pasting industry; iii) ice cream industry; iv) cassava starch industry	Prohibited on the basis of national security	Health service facilities Private maternity facilities Pharmacy services/public drugstore Pharmaceuticals wholesale/pharmaceutical	100% domestic capital requirement

(Continued)

Appendix 7.2 (Continued)

Country	Temporary exclusion list/restricted investment: sector/industry	Restriction/ conditionality requirements	Sensitive list: sector/industry	Restriction/ conditionality requirements
	Agricultural cool rooms	Restricted to localities near wholesale market	raw materials wholesale	
	Agriculture: packaging	Restricted to exported fresh horticultural		
	Agricultural: warehousing	Restricted to localities associated with wholesale market	Pension funds	
		Maximum foreign equity participation of 49%	Private broadcasting service/subscribed broadcasting service/ press company	
	Scheduled domestic/ international public transport services		service/press company Retailing through the media	
	Specialized air transport services (medical, crew training, air transport sales agency)		Film distribution (import/export and domestic distribution)	
	General cargo transport services		Technical film/ production services/	
	Hazardous materials transport services		facilities/processing Pit sand mining	
	Container transport services		General medical services/ hospital/	
	Educational services (basic and middle education, higher education)		general clinic	
	Architectural services	Maximum foreign equity participation of 55%		
	Engineering and design services	Maximum foreign equity participation of 80%		
	Construction services			
	Insurance (life, general, reinsurance, broker)			
Malaysia			Services incidental to manufacturing activities undertaken on a fee/contract basis associated with	As stipulated on the general sensitive list (see Appendix 7.1)

(Continued)

Appendix 7.2 (Continued)

Country	Temporary exclusion list/restricted investment: sector/industry	Restriction/ conditionality requirements	Sensitive list: sector/industry	Restriction/ conditionality requirements
			pineapple canning, palm oil milling, palm oil refining, sugar refining, liquors and alcoholic beverages, tobacco processing and cigarettes, sawn timber, veneer and plywood production, wood-based products utilizing local logs as raw materials (as specified on the sensitive list and the conditions stipulated therein). See Appendix 7.1	
			Timber extraction and harvesting services	Closed to foreign investment in Peninsular Malaysia and Sabah. 30% maximum foreign equity participation for Sarawak and/or subject to case by case determination

(Continued)

Appendix 7.2 (Continued)

Country	Temporary exclusion list/restricted investment: sector/industry	Restriction/ conditionality requirements	Sensitive list: sector/industry	Restriction/ conditionality requirements
			Specialized consultancy, advisory and operation services in agriculture, animal husbandry, fishery industry Services incidental to oil and gas extraction	Restricted to maximum of 30% foreign equity participation and/or considered on a case by case basis
Philippines			Services incidental to the utilization of marine resources in archipelagic waters, territorial sea and exclusive economic zone (i.e. taking of marine or freshwater crustaceans, molluscs, aquatic animals, marine materials, operation of fish hatcheries, cultivation of edible seaweeds, fish farming, breeding, rearing, cultivation of oysters for pearls or food)	Prohibited
			Services related to smallscale mining operations and related services (incidental to quarrying stone, sand or clay, mining of	Prohibited

(Continued)

Country	Temporary exclusion list/restricted investment: sector/industry	Restriction/conditionality requirements	Sensitive list: sector/industry	Restriction/conditionality requirements
			chemical and fertilizer minerals, extraction of salt)	
Thailand			Services incidental to the newspaper business	Foreign equity participation restricted to less than 50% of registered capital
			Services incidental to rice farming, farming or gardening and services related to animal farming	
			Services related to fishery for marine animals	
Singapore			Services incidental to the manufacture of chewing gum, bubble gum, dental chewing gum or any like substance	Prohibited on grounds of safety and social reasons
			Services incidental the manufacture of firecrackers and matchsticks	
			Services incidental to quarrying	No more licences issued
			Services related to pig farming	

(Continued)

Country	Temporary exclusion list/restricted investment: sector/industry	Restriction/ conditionality requirements	Sensitive list: sector/industry	Restriction/ conditionality requirements
Cambodia		Not available		
Lao People's Democratic Republic			Services incidental to the manufacture of weapons/ ammunition	Prohibited for reasons of national security, natural environment, public health and/or national culture
			Services incidental to the manufacture of narcotic drugs	
			Services incidental to the manufacture of cultural items/ destructive of the national culture and tradition	
			Services incidental to the manufacture of chemical substances and industrial waste hazardous to the human life and the environment	
Myanmar[a]	Services related to manufacture of pharmaceuticals	Subject to permission from Food and Drug Administration		
	Services for manufacturing of	Prohibited and confined		

(Continued)

Appendix 7.2 (Continued)

Country	Temporary exclusion list/restricted investment: sector/industry	Restriction/ conditionality requirements	Sensitive list: sector/industry	Restriction/ conditionality requirements
	barites powders from indigenous ores Services relating to manufacture of refined petroleum products	to state-owned corporation Prohibited unless notified by the government and subject to State-Owned Economic Enterprises Law		
Vietnam[a]	Advertising services Services related to the production of electronic scales for postal operation	Foreign investment permitted only in the form of a joint venture (JV) or business cooperation contract (BCC)		
	Services related to the production of small capacity microwave equipment, main distribution frame component, subscriber local loop equipment, terminal boxes, wiring cables (telephony) Services related to producing small capacity telephone switching systems, optical fibre terminals, telephone sets	Subject to export, technology and export requirements		
	Services related to maintaining and repairing electrical and mechanical equipment used in the steel industry	Prohibited. No investment licences will be issued		
	Maritime and aviation business services	Subject to BCC/JV or as stipulated by government		

Source: ASEAN Secretariat, Jakarta, Indonesia.

Notes

a Brunei Darussalam, Thailand and Myanmar do not publish a 'sensitive list' as such but include on their temporary exclusion list restrictions and/or conditionality clauses. These are not indicated for phasing out but only for 'periodic review'.

b Presidential Regulation of the Republic of Indonesia, Number 77 of 2007, Concerning the List of Lines of Business Closed and Open with Conditions of Investment.

8 Economic impact of investment provisions in Asian RTAs

Sébastien Miroudot

Introduction

The proliferation of Regional Trade Agreements (RTAs) is a well-known fact of international trade and this trend is not likely to subside, as many agreements are under negotiation or in the process of ratification. As of July 2007, 380 agreements had been notified to the World Trade Organization (WTO).[1] There is however more to this 'proliferation' than just an increase in the number of agreements signed (Fiorentino *et al.* 2007). One distinguishing feature of recent RTAs is their wide-ranging coverage and complexity. Tariff reductions are accompanied by provisions on non-tariff barriers (NTBs), customs procedures, sanitary and phytosanitary measures and intellectual property protection. Most of the new agreements cover trade in services and a number of regulatory issues that go beyond multilaterally agreed disciplines – such as government procurement, competition policy and the environment.

Among these provisions that characterize the 'new regionalism' (Ethier 1998), investment is particularly important and has changed the nature of RTAs as they jointly liberalize trade and investment in a different way from multilateral agreements or bilateral investment treaties (BITs). For a long time, rule-making in international trade and investment largely evolved along two separate tracks (Houde *et al.* 2007). Since the conclusion of the North American Free Trade Agreement (NAFTA) in 1994, most RTAs[2] have combined BIT-like provisions on the protection and promotion of investment with provisions on the liberalization of foreign investment and comprehensive trade in services disciplines. A similar evolution occurred at the WTO with the entry into force of the General Agreement on Trade in Services (GATS) in 1995 that includes 'commercial presence' as one of the four modes of supply of services. There is however no multilateral agreement on investment that covers both goods and services and includes the provisions formerly found in BITs. Only RTAs provide a wide coverage of investment issues and deal with the interaction between investment disciplines and services trade.

Asia has appeared as a latecomer to regionalism with very few agreements signed prior to 2000 (Lloyd 2002). However, in the past five years, many deals have been concluded and even more are under negotiation, giving rise to the 'noodle bowl syndrome' explored by Jayant Menon in Chapter 9 of this book. This shift to regionalism can be explained by the financial crisis of 1997 and the necessity to promote regional economic cooperation as well as by the slow progress of multilateral trade negotiations in the Doha Development Agenda (Park 2006). The proliferation of RTAs has occurred mainly in East Asia and illustrates the 'domino effect' described by Richard Baldwin. As emphasized by the editors in the introduction to this book, the entry of China into the WTO and its current RTA strategy also contribute to the increase in the number of agreements under negotiation. With the exception of the Association of Southeast Asian Nations (ASEAN), most of these RTAs are bilateral trade agreements. But they include deep commitments, in particular in the area of services trade and investment, and as such are good candidates for studying the economic impact of their investment provisions in the context of 'factory Asia' and the fragmentation of world production.

Because Asia started to negotiate trade and investment agreements later, and with partners outside Asia who had already developed their own sets of rules, Asian RTAs are found to be the most divergent in terms of their investment and services provisions and to have greater complexity. Another characteristic of the region is that trade in intermediate goods and services represents a larger share of regional trade than in other parts of the world. This reflects the fact that the fragmentation of production is at a more advanced stage in Asian value chains (Ando and Kimura 2007).

This chapter builds on the work of Lesher and Miroudot (2006) and refines the analysis of the economic impact of investment provisions in RTAs, in particular by looking at the scope of commitments in services industries where most of the restrictions on foreign investment occur. The focus is on Asia where many of the recent and most innovative agreements have been signed and for which a detailed analysis of preferential commitments is available (Fink and Molinuevo 2007). The chapter first describes the complex interrelationships between trade and investment and the extent to which RTAs may have an impact. It then analyses the investment provisions in Asian RTAs and outlines the methodology used to quantify them. The rest of the chapter describes the data and the empirical model used, before discussing the results of the regressions performed and offering concluding remarks.

The drivers of trade and investment in Asia: what role for RTAs?

Trade and investment can be seen as two sides of market access. Firms have different means to serve foreign markets and in particular they can choose between exporting and creating a subsidiary within the foreign economy to produce locally. The choice between exports and FDI has been the focus of the recent literature on firm heterogeneity and global sourcing (Antràs and Helpman 2004; Helpman 2006).

When trade costs are high and the firm's market access motives are 'market-seeking', a company is encouraged to invest and to sell goods and services produced locally through its affiliate rather than to trade at arm's length through the parent company. Horizontal FDI is thus expected to create a relationship where trade and investment are substitutes and where the removal of trade barriers between countries is likely to reduce FDI. In the presence of economies of scale, there are additional reasons to geographically concentrate the production in the home country and to choose international trade rather than foreign investment to access foreign markets. This situation has been described in the literature as the 'proximity-concentration trade-off'[3] (Brainard 1997).

In the context of vertical FDI ('export-platform' FDI or 'efficiency-seeking' FDI), trade and investment can be seen as complements instead of substitutes. The motivation for investing is to fragment the production process to achieve higher efficiency by taking advantage of specific location advantages in the host economy. Flows of capital are likely to be accompanied by greater trade flows. The sequencing of production requires intermediate inputs to be moved from one country to another, as well as the final products to be exported to third-country markets. In addition to trade costs and economies of scale, factor endowments are important determinants in the complex patterns of trade and investment that emerge with the 'unbundling' of production. These patterns are made all the more complex by the fact that firms' strategies generally combine horizontal and vertical FDI.

Regional trade agreements affect firms' strategies at several levels. Through their trade liberalization provisions, they can lower the costs of intra-regional trade and in some cases increase the costs of extra-regional trade. In this sense, even an agreement without investment provisions is likely to have an impact on the choice between exports and FDI. When RTAs have investment disciplines and in particular non-discrimination or protection provisions, the entry cost for investors is also lower. Whether the agreement eventually increases or reduces FDI flows is an empirical question. The answer depends on the relative strength of the reduction in trade costs and investment entry costs, as well as the firm's FDI motives (efficiency-seeking or market-seeking).

The picture is further complicated by network effects and third-country effects that arise because firms can choose their production location from among several countries that belong to different regional integration schemes. When economic integration is deepened in a group of countries, trade liberalization can have a redistributive effect on intra-regional investment patterns where one country might attract more FDI and other countries less (although they signed the same agreement). This should be kept in mind when analysing the economic impact of investment provisions in RTAs and explains the approach followed in this chapter where an index is created for each signatory of the agreements.

While studies on regionalism have flourished, few have attempted to assess the economic impact of new provisions found in a wide range of RTAs. This is in part because agreements are not only numerous, but also because they take a very different approach from one another to incorporating 'new' non-trade provisions. Moreover, there are few indicators available that distinguish the different types of agreements, a necessary step for quantitative analysis. Thus, much of the previous work on trade and investment in RTAs has focused either on a description of the investment provisions found in trade agreements (e.g. UNCTAD 2005) or on the econometric analysis of determinants of FDI in which RTAs are included as a dummy variable (e.g. World Bank 2005).

A small but growing number of studies have investigated the impact of investment-related provisions in RTAs on trade and investment flows. Interestingly, most of these studies focus on Asian RTAs. The first study looking at the impact of trade liberalization on investment was by Jeon and Stone (2000). They studied the impact of ASEAN on trade and investment in the Asia-Pacific economies and found that intra-bloc trade flows increased as a result of ASEAN, but that ASEAN's effect on intra-bloc investment was insignificant. Adams *et al.* (2003) were the first to construct an index of liberalization to measure the breadth and depth of RTAs, including their investment provisions. Dee (2006) provides a similar analysis for the Asia-Pacific region with a more elaborate FDI empirical model that takes into account the recent developments in the literature outlined above.

While Adams *et al.* (2003) and Lesher and Miroudot (2006) find a significant and positive impact of RTAs on investment flows, Dee (2006) argues that the provisions of RTAs have a very minor role and that in the case of the Asia-Pacific region investment patterns are mainly explained by complex network behaviour of multinational corporations. In her study, trade provisions appear to have a greater impact than investment provisions. One question remains: Is the minor role attributed to the investment provisions of RTAs specific to the Asia-Pacific region where the fragmentation of world production is more pronounced? Or is it attributable to the econometric analysis conducted and the choice of empirical model? To answer this question, the remainder of the chapter proposes an alternative methodology to characterize the extensiveness of investment provisions in Asian RTAs and to test their economic impact on trade in goods, trade in services and foreign investment in a dataset where all reporter countries are part of Asian production networks.

The extensiveness of investment provisions in Asian RTAs

The study covers 22 RTAs where at least one party comes from Asia.[4] Only agreements with substantive investment provisions in force in 2006 – the last year in the panel of data – are analysed. They constitute the tip of the iceberg or of the noodle bowl as the number of agreements under negotiation or signed but not yet in force is much higher (about four times higher). It is however not possible to undertake any quantitative analysis on the impact of agreements not yet implemented.

Table 8.1 summarizes the provisions regarding the right of establishment and non-discrimination in the pre- and post-establishment phase (national treatment and most-favoured-nation treatment) for investment in goods and services. Additional provisions (not reported in Table 8.1) have also been analysed to create the index used in this study. In particular, these include provisions on investment regulation and protection (provisions on performance requirements, expropriation, fair and equitable treatment, free transfer of funds and temporary entry and stay for key personnel) and dispute settlement.[5]

Table 8.1 RTAs included in the study and non-discrimination provisions for investment in goods and services

Agreement	Countries	Year in force	Investment in goods			MFN	Investment in services			
			Pre-estab-lishment	National treatment	Limitations		'NAFTA-inspired' or 'GATS-inspired'?	Market access or pre-establishment	National treatment	Limitations
PATCRA	Australia, Papua New Guinea	1977	no	no	–	yes	–	no	no	–
ANZCERTA (services)	Australia, New Zealand	1989	no	no	–	no	NAFTA	yes	yes	negative list
ASEAN framework agreement on services	Brunei, Cambodia, Indonesia, Lao PDR, Malaysia, Myanmar, Philippines, Singapore, Thailand, Vietnam	1995	no	no	–	no	GATS	yes	yes	positive list
ASEAN Investment Area	Brunei, Cambodia, Indonesia, Lao PDR, Malaysia, Myanmar, Philippines, Singapore, Thailand, Vietnam	1998	yes	yes	negative list	yes	–	–	–	–
NZSCEP	New zealand, Singapore,	2001	yes	yes	negative list	yes	GATS	yes	yes	positive list

Agreement	Countries	Year								
JSEPA	Japan, Singapore	2002	yes	yes	negative list	no	GATS	yes	yes	positive list
EFTA-Singapore	Iceland, Liechtenstein, Norway, Singapore, Switzerland	2003	yes	yes	negative list	yes	GATS	yes	yes	positive list
SAFTA	Australia, Singapore	2003	yes	yes	negative list	no	NAFTA	yes	yes	negative list
CEPA	China, Hong Kong	2004	no	no	–	no	–	yes	yes	positive list
Chinese Taipei–Panama	Chinese Taipei, Panama	2004	yes	yes	negative list	yes	NAFTA	yes	yes	negative list
Korea–Chile	Chile, Korea	2004	yes	yes	negative list	yes	NAFTA	yes	yes	negative list
USA–Singapore	Singapore, USA	2004	yes	yes	negative list	yes	NAFTA	yes	yes	negative list
AUSFTA	Australia, USA	2005	yes	yes	negative list	yes	NAFTA	yes	yes	negative list
CECA	India, Singapore	2005	yes	yes	positive list	no	GATS	yes	yes	positive list
JMSEP	Japan, Mexico	2005	yes	yes	negative list	yes	NAFTA	yes	yes	negative list
NZTCEP	New Zealand, Thailand	2005	yes	yes	negative list	no	–	no	no	–
TAFTA	Australia, Thailand	2005	yes	yes	positive list	yes	GATS	yes	yes	positive list
Chinese Taipei–Guatemala	Chinese Taipei, Guatemala	2006	yes	yes	negative list	yes	NAFTA	yes	yes	negative list
EFTA-Korea	Iceland, Korea,	2006	yes	yes	negative list	yes	GATS	yes	yes	positive list

(Continued)

Table 8.1 (Continued)

Agreement	Countries	Year in force	Investment in goods				Investment in services			
			Pre-estab-lishment	National treatment	Limitations	MFN	'NAFTA-inspired' or 'GATS-inspired.'	Market access or pre establishment	National treatment	Limitations
	Liechtenstein, Norway[a] and Switzerland									
JMEPA	Japan, Malaysia	2006	yes	yes	negative list	yes	GATS	yes	yes	positive list
Korea–Singapore	Korea, Singapore	2006	yes	yes	negative list	no	NAFTA	yes	yes	negative list
Trans-Pacific SEP	Brunei, Chile, New Zealand, Singapore	2006	no	no	–	no	–	yes	yes	negative list

Source: Fink and Molinuevo (2007), Houde et al. (2007), Lesher and Miroudot (2006).

Note

a In the EFTA–Korea RTA, Norway is not part of the investment agreement.

Abbreviations

PATCRA, Agreement on Trade and Commercial Relations Between the Government of Australia and the Government of Papua New Guinea; ANZCERTA, Australia New Zealand Closer Economic Agreement; NZSCEP, New Zealand–Singapore Closer Economic Partnership; JSEPA, Japan–Singapore Economic Partnership Agreement; EFTA–Singapore, European Free Trade Association-Singapore Agreement; SAFTA, The Agreement on the South Asian Free Trade Area; CEPA, (Mainland and Hong Kong) Closer Economic Partnership Arrangement; AUSFTA, Australia–United States Free Trade Agreement; CECA, Comprehensive Economic Cooperation Agreement (between India and Singapore); JMSEP, Agreement between Japan and United Mexican States for the Strengthening of the Economic Partnership; NZTCEP, New Zealand and Thailand Closer Economic Partnership; TAFTA, Thailand–Australia Free Trade Agreement; EFTA–Korea, European Free Trade Association–Korea Agreement JMEPA, Japan–Malaysia Economic Partnership Agreement ; Trans-Pacific SEP, Trans-Pacific Strategic Economic Partnership.

Looking at Table 8.1, one can see the diversity of provisions in these 22 agreements and the different 'models' that are followed, in particular regarding the interaction between investment and trade in services disciplines. Some of these agreements deal only with investment in services sectors (e.g., the Agreement between New Zealand and Singapore on a Closer Economic Partnership (*NZS-CEP*) or the Trans-Pacific Strategic Economic Partnership). ASEAN has two separate agreements for investment and trade in services (including investment in services): the Framework Agreement on the ASEAN Investment Area (AIA) and the ASEAN Framework Agreement on Services (AFAS). These are two sequentially related agreements that together define the policy architecture of ASEAN's investment regime (Jarvis *et al.*, Chapter 7 of this book). These agreements have been amended several times and there is even a third one on the promotion and protection of investment.[6]

Nine agreements have provisions on investment that can be said to be 'NAFTA-inspired'.[7] As in NAFTA, there is a single chapter on investment covering both goods and services and limitations to the non-discrimination principles (national treatment and most-favoured-nation treatment both in the pre- and post-establishment phase) are indicated in a negative list. NAFTA-inspired agreements also tend to include broad provisions on the regulation and protection of investment similar to those found in BITs or going further than WTO disciplines (for example regarding performance requirements). Seven agreements have provisions on investment that are different for goods and services with a services chapter including the 'commercial presence' (Mode 3) and another chapter on investment covering goods but also providing to *all* investments the kind of protection principles coming from the universe of BITs (for example on expropriation, fair and equitable treatment and the free transfer of funds). By contrast, GATS-inspired agreements list their limitations to national treatment and market access in a positive list of sectors.[8]

These architectural considerations do not create a radically different treatment for services and goods. In the end, all types of investment benefit from the liberalization and protection provisions, to the extent that through their list of reservations countries do not reduce the sectoral coverage of the agreement too much. There are however slight differences that can matter. For example, investment chapters have an asset-based definition of investment broader than that of the services chapters, where investment is defined as 'commercial presence'. There is also a debate on the virtues of the negative scheduling approach – where all reservations have to be listed in the agreement – as opposed to the GATS hybrid approach where countries can remain silent on discriminatory rules in sectors where they make no commitment. Another interesting difference is the 'ratchet mechanism' implied by NAFTA-inspired agreements where any new autonomous liberalization of foreign investment is regarded as a commitment in the agreement and it is not possible to revert to the former regime (unless a fair compensation is given to other parties).

Moreover, as part of the innovations mentioned earlier regarding Asian RTAs, there are examples of agreements departing from the NAFTA or GATS models and introducing a negative scheduling approach in GATS-inspired agreements (e.g. the Trans-Pacific Strategic Economic Partnership (SEP)), adding some kind of ratchet mechanism to GATS-like commitments (e.g. the 'SS' entries in the Japan–Malaysia agreement), simplifying the way schedules of commitments are presented (e.g. the Singapore–New Zealand and Thailand–Australia agreements) or resorting to a third approach (e.g. a full positive scheduling approach rather than a GATS hybrid approach in the agreement between mainland China and Hong Kong known as the Mainland and Hong Kong Closer Economic Partnership Arrangement (CEPA)).

More than the GATS or NAFTA approach, what really distinguishes agreements and should be accounted for in any quantification exercise is the scope of commitments. Table 8.2 indicates for each country the percentage of services sub-sectors where commitments are made for investment (Mode 3 in the case of GATS-inspired agreements) and the percentage of sub-sectors where GATS-plus commitments are made.[9] The second column of percentages reveals the extent to which the RTA grants preferential treatment. The analysis is limited to services as about 85 per cent of reservations to non-discrimination principles are in services industries (UNCTAD 2005). It is also in services that more than 60 per cent of foreign investment takes place.

Looking at Table 8.2, one can see that the scope of commitments can be fairly low for some countries. Putting aside agreements that do not cover investment in services (where the percentage of commitments beyond GATS is zero) or where countries have not yet scheduled their commitments (e.g. Brunei in the Trans-Pacific SEP), the coverage can be as low as 24 per cent for Myanmar in ASEAN. Brunei and Indonesia also have quite a low number of sub-sectors with liberalization commitments (32 per cent and 34 per cent, respectively). These figures take into account the five liberalization packages negotiated up to 2006.[10] In the same agreement, Thailand and Vietnam have made commitments in a larger number of sub-sectors (51 per cent and 62 per cent, respectively).

It should be noted however that these figures include commitments that are already in GATS. This is why the second percentage given in Table 8.2 – the percentage of commitments beyond GATS – is also important.[11] While Vietnam applies national treatment and allows market access in 62 per cent of services industries, the preferential treatment offered to its ASEAN partners is very low (3 per cent). Indonesia, as mentioned above, has commitments in 34 per cent of services sub-sectors but 20 percentage points out of 34 correspond to sub-sectors not committed vis-à-vis other WTO Members. The scope of commitments is lower but their preferential content is higher.

To create the index presented in the last column of Table 8.2, the information gathered on investment provisions in RTAs is coded on a zero-to-one scale, where zero indicates the absence of a given provision and one represents the most FDI-friendly provision in the list of possible options.[12] Table 8.3 summarizes the score assigned to each type of provision. The two variables reported in Table 8.2 regarding the percentage of services sectors in which liberalization commitments are undertaken and the percentage of commitments beyond GATS are included in the index (their value is also between 0 and 1). This explains why the index score is different for the signatories of the same agreement.

Country	Agreement(s)	Partner(s)	Investment in services[a]		Index score[a]
			% commitments	% beyond GATS	
Australia	ANZCERTA	New Zealand	97	54	0.492
Australia	AUSFTA	USA	99	34	0.727
Australia	PATCRA	Papua New Guinea	0	0	0.050
Australia	SAFTA	Singapore	81	17	0.530
Australia	TAFTA	Thailand	66	05	0.496
Brunei	ASEAN	Cambodia, Indonesia, Lao PDR, Malaysia, Myanmar, Philippines, Singapore, Thailand, Vietnam	32	25	0.487
Brunei	Trans-Pacific SEP	Chile, New Zealand, Singapore	10	0	0.120
Cambodia	ASEAN	Brunei, Indonesia, Lao PDR, Malaysia, Myanmar, Philippines, Singapore, Thailand, Vietnam	60	5	0.504
China	CEPA	Hong Kong	69	30	0.298
Chinese Taipei	Chinese Taipei–Guatemala	Guatemala	98	45	0.810
Chinese Taipei	Chinese Taipei–Panama	Panama	99	57	0.842
Hong Kong (China)	CEPA	China (mainland)	34	0	0.131
India	CECA	Singapore	45	37	0.496
Indonesia	ASEAN	Brunei, Cambodia, Lao PDR, Malaysia, Myanmar, Philippines, Singapore, Thailand, Vietnam	34	20	0.478
Japan	JMEPA	Malaysia	89	55	0.793

(Continued)

Table 8.2 (Continued)

Country	Agreement(s)	Partner(s)	Investment in services[a]		Index score[a]
			% commitments	% beyond GATS	
Japan	JMSEP	Mexico	95	51	0.812
Japan	JSEPA	Singapore	79	36	0.632
Korea	EFTA–Korea	Iceland, Liechtenstein, Switzerland	69	56	0.710
Korea	EFTA–Korea	Norway	69	56	0.480
Korea	Korea–Chile	Chile	97	88	0.916
Korea	Korea–Singapore	Singapore	75	40	0.644
Malaysia	ASEAN	Brunei, Cambodia, Indonesia, Lao PDR, Myanmar, Philippines, Singapore, Thailand, Vietnam	46	23	0.515
Malaysia	JMEPA	Japan	46	21	0.594
Myanmar	ASEAN	Brunei, Cambodia, Indonesia, Lao PDR, Malaysia, Philippines, Singapore, Thailand, Vietnam	24	23	0.459
New Zealand	ANZCERTA	Australia	98	51	0.487
New Zealand	NZSCEP	Singapore	74	24	0.554
New Zealand	NZSCEP & Trans-Pacific SEP	Singapore	93	40	0.698
New Zealand	NZTCEP	Thailand	0	0	0.176
New Zealand	Trans-Pacific SEP	Brunei, Chile	93	40	0.462
Philippines	ASEAN	Brunei, Cambodia, Indonesia, Lao PDR, Malaysia, Myanmar, Singapore, Thailand, Vietnam	35	13	0.462
Singapore	ASEAN	Brunei, Cambodia, Indonesia, Lao PDR, Malaysia, Myanmar, Philippines, Thailand, Vietnam	39	11	0.466
Singapore	CECA	India	72	50	0.606
Singapore	EFTA–Singapore	Iceland, Liechtenstein, Norway, Switzerland	75	55	0.723

Country	Agreement	Partner(s)			
Singapore	JSEPA	Japan	77	57	0.680
Singapore	Korea–Singapore	Korea	79	56	0.695
Singapore	NZSCEP	New Zealand	69	51	0.610
Singapore	NZSCEP & Trans-Pacific SEP	New Zealand	86	63	0.740
Singapore	SAFTA	Australia	81	62	0.647
Singapore	Trans-Pacific SEP	Chile	86	63	0.505
Singapore	Trans-Pacific SEP & ASEAN	Brunei	86	63	0.738
Singapore	USA–Singapore	USA	93	81	0.884
Thailand	ASEAN	Brunei, Cambodia, Indonesia, Lao PDR, Malaysia, Myanmar, Philippines, Singapore, Vietnam	51	27	0.539
Thailand	NZTCEP	New Zealand	0	0	0.176
Thailand	TAFTA	Australia	41	6	0.436
Vietnam	ASEAN	Brunei, Cambodia, Indonesia, Lao PDR, Malaysia, Myanmar, Philippines, Singapore, Thailand	62	3	0.506

Source: Fink and Molinuevo (2007) for East Asian agreements, the author for other agreements and the index scores.

Notes: The percentage of sectors where commitments are made and the index score have a time dimension reflecting the evolution of RTAs commitments. The values reported in the Table are the latest ones. When several agreements are in force with the same partner(s), the combined impact of their provisions is shown.

Abbreviations

ANZCERTA, Australia New Zealand Closer Economic Agreement; AUSFTA, Australia–United States Free Trade Agreement; PATCRA, Agreement on Trade and Commercial Relations Between the Government of Australia and the Government of Papua New Guinea; SAFTA, The Agreement on the South Asian Free Trade Area; TAFTA, Thailand–Australia Free Trade Agreement; Trans-Pacific SEP, Trans-Pacific Strategic Economic Partnership; CEPA, (mainland and Hong Kong) Closer Economic Partnership Arrangement; CECA, Comprehensive Economic Cooperation Agreement (between India and Singapore); JMEPA, Japan–Malaysia Economic Partnership Agreement; JMSEP, Agreement between Japan and United Mexican States for the Strengthening of the Economic Partnership; JSEPA, Japan–Singapore Economic Partnership Agreement; EFTA–Korea, European Free Trade Association–Korea Agreement; EFTA–Singapore, European Free Trade Association–Singapore Agreement; NZSCEP, New Zealand–Singapore Closer Economic Partnership; NZTCEP, New Zealand and Thailand Closer Economic Partnership.

Table 8.3 Coding of investment provisions and weights attributed to the different components of the index

Category	Score
Component 1: Non-discrimination (non-services sectors)	*Weight: 0.151*
Right of establishment?	
No	0.00
NT	0.50
MFN+NT	1.00
Pre-establishment limitations	
(n/a)	0.00
Positive list	0.33
Negative list	0.66
None	1.00
National treatment	
No	0.00
Yes	1.00
Limitations to national treatment	
(n/a)	0.00
Positive list	0.33
Negative list	0.66
None	1.00
Most favoured nation	
No	0.00
Yes	1.00
Limitations to MFN	
(n/a)	0.00
Positive list	0.33
Negative list	0.66
None	1.00
Component 2: Non-discrimination (services sectors)	*Weight: 0.124*
Provisions on establishment?	
None	0.00
NT	0.50
MFN+NT/Market access	1.00
Pre-establishment limitations	
(n/a)	0.00
Positive list	0.33
Negative list	0.66
None	1.00
National treatment	
No	0.00
Yes	1.00
Limitations to national treatment	
(n/a)	0.00
Positive list	0.33
Negative list	0.66
None	1.00
Most Favoured Nation	
No	0.00
Yes	1.00
Exceptions to MFN	
(n/a)	0.00

(*Continued*)

Table 8.3 (Continued)

Category	Score
Negative list	0.50
None	1.00
Component 3: Investment regulation and Protection	*Weight: 0.209*
Provisions prohibiting performance requirements?	
No	0.00
Yes	0.50
Yes, beyond TRIMS	1.00
Free transfer of funds	
No	0.00
Yes	1.00
Temporary entry and stay for key personnel?	
No	0.00
Yes	1.00
Provisions on expropriation	
No	0.00
Yes	1.00
Specific reference to fair and equitable treatment	
No	0.00
Yes	1.00
State–investor dispute settlement	
No	0.00
Ad hoc/permament arbitration (only one)	0.50
Ad hoc and permanent arbitration	1.00
Component 4: Scope of commitments (services)	*Weight: 0.255*
Percentage of sub-sectors where commitments are made	(Score indicated in Table 8.2)
Component 5: Preferential commitments (services)	*Weight: 0.261*
Percentage of sub-sectors where commitments go beyond GATS	(Score indicated in Table 8.2)

After assigning a numerical value to each type of investment provision, it is necessary to weight them to build an aggregate index. A simple average is first used to
obtain a score for three categories of provisions: (1) non-discrimination for goods;
(2) non-discrimination for services; and (3) investment regulation and protection.
Two other scores are obtained through the analysis of schedules of commitments in
services: (4) the percentage of services sub-sectors covered by liberalization commitments; and (5) the percentage of commitments beyond GATS offering preferential treatment (the two values reported in Table 8.2). The weight given to each of
these five components is shown in Table 8.3. It was obtained through factor analysis (principal component analysis), a statistical approach in which each component
is weighted according to its contribution to the overall variance in the data.

It should be kept in mind that the exercise is not a qualitative assessment of the
value of each provision or agreement per se, but rather a ranking exercise used to
obtain an index clearly separating different types of RTAs with investment provisions. Thus, the index is designed to be used in subsequent quantitative analysis and not to assess the quality of each agreement. Moreover, the analysis is
different from that in Lesher and Miroudot (2006) or Dee (2006), as the index

incorporates an assessment of the preferential content of the agreement with regard to investment provisions.

As a consequence, the agreements with the highest index scores are not the ones with the most extensive coverage (e.g., Australia–USA) but those that in addition to extensive provisions offer a substantially preferential treatment (Korea–Chile has the highest index score in Table 8.2). The preferential treatment however represents only one quarter of the overall index score. Agreements such as the Australia–USA one still score high in the index due to their extensive provisions even if the preferential treatment is lower. Through this approach we expect a better measurement of the impact of investment provisions in RTAs, as the index tells us something about the preferential treatment resulting from the agreement.

Data used and specification of the empirical model

The dataset created for the study includes 18 reporter countries: Australia, Bangladesh, Brunei, Cambodia, China, Chinese Taipei, Hong Kong (China), India, Indonesia, Japan, Republic of Korea, Malaysia, Myanmar, New Zealand, the Philippines, Singapore, Thailand and Vietnam. Bilateral trade and investment with 190 partner countries are reported over the period 1990–2006. Due to the unavailability of data and gaps in the period covered for some countries, the panel is unbalanced.

Three kinds of flows are used as dependent variables in the quantitative analysis:

1   trade in goods (imports and exports);
2   cross-border trade in services (imports and exports); and
3   foreign direct investment (inward and outward, covering both goods and services).

Data on imports and exports of goods are taken from the United Nations Statistical Division Commodity Trade Database (Comtrade). Cross-border trade in services is assessed using the OECD Trade in Services by Partner country (TISP) database (with mirror data for non-OECD countries). Lastly, data on foreign direct investment come from the OECD International Direct Investment Statistics and are completed with UNCTAD data from the FDI Statistics database. In both cases, data on FDI inward and outward stocks are used as they are generally regarded as more reliable.

While trade data on goods are available for most of the countries included in the analysis, the number of observations is smaller for cross-border trade in services and FDI stocks. The dataset mainly consists of data on services trade and investment between OECD countries (as reporters or partners) and non-OECD countries. Even in the UNCTAD dataset, the information on FDI inward and outward stocks between non-OECD countries is scarce. It is however not a limitation in the analysis, as the bulk of investment in the region is between OECD countries and their partners (as host or parent countries). Also, the trade agreements signed are predominantly (or have been until recently) of a North–South type. For most of the agreements presented in Table 8.1, there are observations in the dataset. It is only cross-border trade in services and investment stocks between ASEAN countries that tend to be not fully covered.

To evaluate the economic impact of RTAs with investment provisions on trade, the analysis relies on the gravity model and its standard variables: distance, gross domestic product (GDP) and a set of geographical and cultural 'dummies'. Average applied tariff rates are also included in a specification to ensure that the index does not capture the impact of trade liberalization on trade flows but rather the impact of investment liberalization. The data on distance, common border, common official language and past colonial relationship are taken from the Centre d'Etudes Prospectives et d'Informations Internationales (CEPII) database, while GDP data (current GDP in thousands of US dollars[13]) come from the World Development Indicators (WDI) of the World Bank.

The specification to assess the impact of investment provisions on trade in goods or cross-border trade in services is:

$$\begin{aligned}
\text{Trade}_{ijt} = {} & \beta_0 + \beta_1 \ln(\text{distance}_{ij}) + \beta_2 \text{ common border}_{ij} \\
& + \beta_3 \text{ common language}_{ij} + \beta_4 \text{ colonial rel}_{ij} \\
& + \beta_5 \ln(\text{joint GDP}_{ijt}) + \beta_6 \ln(\text{RTA index}_{ijt}) \\
& + \alpha_i + \gamma_j + \lambda_t + \varepsilon_{ijt}
\end{aligned} \tag{1}$$

where Trade_{ijt} can be imports of goods, exports of goods, cross-border imports or exports of services from country i to country j in year t. The RTA index measures the extensiveness of investment provisions in RTAs and is calculated following the methodology described in the previous section. The value is specific to country i in its bilateral relationship with country j in year t.

While the impact of investment provisions found in RTAs on investment stocks could also be assessed through the standard gravity equation, the literature has recently highlighted that a better theoretical and empirical approach relies on the knowledge-capital model developed by James Markusen.[14] As highlighted in the section entitled 'The drivers of trade and investment', FDI can be horizontal or vertical. The model assumes that horizontal FDI takes place between countries with similar skill endowments while vertical FDI is driven by differences between skill-abundant and skill-scarce countries. Recently, Bergstrand and Egger (2007) have shown that the gravity equation for FDI could be derived from a similar model. Variables to estimate the knowledge-capital model, such as the information on trade and investment costs are however not readily available. Most of the proxies that could be used (e.g. trade policy or investment policy indices) create econometric issues in panel estimation with fixed effects as they have little variation over time and are likely to be collinear with the fixed effects.

A 'simplified' version of the knowledge-capital gravity equation is therefore used. As in Egger and Merlo (2007), two variables are added to the FDI specification: the relative GDP and the relative skilled-labour endowment. The relative

GDP is defined as the ratio of the real GDP of the partner country to its reporter, while the relative skilled-labour endowment is the ratio of the tertiary school enrolment in the partner country to its reporter. Data come from the *World Development Indicators* (World Bank 2008).

The specification is:

$$\begin{aligned}
\text{FDI}_{ijt} = &\beta_0 + \beta_1 \ln(\text{distance}_{ij}) + \beta_2 \text{ common border}_{ij} \\
&+ \beta_3 \text{ common language}_{ij} + \beta_4 \text{ colonial rel}_{ij} \\
&+ \beta_5 \ln(\text{joint GDP}_{ijt}) + \beta_6 \ln(\text{relative GDP}_{ijt}) \\
&+ \beta_7 \ln(\text{relative skill}_{ijt}) + \beta_8 \ln(\text{RTA index}_{ijt}) \\
&+ \alpha_i + \gamma_j + \lambda_t + \varepsilon_{ijt}
\end{aligned}$$

$$(2)$$

In equations (1) and (2), there are fixed effects for reporters, partners and years. It is through these fixed effects that the multilateral price resistance term is taken into account and the heterogeneity of reporters and partners is accounted for (Anderson and van Wincoop 2004; Cheng and Wall 2005). Another issue in the estimation of gravity equations is the treatment of zeros that cannot be logged. At the aggregate level, trade in goods between countries is rarely zero but there are zero trade flows in the dataset for cross-border trade in services and about half of the observations for FDI stocks have a value of zero.[15] Ignoring zeros could introduce a bias in the analysis (Santos Silva and Tenreyro 2006). Instead of ordinary least squares (OLS) estimations, equations (1) and (2) are estimated with Poisson regressions where the dependent variable is not logged (and zeros are kept). In contrast to Tobit regressions (that are also used to deal with zeros), it is possible in a Poisson panel regression to keep the fixed effects and to obtain consistent estimators. In addition, to distinguish between 'true' zeros (that are consistent with the gravity or knowledge-capital model) and 'false' zeros (that could be missing data reported by mistake as zeros) zero-inflated Poisson regressions have also been estimated.

Results of the quantitative analysis

Table 8.4 summarizes the results of the regressions. All variables are significant at the 1 per cent level. Due to the presence of fixed effects that can account for unobserved variables and the robustness of the gravity framework, the pseudo R-squared that measures the 'goodness of fit' has a high value (above 90 per cent) in all regressions.[16] This means that the empirical model accounts well for the trade and investment flows observed.

Starting with inward FDI stocks, an interesting result is that the goodness of fit is not substantially increased between column (1) – the standard gravity equation – and column (2) – the knowledge-capital version of the gravity equation. The two additional variables in the second specification, the relative GDP and relative skilled-labour endowment indicate that inward FDI in Asia is positively affected by

Table 8.4 Results of the econometric analysis

Dependent variable	Inward FDI		Outward FDI		Cross-border imports of services	Cross-border exports of services	Imports of goods		Exports of goods	
	(1)	(2)	(3)	(4)	(5)	(6)	(7)	(8)	(9)	(10)
Distance	-0.947	-1.046	-0.950	-1.646	-0.711	-0.579	-0.402	-0.445	-0.440	-0.476
	(432.73)**	(326.69)**	(319.64)**	(256.60)**	(7497.07)**	(6200.55)**	(21849.25)**	(19279.20)**	(24573.57)**	(21806.45)**
Common border	3.386	3.079	(dropped)	(dropped)	1.796	1.612	0.984	0.707	0.915	0.763
	(47.76)**	(37.25)**			(11773.03)**	(10141.59)**	(29947.73)**	(15503.45)**	(30373.00)**	(19576.90)**
Common language	1.142	1.142	1.611	2.355	0.120	0.134	0.427	0.398	0.118	0.028
	(559.39)**	(376.26)**	(379.42)**	(347.91)**	(1018.49)**	(1135.13)**	(17172.70)**	(13076.84)**	(4968.62)**	(974.87)**
Colonial relation-ship	-1.034	-1.192	-1.937	-4.771	-0.151	-0.202	-0.374	-0.482	-0.022	-0.049
	(331.72)**	(250.64)**	(351.62)**	(362.95)**	(1226.27)**	(1704.24)**	(11320.38)**	(12127.62)**	(694.25)**	(1307.24)**
Joint GDP	0.645	0.193	1.235	1.112	0.692	0.479	0.745	0.778	0.936	1.077
	(251.89)**	(35.34)**	(436.40)**	(221.95)**	(3613.24)**	(2370.46)**	(27003.69)**	(23051.14)**	(34378.00)**	(32725.37)**
Applied tariff								-0.064		-0.027
								(7467.87)**		(2927.07)**
Relative GDP		0.488		-1.737						
		(51.21)**		(175.36)**						
Relative skill		-0.441		0.589						
		(79.17)**		(108.86)**						
RTA index	0.033	0.028	0.097	0.103	0.016	0.028	0.001	0.010	0.027	0.029
	(120.90)**	(65.72)**	(218.56)**	(89.46)**	(1173.62)**	(2025.25)**	(354.79)**	(1993.26)**	(7.467.66)**	(6738.57)**

(Continued)

Table 8.4 (Continued)

Dependent variable	Inward FDI		Outward FDI		Cross-border imports of services	Cross-border exports of services	Imports of goods		Exports of goods	
	(1)	(2)	(3)	(4)	(5)	(6)	(7)	(8)	(9)	(10)
Fixed effects										
Reporter and partner	yes	yes	yes	yes	yes	yes	yes	yes	yes	yes
Year	yes	yes	yes	yes	yes	yes	yes	yes	yes	yes
Number of observations	4,922	1,890	2,851	1,251	2,574	2,612	34,124	20,080	36,337	19,739
Pseudo R-squared	0.9303	0.9367	0.9436	0.9705	0.9577	0.9422	0.9475	0.9514	0.9574	0.9612

Notes: Poisson maximum-likelihood estimations. Independent variables are logged. Absolute value of z statistics in parentheses.
* Significant at 5%.
** Significant at 1%.

the parent-to-host relative GDP and negatively impacted by the ratio of the parent-to-host skilled-labour endowment. Egger and Merlo (2007) obtained a similar result in a dataset of OECD countries and economies in transition. Turning back to the discussion in the 'Drivers of trade and investment in Asia' section, this suggests that FDI is mainly of the horizontal type with capital moving between countries with a rather similar skilled-labour endowment (if one assumes that the assumption of the knowledge-capital model about the difference between horizontal and vertical FDI is correct) and from large to small economies. The negative coefficient for the relative skill endowment is also consistent with the idea that multinational firms are headquartered in skilled-labour abundant countries and that there is a complementarity between capital and skilled-labour (two assumptions that are also part of the knowledge-capital model).

Looking at the coefficient for investment provisions in RTAs, there is a positive and statistically significant coefficient for the RTA index variable (in both specifications) indicating that FDI is influenced by the content of RTAs and the preferential treatment granted to foreign investors. The economic significance is however lower than in previous studies and in particular compared to that of Lesher and Miroudot (2006). The elasticity measured is about 0.03. This means that a 100 per cent increase in the index is likely (holding other variables constant) to increase inward FDI by 3 per cent. This impact is however not negligible. Going from the index score of the Thailand–New Zealand agreement (0.176 – this agreement does not cover services yet but foresees a future negotiation to liberalize trade in services) to the score of the Korea–Chile FTA (0.916 for Korea) implies a 13.8 per cent increase in inward FDI according to the coefficient estimated.

Interestingly, the coefficient is stronger (and also positive) for the impact of investment provisions on outward FDI. The elasticity measured in the two specifications in columns (3) and (4) is around 0.1. Parent companies seem to benefit more than affiliates from the agreements negotiated. It reveals also that a country's own liberalization efforts can encourage outward FDI. Accepting more foreign companies in the domestic economy will make it easier for domestic companies to invest abroad.

In the second specification referring to the knowledge-capital model, the results are consistent with those obtained for inward FDI. The relative GDP (partner relative to reporter and hence host to parent this time) has a negative sign and the relative skilled-labour endowment a positive sign. Outward FDI is more important in countries with similar skill endowments and with a relatively smaller GDP.

In columns (5) and (6) of Table 8.4, the dependent variable is cross-border trade in services (imports and exports). The positive coefficient found for the RTA variable highlights that there are complementarities between cross-border trade in services and investment (in goods or in services). Not only is a more liberal investment regime as a consequence of a trade agreement with investment liberalization likely to increase investment in services (Mode 3 in GATS parlance) but it also has a positive impact on Mode 1 and Mode 2 (cross-border trade in services).[17] Such complementarities have been identified in several empirical studies at the sector level.[18] In the 'exports versus FDI' debate, trade in services is generally found to be a complement to FDI (in services but also in the manufacturing sector). This can be explained by the supporting services implied by international production (e.g. logistics services, telecoms services, financial services among others) and the fact that affiliates of foreign companies tend to rely on services provided by suppliers from the parent country. But as the coefficient of the RTA index is higher for exports than for imports of cross-border trade in services, one can assume that liberalizing investment in the home economy also has a positive impact on services exports.

Regarding trade in goods in columns (7) to (10), there is also a positive impact on investment provisions in RTAs. Two specifications are used to assess the impact of agreements, one with the weighted applied tariff (between the reporter and partner) and one without. This is to show that the positive and significant coefficient found for the RTA variable is not capturing the trade liberalization provisions of the agreements through a reduction of trade costs. The impact of investment liberalization on imports of goods is very small (even smaller when trade liberalization is not controlled for) but the impact on exports is not negligible.

Concluding remarks

This chapter has presented new quantitative work on the economic impact of investment provisions found in RTAs, with a focus on Asia where multinational enterprises have been particularly active in reorganizing their production across countries and where many agreements with deep commitments have been recently signed. The results confirm that investment provisions in RTAs are associated with higher inward and outward investment flows, as well as increased cross-border trade in services and higher trade flows in goods. The impact measured is however somewhat lower than in previous studies such as that of Adams *et al.* (2003) or Lesher and Miroudot (2006). This impact is nonetheless economically significant and quite substantial for outward FDI and to a lesser extent inward FDI.

By creating an index measuring the extensiveness of investment provisions and by including in this index a measure of the scope of liberalizing commitments and of their preferential nature, the RTA variable is sufficiently different for each reporter and shows enough variation over time to avoid many of the collinearity issues generally associated with the estimation of the gravity equation with policy variables. The panel dimension is also particularly suitable to deal with complex agreements such as the three ASEAN agreements related to investment that have been regularly amended. The index created has been found robust to changes in specifications, the use of robust standard errors and the use of different types of fixed effects.

A question remains regarding the causal relationship between investment provisions in trade agreements and increased investment stocks. It is still a possibility that countries tend to sign RTAs with partners where investment is (potentially or not) high and that these RTAs are more likely to include extensive investment provisions.

However, the nature of the RTA variable created for this study makes this unlikely as the index score changes over time and there are several examples of agreements (such as the ASEAN, the ANZSCEP, or the Trans-Pacific SEP) where the liberalization of investment in services or in goods comes several years after the entry into force of the trade agreement (or where investment is first liberalized in goods and then in services or vice versa). The fact that such a variable is more significant than an RTA dummy variable or an index taking the same value for all years hints at a causality going from the investment provisions to the increased investment flows.

A more fundamental question regarding the causal relationship between RTAs and investment is whether the RTA variable really measures the impact of disciplines introduced by the agreement or picks up domestic investment policies. It has been highlighted that investment and services commitments in RTAs generally lock in what already exists at the domestic level. Even GATS-plus commitments could be seen as bringing commitments closer to the actual level of liberalization, as found in the domestic investment regime, rather than opening up new markets for investors. The quantitative analysis however captures something specific to the RTAs (as we have fixed effects to account for domestic policies). The RTA could have a credibility effect (for example due to the binding of domestic policy under international law) or advertise the country to potential investors, if it does not per se add any new disciplines to the existing investment regime.

Assuming that RTAs have a positive impact on FDI leads to several conclusions or implications. First, there are strong complementarities between trade and investment liberalization and, although bilateral investment treaties are also found to be associated with higher investment flows (Egger and Merlo 2007), the combination of trade and investment liberalization seems to have a greater impact and justifies the new generation of RTAs with 'deep integration' provisions on investment and trade in services. As disciplines on investment in services are partly in investment agreements and in the GATS, RTAs really add to existing rule-making and can provide investors with an investment regime that takes a more coherent approach towards goods and services. However, there is no reason for this greater coherence to be limited to the bilateral or regional level. It could also be achieved plurilaterally or multilaterally.

Looking at the index scores in Table 8.2, the 'fragility' of Asian regionalism (Baldwin 2006) seems to be confirmed. It is true that many agreements have been signed and have extensive provisions in the area of services and investment but the scope of commitments in several of the agreements is surprisingly low. Or when it is not low, the surprise sometimes comes from the very small number of improved commitments, as shown by the analysis of Fink and Molinuevo (2007). In a sense, to the extent that preferential treatment can create trade or investment diversion, it may be better. But there is nonetheless a contrast between the extensive provisions of some agreements providing market access, national treatment and most-favoured-nation treatment and how in fact very few additional sectors benefit from these provisions. This is however not the case for all agreements and a certain number of them are ambitious both in the scope of their provisions and the sectors covered.

What the quantitative analysis suggests is that even when they are limited, the provisions of the agreements matter. This finding should encourage countries to be more ambitious as even a partial liberalization is associated with non-negligible positive effects on trade and investment flows. And one should also keep in mind that in the quantitative analysis we have treated 'full' and 'partial' commitments as equivalent. This means that agreements with a high index score still have many reservations listed to accommodate all their specific policy needs in sectors where investment might be detrimental to other policy objectives (e.g. social and environmental goals). The positive impact that the study measures is on the basis of a diminution of sub-sectors fully excluded from liberalizing commitments rather than the removal of all reservations previously listed.

Lastly, while one reason for studying Asia was the higher prevalence of vertical FDI and network patterns in FDI, the results of the quantitative analysis do not seem to be different or to indicate that the determinants of FDI are different. The relative GDP and relative skilled-labour endowment variables have shown results consistent with the knowledge-capital model but not suggesting a greater role on average for vertical FDI in Asia. The empirical model could be refined to further investigate the relationship between investment provisions in RTAs and different types of foreign investment with a better treatment of third-country effects, as suggested by Dee (2006). Further research could also be devoted to an analysis of the role of rules of origin. These rules are more liberal for services and investment than for goods (Fink and Jansen 2007). But still the results of the quantitative analysis suggest that a preferential treatment for investment can have an impact on FDI and trade flows.

Acknowledgements

Although based on OECD research, the findings and conclusions expressed in this chapter are those of the author and do not represent those of the OECD or its member countries. The author would like to thank Carsten Fink and Martin Molinuevo for having shared their data on East Asian RTAs and for helpful comments. Thanks are also extended to Julien Chaisse, Jonathan Gage, Mike Gestrin, Marie-France Houde and Molly Lesher for useful suggestions, as well as participants at the World Trade Institute/National Centre of Competence in Research (WTI/NCCR) conference on 'Expansion of FDI in Asia' organized with the National Institute of Development Administration in Bangkok in January 2008.

Notes

1 http://www.wto.org/english/tratop_e/region_e/region_e.htm *(accessed 12 June 2008)*.
2 According to UNCTAD (2007), about 240 RTAs have provisions on investment.
3 When firms export they face transport costs and trade barriers. If a firm produces directly in the foreign market through an affiliate, it is closer to foreign consumers and can save the trade costs. However, the production is split between the home economy and the foreign economy and economies of scale are lost. There is also a fixed cost when

the firm establishes in the foreign market, i.e. an entry cost. In short, there is a trade-off between achieving proximity to consumers and concentrating production to exploit economies of scale.

4 As Australia and New Zealand have developed an important network of RTAs with their Asian partner countries, these two economies are included as reporters in the dataset. Because they have signed more RTAs with investment provisions, most of the reporting countries are from East Asia. Only Bangladesh and India are from South Asia. The dataset includes all agreements in force in 2006 which had substantive investment provisions. The full list of reporters is given in the section 'Data used and specification of the empirical model' and can be seen in Table 8.2.

5 The complete taxonomy can be found in Lesher and Miroudot (2006) with a description of the role of these provisions and how they are likely to influence investors' decisions.

6 The ASEAN Agreement for Promotion and Protection of Investment (1987). In the subsequent analysis, the three ASEAN agreements dealing with investment (and their amendments) are taken into account. The use of panel data allows the index score calculated for ASEAN members to reflect the evolution of the provisions. As a separate index is created for each reporter, differences between ASEAN members are also incorporated into the analysis (with regard to their schedules of commitments).

7 See Houde *et al.* (2007) for a discussion and illustration of 'NAFTA-inspired' vs. 'GATS-inspired' agreements and the interaction between investment and services chapters.

8 The GATS approach is referred to as a 'positive list' scheduling approach in Table 8.1, but more accurately is of a 'hybrid' type. Countries indicate a positive list of sectors where commitments are made but limitations to national treatment and market access in these sectors are reported in a negative list.

9 The data for East Asian economies come from Fink and Molinuevo (2007). In their study, a distinction is made between 'partial' and 'full' commitments. When there is a commitment for a specific sub-sector but reservations are scheduled in this sub-sector, the commitment is regarded as 'partial'. However, it is difficult to assess the extent to which limitations are binding for investors and how 'partial' commitments can be weighted as opposed to 'full' commitments in a quantitative analysis. The coverage ratio is therefore calculated on the basis of all commitments (whether partial or full). Agreements listing many limitations to national treatment and market access are generally also selective about the number of sub-sectors where commitments are made. Conversely, agreements with very few limitations in committed sectors tend to have a high sectoral coverage. Thus, the distortion introduced by the aggregation of 'partial' and 'full' commitments should not be too large.

10 A sixth package was concluded in November 2007.

11 When calculating the percentage of sub-sectors with commitments going beyond GATS, the percentage reflects an improvement in commitments already made. For example, a sub-sector where limitations are listed in GATS but removed in the RTA counts as an improved commitment.

12 More detail on the methodology used to code particular provisions can be found in Lesher and Miroudot (2006).

13 Current rather than real GDP is used, as price effects are accounted for in the model through the country and year fixed effects. See Baldwin and Taglioni (2006) for a discussion of the issues related to the (mis)use of GDP deflators in the estimation of gravity equations.

14 The knowledge-capital model first appeared in a publication by Markusen (1984). An empirical estimation of the model is provided by Carr *et al.* (2001).

15 Since FDI stocks are expressed in millions of US dollars, these 'zeros' can be negligible values.
16 The McFadden's pseudo R-squared in a Poisson regression is different from the standard R-squared in an OLS regression and should not be interpreted as its equivalent.
17 One should however be cautious in the interpretation, as the agreements generally liberalize cross-border trade in services together with investment. The increase in exports and imports of services could be the consequence of provisions in Mode 1 and Mode 2. There are however agreements in the dataset where only investment in services benefits from non-discrimination commitments.
18 For an illustration in the banking sector, see Buch and Lipponer (2007).

References

Adams, R., Dee, P., Gali, J. and McGuire, G. (2003) 'The trade and investment effects of preferential trading arrangements – old and new evidence', *Australian Productivity Commission Staff Working Paper*, Canberra.

Anderson, J. and van Wincoop, E. (2004) 'Trade costs', *Journal of Economic Literature*, 42, 691–751.

Ando, M. and Kimura, F. (2007) 'Fragmentation in East Asia: Further evidence', Working paper, Hitotsubashi University, Tokyo.

Antràs, P. and Helpman, E. (2004) 'Global sourcing', *Journal of Political Economy*, 112: 552–80.

Baldwin, R. (2006) 'Managing the noodle bowl: The fragility of East Asian regionalism', *CEPR Discussion Paper* No. 5561, London: Centre for Economic Policy Research.

Baldwin, R. and Taglioni, D. (2006) 'Gravity for dummies and dummies for gravity equations', *NBER Working Paper* No. 12516, Cambridge, MA: National Bureau of Economic Research.

Bergstrand, J.H. and Egger, P. (2007) 'A knowledge-and-physical-capital model of international trade flows, foreign direct investment, and multinational enterprises', *Journal of International Economics*, 73, 278–308.

Brainard, S.L. (1997) 'An empirical assessment of the productivity-concentration trade-off between multinational sales and trade', *American Economic Review*, 87: 520–44.

Buch, C. and Lipponer, A. (2007) 'FDI versus exports: Evidence from German banks', *Journal of Banking & Finance*, 31: 805–26.

Carr, D.L., Markusen, J.R. and Maskus, K.E. (2001) 'Estimating the knowledge-capital model of the multinational enterprise', *American Economic Review*, 91: 693–708.

Cheng, I. and Wall, H. (2005) 'Controlling for heterogeneity in gravity models of trade and integration', *Federal Reserve Bank of St Louis Review*, 87: 49–63.

Dee, P. (2006) 'Multinational corporations and Pacific regionalism', *Pacific Economic Papers*, No. 358.

Egger, P. and Merlo, V. (2007) 'The impact of bilateral investment treaties on FDI dynamics', *The World Economy*, 30: 1536–49.

Ethier, W. (1998) 'The new regionalism', *The Economic Journal*, 108: 1149–61.

Fink, C. and Jansen, M. (2007) 'Services provisions in regional trade agreements: Stumbling or building blocks for multilateral liberalization?', paper presented at the conference on Multilateralising Regionalism, WTO-HEI-CEPR, Geneva, September 2007.

Fink, C. and Molinuevo, M. (2007) 'East Asian free trade agreements in services: Roaring tigers or timid pandas?', *East Asia and Pacific Region, Report* No. 40175, Washington, DC. World Bank.

Fiorentino, R.V., Verdeja, L. and Toqueboeuf, C. (2007) 'The changing landscape of regional trade agreements: 2006 Update', *Discussion Paper* No. 12, Geneva: World Trade Organization.

Helpman, E. (2006) 'Trade, FDI, and the organization of firms', *Journal of Economic Literature*, 44: 589–630.

Houde, M.F., Kolse-Patil, A. and Miroudot, S. (2007) 'The interaction between investment and services chapters in selected regional trade agreements', *OECD Trade Policy Working Paper* No. 55, Paris: Organisation for Economic Co-operation and Development.

Jeon, B.N. and Stone, S.F. (2000), 'Foreign direct investment and trade in the Asian-Pacific region: Complementarity, distance and regional economic integration', *Journal of Economic Integration*, 15: 460–85.

Lesher, M. and Miroudot, S. (2006) 'Analysis of the economic impact of investment provisions in regional trade agreements', *OECD Trade Policy Working Paper* No. 36, Paris: Organisation for Economic Co-operation and Development.

Lloyd, P. (2002) 'New bilateralism in the Asia-Pacific', *World Economy*, 25: 1279–96.

Markusen, J.R. (1984) 'Multinationals, multiplant economies, and the gains from trade', *Journal of International Economics,* 16: 205–226.

Park, I. (2006) 'East Asian regional trade agreements: Do they promote global free trade?', *Pacific Economic Review,* 11: 547–68.

Santos Silva, J. and Tenreyro, S. (2006) 'The log of gravity', *Review of Economics and Statistics*, 88: 641–58.

UNCTAD (2005) *Investment provisions in economic integration agreements*, Geneva: United Nations Conference on Trade and Development (UNCTAD/ITE/IIT/2005/10).

UNCTAD (2007) 'Development implications of international investment agreements', *IIA Monitor* No.2 (UNCTAD/WEB/ITE/IIA/2007/2).

World Bank (2005), *Global Economic Prospects: Trade, regionalism and development,* Washington, DC: World Bank.

World Bank (2008) *World Development Indicators 2008* Database, Washington, DC: World Bank.

Part III

Asian interest in multilateral rules on trade and investment

A new paradigm?

9 Dealing with the noodle bowl effect in Asia

Consolidation, multilateralization, harmonization or dilution?

Jayant Menon

'I think the noodle bowl will become an inedible quagmire – it may take a long time to throw out but sensible businesses will simply order up other dishes'.[1]
(Hugh Patrick, Columbia University)

Introduction

Every country in the world today, with the exception of Mongolia, is a member of at least one plurilateral free trade agreement (PTA) and one bilateral free trade agreement (BTA), and most are members of multiple BTAs. If PTAs were considered the main threat to the world trade system in the 1990s, the concern has since shifted to BTAs. The number of BTAs has been growing at an astounding pace. The outcome of this proliferation of often overlapping BTAs and PTAs is described as the spaghetti bowl effect or, in the Asian region, the noodle bowl effect. It refers to the increased cost of doing business, and welfare losses associated with trade diversion due to inconsistencies between various elements of the agreements. These include, for instance, different schedules for phasing out tariffs, different rules of origin, exclusions, conflicting standards, and differences in rules dealing with anti-dumping and other regulations and policies (Pangestu and Scollay 2001).

How do we remedy the situation? There appears to be widespread agreement that a successful conclusion to the stalled Doha Round of the WTO would be the best way forward in minimizing the negative impacts of the current mess. Given the current uncertainty as to the timing and nature of such a conclusion, and concern that any expedited resolution may involve significant compromises that could undermine the outcome itself, interest has shifted to alternative measures for addressing this problem. Some see these as interim steps in addressing the problem, while others propose them as fully fledged remedies. All of them are premised on the assumption that even a *bona fide* conclusion to the Doha Round may no longer be sufficient to remedy the chaotic trading environment of crisscrossing BTAs and overlapping PTAs.

A general limitation of the proposals put forward for dealing with the noodle bowl effect is that they tend to implicitly group all kinds of BTAs and PTAs together as a homogeneous group. In other words, the proposals ignore underlying differences in motivation in forming BTAs and PTAs. It is argued that the underlying motivation will be critical in determining whether or not a particular remedy is likely to be effective in minimizing the impacts of the noodle bowl effect. In other words, unless the proposed remedy does not directly conflict with the underlying motivation in forming the BTA, it is likely to be resisted by the parties concerned, and is unlikely to work.

A second limitation relates to how some of the proposed remedies are presented. In general, they are promoted only in terms of neutralizing the distortions associated with the noodle bowl effect. A related, but often ignored issue is the impact that the proposed remedies have in terms of promoting trade liberalization beyond the neutralization of the noodle bowl effect. In other words, to what extent can a proposed remedy go beyond dealing with the distortions associated with overlapping BTAs and PTAs with their differing rules and requirements, and further the cause of promoting freer trade?

With these limitations in mind, this chapter develops a taxonomy for classifying BTAs by underlying motivation before considering the effectiveness of the different remedies proposed, both in terms of addressing the noodle bowl effect and more generally in terms of the pursuit of liberalization. We begin, however, by providing some facts and figures relating to BTAs, including their proliferation in the next section. The third section adapts a taxonomy developed by Menon (2007a) to classify BTAs by their main driving force, or motivation, to provide the backdrop for the ensuing analysis. The fourth section begins by outlining the various options proposed for dealing with the consequences of the noodle bowl effect, before providing an assessment of their ability to do so. The final section contains a summary of the main points.

BTAs: some facts and figures

A complete listing of the BTAs that involve at least one country from the Asia-Pacific region,[2] together with their status, is provided in Table 9.1, and summarized in Table 9.2. The same information is provided in diagrammatic form in Figure 9.1.

Between 1983 and 1999, the interest in forming BTAs was growing at a slow but steady pace. From 2000 however, this growth started to accelerate. Between 2000 and 2004, the number of BTAs concluded more than doubled, and doubled again in the next four years to reach 77 by January 2008. At the moment, another 65 BTAs are currently under negotiation, and 44 more have been proposed. This last number in particular keeps increasing.

Of the BTAS that have been concluded or are under implementation, the United States tops the list with 16 of them, followed by Chile (12), Singapore (10), Mexico (9), and Japan (8). Of the BTAs for which framework agreements have been signed or are currently being negotiated, Singapore tops the list with 10, followed by India with 9, and Australia, Japan, Pakistan and People's Republic of China (PRC) with 7 each. The majority of these BTAs, whether concluded, being negotiated or proposed, are inter-regional in nature, in that one partner lies outside the 'region', however defined. From Table 9.3, which considers

Table 9.1 BTAs of countries in ASEAN, APEC and South Asia, as of January 2008

	Concluded[a]/under implementation[b]			Framework agreement signed[c]/under negotiation[d]			Proposed/under consultation/study[e]	
No.	Parties	Date	No.	Parties	Date	No.	Parties	Date
1	ASEAN–Korea	Jul 06	78	ASEAN–Australia and New Zealand	Feb 05	143	Australia–Korea	Dec 06
2	ASEAN–PRC	Jan 05	79	ASEAN–EU	May 07	144	Australia–Mexico	Jan 06
3	Australia–New Zealand	Jan 83	80	ASEAN–India (FA signed)	Jan 04	145	India–Australia	Jan 08
4	Canada–Chile	Jul 97	81	ASEAN–Japan (FA signed)	Nov 07	146	India–Colombia	Mar 01
5	Canada–Costa Rica	Nov 02	82	Australia–Chile	Dec 06	147	India–EFTA	Nov 07
6	Canada–EFTA[f] (concluded)	Jun 07	83	Australia–GCC	Jul 07	148	India–Indonesia	Aug 05
7	Canada–Israel	Jan 97	84	Australia–UAE	Mar 05	149	India–Israel	Aug 07
8	Canada–United States[g]	Oct 87	85	Canada–Andean Community	Jun 07	150	India–Russian Federation	Oct 07
9	Chile–Colombia (signed)	Nov 06	86	Canada–Caribbean Community	Oct 07	151	India–Uruguay	2004
10	Chile–EFTA	Dec 04	87	Canada–Central America	Nov 01	152	India–Venezuela	2004
11	Chile–MERCOSUR	Aug 99	88	Canada–Dominican Republic	Jun 07	153	Indonesia–Australia	Nov 05
12	Chile–Mexico	Oct 96	89	Canada–Singapore	Jan 02	154	Indonesia–EFTA	Jul 07
13	Chile–Panama (signed)	Jun 06	90	India–Egypt	Jan 02	155	Japan–Canada	Nov 05
14	Chile–Peru (signed)	Aug 06	91	India–EU	Sep 05	156	Korea–GCC	Nov 07
15	EFTA–Singapore	Jan 03	92	India–GCC[h] (FA signed)	Aug 04	157	Korea–MERCOSUR	Dec 07
16	India–Afghanistan (signed)	Mar 03	93	India–Korea	Mar 06	158	Korea–South Africa	Jun 05
17	India–Chile (signed)	Mar 06	94	India–Mauritius	Aug 05	159	Korea–Thailand	Aug 03
18	India–MERCOSUR (signed)	Jan 04	95	India–SACU[i] (FA signed)	Nov 04	160	Malaysia–India	Jan 05
19	India–Singapore	Aug 05	96	India–Thailand (FA signed)	Oct 03	161	Malaysia–Korea	Nov 05
20	India–Sri Lanka	Dec 98	97	Japan–Australia	Apr 07	162	New Zealand–India	May 07
21	Indo–Nepal Treaty of Trade	Jun 02	98	Japan–GCC	Sep 06	163	New Zealand–Korea	Dec 06
22	Japan–Brunei (signed)	Jun 07	99	Japan–India	Feb 07	164	New Zealand–Mexico	Nov 02
23	Japan–Chile	Sep 07	100	Japan–Korea	Dec 03	165	Pakistan–Afghanistan	Jun 06
24	Japan–Indonesia (signed)	Aug 07	101	Japan–Switzerland	May 07	166	Pakistan–Brunei	Mar 06
25	Japan–Malaysia	Jul 06	102	Japan–Vietnam	Oct 06	167	Pakistan–Jordan	Jun 06
26	Japan–Mexico	Apr 05	103	Korea–Canada	Jul 05	168	Pakistan–Kazakhstan	Dec 03
27	Japan–Philippines (signed)	Sep 06	104	Korea–EU	May 07	169	Pakistan–Philippines	Apr 04
28	Japan–Singapore	Nov 02	105	Korea–Mexico	Mar 06	170	Pakistan–Tajikistan	Dec 05
29	Japan–Thailand	Nov 07	106	Malaysia–Australia	May 05	171	Pakistan–Thailand	Sep 06
30	Korea–Chile	Apr 04	107	Malaysia–Chile	2007	172	PRC–India	Jun 03

(Continued)

Table 9.1 (Continued)

Concluded[a]/under implementation[b]			Framework agreement signed[c]/under negotiation[d]			Proposed/under consultation/study[e]		
No.	Parties	Date	No.	Parties	Date	No.	Parties	Date
31	Korea–EFTA	Sep 06	108	Malaysia–New Zealand	May 05	173	PRC–Korea	Mar 06
32	Korea–Singapore	Mar 06	109	New Zealand–GCC	Jul 07	174	PRC–Norway	Mar 07
33	Korea–United States (signed)	Jun 07	110	New Zealand–Hong Kong	Nov 00	175	PRC–South Africa	Jun 04
34	Laos–Thailand	Jun 91	111	New Zealand–PRC (FA signed)	Dec 04	176	Singapore–Bahrain[j]	Oct 03
35	Malaysia–Pakistan	Jan 08	112	Pacific ACP–EC	Sep 04	177	Singapore–Sri Lanka	Aug 03
36	Mexico–Bolivia	Jan 95	113	Pakistan–Bangladesh	Nov 03	178	Singapore–UAE[j]	Mar 05
37	Mexico–Costa Rica	Jan 95	114	Pakistan–GCC (FA signed)	Aug 04	179	Thailand–Chile	Mar 06
38	Mexico–EFTA	Jul 01	115	Pakistan–Indonesia (FA signed)	Nov 05	180	Thailand–MERCOSUR	Mar 06
39	Mexico–EU	Jul 00	116	Pakistan–MERCOSUR (FA signed)	Jul 06	181	United States–Brunei	May 07
40	Mexico–Israel	Jul 00	117	Pakistan–Morocco	2005	182	United States–Indonesia	Jan 07
41	Mexico–Nicaragua	Jul 98	118	Pakistan–Singapore	Aug 05	183	United States–Pakistan	Aug 07
42	Mexico–Uruguay	Jul 04	119	Pakistan–Turkey (FA signed)	May 04	184	United States–Philippines	1989
43	New Zealand–Singapore	Jan 01	120	Peru–EFTA	Apr 06	185	United States–Sri Lanka	2002
44	Pakistan–Iran	Sep 06	121	PRC–Australia (FA signed)	May 05	186	United States–Taipei, China	2002
45	Pakistan–Mauritius	Jun 05	122	PRC–GCC	Apr 05			
46	Pakistan–Sri Lanka	Jun 05	123	PRC–Iceland (FA signed)	2006			
47	Papua New Guinea–Australia	Sep 91	124	PRC–Peru	Jan 08			
48	PRC–Chile	Oct 06	125	PRC–SACU	Oct 06			
49	PRC–Hong Kong	Jan 04	126	PRC–Singapore	Jul 04			
50	PRC–Macao	Jan 04	127	Singapore–Egypt	Nov 06			
51	PRC–Pakistan	Jul 07	128	Singapore–Kuwait	Jul 04			
52	PRC–Thailand	Oct 03	129	Singapore–Mexico	Jul 00			
53	Singapore–Australia	Jul 03	130	Singapore–Peru	Feb 06			
54	Singapore–EFTA	Jan 03	131	Singapore–Qatar[j]	Nov 06			
55	Singapore–Jordan	Aug 05	132	Singapore–Ukraine	May 07			
56	Singapore–Panama	Jul 06	133	Taipei, China–Dominican Republic	2006			
57	Sri Lanka–Iran (signed)	Nov 04	134	Taipei, China–Paraguay (FA signed)	Aug 04			
58	Taipei, China–Guatemala	Jul 06	135	Thailand–Bahrain (FA signed)	Dec 02			
59	Taipei, China–Nicaragua	Oct 07	136	Thailand–EFTA	Oct 05			
60	Taipei, China–Panama	Jan 04	137	Thailand–Peru (FA signed)	Nov 05			
61	Thailand–Australia	Jan 05	138	Ukraine–Singapore	May 07			

62	Thailand–New Zealand	Jul 05
63	Thailand–Peru (signed)	Nov 05
64	United States–Australia	Jan 05
65	United States–Bahrain	Aug 06
66	United States–Chile	Nov 04
67	United States–Colombia (signed)	Nov 06
68	United States–Israel	Sep 85
69	United States–Jordan	Dec 01
70	United States–Marshall Islands	May 04
71	United States–Micronesia	Jun 04
72	United States–Morocco	Jan 06
73	United States–Oman (signed)	Sep 06
74	United States–Palau	Jun 07
75	United States–Panama (signed)	Apr 06
76	United States–Peru (signed)	Oct 94
77	United States–Singapore	Jan 04

139	United States–Malaysia	Mar 06
140	United States–Thailand	Jun 04
141	United States–SACU	Nov 02
142	United States–UAE	Nov 04

Sources: Author's compilation based on data from the following websites: ADB ARIC (aric.adb.org); Australian Government Department of Foreign Affairs and Trade (www.dfat.gov.au); Bilaterals.org (www.bilaterals.org); Foreign Affairs and International Trade Canada (www.dfait-maeci.gc.ca); Office of the US Trade Representative (www.ustr.gov); Organization of American State's Foreign Trade Information System (www.sice.oas.org); and WTO (www.wto.org).

Notes
a Concluded – Parties have signed the agreement after completing negotiations. Some FTAs would require legislative or executive ratification.
b Under implementation – FTA has entered into force.
c Framework agreement signed – Parties have initially negotiated and signed the framework agreement (FA).
d Under negotiation – Parties have begun negotiations without a framework agreement (FA).
e Proposed/under consultation/study – Parties are considering a free trade agreement, establishing joint study groups or a joint task force, and conducting feasibility studies to determine the desirability of entering into an FTA.
f European Free Trade Association.
g Superseded by NAFTA.
h Gulf Cooperation Council.
i South African Customs Union.
j Now GCC–Singapore FTA.

Table 9.2 BTAs of countries in ASEAN, APEC and South Asia (cumulative), as of January 2008

Year	Concluded[a]/under implementation[b]	FA signed[c]/under negotiation[d]	Proposed/under consultation/study[e]	Total
1983	1	0	0	1
1984	1	0	0	1
1985	2	0	0	2
1986	2	0	0	2
1987	3	0	0	3
1988	3	0	0	3
1989	3	0	1	4
1990	3	0	1	4
1991	5	0	1	6
1992	5	0	1	6
1993	5	0	1	6
1994	6	0	1	7
1995	8	0	1	9
1996	9	0	1	10
1997	11	0	1	12
1998	13	0	1	14
1999	14	0	1	15
2000	16	2	1	19
2001	19	3	2	24
2002	22	7	5	34
2003	27	10	10	47
2004	39	22	14	75
2005	49	36	22	107
2006	67	50	32	149
2007	76	64	43	183
2008	77	65	44	186

Sources: Author's compilation based on data from the following websites: ADB ARIC (aric.adb.org); Australian Government Department of Foreign Affairs and Trade (www.dfat.gov.au); Bilaterals.org (www.bilaterals.org); Foreign Affairs and International Trade Canada (www.dfait-maeci.gc.ca); Office of the US Trade Representative (www.ustr.gov); Organization of American State's Foreign Trade Information System (www.sice.oas.org); and WTO (www.wto.org).

Notes
a Concluded – Parties have signed the agreement after completing negotiations. Some FTAs would require legislative or executive ratification.
b Under implementation – FTA has entered into force.
c Framework agreement (FA) signed – Parties have initially negotiated and signed the FA.
d Under negotiation – Parties have begun negotiations without an FA.
e Proposed/under consultation/study – Parties are considering a free trade agreement, establishing joint study groups or a joint task force, and conducting feasibility studies to determine the desirability of entering into an FTA.

various definitions of the region, we can see that the share of intra-regional BTAs is very low for both Association of Southeast Asian Nations (ASEAN)+3 and ASEAN+6 definitions, and even when we define the region to include the full complement of countries covered in this paper, the share is still only about half.

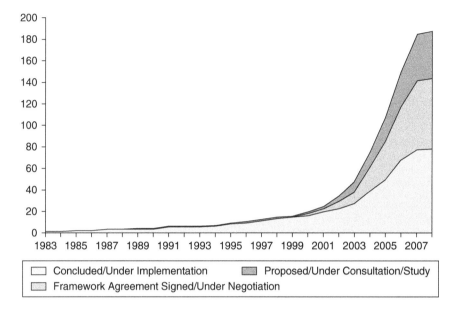

Figure 9.1 BTAs of countries in ASEAN,[3] APEC and South Asia by status, cumulative as of January 2008

Sources: Author's compilation based on data from the following websites: ADB ARIC (aric.adb.org); Australian Government Department of Foreign Affairs and Trade (www.dfat.gov.au); Bilaterals.org (www.bilaterals.org); Foreign Affairs and International Trade Canada (www.dfait-maeci.gc.ca); Office of the US Trade Representative (www.ustr.gov); Organization of American State's Foreign Trade Information System (www.sice.oas.org); and WTO (www.wto.org).

Factors driving the proliferation of BTAs

Why are BTAs so popular? In answering this question, we identify a set of *general* as well as *specific* factors or motivations for the popularity of BTAs. The general motivations apply to most, if not all, BTAs, but there is always at least one additional *specific* factor that drives the formation of a BTA. Usually there is more than one *specific* factor involved however. For instance, each party to the BTA may have its own motivation for pursuing the agreement, and this may not coincide with the interests of the other party. It is also possible that each party has more than one motivating factor. When there are two or more factors motivating the BTA, the dominant one is used in classifying it.

General factors

An important reason for the popularity of BTAs is the apparent disenchantment with the pace of progress of liberalization at the multilateral level. The difficulties associated with concluding the Doha round have simply reinforced this view. Many feel that the WTO has failed to deliver and so have pursued BTAs (and PTAs) as a means of pressing ahead with their trade and liberalization agendas.[4]

Table 9.3 The share of intra-regional BTAs for different definitions of 'region'

Group	Concluded[a]/under implementation[b]		FA signed[c]/under negotiation[d]		Proposed/under consultation/study[e]		Total	
	No.	Share	No.	Share	No.	Share	No.	Share
ASEAN+3	11	14%	1	2%	1	2%	12	6%
ASEAN+6	17	22%	14	21%	11	25%	42	23%
ASEAN+6 + other APEC[f]	34	44%	27	41%	20	45%	81	44%
ASEAN+6 + other APEC + other South Asia	40	52%	30	63%	26	59%	96	52%

Sources: Author's compilation based on data from the following websites: ADB ARIC (aric.adb.org); Australian Government Department of Foreign Affairs and Trade (www.dfat.gov.au); Bilaterals.org (www.bilaterals.org); Foreign Affairs and International Trade Canada (www.dfait-maeci.gc.ca); Office of the US Trade Representative (www.ustr.gov); Organization of American State's Foreign Trade Information System (www.sice.oas.org); and WTO (www.wto.org).

Notes
a Concluded – Parties have signed the agreement after completing negotiations. Some FTAs would require legislative or executive ratification.
b Under implementation – FTA has entered into force.
c Framework agreement (FA) signed – Parties have initially negotiated and signed the FA.
d Under negotiation – Parties have begun negotiations without an FA.
e Proposed/under consultation/study – Parties are considering a free trade agreement, establishing joint study groups or a joint task force, and conducting feasibility studies to determine the desirability of entering into an FTA.
f Lao People's Democratic Republic is a member of ASEAN, but not APEC.

A kind of snowball or domino effect, as seen with PTAs in the past (see Baldwin 1996), has also been driving the growth in BTAs. In the Asia-Pacific region, interest in forming BTAs began in the late 1990s with Japan, Singapore, South Korea and New Zealand. By 2000, the United States, Australia, Thailand and the People's Republic of China had joined the trend, with more than 40 new BTAs being proposed or negotiated (see Table 9.2). The momentum gathered over subsequent years to the point where other Asia-Pacific countries may have felt disadvantaged if they did not join the club. The number of BTAs thus continued to grow, and almost doubled to 109 between 2002 and 2004. There is clearly a momentum effect driving some of the growth in BTAs with countries not wanting to be left behind in this apparent race.[5]

It is often claimed that some, if not most, BTAs are essentially politically motivated. There is no doubt that political economy considerations, and indeed political parties or politicians themselves, play a major role in driving the proliferation of BTAs. A recent example of this from the United States, is how the control of both Houses by the Democrats has put at risk a number of the BTAs that the Bush administration has been pursuing. Although we try to take into account political, strategic and foreign policy related issues, we focus on economic and economic-related considerations because they are easier to identify and measure. Thus, the discussion that follows is likely to understate the role that politics and politicians play in the proliferation of BTAs, simply because these influences are often difficult to measure or model, let alone classify.

Specific factors

In trying to classify BTAs, with a view towards a better understanding of them and their motivating factors, previous researchers have focused on issues such as relative size of the partners (Bonapace 2004; Whalley 2008) or geographical dispersion (Scollay 2003), while others have referred to a range of trade, political and other non-economic issues (e.g. Pangestu and Scollay 2001; Baldwin 2004; Ravenhill 2006). These studies have generally failed to identify any clear or consistent pattern relating to size or geography, and have usually concluded that myriad factors are probably involved. Menon (2007b) brings together, in a systematic way, various economic, political and strategic factors underlying the proliferation of BTAs in an attempt to redress this ambiguity.

In this section, we adapt the taxonomy of Menon (2007a) to focus on economic motivations. There is no claim that this adaptation, or the original taxonomy, is comprehensive in the sense that it can explain, or classify, all BTAs. It only attempts to explain most of them. There are apparently a host of BTAs that are basically single or limited-issue agreements, which may not even try to address tariff or non-tariff barriers. Furthermore, these may be sector or product specific, which makes generalization even more difficult.[6] There is not much we can do to accommodate these single- or limited-issue BTAs in a taxonomy, apart from recognizing that they exist and that they may need to be considered separately.

We identify three broad categories of specific economic factors, namely: sector driven, market access and PTA based. As depicted in Figure 9.2, each of these three categories has two sub-categories. Thus, in total, we identify six specific economic factors to explain the proliferation of BTAs.

Sector driven BTAs

Sector driven BTAs are subdivided into sector excluding and sector expanding BTAs. These BTAs are motivated mainly by one or a few key sectors. There is both a positive and a negative element to this sector based motivation, with some BTAs designed to expand liberalization into sectors or areas that have previously been ignored at the multilateral level, while others exclude sensitive sectors or issues.

SECTOR EXPANDING BTAs

It is easy to see why BTAs are easier to negotiate and conclude than PTAs or a multilateral deal: with only two parties involved, the potential for disagreement is reduced. As the focus of liberalization shifts away from the relatively easier task of reducing trade taxes on industrial products, achieving agreement on a multilateral level has

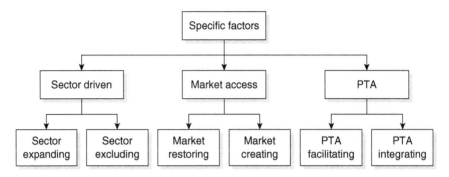

Figure 9.2 The different motivations for forming BTAs: specific factors

become more difficult as the agenda broadens to address less transparent forms of protection, more complex issues and new sectors. By requiring only two parties to agree, a BTA could face fewer obstacles than a regional or multilateral pact. BTAs may thus have the potential to achieve a deeper level of integration than that possible through the multilateral approach alone. Even if it is not any deeper, it is often argued that we might be able to get there more quickly using the bilateral approach than the multilateral one. Thus, sector expanding BTAs are often described as 'WTO Plus' or 'New Age' BTAs. The USA–Singapore BTA is one of the first such BTAs and, subsequent BTAs being pursued by the United States with the other ASEAN countries as part of its 'Enterprise for ASEAN Initiative' are using it as a model.

Of the various so-called 'Singapore issues' that were raised at the WTO Ministerial Conference in Singapore in 1996, only the rather fuzzy concept of trade facilitation measures appears to have survived on the WTO agenda. Other Singapore issues such as establishing rules for investment, competition policy and government procurement are being pursued in some sector expanding BTAs. Progress with liberalization of services in general has been slow at the multilateral level and fraught with difficulties over country-specific sensitivities. A wide-ranging multilateral deal in the near future looks unlikely. Some sector specific BTAs have emerged in response to such an environment. In this environment, BTAs have also been driven by the fact that preferential access may enable a supplier to steal an irreversible march on the competition, and cement a long-term advantage in the market. Many of the US BTAs with developing countries are pursuing more favourable rules relating to investment and intellectual property rights. Most of these BTAs involve countries that have had long-standing and strong trade relations, but are now looking to extend that relationship to new areas, especially in services.

SECTOR EXCLUDING BTAs

Apart from services, the most sensitive sector as far as liberalization is concerned is agriculture. Most sector excluding BTAs relate, in one way or another, to this sector. An example of the negative element would be the BTA between Japan and Singapore, known as the Japan–Singapore Economic Partnership Agreement (JSEPA). Japan has long resisted joining PTAs because of its reluctance to liberalize its agriculture sector, but the absence of any significant agricultural sector in the city state of Singapore has facilitated the signing of this BTA. Even the few agricultural products that Singapore does export, such as cut flowers and ornamental fish, were easily excluded from the JSEPA. Less than 10 per cent of the volume of exports of agricultural products from Singapore to Japan is provided with duty-free access, and the JSEPA did not create any new preferences in the agricultural sector (Ravenhill 2006).

A similar set of exclusions of sensitive sectors can be found in Japan's BTA with Mexico. Unlike Singapore, Mexico does have a large agricultural sector and is a major exporter of meat (pork in particular) to Japan, so the exclusions have been so widespread that about 13 per cent of Mexico's exports to Japan are excluded from the BTA. Thus, even when agriculture is important to one partner but sensitive for the other, it appears that BTAs can still be concluded by excluding this sector. Apart from exclusions, there is also greater room to manipulate rules of origin in a one-on-one setting to limit liberalization of sensitive sectors. Clearly the flexibility provided by BTAs through one-on-one negotiations allows such compromises to be made and trade agreements to be concluded when they might otherwise stall or fail.

Market access BTAs

As mentioned above, we divide market access BTAs into two groups: market restoring and market creating.

MARKET RESTORING BTAs

In the earlier discussion on general factors behind the popularity of BTAs, we noted that one of the reasons was the apparent disenchantment with the pace of progress of liberalization at the multilateral level. The same disenchantment with the WTO was one of many factors driving the original interest in PTAs. It also set off a kind of snowballing or domino effect (see Baldwin 1996). As the world trade system started to be carved up into blocks, countries that did not belong to a PTA felt compelled to form or join one in order to secure regional markets, or compensate for markets in other regions that were becoming more isolated and less accessible as a result of preferential arrangements.

Some BTAs have developed in response to such a global trading environment. The motivation behind them is the desire to restore trade links that existed prior to a trading partner joining a PTA. They generally apply to non-regional but traditional trade partners where one or both have become members of a relatively integrated PTA, which has weakened trade links between them as a result. These BTAs are designed to bypass, or at least reduce, the discriminatory treatment imposed upon them as a result of the PTA. Lloyd (2002: 6) describes this as the one factor that is common to all new PTAs and sees it as becoming more important relative to the other factors.

> As he puts it (p. 6): This is the fear of exclusion from major markets. In this context, exclusion does not mean that a country is denied access to a market, that is, total exclusion. It means that it has access on terms less favorable than some other country or countries.

With the European Union (EU) and the North American Free Trade Agreement (NAFTA) as centres of regional preferential trade, and with little or no prospect of other countries becoming members of these regional trade blocs, many of the BTAs being pursued with them (either with the EU or NAFTA or with individual member countries) would serve as examples of restoring market access BTAs.

The United States is a major trading partner for most of the ASEAN countries. As noted earlier, with the exception of Cambodia and Myanmar, all ASEAN countries have either concluded or are pursuing BTAs with the United States. For the ASEAN countries, the BTAs are viewed as a means of restoring market access in the post-NAFTA era.

MARKET CREATING BTAs

Market creating BTAs usually involve countries seeking to strengthen trade and investment relations when there have been few or only weak economic relations in the past. To the extent that limited trade in the past has been the result of trade barriers or other regulatory or commercial restrictions, market creating BTAs may be successful in achieving their objective of promoting bilateral trade. They could also involve one party with an economy that is highly trade liberalized, such as Singapore or Chile. These countries have little left to liberalize on the tariff front but are looking for better access to new markets. Countries looking to conclude BTAs with such low or zero tariff countries are usually motivated by access to non-trade sectors, particularly services. In this respect, these BTAs are similar to sector expanding BTAs, but differ from them in that they involve new or non-traditional trading partners. These highly liberalized countries also provide the best gateway, or conduit, to the region that they belong to, if the partner country is looking for such regional access. For example, many of the countries pursuing BTAs with Chile are looking for a foothold in the broader Latin and South American markets.

Another instance could involve two countries having relatively high trade barriers with the rest of the world, but then each removes them preferentially among regional partners in a PTA. In this case, there may be potential for boosting trade between the two countries through a BTA that opens up a conduit between the PTAs of which each country is a member. If, on the other hand, the trade relations are historically weak due to economic reasons based on comparative advantage, such as competitive rather than complementary resource endowments, then such BTAs will have little, if any, effect on boosting bilateral trade, unless the preference margins are very large.

PTA based BTAs

The PTA based category is also divided into two sub-categories: PTA facilitating and PTA integrating BTAs.

PTA FACILITATING BTAs

These are BTAs that are designed to hasten the pace of integration of a country seeking to join a PTA of which the other country is already a member. In other words, it is a BTA between a non-member and a member of a BTA. Although both parties are usually countries, they need not be so; they could also be BTAs or PTAs. An example of this would be the India–Thailand BTA, with India aiming to strengthen ties with the ASEAN Free Trade Area (AFTA). The same is true of the 'Plus 3' countries of ASEAN, with the People's Republic of China, Japan and Korea pursuing individual BTAs with ASEAN members. Such BTAs can also be pursued with the PTA as a whole, and all the 'Plus 3' countries are doing so with ASEAN.

PTA INTEGRATING BTAs

These are BTAs between members of a PTA. These types of BTAs stand out because unlike all other BTAs, the parties involved already have some form of a preferential trade agreement designed to promote closer economic relations between them. Examples of such BTAs include the Lao People's Democratic Republic–Viet Nam BTA and the Singapore–Thailand BTA, all member countries of which are also members of AFTA.

Alternative approaches to dealing with the proliferation of BTAs, and effectiveness

There are four broad approaches that have been proposed for addressing the proliferation of BTAs, and minimizing the damage that the noodle bowl effect is having on the world trade system. These are: (a) *consolidation* of BTAs into PTAs (e.g. Brummer 2007; Kawai 2007; Kawai and Wignaraja 2007); (b) *multilateralization* of preferential tariffs and other accords (e.g. Feridhanusetyawan 2005; Menon 2007b); (c) *harmonization* of MFN tariffs through coordinated reduction (Pangestu and Scollay 2001; Baldwin 2004; Estevadeordal *et al.* 2007a; Hoekman and Winters 2007); and (d) *dilution* of rules of origin (ROOs) through liberalization (Baldwin 2006a; Estevadeordal *et al.* 2007b; Gasiorek 2007).

We begin by examining the rationale provided for each approach before assessing how effective it is likely to be in achieving its objectives.

Consolidation

We start with the consolidation of BTAs into region-wide FTAs, or blocks, where the various BTAs between members belonging to the same region are supposed to become largely redundant. There are numerous examples of defunct BTAs following the establishment of the EU that lend credence to this approach. In the Asia-Pacific region, the USA–Canada BTA was superseded by the establishment of NAFTA. An Asia-wide free trade agreement (FTA) could supersede a host of regional BTAs, and consolidate them into one region-wide agreement, if the rules were changed to accommodate this.

The consolidation approach has the potential to reduce and perhaps even eliminate, intra-regional BTAs. In terms of our taxonomy, this would cover PTA integrating BTAs and, depending on the size of the consolidated PTA, some or all PTA facilitating BTAs as well. It is hard to imagine how it would neutralize any other type of BTA however. Most BTAs in the Asia-Pacific region are inter-regional in nature, as can be seen from Table 9.3. In the Asia-Pacific region, Kawai and Wignaraja (2007) propose an ASEAN+3 FTA initially, then an expansion to ASEAN+6 in their main consolidation proposal. From Table 9.3, we see that an ASEAN+3 FTA could potentially address only 6 per cent of all BTAs, while an ASEAN+6 FTA would cover less than a quarter of them. In short, it would not affect the vast majority of BTAs, at least not in terms of neutralizing them.

On the negative side, it may not always be easy to implement, as there are serious technical and implementation problems associated with 'folding several FTAs together that have different tariff rates and innumerable rules of origin (often defined differently by product) for preferences to kick in' (Bhagwati 2006).

Even if it were possible to implement, would there be any incentive to do so? A real-life example is provided in South Asia with the establishment of the South Asia Free Trade Area (SAFTA) in 2004, after a number of intra-regional BTAs had been concluded (see Table 9.1), such as the India–Sri Lanka pact. According to Weerakoon (2008), the India–Sri Lanka BTA is superior in its provisions to SAFTA in almost all respects, and as a result 93 per cent of Sri Lanka's exports to India currently enter duty free using the provisions of this BTA. Rather than consolidating and neutralizing this or other BTAs, it would appear that SAFTA has been rendered irrelevant by the presence of these BTAs. It could be argued that this may be a timing issue, since the full implementation of the SAFTA accords will not occur until 2016. Although this may be so and can only be determined in the future, there are underlying reasons to suspect that it is more than just a timing issue.

Once again, it may be a question of underlying motivation, and this view is captured in the following quotation from the Bangladeshi Minister of Commerce, Amir Chowdury: 'When it comes to [our] regional FTA, big economies like India and Pakistan may not offer handsome duty cuts due to distinct interests with an individual country. But they may offer large duty cuts in bilateral FTAs with Bangladesh.'[7] This position implies that not only would existing intra-regional BTAs continue in operation following the creation of a consolidated regional FTA, the incentive to pursue new intra-regional BTAs would still remain. If this is true, then the consolidated regional FTA would simply add another strand to the noodle bowl. In short, it is questionable whether the consolidation approach is a practical and effective way to address even intra-regional BTAs.

Thus, we need to put the ball back in the court of the 'consolidators', who advocate this approach. So far, we appear to have very little detail to go on. Moreover, the contrary case, that it would be very difficult to achieve, is compelling. This is because the BTAs are a highly heterogeneous group of agreements. They invariably have different tariff rates, different treatment of quantitative restrictions (QRs), different sector exemptions (and often different 'phase-in' rates for them), different ROOs (often defined product by product), and a host of other arrangements ranging from some service sector liberalizations to labour and standards provisions. If consolidation were to proceed, the more likely outcome is some sort of 'lowest common denominator' result, which would achieve very little (Hill and Menon 2008).

But there is a greater concern associated with employing this approach to address the proliferation of BTAs. This approach could serve to further fragment the world trade system, if it is perceived to be carving it up further, by introducing another distinct regional block. That is, apart from the EU and NAFTA, a consolidated Asian FTA may be viewed as the third block, or the third carved up, and thereby isolated, region. It is therefore critical that consolidation involves a concerted effort to ensure that the FTA is open, and is perceived to be so.

If the consolidated FTA is perceived as being isolating, or discriminatory in any way, it may provide fresh impetus for a new wave of market restoring BTAs, as traditional trade partners outside the region seek to retain trade access with members of the newly formed FTA. Perception and reality can vary, but, in this context, it may be perceptions that matter in the end, whatever the reality. It is hard to imagine how a new, large, consolidated block could be perceived as anything other than threatening, if not sinister, to non-member traditional trading partners, however open it is designed to be. If this is indeed the perception, and if there are more countries outside the region than inside, it is possible that the total number of BTAs could actually increase as a result. This could happen if the reduction in the number of intra-regional BTAs through a consolidated FTA is more than offset by the number of inter-regional market restoring BTAs that it indirectly induces. This is hardly a remedy to the problems facing the world trade system. To the contrary, it could add to the noodle bowl effect.

Multilateralization

Once a country has concluded BTAs with most, if not all, of its major trading partners, it may then make sense to: (a) equalize preferences across these BTAs; and (b) offer them to non-BTA countries on a most-favoured nation (MFN) basis. This would remove the administrative burden and eliminate distortions of country and global trade patterns. As is often the case with reversing second-best policies, however, it is the actual realized cost of implementation rather than any potential unrealized benefits that usually drives the process. And there are significant unrealized benefits that will accrue to the country concerned as well as the world trade system if this process of multilateralizing preferences is pursued, irrespective of the reason for doing so.

Although this approach is appealing in theory, and has the potential to remedy the noodle bowl effect, how realistic is it in practice? There are precedents to the voluntary multilateralization of preferential accords, so this is not a pipe dream. Indeed, AFTA and the actions of its original members confirm this possibility (see Feridhanusetyawan 2005; Menon 2007b). At the Asia-Pacific Economic Cooperation (APEC) Leaders Summit in Subic Bay in 1996, President Ramos of the Philippines raised the option of multilateralizing, within APEC, the AFTA accords. At the time, Indonesia had already begun providing its AFTA accords to other APEC countries. Although this proposal was never formally adopted by AFTA members, the original members have been pursuing multilateralization of their accords, not just within APEC, but on an MFN basis on a wide range of products. In 2002, preferences were fully multilateralized, or the margin of preference (MOP) was zero, for more than two-thirds of the tariff lines for the original ASEAN countries (Feridhanusetyawan, 2005). This share continues to increase year by year, although the MOP for a range of sensitive products remains high.

In terms of supporting global trade liberalization, the multilateralization process fares well. Because preferential tariff reduction schedules are generally more ambitious and rapid, this approach can accelerate the pace of multilateral trade liberalization.

To illustrate the process using AFTA as an example, Figure 9.3 compares, in stylized form, trade liberalization outcomes under various scenarios involving WTO and AFTA. WTO negotiations and outcomes reduce the amount of time required for countries to move towards their goal of free and open trade (defined here as 0–5 per cent average tariff rates). How does multilateralization of AFTA accords affect this outcome? If AFTA is implemented on a purely minimalist basis, or without any multilateralization of tariff preferences, then the time taken to arrive at the above-mentioned goal is unchanged. Average tariff rates do fall more rapidly however, particularly up to AFTA's 2003 deadline for 0–5 per cent internal tariff rates for its original members, but this gain could be offset by the trade diversion that it would also induce. If, however, members choose to fully multilateralize their preferences for all tariff lines soon after AFTA commences, then the deadline for free and open trade is moved forward to coincide with AFTA's deadline of 2003. In reality, we observe that preferences for a majority of tariff lines have been fully multilateralized and if the remaining one-third or so of tariff lines are dealt with in the same way relatively soon, then the deadline will fall somewhere between 2003 and the WTO based deadline. If this happens, AFTA would have served as a building block enabling countries to pursue multilateral goals at a faster pace.

How about the capacity of multilateralization to neutralize the noodle bowl effect? Returning to our taxonomy, what kind of BTAs would this approach be able to cater to? It could cover most, if not all, market access BTAs, since the objective is mainly to restore or expand trade, and not to exclude or protect it in any way. For similar reasons, it could also apply to all types of PTA based BTAs.

It is often argued that preferential accords in the non-tariff arena, such as those applying to the services sector, are quite easily multilateralized once they have

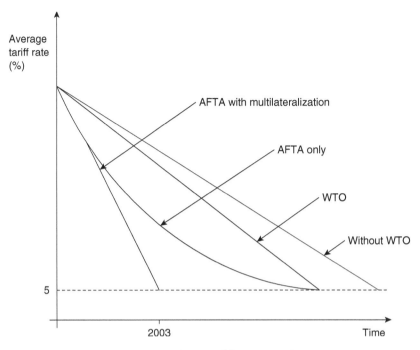

Figure 9.3 WTO and AFTA liberalization: different scenarios

Source: Menon, 2007a.

been negotiated (see Lloyd 2002; Hoekman and Winters 2007). This is because the instrument of protection in many service sector industries is regulation in one form or another, such as rules relating to foreign investment, competition policy, and government procurement. The same applies to the myriad measures that relate to trade facilitation, as well as technical product standards, sanitary and phytosanitary measures, certification procedures and processes, and mutual recognition arrangements relating to professional qualifications, among others. Such regulations are quite naturally applied in a non-discriminatory fashion, treating domestic and foreign firms[8] equally. This is quite different from tariffs affecting trade in goods, where domestic/foreign and intra-foreign discrimination is the objective. If this is the case, then this approach would appeal to sector expanding and some of the market creating BTAs.

Harmonization

There is often resistance to multilateralizing preferences however; after all, preferences form the basis of BTAs and PTAs. If such resistance cannot be overcome, another way of reducing the MOP and the distortions it creates is to bring down the MFN tariffs themselves. When brought down gradually, the MOP is not zero in the interim or at the end, but is much smaller. This approach may be more realistic when members feel committed to the preferential arrangement and therefore prefer a measured approach that retains some integrity of the arrangement, especially in the interim. When employing this method, an aggressive stance would involve a coordinated approach, such as harmonizing MFN tariffs, as with a customs union, to the lowest rate applied in the region. This approach does not require a customs union to be established however, as demonstrated by Estevadeordal *et al.* (2007a) in the case of Latin American PTAs. This aggressive approach is to be preferred, if practicable, in implementing the harmonization of MFN tariffs through coordinated reduction.

To some extent, this approach can be considered the dual to the multilateralization approach discussed earlier, but it employs a more pragmatic means that involves gradualism, and an eventual result that is less ambitious (non-zero MOP). It also differs from multilateralization in that it applies only to tariff measures and not non-tariff measures.

So, in terms of our taxonomy, it could cater to the same BTAs as the multilateralization approach with the exception of sector expanding BTAs, and some of the market creating BTAs. But, as with the multilateralization approach, it will not appeal to countries motivated to conclude BTAs which are sector excluding.

Dilution

The final approach that we consider is the dilution of rules of origin (ROOs) through liberalization. An interim measure towards full multilateralization of accords may take the form of loosening up ROOs and diluting their restrictive effect. If members of the BTA or PTA are not yet ready to give up reciprocal preferences, then this approach could be seen as preparing the groundwork for that process. This could be done by harmonization and expanding rules of cumulation. If rules of cumulation are sufficiently expanded and then harmonized across different agreements, the outcome might no longer require complete multilateralization of tariff accords. In this sense, liberalizing ROOs, like harmonized reduction of MFN tariffs, can be thought of as an alternative means of achieving the same result.

Like the harmonized reduction approach, it would apply mainly to tariff measures, and cater for similar types of BTAs. But it can be more effective in limiting future growth in extra-regional BTAs such as market restoring BTAs. This is because a system of bilateral hub–spoke agreements with constraining ROOs is likely to greatly encourage hub–spoke trade at the expense of spoke–spoke trade. So, if the ROOs are sufficiently liberalized and rules of cumulation adequately expanded, it can remove distortions associated with artificial sourcing of inputs simply to meet regional cumulation requirements. This will reduce the incentive for spoke countries to pursue BTAs with either the hub or other spokes to prevent (non-preferential) spoke–spoke trade being diverted to (preferential) hub–spoke trade.

In this way, this approach has an edge over the harmonized approach. It has the same advantage over the multilateralization approach in being better suited to

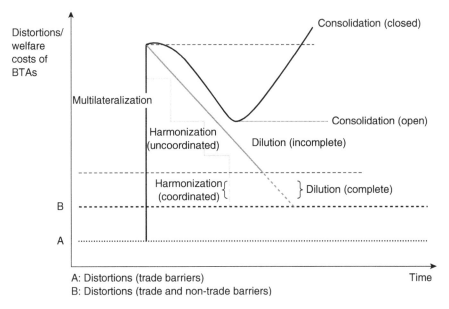

Figure 9.4 Stylized welfare effects of different remedies

addressing market restoring BTAs, but is not as effective in neutralizing sector expanding BTAs, since it deals mainly with tariff but not non-tariff measures.

A summing up

In this section, we summarize the assessment and likely impacts of the four proposed remedies for addressing the effects of the proliferation of BTAs, as well as promoting liberalization more generally. Figure 9.4 portrays, in stylized form, the likely welfare effects of each remedy, and variants therein, while Table 9.4 summarizes the ability of each remedy to address the different types of BTAs presented in our taxonomy.

Although Figure 9.4 is largely self-explanatory, two points are worth highlighting. The first is that the multilateralization approach produces the most significant reduction in distortions, as well as being able to do so in the shortest time. It has the capacity to eliminate not only the MOP, but also some of the distortions associated with discriminatory restrictions in the non-trade sector, especially services. It can achieve this in the shortest time because it involves a one-off decision, as opposed to staggered (harmonization) or gradual (dilution) changes.

If multilateralization is therefore the most preferred approach, the least preferred is consolidation. Although distortions fall initially, as (some) intra-regional BTAs are neutralized, they can rise again if a 'lowest common denominator' outcome prevails, whereby the average level of distortions actually increases and/or they induce new extra-regional, or market restoring, BTAs. If the consolidated

Table 9.4 Effectiveness of proposed remedy/approach versus type of BTA

Type of BTA	Proposed remedy\approach			
	Consolidation	Multilateralization	Harmonization	Dilution
Sector expanding		Yes		
Sector excluding	Partial	Partial	Partial	Partial
Market restoring		Yes	Yes	Yes
Market creating		Yes		
PTA facilitating	Yes	Yes	Yes	Yes
PTA integrating	Yes	Yes	Yes	Yes
Impact				
Induce new BTAs	Yes (closed) No (open)	No	No	No

FTA is perceived as being relatively closed, then it is likely that distortions could increase substantially. Even if the consolidated FTA is designed to be 'open' and is perceived to be so, the reduction in distortions is the lowest of the four approaches, because it can only address a limited range of BTAs, as highlighted in Table 9.4, and more likely on a lowest common denominator basis.

The consolidation approach has the capacity to address only two types of BTAs, namely PTA facilitating and PTA integrating, and these two types of BTAs can also be addressed using any of the other three approaches (Table 9.4). In addition to these two types of BTAs, the harmonization and dilution approaches can also deal with market restoring BTAs, whereas the multilateralization approach can additionally neutralize sector expanding BTAs. All four approaches are partially able to address sector excluding BTAs (discussed in more detail below).

The consolidation approach may also be an overreaction to the problems associated with the noodle bowl effect, or the general proliferation of BTAs. A fact that is being increasingly recognized, and confirmed by data on rates of utilization of preferences, is that many BTAs have no significant real effect on trade and other flows. Some BTAs are simply paper agreements that have no impact at all, apart from the resources wasted in their preparation, negotiation, and maintenance. Others, which are being implemented, have a much smaller impact than the sectors that they cover would suggest, because of low utilization rates. Various surveys of rates of utilization of preferences lend support to this view (see Grether and Olarreaga, 1998). For instance, a survey by the Japan External Trade Organization (JETRO 2003) found that in 2002 within AFTA, the rate was only 4 per cent for Malaysia and 11 per cent for Thailand. That is, the costs of complying with ROOs and other requirements are perceived to be higher than the benefit accorded by preferential treatment, and so exporters choose to ignore the preferential tariff and apply for MFN treatment. Pomfret (2007) claims that most of the world's trade continues to be conducted in this way, despite the proliferation of preferential agreements.

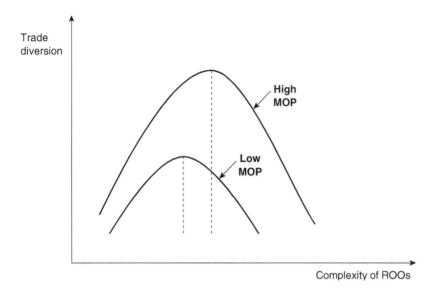

Figure 9.5 Rules of origin and trade diversion

Figure 9.5 illustrates this in stylized form. As the complexity of ROOs increases, the amount of trade diversion also increases initially. That is, in order to satisfy increasingly demanding domestic content requirements as well as other requirements, the sourcing of more and more inputs needs to be switched from the lowest cost supplier (assumed to be extra-regional) to regional member countries. Depending on the MOP, a turning point is eventually reached, which corresponds to a certain critical level of complexity. Beyond this level, it is no longer perceived as being profitable to try and satisfy the requirements of the preferential agreement, and it is more cost-effective to switch back to the lowest cost supplier. The level of trade diversion induced starts to taper off. The recorded low rates of utilization of preferences would suggest that the level of complexity of most ROOs lie somewhere beyond this critical level.

Another reason why consolidation may be an overreaction relates to the role that export processing zones play in providing a refuge for firms seeking to escape the quagmire of the noodle bowl. For example, the fastest growing segment of world trade is in electronics and components. Here production is being 'sliced up' across international boundaries more than ever, as multinational enterprises (MNEs) continue the search for efficient, low-cost production centres that are integrated into their multi-country production and distribution systems.

Asia is the driving force behind the growth of this trade.[9] The big MNEs in these sectors – Intel, Dell, Sony and others – typically produce, source and distribute in a dozen or more countries. It is inconceivable that these globally integrated giants could operate effectively across so many customs zones, each with their own set of ROOs. In fact they do not. Instead they generally choose to operate in export zones, where goods flow in and out on a duty-free basis, beyond the reach of PTAs or BTAs. The more these PTAs and BTAs spread, the more these firms will be driven into export zones to escape from them, and, in the process, will create an unhealthy dualism between the zones and the rest of the economy. Unless, of course, the countries continue down the path of unilateral liberalization and become, like Hong Kong and Singapore, one big free trade area. For this reason, BTAs are ultimately likely to collapse under their own weight (Hill and Menon 2008).

A feature that is clearly apparent from Table 9.4 is that none of the approaches appear to be able to address sector excluding BTAs fully. While any of the approaches could be employed to neutralize preferences in sectors other than the ones being specifically excluded (thus the reference to 'partial' in Table 9.4), the liberalization of these excluded sectors remains problematic for all approaches. It is important to note, however, that the distortions that result from excluding these sectors are different from those associated with the noodle bowl effect. These distortions do not arise from preferences or explicit discriminatory treatment, but from domestic subsidies and other forms of national support, as well as various non-tariff measures. But as we noted in the Introduction, it is important to consider these proposals not only in terms of dealing with the noodle bowl, but more broadly in terms of the overall liberalization process.

What can be done about these BTAs or, more specifically, the sectors excluded in these BTAs? This is where we return to the WTO, and the potential role that the Doha Round could play. This is because it is the multilateral approach that is arguably the best forum to deal with liberalization of these excluded sectors. The reason for this relates to the fact that the multilateral approach has one key advantage over the bilateral (or regional) approach in this respect. This is the ability to trade concessions across disparate interests; that is, to weigh the costs to countries of conceding protection in sensitive sectors (such as agriculture) against the benefits from increased market access in areas in which they have a comparative advantage (e.g. through changes to rules relating to investment, intellectual property or services).[10] This constrains negotiating positions and options within the WTO. Every time a BTA allows a country to bypass this trade-off simply through its choice of partner, and secure benefits without incurring costs, the task of liberalizing such sensitive sectors is made more difficult.

Summary and conclusions

The interest in forming BTAs has been growing at a phenomenal rate. In the Asia-Pacific region, defined as covering most of APEC and South Asia, the number of BTAs concluded has almost tripled over the past five years, from 27 in 2002 to 77 in January 2008. Furthermore, this interest appears to be increasing at an ever faster rate, with the number of proposed BTAs rising from 5 to 44 over the same period. The outcome of this proliferation of often overlapping BTAs and PTAs is described as the spaghetti bowl effect or, in the Asian region, the noodle bowl effect. Whatever one chooses to call it, there is little doubt that it is not a good way to organize trade, and that it is welfare-reducing.

This chapter has considered the various options proposed for dealing with this proliferation, and assessed their ability to do so. But previous assessments have ignored underlying differences in motivation for forming BTAs. To overcome this limitation, we have developed a taxonomy for classifying BTAs by motivation before considering the effectiveness of the different remedies proposed. Each proposal has its pros and cons, and any one may be more effective in neutralizing a BTA depending on why the BTA was formed. In short, motivation matters! Thus, a combination of the various proposals may be warranted, given the myriad motivations.

Although multilateralization of preferential accords is the most preferred approach to dealing with the problem, incentives to do so might be lacking. The least preferred approach is consolidation into region-wide FTAs, because it is both impractical and potentially counter-productive. That is, it could induce a larger number of inter-regional BTAs than the number of intra-regional BTAs that it may neutralize.

Because of differences in motivation, these proposals will have a role to play even in the event of an expeditious and *bona fide* conclusion to the Doha Round. But the WTO remains the best forum within which to try and address the most stubborn of BTAs, the sector excluding ones, and the most difficult of sectors, agriculture, because of its ability to trade concessions across disparate interests in a multilateral setting.

Acknowledgement

This is a revised version of a paper presented to a Conference on International Rules on Trade and Investment held in January 2008 in Bangkok. I am grateful for comments received from Charles Adams, W. Max Corden, Hal Hill, Ted James, Hugh Patrick and Richard Pomfret, and to Anna Melendez-Nakamura and Dorothea Lazaro for excellent research assistance. The views expressed herein are those of the author and should not be taken to reflect those of the Asian Development Bank.

Notes

1 Personal communication.
2 There are several definitions of the Asia-Pacific region. In this chapter, we use the members of the Association of Southeast Asian Nations (ASEAN) Asia-Pacific Economic Community (APEC) plus South Asia. The Central Asian Republics and Russia are excluded however, but considered in Menon (2007b).
3 Lao People's Democratic Republic is a member of ASEAN, but not APEC.
4 In a paradoxical twist, it seems WTO meetings themselves are being overshadowed and provide an opportunity for members to pursue new BTAs with other member countries. In the Bangkok-based daily newspaper, *The Nation*, dated 17 June 2004, an item entitled 'Peru seen as FTA Gateway' reports that: 'In the corridors of the WTO meetings, Thai officials discussed the possibility of FTAs with Mexico, Chile and Peru'. In the same vein, it is somewhat ironic that the Japan–Singapore BTA was concluded at the APEC summit meeting in Shanghai in October 2001.

5 Baldwin (2006b, p. 22) argues that it could continue to play a role in the proliferation of BTAs in the region in the coming years: 'If history is any guide, the domino effect in East Asia will spread to many, many more countries in the neighborhood. In Europe, for example, the playing out of several waves of domino effects has left the EU with preferential trade deals with every WTO member except nine. It is therefore conceivable that the 13 members of the ASEAN+3 group will end up signing a very large number of bilaterals in the coming years.'

6 For example, out of season fruit and vegetables could motivate a BTA, such as the USA–Chile agreement (that also included copper) or the proposed Pakistan–Indonesia one (seasonal differences in citrus fruit).

7 '"Dhaka needs bilateral FTAs to get maximum from SAFTA", says Commerce Minister', *The Daily Star*, Dhaka, 1 March 2004.

8 The nationality of a firm is defined here in terms of location of production rather than ownership.

9 Between 1969–1970 and 2005–2006, the share of Asian (almost entirely East Asian) countries in global non-oil exports reported a three-fold increase, from 11.1 per cent to 33.4 per cent. The fastest growing sectors have been within the machinery and transport equipment group of manufacturing, in particular information and communication technology (ICT) products. These have played a pivotal role in this major relocation of global trade to East Asia. By 2005–2006, over 67 per cent of total world ICT exports originated from Asia.

10 See Menon (1998) for more details. A potent example of this trade-off was provided in the lead-up to the WTO meeting in Hong Kong in December 2005. Brazil and India, representing the apparent position of the majority of developing countries, proposed opening their markets further to industrial goods and services in exchange for the EU and the USA dismantling the elaborate system of support to their agricultural sectors.

References

Baldwin, R.E. (1996) 'A domino theory of regionalism' in R.E. Baldwin, P. Haaparanta and J. Kiander (eds) *Expanding Membership of the EU*, Cambridge: Cambridge University Press.

Baldwin, R.E. (2004) 'The spoke trap: Hub and spoke bilateralism in East Asia,' *CNAEC Research Series 04-02*. Seoul: Korea Institute for International Economic Policy.

Baldwin, R.E. (2006a) 'Multilateralising regionalism: Spaghetti bowls as building blocs on the path to global free trade', *World Economy*, 29(11): 1451–1518.

Baldwin, R.E. (2006b) 'Managing the noodle bowl: The fragility of East Asian regionalism', *CEPR Discussion Paper No. 5561*, London: Centre for Economic Policy Research.

Bhagwati, J.N. (2006) 'Why Asia must opt for open regionalism on trade', *The Financial Times*, 3 November.

Bonapace, T. (2004) *Regional Trade Agreements: ESCAP Situation and Interaction with WTO Rules*, Bangkok: UN-ESCAP.

Brummer, C.J. (2007) 'Ties that bind: Regionalism, commercial treaties, and the future of global economic integration', *Vanderbilt Law Review*, 60(5): 55–72.

Estevadeordal, A., Freund, C. and Ornelas, E. (2007a) *Does Regionalism Affect Trade Liberalization towards Non-Members?* Washington, DC: Inter-American Development Bank.

Estevadeordal, A., Harris, J. and Suominen, K. (2007b) 'Harmonizing rules of origin regimes around the world', paper presented to the Conference on Multilateralizing Regionalism, WTO and CEPR, Geneva, September.

Feridhanusetyawan, T. (2005) 'Preferential trading agreements in the Asia-Pacific Region', *IMF Working Paper 149,* Washington, DC: International Monetary Fund.

Gasiorek, M. (2007) 'Multilateralizing regionalism: Relaxing rules of origin', paper presented to the Conference on Multilateralizing Regionalism, WTO and CEPR, Geneva, September.

Grether, J.-M. and Olarreaga, M. (1998) 'Preferential and non-preferential trade flows in world trade', *Staff Working Paper ERAD-98-10.* Geneva: World Trade Organization.

Hill, H. and Menon, J. (2008) 'Back to basics on trade', *Far Eastern Economic Review,* 171(5): 44–7.

Hoekman, B. and Winters, L.A. (2007) 'Multilateralizing "deep regional integration": A developing country perspective', paper presented to the Conference on Multilateralizing Regionalism, WTO and CEPR, Geneva, September.

JETRO (2003) *Current Status of AFTA and Corporate Responses,* Tokyo: Japan External Trade Organization.

Kawai, M. (2007) 'Evolving economic architecture in East Asia', *Discussion Paper No. 84,* Tokyo: ADB Institute.

Kawai, M. and Wignaraja, G. (2007) 'Multilateralizing regional trade arrangements in Asia', paper presented to the Conference on Multilateralizing Regionalism, WTO and CEPR, Geneva, September.

Lloyd, P. (2002) *New Regionalism and New Bilateralism in the Asia-Pacific*, Singapore: Institute of Southeast Asian Studies.

Menon, J. (1998) 'The expansion of the ASEAN Free Trade Area', *Asian-Pacific Economic Literature*, 12(2): 10–22.

Menon, J. (2007a) 'Bilateral trade agreements', *Asian-Pacific Economic Literature*, 21(2): 29–47.

Menon, J. (2007b) 'Building blocks or stumbling blocks? The GMS and AFTA in Asia', *ASEAN Economic Bulletin*, 24(2): 254–66.

Pangestu, M. and Scollay, R. (2001) 'Regional trading arrangements: Stock take and next steps', paper presented to the PECC Trade Policy Forum, Thai Ministry of Commerce, Bangkok, 12–13 June.

Pomfret, R. (2007) 'Is regionalism an increasing feature of the world economy?', *The World Economy*, 30(6): 923–47.

Ravenhill, J. (2006) 'The political economy of the new Asia-Pacific bilateralism: Benign, banal, or simply bad?', in V.K. Agarwal and S. Urata (eds) *Bilateral Trade Agreements in the Asia-Pacific*, London: Routledge, 27–49.

Scollay, R. (2003) 'RTA developments in the Asia-Pacific region: State of play', paper presented to the Focus Workshop on Trade, Fifteenth PECC General Meeting, Brunei Darussalam.

Weerakoon, D. (2008) 'India's role in SAARC: Integration and the way ahead', paper presented to the ADB–ICREAR Workshop on South Asian Integration, New Delhi, March.

Whalley, J. (2008) 'Recent regional agreements: Why so many, why so much variance in form, why coming so fast, and where are they headed?' *The World Economy*, 31(4), forthcoming.

10 India's multilayered FDI regulation

Between resistance to multilateral negotiations and unilateral proactivism

Julien Chaisse, Debashis Chakraborty and Arup Guha

Introduction

Like the other BRICs countries (Brazil, the Russian Federation, and China), India has participated in a 'deep integration' process. It was primarily achieved through *inward* investment. But firms from these four countries are becoming sources of *outward* foreign direct investment (as part of the growth of such investment from emerging markets in general), to establish portfolios of locational assets as increasingly important sources of their international competitiveness (Sauvant 2005). While these countries are on the verge of becoming important outward investors, many of their firms still need to acquire the necessary know-how and their governments need to put in place an appropriate enabling framework.

Since the liberalization of its economy in 1991, India has undergone major economic reforms, which have caused deep changes in its economy and consequently in its influence at the global level. These reforms consisted of opening up the economy to more foreign trade and investment, and the dismantling of the industrial licensing system. Over the last decade, India's growth rate has picked up, foreign exchange reserves have increased considerably, and the information technology sector has taken off, making India a major economic player in the global setting. These developments have led to a worldwide interest in the Indian economy, such as has not been witnessed since the time of India's independence. However, despite this growing association with the global flow of goods and investment, India has always shown a reluctance to engage in negotiations on a multilateral framework for investment.

It is widely held by scholars that in recent times trade and investment have been complementary (Egger et al. 2007), and achieving one is impossible in the absence of the other. However, the inclusion of the relationship between trade and investment (henceforth TI) in the World Trade Organization (WTO) forum for negotiation with the establishment of a Working Group on Trade and Investment (WGTI), one of the four Singapore Issues,[1] was the subject of fiery debates right from the beginning (Sauvé 2006). Moreover, investment had been the subject matter leading to the derailing of the WTO's Cancún meeting.[2] Important differences of opinion made negotiations impossible and contributed, in part, to the breakdown of the meeting. In the summer of 2004, in the aftermath of the discussions of July 2004,

WTO Members conceded that 'no work towards negotiations on [investment] will take place within the WTO during the Doha Round'.

The conflict of interest between the two groups of countries plays a key role in creating the current scenario. In general the developed countries believe that the inclusion of TI under the negotiating agenda of the WTO would be a major step forward in ensuring attainment of the WTO objectives of freer trade and a liberal investment regime, leading to increased foreign direct investment (FDI) to members with freer investment regimes. Adopting this perspective, Japan and the European Union pushed forcefully for the commencement of negotiations on investment while the United States did not strongly support this initiative (Kurtz 2002). The 'flying geese model' experienced by Asian tigers has always been a case in the developing countries point (de Mello 1997). However, a number of developing countries remained averse to the idea of a multilateral investment agreement, mostly owing to the potential risk involved with capital flight and the development consequences observed following the Southeast Asian currency crisis, which led even the International Monetary Fund (IMF) and the World Bank to acknowledge the importance of maintaining a strict investment regime in developing countries.[3] In this connection, the idea of making capital mobility conditional upon the access gained in labour mobility of the South as a bargaining tool has surfaced from time to time (Hoekman and Saggi 2001). Nonetheless, the effectiveness of such a policy has been questioned (Das 2003).

The international investment framework currently consists of thousands of individual agreements without any formal coordination. In the absence of global investment rules, States have no other choice but to continue concluding bilateral or regional agreements. As an immediate consequence this further accentuates the diversity and fragmentation of the international investment agreement universe (Chaisse and Gugler 2008). This scenario has justified and given rise to the current project, which intends to create an effective multilateral framework for investment.

Of course, investment provisions are already embraced in several international agreements (e.g. North American Free Trade Agreement (NAFTA), General Agreement on Trade in Services (GATS) and the Agreement on Trade Related Investment Measures (TRIMs)) and further negotiations on investment would not necessarily represent major progress. However, the coverage under these agreements deals only with limited investment provisions. Indeed, these investment provisions do not comprehensively address the key investment concerns such as legal security, policy coherence or the transparency of government commitments. Undoubtedly, addressing these issues in greater detail would considerably improve the global business environment and facilitate investment. In short, the current state of affairs challenges all countries and their economic policies to commit themselves to ongoing efforts towards the improvement and further liberalization of investment regimes.

The thesis of this contribution is as follows: the potential inclusion of a multilateral framework for investment at the WTO is intended to coordinate the global regulation on trade and investment. In addition to the difficulties arising during these negotiations (Sauvé 2006),[4] a major concern is that certain countries such as India are not interested in a full-scale capital account convertibility (CAC). As a part of the G4, India is currently a major player in the trade-related international regulatory framework, a fact of which it was once again reminded during the WTO Doha Ministerial Meeting (held in Geneva from 21 to 30 July 2008). The concerns of China and India deserve attention at the WTO. It is argued here that the question of a multilateral framework for investment cannot be resolved without taking into account the reluctance of India to adopt a freer investment regime. There is a historical reluctance of developing countries to establish freer investment regimes. The project on a new international economic order (NIEO) has already assigned preeminence to the sovereignty of States and their necessary control of the private sector, notably of foreign capital. But that political approach is reinforced by objective arguments analysed here.

This chapter is organized along the following lines. First we briefly discuss the debate on having a freer investment framework and foreign investment regime in India. India's submissions to the WTO on this front are reviewed next. Then, in order to evaluate the legitimacy of India's concerns, the potential impact of a destabilizing shock on her capital account is analysed through an empirical model. Finally, based on the findings, policy lessons are drawn.

Foreign investment and financial mobility regime in India

Before going into the WTO negotiations on TI, the theoretical perspective behind the developing country concerns needs to be reviewed. According to open economy macroeconomics, a large capital inflow into a country causes the relative prices of the goods to change (the speed of which depends on the exchange rate regime), and makes exports relatively dearer (and imports relatively cheaper). This causes a worsening of the current account balance and vice versa. To complicate the situation, a balance of payments (BOP) crisis may occur reflecting the dynamics of short-term debt, when speculators try to get rid of the domestic currency in exchange for the central bank's foreign exchange reserves in crisis situations, resulting in the collapse of the exchange rate (Rao 2006). The long adjustment period required in the aftermath of such a crisis causes the developing countries to be hesitant about freer investment regimes. However, it has been argued that CAC is neither necessary nor sufficient for a foreign exchange crisis (Agarwal 1998).

Until the early 1990s, India maintained a controlled exchange rate regime and various components of capital accounts transactions (e.g. FDI, portfolio equity investment, external commercial borrowing, non-resident deposits, short-term credit and outward investment) were subject to restrictions.[5]

The situation improved after the BOP crisis in July 1991, when India applied for IMF loans and hence had to adopt a liberalized framework in return. Subsequently, in January 1994, India joined the Multilateral Investment Guarantee Agency (MIGA), which protected the inward investment against a probable expropriation or nationalization. Later, in August 1994, the Indian rupee was made fully convertible on India's current account (as per IMF Article VIII). In order to explore the possibility of having CAC, the Tarapore Committee was set up and, in May 1997, the Committee recommended the introduction of CAC by 1999–2000 in a phased manner.[6]

However, the recommendation was subject to criticism in light of the Southeast Asian experience,[7] and India preferred to follow a cautious approach. The debate on the preparedness of the country for CAC has been revisited from time to time, and it is held that provided the preconditions suggested by the Tarapore Committee are met and the process is implemented taking into account relevant considerations (Jadhav 2003), a movement towards full convertibility is possible.[8] However, the preparedness of the country for going towards full CAC is still doubted by scholars (Gupta and Milind 2004).

A gradual reform of foreign investment and financial flow regulations took place in India in the period following the recommendations of the Tarapore Committee. It was realized that the draconian Foreign Exchange Regulation Act (FERA), enacted in 1973 during the severe shortage of foreign exchange in the country, had outlived its utility, and a new Foreign Exchange Management Act (FEMA) was introduced in June 2000. In 2003, the overseas investment norms for corporate houses were eased by allowing the prepayment of foreign loans over US$100 million. Later, in April 2005, the limit on overseas investment under the automatic route was increased from 100 per cent of the net worth of the Indian entity to 200 per cent and remittance limits have also been substantially relaxed.[9]

More recently, the Reserve Bank of India (RBI) has increased the upper limit on overseas investment by mutual funds. Moreover, the Committee on Fuller Capital Account Convertibility has recommended that the limit for a company's investment in overseas ventures be raised to 250 per cent of net worth in 2006–2007 and then gradually up to 400 per cent of net worth by 2011.

The FDI reporting system in India has also undergone a change over the years. Previously, only figures on 'equity capital' were included in the reported FDI data. However, in May 2000, the Department of Industrial Policy and Promotion (DIPP) constituted a committee charged with bringing the Indian system in line with international best practices (the IMF definition), which recommended a revised definition. According to the revised definition, 'equity capital', 'reinvested earnings' and 'other direct capital' are currently included in reported FDI statistics.

India's regime for FDI

The current Indian FDI regime is incorporated in the Foreign Exchange Management Regulations, 2000.[10] Since 1991, the investment regime in India has been considerably simplified and liberalized, and is now open to foreign investment with the exception of certain specific areas (e.g. railways, print media, retail and agriculture).

At the international level, India has been very active and has negotiated several bilateral agreements on investment. Since 2002, it has signed 16 such agreements, of which 8 have yet to be ratified.[11] Of the agreements signed before 1 January 2002, 10 have entered into force since 1 January 2002.[12] This shows the willingness of the Indian Government(s) to attract FDI into the country (UNCTAD, 2004). However that willingness is essentially unilateral and demonstrates the quest for a progressive and controlled liberalization. Indian bilateral investment treaties (BITs) contain broad provisions without delineating in detail circumstances that would allow India to move away from investor protection to exercise regulatory discretion to pursue public policy objectives. One important safeguard in the Indian BITs that preserves regulatory discretion is that all investments are subject to national laws (UNCTAD, 2006). Nevertheless, Prabhash Ranjan argues in a recent paper that, against the backdrop of the emerging investor–state case law, Indian BITs need to be drafted more precisely to strengthen India's regulatory discretion (Ranjan 2008a).

These gradual reforms have resulted in continued growth in annual FDI inflows. Indeed, annual FDI inflows into India grew from US$3.13 billion in 2002–2003 to US$5.6 billion in 2005–2006.[13] However, India has never matched the inward success story of other Asian neighbours like China for various reasons:

> A May 2002 report on reforming the investment approval and implementation procedures concluded that, despite economic liberalization, FDI had not entered India to the degree expected; and this was due to several constraints, including the complexity of procedural requirements of several laws and regulations, as well as transparency in the approval procedures.[14]

The impact of the investment-related disputes involving India as a respondent and the unilateral reform measures undertaken by it are worth mentioning here. India had to amend its policies to bring them into line with the WTO investment regime after losing a case against the USA[15] and the EU[16] on TRIMs. In 2001, the *India – Measures Affecting the Automotive Sector* case involved a TRIM requiring 'trade balancing'. In May 1999, the US Government lodged a complaint against the Indian Government concerning the motor industry measures it had introduced in November 1997. Under the 1997 law, the Indian Government required all new foreign motor vehicle manufacturing investors to sign a standard memorandum of understanding (MOU) with the Government establishing:

- a minimum US$50 million investment in joint ventures with majority foreign ownership;
- a waiver of import licences if local content exceeds 50 per cent; and
- the obligation to export within 3 years, with possible restrictions on imports for completely knocked-down (CKD) and semi-knocked down (SKD) kits if export requirements are not met.

According to the Panel, as of the date of the establishment of the trade-balancing condition:

> there would necessarily have been a practical threshold to the amount of exports that each manufacturer could expect to make, which in turn would determine the amount of imports that could be made. This amounts to an import restriction. The degree of effective restriction which would result from this condition

may vary from signatory to signatory depending on its own projections, its output, or specific market conditions, but a manufacturer is in no instance free to import, without commercial constraint, as many kits and components as it wishes without regard to its export opportunities and obligations.[17]

Article XI of the General Agreement on Tariff and Trade (GATT) 1994 stipulates the general elimination of quantitative restrictions. Article XI of the GATT 1994 prohibits any measure other than duties, taxes or other charges 'or other measures having equivalent effect'. Therefore, it is not the legal form of the measure but its effect on trade which is important.[18] In the above case, the Panel found that:

> the trade balancing condition contained in Public Notice No. 60 and in the MOUs signed thereunder, by limiting the amount of imports through linking them to an export commitment, acts as a restriction on importation, contrary to the terms of Article XI:1.[19]

After finding that the trade balancing requirements violate GATT Article XI:1, the Panel in *India – Measures Affecting the Automotive Sector* invoked the principle of judicial economy and concluded that it was not necessary to analyse the measures under the TRIMs Agreement.[20]

Among other reform measures with implications for smoothing capital flows, the gradual deregulation of financial services and liberalization of the procedure concerning FDI in the banking, insurance and infrastructure sectors; increased coverage of FDI inflow under the automatic route; and the relaxation of procedures relating to external commercial borrowings (ECBs) need to be mentioned. However, developed countries are still unhappy about the remaining restrictions on foreign equities in India. For instance, the US Government underlined in 2004 that:

> the rules vary from industry to industry and are frequently changed, most often in the direction of further deregulation. The process is not always transparent and the restrictions on combined FDI and portfolio investment are inconsistent across industries... The automatic approval route is not available to foreign investors who wish to set up new ventures in India or who wish to enter into new technical collaborations or trademark agreements in India, if such foreign investors have or have previously had any joint venture, technology transfer or trademark agreement in the same or allied field in India ... Such foreign investors would have to obtain an approval from the Indian government; ... In its application, such foreign investor would have to give reasons why it finds it necessary to set up a new venture or enter into a technical collaboration or trademark agreement. The onus is on the investor to provide adequate justification to the satisfaction of the Indian government that its new proposal would not jeopardize the interests of the existing venture or the stakeholders thereof. The government may, at its discretion, approve or reject the application giving reasons for such rejection.[21]

Despite the attempts by India to simplify the procedure, the trade partners remained sceptical about the changes, as re-stressed by the United States in 2007:

> Foreign purchaser attempts to acquire 100 percent ownership of a locally traded company, permissible in principle, face regulatory hurdles that render 100 percent ownership unobtainable under current practice ... Press Note 18, promulgated in 1998 by the Ministry of Industry, poses major impediments to investment in India by requiring prior approval of the Indian party to a joint venture before the foreign partner can pursue other investment opportunities in India. This provision was widely abused, holding foreign partners hostage, even for failed joint ventures.[22]

India is still trying to clarify and improve its domestic regulation of FDI and a number of steps have been taken in this regard:

> In the latest move to rationalize policy further, in February 2006 equity restrictions were lifted in several activities, including brewing and distillation of alcohol; manufacturing activities in products subject to industrial licensing within 25 km of large cities; and in sensitive sectors such as the manufacture of explosives and hazardous chemicals, and 'greenfield' airports, where investment has been permitted under the automatic route subject to sectoral regulations and, where applicable, an industrial licence under the Industries (Development and Regulation) Act.[23]

The revised investment procedures for various sectors in India and the foreign equity limits following the changes made to the FDI policies during 2006 can be seen in Annex 10.1.

The country's gradually changing perspective on investment can be captured through a comparison of India's Conditional Initial Offer[24] and the Revised Offer[25] to the Council for Trade in Services. While the initial offer tabled in 2004 had imposed an upper limit on foreign investment in a number of sectors, that condition has been removed for several categories (e.g. computer and related services, technical testing and analysis services among others) in the revised offer to be submitted to the WTO in 2005. The revised offer generally requires that the establishment should be through incorporation and subject to approval by the Foreign Investment Promotion Board (FIPB)/Reserve Bank of India (RBI). Also the foreign equity participation limit has been revised upwards for several categories (e.g. telecommunication services). A detailed analysis of India's revised offer may be seen in Annex 10.2. Given the recent revisions incorporated in 2006, it could be expected that the subsequent offers would be more liberal on FDI procedures and equity limits.

Issues in the international regulation of investment

India's concerns under WTO

Under the WTO, while TRIMs refers to provisions related to trade in goods, GATS deals with investment measures in the services category. GATS deals mostly with investment issues of all the existing WTO obligations. The investment implications of GATS are largely derived from the key definition of Article I.2, which identifies modes by which services can be supplied. Several of these imply a significant presence (referred to as a 'commercial presence' in the legal texts) in the country where the service is provided, and provide the basic protective measures of GATS to the investments that are an integral part of this presence. The supply of trade in services through 'commercial presence', which is in essence an investment activity, is covered by Mode 3.

Nevertheless, Mode 4 of GATS also concerns investment issues because it deals with the temporary entry of managerial and other key personnel. Or, in less opaque language, the admission of foreign nationals to another country to provide services there, an aspect which is of considerable interest to India.[26]

GATS uses in large part the selective liberalization approach to provide access to foreign service suppliers, i.e. to foreign investors in the field of services. However, it also contains elements of both the national and most-favoured-nation treatment principles and it relies on the use of both positive lists of commitments and negative lists of exemptions for different purposes (Chaisse and Gugler 2008).

The TRIMS Agreement bans a limited number of performance requirements in so far as they are inconsistent with GATT provisions on national treatment and quantitative restrictions. All members are required to notify and phase out contravening measures, although developing and least-developed countries were granted generous transition periods. The agreement has considerably enhanced the transparency of investment policies throughout the world. Nevertheless, the agreement is limited to measures affecting trade in goods.

Three further agreements – the Agreement on Trade-Related Aspects of Intellectual Property Rights (TRIPS), the Government Procurement Agreement (GPA), and the Agreement on Subsidies and Countervailing Measures (ASCM) – have only indirect effects on investment. Hence we do not consider them in the current analysis (Gugler and Tomsik 2007).

In order to strengthen the provisions of the GATS and TRIMs Agreements, the Singapore Ministerial Declaration (1996) introduced the relationship between trade and investment as a matter for future discussion at WTO forums. Technically, TRIMs could be expanded by adding more examples to the Illustrative List. This adds to the uncertainty about which aspects of a national industrial policy can or will be challenged in the WTO, either through a loose interpretation of TRIMs or additions to the Illustrative List. But negotiations on this point were unsuccessful.

A working group was constituted to look into the relevant concerns; it submitted its report in December 1998 recommending further studies on FDI-related issues.[27] Furthermore, the study put the evaluation of the relationship between the mobility of capital and the mobility of labour among other issues on the future checklist.

In the initial period of the discussion during the late 1990s, India interestingly considered the question of linking capital and labour mobility for some time, as observed from its submission to the Working Group on Trade and Investment:

It is important for the Working Group on the Relationship between Trade and Investment to hold discussions to explore the nature and extent of issues in labour resources faced by different sectors. The Working Group can consider ways to overcome the labour crunch and improve productivity of capital by improving the mobility of labour... Even if the Working Group considers ways for the mobility of capital, there is little or no guarantee that appropriate labour inputs would become available for utilization of that capital. Hence, the Working Group can help align grassroots realities and suggest easy mobility of selected categories of labour apart from the higher categories of personnel for which most Member countries of the WTO have already undertaken commitments under the GATS. For complementing immediate production purposes, the Working Group can suggest ways for selected labour to move from surplus regions to deficit regions.[28]

This outlook continued to be expressed in the subsequent period as reflected by India's submission to the WTO in 1999:

The extensive debate on free mobility of capital may have to be supplemented by an equally extensive study on free mobility of labour. If cheap labour is an important determinant of investment decisions, and results in higher profitability for investors which can be ploughed back into the home country economy, it may be, at the least, equitable to augment host country economies by returns from a mobile labour working in the investors' home country ... mobility of labour should be inextricably linked with the discussions on trade-investment linkage if the WTO is to go beyond looking at delivery systems to look at production systems.[29]

Even after the failure of the Seattle Ministerial Declaration of 1999, as reflected through its submissions to the WTO, India did not abandon the idea of linking labour and capital mobility. For instance, during the Seattle-to-Doha period, it focused on a number of questions involving the optimality of barrier-free FDI inflow into developing countries, foreign investors' obligations, issues pertaining to investment incentives, the costs of adjustment and impact on social gains in developing countries and the comparative flexibility with bilateral investment agreements, among others. The submission maintained that there is a need to check the following to ensure the above-mentioned issues are taken into account:

Whether mobility of labour should also not be meaningfully addressed when movements relating to the other three factors of production namely, goods, services and capital are being taken up in one form or the other.[30]

However, in the subsequent period, India slowly started to move away from this position, probably in the light of the East-Asian Experience. Before the Doha Round, India had expressed dissatisfaction over the progress of technology transfer

Table 10.1 The global FDI inflow scenario as a proportion of world flows (%)

Country	1992–1997[a]	1998	2000	2001	2002	2004	2005
Brazil	2.13	4.18	2.36	2.75	2.44	2.55	1.64
Chile	0.94	0.67	0.35	0.51	0.28	1.01	0.73
China, PR	10.54	6.58	2.94	5.73	7.77	8.53	7.90
India	0.54	0.38	0.17	0.42	0.51	0.77	0.72
Malaysia	1.87	0.39	0.27	0.07	0.47	0.65	0.43
Mexico	3.09	1.78	1.20	3.28	2.17	2.63	1.97
Singapore	2.67	1.11	1.24	1.84	0.84	2.09	2.19
Thailand	0.73	1.08	0.24	0.47	0.16	0.20	0.40

Source: World Investment Report (2006).

Note
a Annual average.

into developing countries, and cited the following argument as an obvious reason for regulating FDI inflow or investment:

> One major reason why FDI is sought by countries, especially developing countries, is that FDI generally brings with it the much needed state-of-the-art technology that developing countries lack. However, available facts and figures do not vindicate this expectation of developing countries ... more striking, particularly for the developing countries, is the fact that while their share of FDI inflows has gone up, their share in global technology transfers has come down. .... the inevitable conclusion that developing countries should preserve their right and ability to influence foreign direct investment flows into their territories with a view to ensuring that it is accompanied by appropriate technology ...[31]

This motive, along with the volatility concern, has been one of the key factors behind India's decision to oppose the initiation of discussion on TI at both the Doha and Cancún Ministerial Declarations of the WTO. As can be seen from Table 10.1, India's share in world FDI inflow has increased since 2001, but this has not been commensurate with its expectations. However, in general all of the countries listed in the table experienced a fluctuating trend in terms of proportional FDI inflow. Perhaps the intention of maintaining a smooth growth curve (Stiglitz 2000), in light of the volatility associated with FDI-led growth elsewhere, was instrumental behind India's decision to adopt a cautious approach.

At the Doha Ministerial Declaration in 2001, India decided against discussion on any of the Singapore issues, until and unless the level of market access promised to the developing countries at the Uruguay Round is realized.[32] It is interesting to note that apart from developed countries, a number of developing countries including Chile, Costa Rica, South Korea, Morocco, the Czech Republic and Hungary were not averse to the idea of discussing TI at the ministerial meeting (Singh 2001). Finally in line with India's argument the ministerial declaration, i.e. the 'Doha Development Agenda', announced that the negotiations on TI would take place after the Fifth Session of the Ministerial Conference (paragraphs 20–22). The ministerial declaration promised that in future:

> Any framework should reflect in a balanced manner the interests of home and host countries, and take due account of the development policies and objectives of host governments as well as their right to regulate in the public interest. The special development, trade and financial needs of developing and least-developed countries should be taken into account as an integral part of any framework, which should enable members to undertake obligations and commitments commensurate with their individual needs and circumstances.[33]

It is argued that developing countries are more likely to enter into BITs if there is competition with their counterparts for attracting investments. In looking at the historical steps it should be underlined that between 1995 and 2001, India entered into BITs with 41 countries, and that this development was reflected in its submissions to the WTO stressing their advantages during the subsequent period:

> Developing countries need to retain the ability to screen and channel FDI in tune with their domestic interests and priorities. Bilateral investment treaties have been favoured the world over for precisely the flexibility they provide to the host country while at the same time extending necessary protection to foreign investors.[34]

This trend towards bilateral negotiations is still relevant. As mentioned above, between 2002 and 2006, India entered into several negotiations and concluded 16 BITs, 10 of which have already entered into force.[35]

Before the Cancun Ministerial Declaration, India focused on a wide range of issues, spanning from the extent of constitutional powers available to the authorities to make rules and regulations related to foreign investment, to the disclosure and accounting procedures, effects of technology transfer, and restrictive business practices among others. It further noted that the developed countries favouring a multilateral agreement on investment should keep the special characteristic of capital in mind and should learn from past experiences at other forums (e.g. the OECD):

> the question of non-discrimination in capital flows becomes more complex. There is no clear buyer–seller linkage, as is the case of goods and services, and no certainty regarding the source of funds. There is also no certainty regarding the manner in which funds will be retained in the host country and at what point in time, in what manner, and to what extent funds will flow out ... A certain degree of discrimination between different kinds of investment is unavoidable ... A case in point is the OECD Code for the Liberalization of Capital Movements in which right of establishment was introduced in 1984. Another instance is that of the APEC non-binding investment principle. A multilateral Agreement on Investment under the auspices of the economically well-off countries of the OECD, which envisaged in the draft agreement binding

national treatment obligations, did not find favour with many of these countries, and had to be abandoned. How then can an agreement of this nature, envisaging national treatment and MFN provision of a binding nature, be considered in a much more heterogeneous group like WTO?[36]

Subsequently, in 2002, the argument of the worsening BOP situation in case of a potential currency crisis was also brought to the forefront for the first time by India, as is evident from its submission to the WTO at that time:

> Any movement of capital that would cause serious damage to the domestic industry, particularly small and medium-sized enterprises and have adverse effects on employment would need to be carefully regulated. Developing countries need to retain the ability to screen and channel foreign investment in accordance with their domestic interests and priorities. Another point to which attention needs to be drawn is the possible damaging effect of capital outflows on balance-of-payments . . . there is also a strong case for performance requirements such as export obligations and foreign exchange neutrality to moderate the adverse effects of capital outflows.[37]

At the Cancún Ministerial Declaration in 2003 India was upset that despite the promise made at Doha to have future discussions on the Singapore issues only after arriving at a consensus, several developed countries attempted to include TI in the negotiating agenda.[38] India in association with other developing countries rejected the 'Derbez Draft'[39] and the negotiation process was stalled for almost a year. It was decided in the July 2004 declaration of the WTO that no negotiation on TI would take place within the WTO during the Doha Round.

After the Doha Ministerial, Declaration buoyed by the upsurge in outward movement (both short-term and long-term) of professionals from the country, India stopped linking the movement of labour with capital and attempted to convince the developed countries of the gains they could make by allowing free movement of labour from their developed counterparts:

> There is a much greater convergence of interests in Mode 4 between the developed and the developing countries in the current negotiations as compared to [the] Uruguay Round. A strong impetus to such movement is the large gap between the projected needs and the local availability of certain categories of personnel in developed countries, further accentuated by their increasingly aging populations. Welfare gains from freer movement of natural persons would, therefore, accrue to both groups of countries as has been documented in recent studies... Some Members have not introduced any improvement to the existing commitments, others have introduced some minor changes aimed at clarifying and in some cases expanding the scope of commitments ... The problem (in administrative procedures) seems to be the inability to clearly separate the temporary movement of service suppliers from permanent immigration and the application of the normal immigration rules and procedures to even temporary movement under GATS ....[40]

It was furthermore pointed out by India in the following period that the WTO negotiation process has largely failed to meet the expectation of the developing countries. It also stressed the importance of de-linking Mode 4 from other categories of services, given their significance for developing countries, in no uncertain terms:

> After analysing the initial offers presented by developed Members, in our assessment, most of these offers do not show any real improvement to the existing commitments in Mode 4. Some Members have not introduced any improvement to the existing commitments; others have only introduced some minor changes aimed at clarifying and only in a few cases expanding the scope of commitments. Basically commitments continue to be limited to categories of personnel related to commercial presence despite the expressed interest of developing Members for commitments in categories de-linked from commercial presence as well ... Developing Members in general have comparative advantages only in a narrow range of services activities. The primary mode for most of these relates to Mode 4. The liberalisation of this mode of supply would, therefore, provide effective market access to service providers from developing Members and contribute significantly to the implementation of Article IV of the GATS.[41]

India also pointed out in the following period[42] the ineffectiveness of the existing GATS rules in improving the transparency of the regulatory procedures on Mode 4 and concluded that there is enormous scope for improving it. From this point on, the link between mobility of capital and labour has no longer been stressed by India. Against this background, this chapter analyses India's potential ability to utilize CAC as a policy tool to extract benefits in other areas (e.g. mobility of labour) from the developed countries and comments on its reluctance to adopt the CAC or a freer investment regime.

India's regionalism

One key reason behind India's lack of interest in TI negotiations may result from its recent regional trade agreement (RTA) strategy. Before the Cancún Ministerial Declaration, India depended heavily on multilateralism and did not join any vibrant trade bloc. But the WTO has been unable to progress with Doha Development Agenda negotiations (Lescher and Miroudot 2006), effectively weakening the multilateral arrangement. The EU is expanding its structure while the Americas are attempting to establish the Free Trade Area of the Americas (FTAA). Free trade agreements (FTAs) are also increasing. Mexico and Chile, although they belong to the Asia-Pacific Economic Cooperation (APEC) forum, have signed FTAs with the EU. As more countries resort to their own FTAs, APEC appears to have been marginalized and its collective identity and credibility are under threat. APEC began its cooperation in the early 1990s when the biggest consumer markets in North America needed more supplies and East Asian countries needed bigger markets for their products. The United States took the lead in pursuing free trade and investment in the

Asia-Pacific region with the aim of opening the dynamic East Asian market. India was instrumental in setting up the South Asian Association for Regional Cooperation (SAARC), whose major achievement in 1995 was the conclusion of the negotiations on trade preferences within the framework of the SAARC Preferential Trading Arrangement (SAPTA). The Agreement on setting up the South Asian Free Trade Area (SAFTA) was signed by member countries of SAARC in January 2004 and a phased tariff liberalization programme under its aegis began on 1 July 2006.

Since 2003 India has entered into a number of RTA negotiations initially with countries located in Asia, Africa and Latin America. More recently, discussions with Canada and the EU on a broad-based trade and investment agreement have started.

India's interest in the FTAs with the Association of Southeast Asian Nations (ASEAN) can be explained by its willingness to be a part of the broader trade and investment network developed between ASEAN members. Similarly the reason for its interest in entering into FTAs with the capital-rich economies of the region (e.g. Japan and Korea) is obvious. The recent discussions indicate that India would prefer to enter into a bilateral investment promotion and protection agreement (BIPA) with China rather than a simple FTA in goods. To boost investment inflow, the Comprehensive Economic Cooperation Agreement (CECA) with Singapore includes an investment cooperation agreement as well as a Double Taxation Avoidance Agreement (DTAA). Investment cooperation is also incorporated in the Bay of Bengal Initiative for Multi-Sectoral Technical and Economic Cooperation (BIM-STEC), which links the SAARC countries (except Pakistan) with regionally closer ASEAN countries (Myanmar and Thailand), and in the Trade and Economic Framework Agreement with Australia. It is possible that the developments under these forums to a certain extent dilute the incentives for supporting TI.

The empirical analysis[43]

The current analysis attempts to estimate the potential destabilizing effects of capital and current account balances (KAB and CAB, respectively) on each other using the Indian time-series data to analyse the potential threat to the country. The quarterly data on CAB and KAB are obtained from various issues of RBI Bulletins and the *Handbook of Statistics on the Indian Economy*. The first quarter of 1979 to the second quarter of 2005 is taken as the sample period for our analysis. The following underlying relationship is tested here following Wong and Carranza (1999):

$$CAB = f(KAB, \varepsilon) \; ceteris \; paribus$$

where ε stands for any other determinants of the CAB.

Stationarity test

The augmented Dicky–Fuller (ADF) test reported in Table 10.2 shows that the CAB and the KAB series are stationary and non-stationary, respectively. Hence for further analysis we consider the first difference of the series (DKAB), which is stationary.

Table 10.2 Augmented Dickey–Fuller test results (CAB and KAB)

Series	ADF test statistics	5% Critical values
CAB	−3.7693	−3.4543
KAB	1.9382	−3.4543
DKAB	−5.9605	−3.4548

Table 10.3 The Granger causality results

Null hypotheses	A. Pre-liberalization 1979: 1–1994: 2 (4 lags)
CAB does not Granger cause DKAB	Rejected (0.02697)
DKAB does not Granger cause CAB	Rejected (0.00000)

Granger causality tests

Using these two stationary series, we next test for Granger causality, which shows the causal relationship between the two series. For selecting the best fit, a bivariate VAR model is estimated with the sample period, and optimum lag length is determined by looking at the Akaike Information Criteria (AIC). The results are reported in Table 10.3.

The results indicate that there is a causal relationship between CAB and DKAB, i.e. both the series are influenced by the other. The finding is in line with the literature.[44]

Current account and capital responses to capital inflows

A further analysis of Impulse Response Functions enables us to trace the effect of a once-and-for-all unanticipated shock (i.e. a crisis) in capital account on the current account balance. The results are reported in Figure 10.1. The CAB and the KAB series take around 12 quarters each to return to equilibrium in the aftermath of a shock and the fluctuations are both negative and positive, generally beginning with an initial huge fall in the series causing the crisis. The indirect effects through the working of other macro variables perhaps also play a role here.

Conclusions

Conflict over the interpretation of TRIMs reflects the fact that it was a compromise agreement in the first place. Difference of opinion between trade officials from developing and developed countries could not be resolved during the

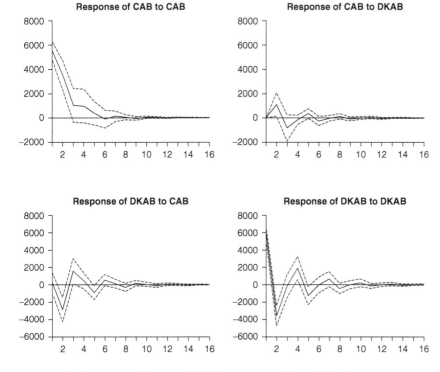

Figure 10.1 Responses of CAB and DKAB to an unanticipated shock

Uruguay Round of GATT talks, and this is reflected in the vague wording of the TRIMs Agreement. Reflecting inconsistencies with the TRIMs Agreement, the domestic motor vehicle industry development policies of India, Indonesia, Brazil and the Philippines have been brought forward or made subject to consultation for dispute settlement. Also, developing countries were not easily able to obtain extensions of the period for removing measures that do not comply with the agreement. In response to these incidents, developing countries remain concerned that adoption of a new agreement would impede their freedom to implement policies with national development priorities.

The chapter initially raised two arguments favouring a freer investment regime in India, namely, facilitating more FDI inflow and the option of ensuring freer mobility of labour in partner countries.

The FDI regime in India has been considerably simplified and liberalized, and is now open to foreign investment with a few exceptions. In 2008 with just a year left for the existing Indian Government to remain in power, it seems to have decided to forge ahead and further liberalize the foreign direct investment policies. The recent fallout of the ruling United Progressive Alliance's leftist partners with the Government over the United States – India nuclear deal and their subsequent withdrawal of support might exacerbate the trend further. The aim is to cash in on the current interest of foreign investors in emerging markets like India rather than let them move on to greener pastures like China and the tiger economies of East Asia. This liberalization results from a unilateral process. By refusing to enter into multilateral negotiations on investment India has been able to gradually facilitate foreign investments. (Some of the most important of the latest decisions in 2008 are the ones to open up the petroleum refining sector and the sensitive area of titanium mining for higher levels of FDI.) This approach can be understood in the light of the Asian crisis. But it is not the only relevant argument.

The scope for a multilateral agreement on investment at the WTO depends on other negotiations. It was not in the interests of India to abandon the control on FDI. At the same time India expected (and still expects) some gains from the ongoing negotiations on GATS and its exports under Mode 4. It seems to us that establishing a link between trade and investment is a strategy to obtain major concessions regarding Mode 4.

Given the recent turn of events, it may be argued that India is ready for full-scale CAC. However, in light of the potential imbalances caused by a hypothetical unanticipated shock in our analysis, India's decision to cautiously open up the domestic economy to FDI inflow and foreign equity holding seems to some extent justifiable. Moreover, it needs to be borne in mind that apart from a potential foreign exchange crisis, the adoption of CAC significantly affects fiscal policy, which is least effective under free mobility of capital. The current high inflation scenario in India needs to be remembered in this context. Perhaps these concerns collectively lead India to adopt a less than enthusiastic approach at the WTO forums on TI.

Given the abundance of 'cheap' skilled professionals in the Indian labour market, the concern over the lower volume of FDI inflow, in comparison with China and other East Asian countries, would be addressed better through targeted policy actions (e.g. creation of better infrastructure). Linking Mode 4 with investment might have its own limitations. In addition, although the dream of achieving free mobility of labour will not come true any time soon, the internal conflicts of interest in the developed countries over the H1-B visa often become visible. A few years ago, Bill Gates, one of the major employers of software professionals from India, demanded of the US policy-makers that the H1-B visa cap on the number of foreign tech workers should be abolished.[45] It is probably not entirely coincidental that a week later the United States granted an additional 20,000 H1-B visas for the fiscal year 2005.[46] The concern for India still exists, as in early 2007 Gates once again had to criticize the US decision to lower the number of the H1-B visas from over 200,000 in the 1990s to the current level of about 65,000. He pleaded for an increase in skilled worker visas emphasizing that the allotment of 65,000 H1-B visas in 2007 had been exhausted some four months before the year began.[47]

The lesson from these events is that as long as the competitiveness of India's 'products', i.e. the expertise of the professional service providers exists, it would be able to achieve its goal slowly, the barriers notwithstanding. Any attempt to facilitate this move by linking it with a freer investment regime is uncertain in terms of outcome, and therefore in the light of these findings, India's current negotiating stance on TI seems reasonably justifiable.

Any project to develop a multilateral agreement on investment should take into account these legitimate expectations. Perhaps the Indian approach shows that an investment agreement could only follow a 'GATS-type' positive list approach in the 'pre-establishment' phase, meaning that countries could pick and choose which commitments they wanted to make. The positive list approach would probably permit a more gradual liberalization, which some countries may prefer. It is common knowledge that in GATS, no member of the WTO is a priori forced to make any commitments in any given sector. Perhaps the stream of negotiations on TI issues over the last decade calls for a similar arrangement here as well. Another suitable solution for India's trade and investment policy would be the negotiation of a 'harbour agreement' within the WTO (Chang-fa Lo, this book, Chapter 11). If there is a substantive multilateral investment agreement, it must tackle the existing BITs and the investment chapters in FTAs. However, it must be recognized that it would be very complicated and not very feasible to change so many BITs, as well as the investment chapters in FTAs, under any multilateral investment agreement. Thus a more workable way is to take a positive decision to recognize in the multilateral arrangement the existing BITs and investment chapters in FTAs. This is the reason not to change the current BITs. Instead, an agreement is suggested that will serve as a harbour for various BITs. Such an option would not discourage India from continuing to negotiate BITs and FTAs. The agreement would serve as a harbour for the countries to have their agreements partly administered by the multilateral organization in two respects:

- The investment committee could collect information about the contents of BITs and make a proper analysis of them.
- Disputes could also be managed by a multilateral mechanism for the parties to a BIT. These will help a *de facto* liberalization of investment policy.

Against the background of an ever more complex system of International investment agreements (IIAs) it has become a major challenge for all countries, in particular developing countries, to negotiate, conclude, and implement the 'right' IIA, to cope with the risks of inconsistencies, and to ensure that the development dimension is properly taken into account. Leaving to India the control of its FDI policies and designing a new harbour agreement could be a realistic way to seek to ensure more coherence in the regulation of international investment.

Notes

1 Alongside trade and competition, trade facilitation and transparency in government procurement.
2 Baldwin, R.E. (undated), 'Failure of the WTO Ministerial Conference at Cancun: Reasons and Remedies' Online. Available HTTP: http://www.ssc.wisc.edu/~rbaldwin/cancun.pdf.

3 The Reserve Bank of India (2004) notes that while *Global Economic Prospects* (World Bank 1999) advised adopting a cautious approach towards capital accounts liberalization, *World Economic Outlook* (IMF 2001) held that capital controls in the short run provide a strong basis for more fundamental reforms in the future. Reserve Bank of India (2004), 'Approach to capital account convertibility'(Chapter VIII) in *Report on Currency and Finance: 2002–03*, Mumbai, pp. 218–52.

4 Concerned namely with the breadth of the definition of 'investment' and 'investors'; the extent of transparency obligations, notably in respect of prior notification requirements; the degree and form of technical assistance required to help developing countries overcome a widely perceived analytical deficit in this area; the operational modalities of development provisions governing the trade and investment interface in a possible WTO investment framework; the desirability of replicating a GATS-like approach to scheduling liberalization commitments, notably in respect of pre-establishment rights; as well as the links between FDI and technology transfer.

5 The proportion of market-determined components in capital account has increased since the early 1980s. Virmani, A. (2001), 'India's BOP crisis and external reforms: Myths and paradoxes', *ICRIER*, December 2001, p. 24.

6 The Committee identified fiscal consolidation, a mandated inflation target and a strengthened financial sector as the three most crucial preconditions to be fulfilled before achieving CAC.

7 EPW Research Foundation (1997), 'Mapping a risky path: Capital account convertibility report', *Economic and Political Weekly* (Mumbai), 7 June, pp. 1300–1303.

8 It should to be mentioned that a significant proportion of the recommendations made by the Tarapore Committee have already been fulfilled. See Annex VIII.1 of RBI (2004) for details.

9 Reserve Bank of India (2006), 'Chronology of major policy announcements: April 2005–July 2006', Annex IV in *RBI Annual Report*, Mumbai, pp. 250–66.

10 Foreign Exchange Management (Transfer or issue of security by a person resident outside India), Regulations, 2000, Notification No. FEMA 20 /2000-RB dated 3 May 2000. Online. Available http: http://www.rbi.org.in/Scripts/BS_FemaNotifications.aspx?Id=174.

11 Trade Policy Review Body – Trade Policy Review – Report by the Secretariat – India, WT/TPR/S/182, 18 April 2007, para. 45.

12 Argentina (12 August 2002), Belarus (23 November 2003), Chinese Taipei (25 February 2005), Croatia (19 January 2002), Cyprus (12 January 2004), Finland (09 April 2003), Hungary (02 January 2006), Indonesia (22 January 2004), Kuwait (28 June 2003), Lao People's Democratic Republic (05 January 2003), Mongolia (29 April 2002), Portugal (19 July 2002), Tajikistan (14 November 2003), Turkmenistan (27 February 2006), Ukraine (12 August 2003), and Yemen (10 February 2004). Ministry of Finance. Online. Available HTTP: http://www.finmin.nic.in/the_ministry/dept_eco_affairs/investment_div/invest_ index.htm#Background_and_salient_features (accessed 8 June 2006).

13 Trade Policy Review Body – Trade Policy Review – Report by the Secretariat – India, WT/TPR/S/182, 18 April 2007, para. 37.

14 Trade Policy Review Body – Trade Policy Review – Report by the Secretariat – India, WT/TPR/S/182, 18 April 2007, para. 39.

15 DS 175 – Measures related to Trade and Investment in the Motor Vehicles Sector – request for consultation on 2 June 1999.

16 DS 146 – on the same issue as in DS 175 – request for consultation on 6 October 1998.

17 India – Measures Affecting the Automotive Sector – Report of the Panel, WT/DS146/R, WT/DS175/R, 21 December 2001, para. 7.277.

18 The Illustrative List annexed to the TRIMs Agreement sets out three categories of 'TRIMs that are inconsistent with the obligation of general elimination of quantitative restrictions provided for in [Article XI :1 of the GATT]' (Annex, para. 2). TRIMs that are inconsistent with Article XI:1 include TRIMs that are: (a) mandatory or enforceable under domestic law or under administrative rulings, or compliance with which is necessary to obtain an advantage, and which restrict 'the importation by an enterprise of products used in or related to its local production, generally or to an amount related to the volume or value of local production that it exports; (b) the importation by an enterprise of products used in or related to its local production by restricting its access to foreign exchange to an amount related to the foreign exchange inflows attributable to the enterprise; or (c) the exportation or sale for export by an enterprise of products'.

19 India – Measures Affecting the Automotive Sector – Report of the Panel, WT/DS146/R, WT/DS175/R, 21 December 2001, para. 7.278.

20 India – Measures Affecting the Automotive Sector – Report of the Panel, WT/DS146/R, WT/DS175/R, 21 December 2001, para. 7.323–7.324.

21 USTR (2004), p. 224.

22 USTR (2007), p. 283.

23 Trade Policy Review Body – Trade Policy Review – Report by the Secretariat – India, WT/TPR/S/182, 18 April 2007, para. 39.

24 India's submission to WTO, 'Conditional Initial Offer', TN/S/O/IND, 12 January 2004.

25 India's submission to WTO, 'Revised Offer', TN/S/O/IND/Rev.1, 24 August 2005.

26 The visiting persons involved may be *employees of a foreign service supplier, or may be providing services as independent individuals*. Mode 4 can be then combined with Mode 3.

27 Document No. WT/WGTI/2, dated 8 December 1998.

28 India's submission to WTO – WT/WGTI/W/39, 4 June 1998.

29 India's submission to WTO – WT/WGTI/W/72, 13 April 1999.

30 India's submission to WTO – WT/WGTI/W/86, 22 June 2000.

31 India's submission to WTO – WT/WGTI/W/105, 26 June 2001.

32 '[N]egotiations (on Singapore Issues) can be launched in these areas only if there is explicit consensus. As far as the proposal to negotiate rules on foreign direct investment is concerned, I would at the outset like to request everybody not to mix up two different issues namely, willingness of a country to receive foreign direct investment and willingness of a country to accept binding multilateral rules on foreign direct investment in the WTO. I would also like to point out that India has a fairly open and liberal foreign investment regime but does not believe that there is need for negotiating rules on this subject in the WTO. In our assessment, the only purpose of such an exercise would be to protect the interests of foreign investors and to take away the policy flexibility available to the developing countries.' Statement by Mr Prabir Sengupta, Commerce Secretary, Government of India, at the informal General Council Meeting of the WTO held in Geneva on 25 June, 2001. *India and the WTO*, June–July 2001, p. 6.

33 WTO 2001. H-1B visa is a non-immigrant visa in force in the United States, which allows foreign nationals to work there for a period of three years. The duration however can be extended to six years.

34 India's submission to WTO – WT/WGTI/W/150, 7 October 2002.

35 Trade Policy Review Body – Trade Policy Review – Report by the Secretariat – India, WT/TPR/S/182, 18 April 2007, para. 45.

36 India's submission to WTO – WT/WGTI/W/152, 19 November 2002.

37 India's submission to WTO – WT/WGTI/W/148, 7 October 2002.

38 '[I]n relation to the Singapore issues, the 13th September draft was even more curious. . . . The Agenda of Doha was very clear on this . . . negotiations on modalities for the

Singapore Issues would commence only after explicit consensus is reached in the next Ministerial Conference. Explicit Consensus means 146 members – now 148 members - have to explicitly say yes, and only then, modalities could begin ... India was the first to speak against the Singapore issues – the 13th September draft, if we had taken the head count of the countries opposing, it should well have been in three figures ... If such a large part of the WTO membership does not agree, how is the 13th September draft produced, which says that modalities will now very shortly commence on investment, and immediately commence on trade facilitation and transparency in Government Procurement ...' Text of keynote address by Mr Arun Jaitley at FICCI–UNCTAD Seminar on 'Reflections on post-Cancun Agenda: The way ahead', 22 October 2003, New Delhi, *India and the WTO Newsletter*, October–November 2003.

39 The Second Revision of the Ministerial Text of the Cancun Ministerial Conference of WTO released on 13 September 2003 is unofficially called the 'Derbez text', named after the Mexican Foreign Affairs Minister Luis Ernesto Derbez.

40 India's submission to WTO – TN/S/W/14, 3 July 2003.

41 India's submission to WTO – TN/S/W/19, 31 March 2004.

42 India's Informal paper submission to WTO – JOB(04)/142, 29 September 2004.

43 The analysis is drawn from Chakraborty, D. and Guha, A. (2007), 'Should India opt for full capital account convertibility? Some exploratory results', Foreign Trade Review, 4: 1–27.

44 The findings of Chakraborty and Guha (2007) indicate that variance in capital inflow into India can be explained by innovations in interest rate differentials and budget deficits as well.

45 'The whole idea behind the H1-B thing is, "Don't let too many smart people come into the country". The thing basically doesn't make sense. That's just wondering ourselves in this global competition', This was part of the statement made by Gates to the policy-makers on Capitol Hill. The Hindustan Times, Friday 29 April 2005.

46 The Hindustan Times, Friday 6 May 2005.

47 'Bill Gates Slams US Visa Policy: More H1-B?', 8 March 2007. Online. Available HTTP: http://onlybombay.blogspot.com/2007/03/bill-gates-slams-us-visa-policy-more-h1.html

Bibliography

Agarwal, M. (1998) 'Capital account convertibility: Fact and frenzy', in M. Agarwal, A. Barua, S.K. Das and M. Pant (eds) *Indian Economy in Transition: Environmental and development issues*, New Delhi: Har-Anand Pvt. Ltd.

Chaisse, J., and Gugler, P. (2008) 'Foreign direct investment issues and WTO Law – Dealing with fragmentation while waiting for a multilateral framework', in J., Chaisse and T. Balmelli, (eds) *Essays on the Future of WTO – Policies and legal issues. Volume 1*, Geneva: Editions Interuniversitaires Suisses, pp. 135–170.

Das, S.P. (2003) 'An Indian perspective on WTO rules on foreign direct investment', in A. Mattoo and R.M. Stern (eds) *India and the WTO*, Washington, DC: The World Bank and Oxford University Press, pp. 141–168.

de Mello, L. (1997) 'Foreign direct investment in developing countries and growth: A selective survey', *Journal of Development Studies*, 34: 1–34.

Egger, P., Larch, M. and Pfaffermayr, M. (2007) 'Bilateral versus multilateral trade and investment liberalisation', The World Economy, 30(6): 567–596.

Government of India, Ministry of Finance, 'Economic Survey', New Delhi (various issues).

Government of India, Reserve Bank of India (2002) 'Report of the Committee on Compilation of Foreign Direct Investment in India', October, Mumbai. Online. Available HTTP: *http://rbidocs.rbi.org.in/rdocs/publicationreport/pdfs/37394.pdf* (accessed 15 September 2008).

Gugler, P. and Chaisse, J. (2008) 'Investment issues and WTO Law – Dealing with fragmentation', in J. Chaisse and T. Balmelli (eds) *Essays on the Future of the WTO*, Geneva: EDIS.

Gugler, P. and Tomsik, V. (2007) 'The North American and European approaches in the international investment agreements', *Transnational Dispute Management Review*, 4(5).

Gupta, D. and Milind, S. (2004) 'Financial developments in India: Should India introduce capital account convertibility?', paper presented at an international conference to mark 10 Years of ASARC (Australia South Asia Research Centre), University House, Australian National University, Canberra, 27-28 April 2004. Online. Available HTTP: http://rspas.anu.edu.au/papers/asarc/2004_07.pdf (accessed 15 September 2008).

Hoekman, B. and Saggi, K. (2001) 'From TRIMS to a WTO agreement on investment?' in B. Hoekman and W. Martin (eds) *Developing Countries and the WTO: A pro-active agenda*, Oxford: Blackwell, pp. 201–214.

IMF (2001) *World Ecinomic Outlook*, Washington, DC: International Monetary Fund.

Jadhav, N. (2003) 'Capital account liberalization: The Indian experience', paper presented at conference organized by IMF and NCAER on A Tale of Two Giants: India's and China's Experience with Reform and Growth, New Delhi, November 2003.

Kurtz, J. (2002) 'A General Investment Agreement in the WTO? – Lessons from Chapter 11 of NAFTA and the OECD Multilateral Agreement on Investment, *Jean Monnet Working Paper No. 6/02*, New York: NYU School of Law.

Lescher, M. and Miroudot, S. (2006) 'Analysis of the economic impact of investment provisions in regional trade agreements', *OECD Trade Policy Working Paper*, No. 36 (TD/TC/WP(2005)40/FINAL).

Ranjan, P. (2008a) 'International investment agreements and regulatory discretion: Case study of India', *Journal of World Trade and Investment*, 9: 209–240.

Ranjan, P. (2008b) 'How long can the G-20 hold itself together? A power analysis', *Centre for Trade and Development, Working Paper*, Number 1, London: Oxfam.

Rao, Manohar, M.J. (1997) 'Macro-economics of capital account convertibility, *Economic and Political Weekly*, 20 December, pp. 3261–3267.

RBI (Reserve Bank of India) (2004) 'Approach to capital account convertibility', in *Report on Currency and Finance: 2002–03*, Mumbai: Reserve Bank of India, pp. 218–252.

Sauvant, K. (2005) 'New Sources of FDI: The BRICS – outward FDI from Brazil, Russia, India and China', *Journal of World Investment and Trade*, 6(5): 639–710.

Sauvé, P. (2006) 'Multilateral rules on investment: Is forward movement possible?' *Journal of International Economic Law*, 9: 325–355.

Singh, Y. (2001) 'India at the Fourth Ministerial Meeting in Doha: Déjà vu – again?' *RGICS Working Paper* No. 32, New Delhi: Rajiv Gandhi Institute of Contemporary Studies.

Stiglitz, J.E. (2000) 'Capital market liberalization, economic growth and instability', *World Development*, 28: 1075–1086.

UNCTAD (2004) *International Investment Agreements: Key Issues Volume II*, New York and Geneva: United Nations.

UNCTAD (2006) *Investment Provisions in Economic Integration Agreements*, New York and Geneva: United Nations.

USTR (United States Trade Representative) (2004) 'National Trade Estimate: Foreign Trade Barriers', *Report on India*, Washington, pp. 213–226.

USTR (United States Trade Representative) (2007) Annual Report of the President of the United States on the Trade Agreements Program, Washington, 108.

Virmani, A. (2001) 'India's BOP crisis and external reforms: Myths and paradoxes', Indian Council for Resreach on International Economic Relations, December.

Wong, Chorng-Huey and Carranza, L. (1999) 'Policy responses to external imbalances in emerging market economies: Further empirical results', *IMF Staff Papers*, 46: 225–237.

World Bank, *Global Economic Prospects*, Washington, DC (various issues).

World Bank (2007) *Developing Countries: Globalisation through overseas investment*. Online. Available HTTP http://www.fdi.net/documents/WorldBank/databases/india/EXIM07.pdf (accessed 15 September 2008).

WTO (1998) *Report of the Working Group on the Relationship between Trade and Investment to the General Council*, Geneva: World Trade Organization (Document No. WT/WGTI/2, 8 December 1998).

WTO (2001a) *Doha Ministerial Declaration*, Geneva: World Trade Organization (Document No. WT/MIN(01)/DEC/1, 20 November 2001).

WTO (2001b) India – Measures Affecting the Automotive Sector – Report of the Panel, WT/DS146/R, WT/DS175/R, 21 December 2001.

WTO (2002a) India – Measures Affecting the Automotive Sector – Communication from India, WT/DS146/14, WT/DS175/14, 13 November 2002.

WTO (2002b) India – Measures Affecting the Automotive Sector – AB-2002-1 – Report of the Appellate Body, WT/DS146/AB/R, WT/DS175/AB/R, 19 March 2002.

WTO (2004) *Text of the July Package*, Geneva: World Trade Organization (Document No. WT/L/579, 2 August 2004).

Annex 10.1 Current FDI scenario in India

Area	New policy
Change of route	FDI has been allowed up to 100% under the automatic route for distillation and brewing of potable alcohol; manufacture of industrial explosives; manufacture of hazardous chemicals; manufacturing activities located within 25 km of the standard urban area limits requiring industrial license under the IDR (Act), 1951; setting up of greenfield airport projects; laying of natural gas/LNG pipelines, market study and formulation and investment financing in the petroleum sector; and cash and carry wholesale trading and export trading.
Increase in equity caps	FDI caps have been increased to 100% and the automatic route extended to coal and lignite mining for captive consumption, setting up infrastructure relating to marketing in the petroleum and natural gas sector, and exploration and mining of diamonds and precious stones.
FDI in new activities	FDI has been allowed up to 100% on the automatic route in power trading, and processing and warehousing of coffee and rubber. FDI has been allowed up to 51% for 'single brand' product retailing, which requires prior Government approval. Specific guidelines have been issued for governing FDI for 'single brand' product retailing.
Removal of restrictive conditions	Mandatory divestment condition for B2B e-commerce has been dispensed with.
Procedural simplification	The transfer of shares by residents to non-residents including acquisition of shares in an existing company has been placed on the automatic route subject to sectoral policy on FDI.

Equity caps on FDI inflow are presently imposed only in select sectors as mentioned in the following:

Up to 20%	FM radio broadcasting.
Up to 26%	Insurance; defence production; petroleum refining in the PSUs[a]; print and electronic media covering news and current affairs.
Up to 49%	Air transport services; asset reconstruction companies; cable network; DTH;[b] hardware for uplinking, HUB, etc.
Up to 51%	Single brand retailing of products.
Up to 74%	Atomic minerals; private sector banking; telecom services; establishment and operation of satellites.

Source: Quoted from the Annual Report, Department of Industrial Policy and Promotion, Government of India (2006–2007 and 2007–2008).

Notes
a PSU, public sector undertakings.
b DTH, direct to home.

Annex 10.2 India's sectoral revised offer for trade in services – select sectors

Sector	Limitations on market access
Architectural services	None except that the establishment would be only through incorporation as partnership firm constituted by architects and subject to the condition that in the case of foreign investors having prior collaboration in that specific service sector in India, FIPB approval would be required.
Integrated engineering services	None except that the establishment would be only through incorporation and subject to the condition that in the case of foreign investors having prior collaboration in that specific service sector in India, FIPB approval would be required.
Urban planning and landscape architectural services	None except that the establishment would be only through incorporation as partnership firm constituted by architects and subject to the condition that in the case of foreign investors having prior collaboration in that specific service sector in India, FIPB approval would be required.
Medical and dental services	Only through incorporation with a foreign equity ceiling of 74% subject to the condition that the latest technology for treatment will be brought in and subject to the condition that in the case of foreign investors having prior collaboration in that specific service sector in India, FIPB approval would be required.
Veterinary services	None except that in the case of foreign investors having prior collaboration in that specific service sector in India, FIPB approval would be required.
Services provided by midwives, nurses, physiotherapists and para-medical personnel	Only through incorporation with a foreign equity ceiling of 74% subject to the condition that the latest technology for treatment will be brought in and subject to the condition that in the case of foreign investors having prior collaboration in that specific service sector in India, FIPB approval would be required.
Computer and related Services	None except that the establishment would be only through incorporation.
R&D services	None except that the establishment would be only through incorporation and subject to the condition that in the case of foreign investors having prior collaboration in that specific service sector in India, FIPB approval would be required.
Real estate services	None for consultancy services, subject to FIPB approval and also subject to the condition that in the case of foreign investors having prior collaboration in that specific service sector in India, FIPB approval would be required.
Rental/leasing services without operators)	None subject to the condition that in the case of foreign investors having prior collaboration in that specific service sector in India, FIPB approval would be required.
Other business services	None subject to the condition that in the case of foreign investors having prior collaboration in that specific service sector in India, FIPB approval would be required.
Telecommunication services	The service will be permitted to be provided only after the operator gets a licence from the designated authority. In the case of foreign investors having prior collaboration in that specific service sector in India, FIPB approval would be

(Continued)

Sector	Limitations on market access
	required. Number of licenses may, however, be limited due to scarce resources such as right of way and spectrum availability, subject to a minimum of two licences in each service area. The private operator should be a company registered in India in which total foreign equity must not exceed 49%.
Motion picture or video distribution services	• Only through representative offices which will be allowed to function as branches of companies incorporated outside India. • Import of titles restricted to 100 per year.
General construction work for civil engineering	None except that the establishment would be only through incorporation and subject to the condition that in the case of foreign investors having prior collaboration in that specific service sector in India, FIPB approval would be required.
Commission agents' services covering sales on a fee or contract	None, subject to approval of RBI/FIPB and conformity with FEMA regulations, as applicable and also subject to the condition that in the case of foreign investors having prior collaboration in that specific service sector in India, FIPB approval would be required.
Wholesale trade services	None, subject to approval of RBI/FIPB and conformity with FEMA regulations, as applicable and also subject to the condition that in the case of foreign investors having prior collaboration in that specific service sector in India, FIPB approval would be required.
Higher education services	• None subject to the condition that service providers would be subject to regulations, as applicable to domestic providers in the country of origin. • None subject to the condition that fees to be charged can be fixed by an appropriate authority and that such fees do not lead to charging capitation fees or to profiteering. Subject further to such regulations, already in place or to be prescribed by the appropriate regulatory authority. In the case of foreign investors having prior collaboration in that specific service sector in India, FIPB approval would be required.
Refuse disposal services sanitation and similar services	None subject to incorporation and the condition that in the case of foreign investors having prior collaboration in that specific service sector in India, FIPB approval would be required.
Life insurance	None, except establishment would be through incorporation with foreign equity not exceeding 26% and subject to the condition that in the case of foreign investors having prior collaboration in that specific service sector in India, FIPB approval would be required.
Non-life insurance	• Unbound except in the case of insurance of freight, where there is no requirement that goods in transit to and from India should be

Sector	Limitations on market access
	insured with Indian insurance companies only. Insurance is taken by the buyer or seller in accordance with the terms of the contract. This position will be maintained. Once under a contract the Indian importer or exporter agrees to assume the responsibility for insurance such as in the case of FOB[a] contracts for imports into India or CIF[b] contracts for exports from India, insurance has to be taken only with an Indian insurance company. • None except establishment would be through incorporation with foreign equity not exceeding 26% and subject to the condition that in the case of foreign investors having prior collaboration in that specific service sector in India, FIPB approval would be required.
Services auxiliary to insurance, such as consultancy, actuarial, risk assessment	None subject to the conditions that foreign companies can be established through incorporation with foreign equity not exceeding 51% and further subject to the condition that in the case of foreign investors having prior collaboration in that specific service sector in India, FIPB approval would be required. In the case of actuarial and advisory services, formal certification by the Actuarial Society of India would be required.
Banking and other financial services	• Operation allowed through branch operations and as a wholly owned subsidiary of a foreign bank licensed and supervised as a bank in its home country and subject to regulations of the RBI. • A limit of twenty licences per year both for new entrants and existing banks. • Banks are allowed to install ATMs at branches and at other places identified by them. Installation of ATM at a place other than in licensed branches is treated as a new place of business and requires a licence. Licences issued for ATMs installed by foreign banks will not be included in the ceiling of twenty licences referred to in item above. • Foreign banks are permitted to invest in private sector banks through the FDI route subject to foreign equity ceiling of 49% and subject to the condition that in the case of foreign investors having prior collaboration in that specific service sector in India, FIPB approval would be required.
Financial leasing	Allowed for foreign financial services companies (including banks) through incorporation and subject to the condition that in the case of foreign investors having prior collaboration in that specific service sector in India, FIPB approval would be required.

Sector	Limitations on market access
Asset management, confined to such as cash or portfolio management, all forms of collective investment management, pension fund management, custodial, depository and trust services	None except establishment would be through incorporation with foreign equity not exceeding 26 % and subject to the condition that in the case of foreign investors having prior collaboration in that specific service sector in India, FIPB approval would be required.
Financial consultancy services, i.e., financial advisory services provided by financial advisers, etc. to customers on financial matters, investment and portfolio research and advice, advice on acquisitions and on corporate restructuring and strategy	• Allowed for foreign financial services companies (including banks) through incorporation. • And subject to the condition that in the case of foreign investors having prior collaboration in that specific service sector in India, FIPB approval would be required.
Hospital services	• None for provision of services on provider to provider basis such that the transaction is between two established medical institutions, covering the areas of second opinion to help in diagnosis of cases or in the field of research. • Only through incorporation with a foreign equity ceiling of 74% and subject to the condition that the latest technology for treatment will be brought in and further subject to the condition that in the case of foreign investors having prior collaboration in that specific service sector in India, FIPB approval would be required. Publicly funded services may be available only to Indian citizens or may be supplied at differential prices to persons other than Indian citizens.
Hotels and other lodging services	Only through incorporation and subject to the condition that in the case of foreign investors having prior collaboration in that specific service sector in India, FIPB approval would be required.
Travel agency tour operator services	Only through incorporation in and subject to the condition that in the case of foreign investors having prior collaboration in that specific service sector in India, FIPB approval would be required.
Tourist guides services	• Only through incorporation and subject to total ceiling of 500 tourist guides conversant in Chinese, Spanish, Portuguese, French and Japanese and in the case of foreign investors having prior collaboration in that specific service sector in India, FIPB approval would be required.

(Continued)

Annex 10.2 (Continued)

Sector	Limitations on market access
	• None for tourist guides conversant in Chinese, Spanish, Portuguese, French and Japanese languages subject to a total ceiling of 500. For others: unbound except as in horizontal commitments.
Entertainment services (including theatre, live bands and circus services Maritime transport services international transport	None and subject to the condition that in the case of foreign investors having prior collaboration in that specific service sector in India, FIPB approval would be required. • At least 40% of cargo carried by liner shipping companies must be reserved for Indian flag ships. • Preference will be given to Indian flag vessels for government cargoes; and government owned/controlled cargo. • Government policy on FOB/FAS^c imports and exports will hold good. • Indian flag vessels will have the first right of refusal for carrying such cargo and only thereafter can foreign flag ships be allowed to be in-chartered/taken on international rental basis.
Maritime cargo handling services	None, except as indicated in horizontal commitment/head note to this schedule and subject to the condition that in the case of foreign investors having prior collaboration in that specific service sector in India, FIPB approval would be required.
Storage and warehousing services in ports	Do
Maritime agency services	Do
Maritime freight forwarding services	Do
International rental/charter of vessels with crew or on bareboat basis (excluding cabotage and offshore transport)	None except obtaining permission from Director General (Shipping) for chartering a foreign flag vessel in the absence of availability of a suitable Indian vessel.
Maintenance and repairs of sea-going vessels	None, except as indicated in horizontal commitment/head note to this schedule and subject to the condition that in the case of foreign investors having prior collaboration in that specific service sector in India, FIPB approval would be required.
Ship broking service	None, except as indicated in the head note and subject to the condition that in the case of foreign investors having prior collaboration in that specific service sector in India, FIPB approval would be required.
Maintenance and repair of aircraft	None and subject to the condition that in the case of foreign investors having prior collaboration in that specific service sector in India, FIPB approval would be required.

Source: Constructed from India's Revised Offer (TN/S/O/IND/Rev.1, 24 August 2005).

Notes
a FOB, free on board.
b CIF, cost, insurance and freight.
c FAS, free alongside ship.

11 Conditions and ways of restoring investment to the WTO negotiation agenda

Establishing a linkage between BITs and the WTO

Chang-fa Lo

Introduction

Despite the large and growing importance of foreign direct investment (FDI) (UNCTAD 2007), the international legal investment framework is highly fragmented. The number of international investment agreements has increased sharply in the last decade (Adlung and Molinuevo 2008) More than 2,500 bilateral investment treaties (BITs) and about 180 trade and economic integration agreements comprising substantive investment provisions have been concluded in this period (Miroudot, this book, Chapter 8). Other agreements are currently under negotiation. The legal content of these agreements has also evolved significantly. International investment disputes have not only become more common, but the cases brought to dispute settlement have also become increasingly complex, creating various interpretations of their provisions and generating huge debates among governments, academics and practitioners. Accordingly, a growing body of jurisprudence and legal literature deals with the interpretation and implementation of the myriad treaties. Furthermore, it seems reasonable to assume that an inscrutable and uncertain investment environment favours large firms with specialized legal departments and preferential access to governments. Thus, the current situation is a potential source of concentrations of power and rent-seeking activities with adverse consequences. International investment is still subject to significant distortions. Specific rules included in a multilateral agreement aiming to remove, or at least to reduce, these policy distortions would increase world GDP. More liberalized markets for investment encourage competition and economic efficiency between and within markets, endorsing a broader dispersion of technology and capital. Probably the most important reason for concluding a multilateral investment agreement is that it offers better protection to investors.

The protection of foreign investment against expropriation is a common clause in BITs and derives from the fact that foreign affiliates are subject to the jurisdiction of the host countries. Prior to the 1980s, decolonization and the socialist movement challenged the property rights of investors. Today, the historical and ideological motivations have changed and the tendency to expropriate has decreased manifestly. Currently 'only' around 60 per cent of FDI stocks invested by OECD countries in non-OECD countries are protected by international investment agreements (IIAs).

It should be noted that these 60 per cent do not include the protection of short-term capital flows.

Investment and trade norms at international level have their respective paths of development. For a long time, international trade rules and international investment norms developed in a parallel way. There were also important points of intersection between investment and trade in terms of their governing rules. However, the meeting points between trade and investment are either occasional or have only limited scope.

This chapter reviews the parallel development and the points of intersection in order to re-examine the possibility of having another intersection between trade and investment at the multilateral level for the purpose of providing a healthy connection between the two. It also aims to explore a suitable approach to coordinate trade and investment rules in a positive manner.

It divides the development of the linkage between trade and investment norms into four stages: the rudimentary stage, the parallel development stage, the re-emerging stage, and the decoupling stage. It then reviews these stages to look at the content and nature of the linkage. This is to help identify the problems and explore the possible approaches for future development. After examining these different stages, the author will try to propose an approach or method to encourage closer ties between these two fields by putting the investment issues back into the WTO negotiation agenda in the future.

History and development of the linkage between trade and investment

There have already been several attempts to negotiate multilateral rules for investment. The most promising attempts were made in the United Nations (UN), in the Organisation for Economic Co-operation and Development (OECD) and in the World Trade Organization (WTO). Nevertheless, all of these attempts failed. A gap left behind following the failure of a multilateral set of rules on investment can explain why bilateral, regional and plurilateral agreements are still a very popular means of formalizing international rules on investment. The degree of integration and cooperation set in these agreements differs depending upon the treaty and the member states. Nevertheless, the key issues to be tackled in all investment agreements are the degree of liberalization of rules governing the entry of foreign investment, the treatment in force in the post-establishment phase, the macroeconomic effects of FDI, the environmental concerns, and the protection of social and human rights. We will explore the successive stages from the Havana Charter to 1995 and the decoupling stage.

Rudimentary stage: the Havana Charter

As early as 1948, the Havana Charter for an International Trade Organization adopted by the United Nations Conference on Trade and Employment (UNCTE 1948) and signed by 53 countries already had investment provisions, although this first comprehensive trade agreement, which included an investment article, was never put into force.

Notwithstanding that the Charter had only one article dealing with investment matters, the coverage of the issues in this article was very broad. Article 12 of the Havana Charter was entitled 'International Investment for Economic Development and Reconstruction'. It recognized international investment as being of great value in the promotion of economic development. It also recognized the right of members to determine the admission of foreign investment, among other matters. Under the article, members were to undertake to provide reasonable opportunities for investments acceptable to them and adequate security for existing and future investments, and to pay due regard to the desirability of avoiding discrimination between foreign investments.

Thus, under the Charter, there were important substantive requirements about the admission of foreign investment and the non-discriminatory treatment. One should note that the requirements were not rigid and the host countries had wide discretion to decide the 'reasonable opportunities for investments' and to give 'due regard to the desirability of avoiding discrimination'. Nonetheless, the recognition of the relations between trade and investment through the inclusion of investment provisions in a trade agreement had shown that countries realized the importance of the linkage between the two.

The parallel development stage

After the failed attempt to put into place the Havana Charter, which included investment matters, there was a long period during which investment rules were developed in parallel with trade rules.

From a trade perspective, the multilateral regime under the General Agreement on Tariffs and Trade (GATT) 1947 had set out the fundamental trade rules, although there were many bilateral or regional trade arrangements in the form of free trade agreements (FTAs) and customs unions (WTOa).

In contrast, international investment rules are mainly composed of numerous BITs concluded between countries. By 1990, 385 BITs had already been signed and the number had increased to about 2,500 at the end of 2005 (UNCTAD 2006). There is a lack of any genuinely multilateral investment treaty covering comprehensively various aspects of investment matters.

International trade rules had little influence on the development of BITs; neither did the BITs have much effect on the development of trade rules, with the exception that in some FTAs, there were investment chapters that also dealt with investment matters. For instance, the Free Trade Agreement between the United States and Canada of 1989 had an investment chapter in Chapter 16, which required each Party to accord to investors of the other Party national treatment regarding the establishment, the acquisition and the operation of business enterprises. It also restricted the use of performance requirements and limited the expropriation (US–Canada FTA 1989). Another example is the North American Free Trade Agreement (NAFTA) concluded in 1992, Chapter 11 (Investment) of which contains comprehensive investment rules on the scope and coverage, national treatment, most-favoured-nation treatment, standard of treatment, minimum standard of treatment, performance requirements, senior management and boards of directors, reservations and exceptions, transfers, expropriation and compensation, special formalities and information requirements, relation to other Chapters, denial of benefits, and environmental measures (NAFTA 1992).

During this parallel development period, there were still two events that had a great deal to do with the linkage between trade and investment. The first was a 1955 resolution on 'International Investment for Economic Development' by the GATT Contracting Parties to urge contracting parties to conclude bilateral agreements to provide protection and security for foreign investment (WTOb). The other is the GATT panel decision on *Canada – Administration of the Foreign Investment Review Act (FIRA)* (BISD 30S/140, 1984; WTOb), in which the panel indicated that the local content requirements were inconsistent with the national treatment obligation of Article III:4 of the GATT, but the export performance requirements were not inconsistent with GATT obligations (WTOc).

The re-emerging stage

In the Uruguay Round negotiations launched in 1986 and completed in 2004, trade-related investment measures were one of the topics of negotiations. During the negotiations, although some developed countries suggested the prohibition of a wide range of trade-related investment measures, there was no agreement about such wide coverage. The result was that the Agreement on Trade Related Investment Measures (TRIMS Agreement) concluded during the negotiations was designed to interpret and clarify the application of GATT provisions in Article III (National Treatment) and Article XI (Elimination of Quantitative Restrictions) to trade-related investment measures (WTOb).

Also the General Agreement on Trade in Services (GATS) was the result of Uruguay Round trade negotiations. Under Article 1, paragraph 2 of the GATS, there are four modes of trade in services, including the supply of a service:

1   from the territory of one Member into the territory of any other Member;
2   in the territory of one Member to the service consumer of any other Member;
3   by a service supplier of one Member, through commercial presence in the territory of any other Member;
4   by a service supplier of one Member, through presence of natural persons of a Member in the territory of any other Member.

Mode 3 is about foreign companies setting up subsidiaries or branches to provide services in another country (commercial presence), which, in essence, refers to investment activities. Thus the GATS can also be seen as a multilateral investment agreement.

Three further agreements arguably have indirect effects on investment (Gugler and Chaisse, 2008): the Agreement on Trade-Related Aspects of Intellectual Property

Rights (TRIPs), the Agreement on Subsidies and Countervailing Measures (ASCM), and the Government Procurement Agreement.

Thus after the Uruguay Round, the linkage between trade and investment was widely recognized, although countries still had very different views about how to tackle the issue. The TRIMS Agreement and the GATS were great achievements in bringing investment issues under the multilateral trading system. The TRIMS Agreement was only able to clarify the application of current trade rules to investment matters. Although it helped to tackle the difficult TRIMS issues, the extent of the breakthrough in terms of establishing additional investment rules was limited. In comparison with TRIMS, the GATS really was an important development in terms of incorporating a wide range of investment matters into the multilateral trading system.

The decoupling stage

After the establishment of the WTO in 1995, the issue of trade and investment continued to be an important one under the WTO negotiations. In the 1996 Singapore Ministerial Declaration, it was decided to establish a Working Group to examine the relationship between trade and investment (paragraph 20) (WTOd).

Later, in the 2001 Doha Ministerial Declaration (WTOe), the issue of the relationship between trade and investment was again tackled (paragraphs 20–22). Under the declaration, members recognized the case for a multilateral framework to secure transparent, stable and predictable conditions for long-term cross-border investment, particularly FDI. They agreed that negotiations should take place after the Fifth Session of the Ministerial Conference (2003 Cancún Ministerial Conference) on the basis of a decision to be taken, by explicit consensus, at that session on modalities of negotiations. However, since there was no consensus, in the 'July Package' (WTOf), concluded on 1 August 2004, the topic of trade and investment was dropped from the Doha Agenda (WTOg), notwithstanding the fact that the range of investment issues which should be tackled within a multilateral agreement remains a controversial matter.

Thus the current situation is that trade and investment issues are decoupled from the present WTO negotiation round and there will be no discussion or negotiation on the linkage between trade and investment during the Doha negotiations.

The conflict of interests between the two groups of countries has played a key role in leading to the current scenario. In general, the developed countries believe that the inclusion of trade and investment under the negotiating agenda of the WTO would be a major step towards ensuring the WTO objectives of freer trade and a liberal investment regime, leading to increased FDI for members with freer investment regimes. To this end, Japan and the EU pushed forcefully for the commencement of negotiations on investment while the United States was not strongly supportive of this initiative. The 'flying geese model' experienced by the Asian tigers has always been a case in point. However, as demonstrated by Chaisse, Chakraborty and Guha in Chapter 10 in this book, a number of developing countries remained averse to that idea, mostly owing to the potential risk of capital flight and the development consequences observed following the Southeast Asian currency crisis, which led even the International Monetary Fund (IMF) and the World Bank to acknowledge the importance of maintaining a strict investment regime in developing countries.

Reasons for the failure

There are multiple reasons for the end of investment negotiations under the Doha Development Agenda (Sauvé 2006). The views or concerns expressed by WTO members during the Working Group meetings held in 2002 and 2003 (WTOh) and those expressed by a non-governmental/organization (NGO) are summarized below.

Possible lack of expertise on investment

The definition of 'investment' represents the first important hurdle in the negotiation of an investment agreement. Should the liberalization and protection clauses within the agreement apply only to specific forms of investment (e.g. only FDI), or should the agreement cover all forms of capital movement? According to general economic theory, all forms of capital movement should be liberalized. The free movement of capital allows the limited resources to be invested where the returns are highest and, therefore, increases allocative efficiency.

Throughout the meetings of the Working Group, some representatives from developing countries expressed their concerns about the complex nature of the relationship between trade and investment, which had gone beyond the domain and expertise of trade negotiators. They considered that their delegations' knowledge of the subject was inadequate to enable them to engage in such comprehensive negotiations. This concern contributed greatly to the eventual failure to incorporate investment issues into the negotiation agenda.

The need to maintain power and discretion to distinguish different kinds of investment

During the discussions of the Working Group, some countries emphasized the importance of investment that would help the expansion of trade. They considered that export-oriented FDI had evidently helped many countries, including East and Southeast Asian countries, to rapidly build their manufacturing and export capabilities. Therefore, it was important to examine the conditions and factors that promoted export platforms or export-oriented FDI.

However, some developing countries certainly had deep concerns about many other kinds of investment not being helpful to their sound economic development. This view was also supported by an NGO, Oxfam International, which urged developing countries to refuse to enter into investment negotiations under the WTO, stating:

> As shown by the experience of many developing countries, foreign direct investment (FDI) has the potential to make an important contribution to

sustainable development. But whether it is beneficial or detrimental to development very much depends on the type and quality of investment and the regulatory environment in the host country. The key questions for sustainable development are what kind of investment and how poor people will benefit.

(Oxfam International)

WTO not being a proper forum

We must underline that the Multilateral Agreement on Investment (MAI) negotiations have shown that NGOs can no longer be excluded from important international negotiations. The MAI negotiations were the beginning of a new era for NGOs, which were transformed from being a set of scattered groups to a 'unified' negotiation partner linked by the Internet. Their growing influence was highlighted by the fact that they were finally invited to participate in the negotiations. Views on the results of this participation diverge. While some note that the NGOs with their different approach have introduced important new aspects, views on the role of the NGOs are mostly critical. Therefore, to exclude NGOs from future negotiations would not only discredit the agreement in the eyes of the wider public, but would constitute a missed opportunity to democratize global governance.

It is claimed by Oxfam International that the WTO is not an appropriate forum for multilateral investment negotiations. Such negotiations would result in a multilateral legal framework whose impact on the sustainable development of developing countries could be very damaging (Oxfam International). This might have contributed to the failure of prolonged discussion or negotiation on investment matters at a multilateral level.

A multilateral investment agreement is not helpful in generating good quality investment

Some developing countries stressed that the positive effects of FDI might not always come about automatically, and that they needed to retain the ability to screen and channel FDI in accordance with their domestic interests and priorities in order to maximize the positive effects and to minimize the negative effects.

Oxfam International also opposed the idea proposed by some countries that an investment agreement under the WTO would be helpful to developing countries for the purpose of attracting more investment. It suggested that the causal link between liberalized investment rules and increased FDI is a tenuous one and that there is no evidence to prove that an international agreement would be capable of generating more investment. It argued that an investment agreement under the WTO would not be capable of generating good quality investment because 'rules are just one of the many factors determining investment decisions' (Oxfam International).

The fundamental differences on the substantive issues

The range of investment issues which should be tackled within a multilateral agreement remains a controversial matter. The MAI negotiations have shown that the most contentious issues are the scope of the future agreement, and whether it should include provisions concerning performance requirements, investment incentives and taxation. In the case of the MAI, the delegations argued in favour of an open, asset-based definition of investment, which covers all forms of investment, including contractual assets and the products of the investments. Accordingly, an investor was defined as any natural or legal person of a contracting party, including permanent residents. Combined with the indirect ownership of the definition of investment, an investor could have been almost anyone, and it is difficult to imagine a broader definition. However, this broad definition of the term 'investment', which would have allowed the scope of the MAI to be adapted to the changing nature of international investment, faced significant resistance from a number of delegations. A second important hurdle is whether to include performance requirements and investment incentives.

In an optimal world with no market distortion, the best policy would be no policy at all. Unfortunately, markets are not perfect and their regulation may be desirable from an economic perspective. It was found that the net welfare effects of export-performance requirements may be positive. A multilateral agreement imposing restrictions on the use of such measures could thus improve the welfare of capital-exporting countries by increasing the returns of multinational enterprises (MNEs), but would simultaneously, at least in the short run, reduce the welfare of the host countries. In general, however, performance requirements tend to render the global economic efficiency suboptimal. On the national level, one finds that most performance requirements in developing countries have actually retarded their development by increasing investment costs and because investors may be deterred from investing in the country in question. Furthermore, performance requirements imply a shift of the benefits from one group to another, which leads to rent-seeking and favours corruption. For example, local content requirements may well benefit input suppliers, but at the expense of final goods producers who are confronted with higher prices and less choice.

During the WTO discussions, there were fundamental differences of opinion on a number of significant substantive issues, mainly between developed and developing countries. On the scope of investment, a number of countries, especially developing ones, preferred a limited definition of investment so as to focus only on FDI. They were concerned about the destabilizing macroeconomic and balance-of-payments effects arising from some types of portfolio investment and they considered FDI to be more predictable and controllable. Developing countries stressed the importance of maintaining flexibility in incorporating the interests of all members.

Developing countries also had concerns that applying some core WTO principles, especially the principle of national treatment, to investment would result in the reduction of the capacity of developing countries to regulate foreign investment. On development and non-discrimination, some members considered the issue of non-discrimination to be a very complex one, and they did not intend to make hasty decisions on this subject. Although FDI could be an important component of their development strategy and policy, some members were concerned about subscribing to an over-idealized view of FDI, as being a kind of panacea for development.

Some developing countries considered that pre-establishment treatment should be left to the discretion of members so that they could make their decisions in accordance with their individual needs and that if they felt comfortable with undertaking further bound liberalization, they should be able to adopt the selective liberalization approach. In essence, developing countries considered that they should be given greater freedom and flexibility to make their investment policies. Lawmakers face a trade-off between protecting the interests of investors and the interests of the host states. A last example is the definition of expropriation, for which investors prefer a broad definition which limits the sovereignty of the host state. In this discussion, it is important to keep the importance of FDI for national competitiveness in mind. FDI is an important source of technology, know-how and labour skills, and what is good for investors is therefore good for the national economy. Nevertheless, the government has important tasks and is also a driver of competitiveness. Striking a balance between these two aspects is a daunting undertaking, but the potential gains make it a very rewarding one.

Possibility of resuming investment negotiation in the future: a new approach needed

The positive elements of the failed discussions

Although countries decided not to continue the negotiations or discussions on investment matters, very positive elements can still be identified from the views expressed during the discussions of the Working Group and from the NGO's proposal to stop negotiating investment issues.

First, there is a view widely shared by developed and developing countries about the importance of technical assistance and capacity building to the success of the negotiations and to the progress in the discussion of investment matters at the multilateral level. Technical assistance and capacity building would help developing countries to evaluate the impact of a multilateral framework on investment within the WTO and to make an informed decision on this matter.

Second, it is also a shared view that the expansion of investment flows in recent years, in the form of FDI, has been of great value through bringing into the host country valuable resources for development, such as capital, technology, managerial and marketing skills and sometimes market access in the case of export-oriented FDI. Some developing countries held a strong view that not all kinds of foreign investment are beneficial to their economies and thus they should be able to maintain power and discretion to take measures to screen the investment and safeguard their economies.

Third, although countries had very different views about the substantive issues, they had less diverse views on procedural ones. For instance, developed and developing countries expressed similar views about the transparency principle being an important element under an investment agreement.

Lessons learned from the Working Group discussions

There are some lessons that we can learn from the discussions of investment matters under the WTO. The basic problem is that it is still premature to enter into substantive negotiations on investment matters. This is partly because many countries are not yet ready to engage in negotiations so as to make informed decisions. If there are a large number of countries that are uncertain or worried about their economies being jeopardized by foreign investment, the WTO can do little to persuade them to establish a comprehensive multilateral investment agreement. In this regard, the continuation of technical assistance and capacity building carried out by the WTO Secretariat would be of immense importance. If there is any multilateral investment agreement in the future, an element establishing the mechanism for continuous technical assistance and capacity building would be a very important part of such an agreement.

Second, some countries were too ambitious about incorporating too broadly the investment matters under the expected investment agreement. During the discussions of the Working Group, developing countries expressed their preference to focus only on FDI, while some developed countries proposed an asset-based definition of investment, which would include portfolio investment. For many countries, the admission of portfolio investment has to do with their financial stability. They do not consider that any safeguard mechanism would be enough to secure their financial stability if they would have to admit foreign portfolio investment. It must be realized that the concern will not be easily allayed and confidence will not be readily established. Any possible requirement on the commitment for the liberalization of portfolio investment will always give rise to deep concern for many developing countries.

In addition to the hesitation about discussing the liberalization of portfolio investment, developing countries also stressed so much on the need of discretion to screen good quality investments from undesirable ones. Apparently, they are not prepared to assume a multilateral obligation, which could put them in a difficult situation in which they would have to admit investments and would have no discretion to refuse undesirable ones. The potential inclusion of a multilateral framework for investment at the WTO is aimed to coordinate the global regulation of trade and investment. In addition to the difficulties arising during these negotiations, another major concern is that certain countries such as India are not interested in going for a full-scale capital account convertibility (Chaisse, Chakraborty and Guha, this volume, Chapter 10).

Certainly, developing countries would very much like to maintain the power to decide the pace of liberalization of their own investment policy, taking into account the nature and the quality of investment.

Taking into account the numerous BITs

The attempted multilateral framework for FDI in the Havana Charter failed to enter into force in 1948, with the result that the legal situation since then has become a patchwork of bilateral, regional, plurilateral and multilateral treaties. The early

1960s witnessed the early process of negotiating bilateral investment promotion and protection agreements between countries. The proliferation of these agreements set up two competing themes within international investment rules. Notably, although an increasing number of developing countries were willing to subscribe to basic standards for investment protection and treatment, they were unwilling to do so at the multilateral level. Bilateral investment treaties have since become the core of the current framework for FDI. More than 2,500 bilateral agreements have been concluded since the early 1960s, most of them in the 1990s.

Bilateral investment treaties prevail as the main form of international investment agreement. Most BITs, however, do not grant investors a 'right to establish' investment. Usually the wording of BITs is such that the parties should encourage investment or perhaps that they should encourage liberalization of their investment regimes. In this kind of agreement, admission clauses are best-effort clauses only encouraging admission. Furthermore, these clauses are often qualified by provisions such as 'subject to each party's laws' and so on. BITs of this kind usually do not grant investors the same conditions that their national companies have for their investments – they do not grant national treatment as far as entry is concerned. The parties to these BITs can usually maintain most of the existing limitations or controls on admission; for example, exclusions of some sectors from FDI, screening procedures, maximum equity conditions, and so on. Put simply, most BITs use what UNCTAD classifies as 'an investment control approach'. This approach does not offer any automatic right of admission or establishment to foreign investment. Therefore governments have a wide range of discretion in this area.

As mentioned earlier, there are thousands of BITs in the world. BITs are concluded not only between developed and developing countries, but also between developing countries. Any possible investment arrangement under the WTO would have to take into account the existence of the large number of BITs and the ways of coping with the relations between the multilateral arrangement and these BITs.

Although many BITs adopt an asset-based definition of investment and thus include portfolio investment as within the scope of the treaties, developing countries tend to be less concerned about this, mainly because it is the result of bilateral negotiations and they would be more able to decide as to the possible negative effect of such bilateral agreements.

However, the huge number of BITs can itself be a barrier to the proper decision on and conduct of international investment activities from the investors' perspective. Thus, a certain degree of coordination would be desirable for the purpose of enhancing the investment environment.

A harbouring agreement to coordinate BITs in the future?

The approach suggested here is that in the future there could be a 'harbouring agreement', the nature and function of which would be as follows:

First, if there is a substantive multilateral investment agreement, it must tackle the existing BITs and the investment chapters in FTAs. However, it must be recognized that it would be very complicated and not very feasible to change so many BITs as well as the investment chapters in FTAs by any multilateral investment agreement. It is important to take into account the reality of international investment law. For instance, since 2003, India has entered into a number of RTA negotiations, initially with countries located in Asia, Africa and Latin America (Chaisse, Chakraborty and Guha, this volume, Chapter 10). Preliminary discussions with Canada and the EU on the preferential trade and investment agreement have just started. India's interest in the FTAs with ASEAN can be explained by its willingness to be a part of the broader trade and investment network developed between the ASEAN members. Similarly, the interest in entering into the FTAs with the capital-rich economies of the region (e.g. Japan and South Korea) is obvious. The recent discussions indicate that India would prefer to enter into a bilateral investment promotion and protection agreement with China rather than a simple FTA in goods. As a consequence BITs and FTAs will be here for a long period. One distinguishing feature of recent RTAs is their wide-ranging coverage and complexity. Tariff reductions are accompanied by provisions on non-tariff barriers, customs procedures, sanitary and phytosanitary measures and intellectual property protection. Most of the new agreements cover trade in services and a number of regulatory issues that go beyond multilaterally agreed disciplines – such as government procurement, competition policy and the environment. Among these provisions that characterize the 'new regionalism', investment is particularly important and has changed the nature of RTAs as they jointly liberalize trade and investment in a way that is not to be found in multilateral agreements or in bilateral investment treaties.

Another convincing example is given in this book by Xiao Jun. His chapter (Chapter 6) underlines that national treatment and investor–state dispute settlement provisions differentiate the Chinese BITs conducted since 2000 from their predecessors. This difference is so important that these new agreements could be regarded as a new generation of Chinese BITs in the twenty-first century.

Thus a more workable way is to take positive steps to recognize in the multilateral arrangement the existing BITs and investment chapters in FTAs. This is the reason not to change the current BITs. Instead, the suggestion is to have an agreement serving as a harbour for various BITs.

On one hand, WTO members could be required to notify an investment committee established under such an agreement of their BITs and investment chapters under the FTAs. The notification should include information that would enable other countries and investors to make a proper evaluation of the investment environment in the relevant host countries. On the other hand, WTO members would be able to use the tools and facilities provided in the agreement and administered by the investment committee. These tools and facilities could include the provision of investment information to members in its raw and processed forms and provision of institutionalized technical assistance and capacity building to developing countries.

Under such an arrangement, developing countries would not have any urgent need to evaluate the extent of values to be gained by the host counties or the possible negative effect of admitting a foreign investment, because there would be no substantive requirement about admitting foreign investment under such an agreement, whether it is an FDI or a portfolio investment. Unless a country has committed to liberalizing its investment measures through a BIT under which the country is obligated to keep its bilateral commitment, it would have the discretion to decide what kind of investment it would admit.

Second, there would be a procedural requirement for transparency, which is an important element under the investment agreement. Countries would be required to have their investment rules published and notified to the investment committee so that other countries and investors would be able to make appropriate investment decisions. The basic idea is simple: in order to make sure that a multilateral agreement is approved, every participating party has to be convinced that their overall net payoff would be positive during the period for which the agreement remains in force.

Third, emphasis should be placed on the discretion of host countries in deciding whether or not to admit foreign investment. This would be an important step in allaying the concerns of developing countries about the restriction of their power to screen foreign investment. If emphasis is not on the discretion, but on the commitment and obligation of the host countries, reaching a consensus would be difficult because it would require both a well-balanced agreement and an efficient environment for negotiations. The benefits of a multilateral investment agreement should be distributed fairly between the different interest groups. In particular, a fair distribution of the benefits between developed and developing countries, producers and consumers (consumer groups and NGOs), and between employers and employees (unions) must be reached. While developing countries and NGOs were officially excluded from the WTO negotiations, communication to and from the Trade Union Advisory Committee (TUAC) located at the OECD headquarters in Paris did not allow for the necessary representation of the employees. Thus, the resulting MAI text showed a 'conception of the agreement as a pure investor and investment protection instrument' biased in favour of the MNEs. While the MAI included important rights for foreign investors, obligations concerning their behaviour would have been introduced only in the form of soft law. The purpose of a harbouring agreement is not to liberalize investment. The liberalization should be voluntary. However, if there were to be transparency and notification requirements, it would greatly help with making the investment decisions and with the expansion of international investment.

Fourth, there should be a voluntary state–state dispute settlement mechanism available for the members to resort to. The investor–state dispute settlement is very controversial. Thus it should be dealt with by the BITs to decide whether once attempts to settle disputes between a foreign investor and the host state by negotiations or consultations had failed, the investor would be free to press charges against the host state. Under the MSI and many BITs, the investor could plead to any competent court under the World Bank Group's International Centre for Settlement of Investment Disputes (ICSID), the ICSID Additional Facility, the Arbitration Rules of the United Nations Commission on International Trade Law (UNCITRAL), or the International Chamber of Commerce (ICC) Rules of Arbitration. They allow investors to choose a tribunal other than one of those mentioned above, under the condition that the parties had agreed on this before the dispute arose. The corresponding provisions within NAFTA have been criticized for lack of transparency as there is no provision for mandatory public access to the litigation documents. While ICSID cases are notified in a public registry, UNCITRAL lacks even this basic requirement. Thus, transparency depends on the access to the legal documents that member countries offer. Especially in the case of Mexico, there is still no guarantee of obtaining such access. Even under the ICSID arbitration system, the decisions of the tribunals have not been made public. The system of international investment arbitration continues to expand its reach. European and American business lobbies, often dominated by service sector companies such as telecommunications, retailers and banks that invest abroad, are keen on new investment treaties and on adding investment rules to broader trade deals. Furthermore, it was argued that the investment dispute settlement provisions favour only the 'big multinationals'. Effectively, the average legal costs are estimated at up to US$0.5 to US$1.5 million for lawyers' fees and US$400,000 or more for the tribunal costs. We know that Argentina has been hit by dozens of arbitration cases since its financial crisis in 2001–2002, when Buenos Aires forcibly changed contracts from dollars into pesos and froze utility prices to cushion the impact on Argentinean consumers. Foreign companies including Mobil, France Telecom and Vivendi have won a string of rulings against Argentina at ICSID, awarding them hundreds of millions of dollars in compensation for lost earnings. Meanwhile, Exxon Mobil is claiming billions of dollars in compensation from Venezuela at ICSID after walking away from an oil project following government attempts to take control. With companies from emerging markets such as India and China investing abroad, the rich countries could increasingly find themselves the targets of litigation. Under the harbouring agreement, the dispute could be about the violation of transparency or notification requirements under the multilateral agreement. It could also concern a breach of a BIT. In the latter situation, only the parties to the BIT should be able to make a complaint, although they would also be allowed to have their dispute settled at the bilateral level under their BIT. The multilateral settlement of bilateral disputes would help to unify the legal views about particular issues commonly occurring under different BITs.

One might reasonably ask about the kind of benefit that this harbouring agreement could generate if there is no substantive commitment. The answer should be straightforward. The agreement serves as a harbour for the countries to have their agreements partly administered by the multilateral organization in two respects: the investment committee can collect information about the contents of BITs and make a proper analysis of them, and the disputes can also be managed by a multilateral mechanism for the parties to a BIT. These will help a *de facto* liberalization of investment policy.

Concluding remarks

This chapter considers that the way of putting the investment issues back into the negotiation agenda does not rely on the possible wide range of substantive commitments. Instead, it depends on allaying concerns and building the confidence of developing countries.

For this purpose, there are a number of elements to be included in the approach: to recognize the existing BITs and their functions; to recognize the power and discretion of host countries to decide on the admission of foreign investment; to impose procedural requirements on notification and transparency; to introduce institutionalized technical assistance and capacity building; and to make available the multilateral dispute settlement mechanism for BIT disputes to unify the legal views on certain commonly occurring issues.

This approach is more modest than the suggestion of GATS-type agreements on investment (Gugler and Chaisse 2008). Applying this hypothesis, an investment agreement could follow a 'GATS-type' positive list approach in the 'pre-establishment' phase, meaning that countries could 'pick and choose' which commitments they wanted to make. The advantage of the positive list approach over the top-down or negative list approach is its greater flexibility. In the case of the NAFTA-type negative list approach, some countries might feel deprived of an important policy tool. The point is that in some sectors and industries it is very difficult to anticipate their future development and character at the moment of writing down the negative list. Here the combined national treatment and most-favoured-nation approach offers less flexibility to host countries in regulating FDI flows into such sectors. In this sense, the GATS provides a realistic approach for dealing with the admission of foreign investment. The positive list approach would probably permit a more gradual liberalization, which some countries may be more comfortable with. In GATS, no member of the WTO is a priori forced to make any commitments in any given sector. Such an approach raised the question of the future of the BITs and FTAs already in existence all over the world and constantly expanding.

Although now might not be the proper time to restore the investment issues to the current WTO negotiation agenda owing to the decision of the members not to include investment in this agenda, we still need to review the failure of the investment negotiations so as to prepare for future possible negotiations of investment matters under the WTO. The author hopes that another point of intersection between trade and investment at the multilateral level for the purpose of providing a healthy connection between these two fields will become a reality with such a mild and practical approach.

References

Adlung, R. and Molinuevo, M. (2008) 'Bilateralism in Services Trade: Is there fire behind the (Bit-)smoke?', *Journal of International Economic Law* 11: 365–409.

Gugler, P. and Chaisse, J. (2008) 'Investment issues and WTO Law – dealing with fragmentation', in J. Chaisse, and T. Balmelli (eds), *Essays on the Future of the WTO*, Geneva: EDIS.

Oxfam International. The Emperor's new clothes: Why rich countries want a WTO investment agreement, *Oxfam Briefing Paper 46*. Online. Available HTTP: http://www.citizen.org/documents/wtoinvestoxfam.pdf (accessed 22 April 2008).

NAFTA (1992) Online. Available HTTP: http://www.nafta-sec-alena.org/DefaultSite/index_e.aspx?DetailID=267 (accessed 22 April 2008).

Sauvé, P. (2006) 'Multilateral rules on investment: is forward movement possible?', *Journal of International Economic Law*, 9(2): 325–55.

UNCTAD (2006) The entry into force of bilateral investment treaties (BITs). *IIA Monitor* No. 3. Online. Available HTTP: http://www.unctad.org/en/docs/webiteiia20069_en.pdf (accessed 22 April 2008).

UNCTAD (2007) *World Investment Report 2007, Transnational Cooperation, Extractive Industries and Development*, New York and Geneva: United Nations. Online. Available HTTP: http://www.conapri.org/download/wir2007_en.pdf (accessed 15 August 2008).

UNCTE (1948) *Havana Charter for International Trade Organization*. Online. Available HTTP: http://www.wto.org/english/docs_e/legal_e/prewto_legal_e.htm (accessed 22 April 2008).

US–Canada FTA (1989) Online. Available HTTP: http://wehner.tamu.edu/mgmt.www/NAFTA/fta/index.htm (accessed 22 April 2008).

WTOa. *Regional Trade Agreements: Facts and Figures*. Online. Available HTTP: http://www.wto.org/english/tratop_e/region_e/regfac_e.htm (accessed 22 April 2008).

WTOb. *Trade and Investment: Technical Information*. Online. Available HTTP: http://www.wto.org/english/tratop_e/invest_e/invest_info_e.htm (accessed 22 April 2008).

WTOc. *Dispute Settlement: GATT Reports List, Adopted Panel Reports within the Framework of GATT 1947*. Online. Available HTTP: http://www.wto.org/english/tratop_e/dispu_e/gt47ds_e.htm (accessed 22 April 2008).

WTOd. *Singapore Ministerial Declaration*. Online. Available HTTP: http://www.wto.org/english/thewto_e/minist_e/min96_e/wtodec_e.htm (accessed 22 April 2008).

WTOe. *Doha Ministerial Declaration*. Online. Available HTTP: http://www.wto.org/english/thewto_e/minist_e/min01_e/mindecl_e.htm#relationship (accessed 22 April 2008).

WTOf. *Text of the 'July Package' – the General Council's Post-Cancún Decision*. Online. Available HTTP: http://www.wto.org/english/tratop_e/dda_e/draft_text_gc_dg_31july04_e.htm (accessed 22 April 2008).

WTOg. *Understanding the WTO: Cross-Cutting and New Issues: Investment, Competition, Procurement, Simpler Procedures*. Online. Available HTTP: http://www.wto.org/english/thewto_e/whatis_e/tif_e/bey3_e.htm (accessed 22 April 2008).

WTOh. *Reports on the Working Group Meetings Held in 2002 and 2003*. Online. Available HTTP: http://www.wto.org/english/tratop_e/invest_e/invest_e.htm (accessed 22 April 2008).

Index

For Product Safety Concerns and Information please contact our EU
representative GPSR@taylorandfrancis.com
Taylor & Francis Verlag GmbH, Kaufingerstraße 24, 80331 München, Germany

www.ingramcontent.com/pod-product-compliance
Ingram Content Group UK Ltd.
Pitfield, Milton Keynes, MK11 3LW, UK
UKHW021833240425
457818UK00006B/180